Excellenc in Fundraising in Canada

THE DEFINITIVE RESOURCE FOR CANADIAN FUNDRAISERS

civil sector press

TORONTO

GUY MALLABONE ET AL.

IMPORTANT:

The following materials are intended as general reference tools for understanding the underlying principles, techniques and conventions of philanthropic fundraising in Canada. The opinions expressed herein are solely those of the authors. To ensure the currency of the information presented, readers are strongly encouraged to solicit the assistance of appropriate professionals.

Further, any examples or sample forms presented are intended only as illustrations. The authors, publishers and their agents assume no responsibility for errors or omissions or for damages arising from the use of published information or opinions.

ISBN-10: 1-895589-92-4
ISBN-13: 978-1-895589-92-4

Excellence in Fundraising in Canada

Published by Civil Sector Press
Box 86, Station C,
Toronto, Ontario, M6J 3M7 Canada
Telephone: 416-345-9403
Fax: 416-345-8010

ACKNOWLEDGEMENTS

Editor
Guy Mallabone

Assistant Editor
Lisa MacDonald

Cover art and book design
John VanDuzer, WISHART.NET

Production
Alan Tang

Publisher
Leanne Hitchcock

GUY MALLABONE

Guy Mallabone, CFRE is a veteran fundraising professional with 32 years' experience as a development officer working in the Arts & Culture, Social Services, and post-secondary educational sectors. Born in Calgary, Alberta, he earned his Bachelor of Commerce degree at the University of Calgary and his Masters of Arts in Philanthropy and Development, at St. Mary's University in Minnesota.

Mallabone is an internationally recognized expert in the practice of fundraising and non-profit management, and currently serves as President and CEO of *Global Philanthropic (Canada)*, an international full-service fundraising consultancy.

He has served AFP as a founding chapter President and international board member, and remains active in support of AFP and the profession as a mentor and presenter. He has served as a member of the International Board for the CFRE certification program, and currently Chairs *Canada Advancing Philanthropy*, the national professional advocacy group working to launch Canada's first Master's degree program in fundraising.

Guy is a frequent speaker at professional conferences locally, nationally, and internationally. He is a professor at the University of Bologna, Italy Master's degree program in fund development, and has authored many articles, a book titled *The Fundraising Audit*, and is co-author of the largest study on donor motivations and barriers completed in Canada.

In 1999, he was selected as the fundraising professional of the year by AFP's Edmonton & Area Chapter and was recognized by Alberta Venture Magazine in 2009 as one of Alberta's *Fifty Most Influential Citizens* and by the Calgary Herald newspaper as one of the city's *Twenty Most Compelling Citizens*. Most recently, AFP Calgary named Guy Outstanding Fundraising Executive for 2011.

PREFACE

As the mouse living next to the elephant, we oftentimes accept, at equal value, the lessons learned and perceptions held from our American cousins as transferable to our Canadian lives. And we know, this isn't always true, and it certainly isn't always practical.

Philanthropy is no exception. Much of what we learn about philanthropy, and the profession of fundraising in particular, comes from examples south of the border. The pioneers in American philanthropy have imprinted upon Canadian leadership and the best practice that we emulate and espouse. In fact, many of the lessons that we've learned and take for granted, come from the giants in US philanthropy. Conferences, in particular offer the opportunity to meet and observe the American centric view of fundraising and philanthropy.

This is not bad thing. But it shouldn't be the only thing.

Canadians have always enjoyed adopting the best from other countries, accepting and rejecting when appropriate, and inventing and creating when needed. EFT (electronic funds transfer) is a good example. Here in Canada, and in fundraising specifically in Canada, EFT rules. It's a very popular practice amongst Canadians to use EFT to pay bills, make donations, and conduct business. But not so in the USA, where EFT has not been developed and honed, or accepted, to the same degree.

While research shows that the "Basic Job Analysis" for fundraising (the blueprint for what fundraising professionals say is the knowledge important for our work) is relatively similar between Canada, the USA, UK, Australia, New Zealand and other countries, there are differences.

In 2009/2010, CFRE International conducted a new job analysis engaging close to 3,000 professional fundraisers around the world, and discovered that in fact, there are some slight differences in how Canadians view the job analysis. In Canada for example, fundraisers rated engaging volunteers in fundraising as more important than did their colleagues in other countries, and as such, spent more time engaging volunteers in fundraising. Canadian fundraisers also indicated that they reported to constituents about the use and impact of donated funds more frequently than fundraisers in other countries.

There is no question that Canadians share more things in common with our colleagues around the world than not, and that the variations tend to be minimal. That is the strength of the fundraising profession. However, while some of these variations are modest, there is a nuance to what it is to be a Canadian fundraiser, and what it means to conduct fundraising successfully in Canada. That is the essence of what we hope to capture in *Excellence in Fundraising in Canada*.

ORGANIZATION OF THE BOOK

The idea for this book came from two great anthologies in fundraising. The first, a classic, *Achieving Excellence in Fundraising* has been a major success and has taught many in our profession about the Rosso model in fundraising. A second edition of the classic, published by Jossey-Bass and edited by Eugene R. Tempel, became an outstanding resource for the profession. The second anthology, *The NonProfit Handbook in Fundraising*, published by AFP/Wiley and edited by Jim Greenfield, is equally ground-breaking in its contribution to the profession.

In both cases, contributions were made by dozens of American scholars and fundraising practitioners. A true collaboration of thought and ideas, these "textbooks" have allowed many practitioners to learn about best practice and put the ideas into action.

And so we are hopeful that *Excellence in Fundraising in Canada* will contribute a uniquely Canadian perspective to the body of knowledge that exists. This book celebrates the contributions from 22 Canadian fundraising professionals, all leaders in their field – each providing a contribution with a Canadian point of view, and a Canadian perspective.

Excellence in Fundraising in Canada has the integrity of an integrated work. Each chapter addresses and contributes to an aspect of a total development program. But the book doesn't have to be read in sequential order - the reader can pick and choose from specific chapters that they wish to access. For example, readers seeking to learn more about online fundraising strategy and its relationship to other fundraising strategies will find chapter fourteen helpful.

Excellence in Fundraising in Canada will make an excellent textbook for college, university, and community courses on fundraising and resource development. It will also serve as a must-have resource for new professionals or those in mid-career who may have a strength in one area of development, but not another.

Many of the contributors to this book have published before, and are recognized as experts in their area of expertise. These authors are committed to the integrity of this profession, and have come together to bring the Canadian perspective to the professional practice of fundraising.

E.H. Guy Mallabone
Calgary, Alberta
August 2011

Foreword
BILL HALLETT, ACFRE

With the publication of *Excellence in Fundraising in Canada*, our understanding of Canada's philanthropic marketplace will change. In the last twenty-five years, a number of Canadian books about fundraising have been written but there has never been a comprehensive fundraising textbook written by Canadians for Canadians until the publication of this work.

Excellence in Fundraising in Canada, edited by Guy Mallabone, an outstanding leader in the fundraising profession, collectively represents more than 400 years of fundraising experience! The authors who contributed chapters to the book represent the geographic diversity of our country but are united in their passion for adding the Canadian fundraising experience to the profession's body of knowledge.

These professionals recognize the value of contributing their best practice learning to the next generation of those in our field who are advocates of "action for the common good."

Consider them the mentors you always wanted – ready to share insightful thoughts, unique reflections and visioning for a professional discipline that has only really emerged in the last forty years.

We know that demographic changes, economic upheaval and technological advances are shifting current philanthropic practices. This book, together with continued research, means we will no longer be dependent on texts and studies from other countries to understand our own unique Canadian philanthropic marketplace.

This text will undoubtedly be a resource for anyone who aspires to be a professional fundraiser, earning the Certified Fundraising Executive (CFRE) credential or any other certificate or degree offered by Canadian universities and colleges. But it is more than an academic resource. Human stories and flowing prose make it a book that is immensely readable, deserving to be on the bookshelf of every fundraiser, senior executive and board member in the not-for-profit, charitable sector in this country.

Editors note: Bill Hallet has provided leadership to the Canadian fundraising sector from the earliest days of the profession's organization. A leader. A best practice practitioner. A mentor. It is fitting that one of Canada's fundraising founding fathers provide the Foreword for this book.

TABLE OF CONTENTS

CHAPTER 1

FUND DEVELOPMENT PLANNING

KEN WYMAN, CFRE

In 2009, more than a thousand Canadian charities shut their doors voluntarily. By the middle of 2010 the numbers seemed headed for a 20% increase, according to data extracted from the Canadian Revenue Agency website. *read more...*

Why did they close? It might have been because of a lack of money, a shortage of volunteers, a merger with another charity, or no ongoing need for the charity's services. It seems safe to say that it involved a lack of planning in most cases.

Planning is hard. Constantly under pressure from the tyranny of the urgent, charities and non-profit groups have a difficult time thinking about the long-term.

Resistance to change also makes it difficult to develop rational plans. Like me, you have probably heard too many fundraising activities justified on the grounds that "we've always done it that way."

What does good planning require? In a nutshell, planning is a *systematic* process of setting *measurable* goals in relations to *needs*, researching relevant *data*, comparing *options*, minimizing *risks*, balancing *resources*, taking appropriate *action* and *evaluating* results so you can make *changes* for the next plan.

This chapter will put most of the emphasis on two essential aspects: planning for the long-term, and data-driven, evidence-based planning.

MORE THAN A FINANCIAL TARGET

Having a monetary goal is an essential part of a plan, but not the whole plan. Worse yet, too many groups have no logical way to decide on their financial targets. Deciding on a goal by taking last year's results and adding 10% is not much better than picking a number out of the air. This is like a child deciding to become a rock star, an astronaut, a doctor, or a millionaire by age 30. It is fun to imagine. It may even be possible to achieve, if you plot out the logical steps needed to arrive at your destination.

The amount you can raise is NOT determined by the amount you need to spend. There may not be any relationship between these two figures. It is certainly true that, whatever you plan to do -- build a hospital, feed the hungry, or celebrate great art -- donors want to know how you plan to spend their money. You must -

- break your big vision and mission into specific projects
- document the methods you will use
- list the skills needed to implement the work

- budget the costs, ideally over a three to five year period
- set-up a system to evaluate whether your efforts are achieving the outcomes you want

This is the essential, painstaking process of translating the architect's first sketches of the exterior into detailed blueprints. Each of these projects is like a brick in a wall, adding up to a complete building.

Developing project details can also solve one of the most serious problems in fundraising: few (if any) funders want to contribute to overhead, administration, and routine maintenance. Instead these costs must be shared among all the projects. This technique, widely used in both business and government, is referred to as "activity based costing."

For example, the cost of a pizza includes not only the dough, sauce, cheese and toppings. It also includes a fair share of the oven and the fuel; the cook's time and the manager's; the delivery vehicle, driver, gas, and insurance; the building and the janitor who keeps it all clean (I hope!); the box, the marketing, the phone to place your order; the return on investment / profit, the accountant, and the cost of a new recipe book, like this one. Each pizza and each project includes an appropriate share of the overhead. A full explanation of how to implement activity based costing in a non-profit organization is a topic for another book.

Developing the details of your projects is essential. However it should not be mistaken for developing a fundraising plan. At best, these details provide just one of the necessary components of the "case for support." At worst, they are like the detailed dreams promoted by lotteries. It is fun to list how you'd spend your millions. How big should your yacht be? Will you build a mansion in a tropical paradise or buy a penthouse in a major city? What colour will you choose for your new sports car? How much will you give to charity and family? Knowing how you'd *spend* the money is not the same as having a plan to *get* the money.

PLAN FOR THE LONG-TERM

Too many groups are so focused on short-term tactics such as their next special event, direct marketing campaign, grant application, or major donor visit that they lose sight of the big picture. Planning for the details of each of these tactics is crucial, but strategic thinking integrates them all over a multi-year period. You'll find details on each of these tactics and more throughout this book. Right now, let's think bigger.

Sustainability means the ability to keep doing what you need to do over many years without using up more resources than you gain. In farming, this means replenishing the soil for future harvests. Sustainable fundraising means you measure success not just in the gross or net dollars you raise this month or this year, but in the ongoing relationships you nurture with donors over a life-time.

Plans that focus only on the dollars raised each year are like depleting the soil until you cannot grow anything on a once fertile farm. As in agriculture, forestry, or any resource-based industry, in fundraising terms, depleting the soil would mean the bad habit of taking out more than you put back.

The best organic fertilizer is known by two initials: not "BS" but "PR." Replenishing donors' willingness to give means thanking them properly and often. They must feel that their donation helped make the world a better place. Newsletters, testimonials, photos, tours of projects, and news coverage are all essential to nourishing their giving nature.

A sustainable plan must be based on the donor pyramid. This is one of the core principles of fundraising. (See Figure 1.1) The main idea it conveys is that you need to have a system to acquire new supporters, keep them loyal, and upgrade their commitments over several years.

Not everyone starts at the bottom and stays with you as you climb the pyramid, of course. That is why it gets smaller toward the top. Major donors may begin near the top, without climbing the bottom levels. Many bequests come from donors who were previously unknown and uncultivated. While it is not a magic answer, it is a useful long-term model.[1] The

smart fundraiser has a plan to move as many people as possible to the next level.

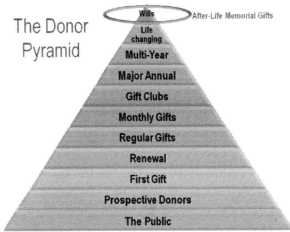

Figure 1.1 - *The Donor Pyramid emphasizes the need for a multi-year plan to acquire new supporters, retain them, and upgrade their giving. This is more important than the amount of money raised from any single campaign. Different versions of the pyramid may have variations in the number of levels.*

Let's climb the pyramid, one level at a time, to develop your plan.

Most of this section focuses on gifts from individuals, since charities in Canada generally get substantially more support from individuals than from corporations and foundations combined. The pyramid can be adapted to sponsorship and grants.

Although grants are not usually repeated yearly, the same cycle applies: you find new supporters, treat them well and attempt to get repeat support at ever higher levels. Another version of the pyramid could describe the relationship with volunteers, from the many who do little or nothing, upgrading carefully to the few who do so much.

THE PUBLIC

The base of the pyramid, which contains the largest number of people, is "The Public." Too many organizations naively plan to raise money from "the public." One of my goals is to banish this phrase. Here is a dose of cold reality:

- 25% of Canadians don't give to any charities at all (according to charitable tax credits claimed - granted this may be under-reported as donations

---

1 Critics of the donor pyramid point out, quite correctly, that it is an imperfect model. Mark Rovner set off a storm of responses in early 2010 when he posted this blog. "Let's start by admitting that the fundraising pyramid is a lie. Most major donors at most organizations do not rise up through the ranks of $15 donors, who become $100 donors, and then ultimately become $100,000 donors. Most major donors come to organizations via other major donors. Most low dollar direct mail or Internet donors hang around for a year or two and then stop giving altogether." See his full argument at *http://seachangestrategies.com/blog/2010/01/08/playing-by-the-wrong-rules/*. Then for the many useful responses, search the internet for "Donor Pyramid is a Lie" and read the responses and reactions. Time well spent.

may not be claimed and may exclude gifts to non-profit groups or directly to people in need).

- Only 5% of Canadians give more than $915 a year to charities. Their donations total 47% of all charity revenue from individual donors. (For those fond of Pareto's 80/20 rule, if you combine the giving of everyone who gave more than $209, you'll see that 25% of the people give 80% of the money.)

- 75% of Canadians give less than a total of $209 a year to all charities combined. (This includes the 25% who claim no charitable tax credits at all. This 75% of the population gives only 20% of total charitable contributions.)

- 20% give more than $209 but less than $915 a year. Their donations total 33% of all giving. (Combined with the 75% who give from zero to $209, this means all the donations from 95% of Canadians amount to only 53% of the financial contributions.)

Major Individual Donors
The few who do more

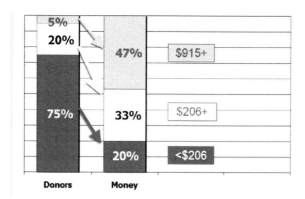

Figure 1.2 - Almost half the donations from Canadian individuals come from the 5% of the population who claim charitable tax credits. To be among these top donors one only needs to make charitable gifts totalling $915 or more in a year. Fully 75% of Canadian tax returns show gifts of less than $206 to all charities combined. (CRA data)

PROSPECTIVE DONORS

The challenge is to develop a plan that focuses on those who are actually likely to support your organization. These are the real prospects.

Who are the best prospects? Other chapters in this book will go into greater depth, but here is a brief overview.

Plan to start by asking for support from the people closest to your organization. They are the most likely to give. Rosso's Concentric Circles of Giving[2] illustrates this. (See Figure 1.3)

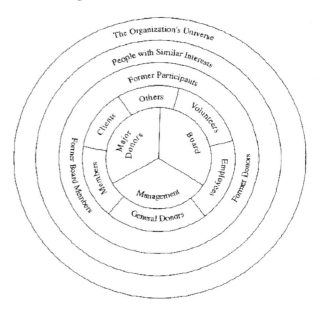

Figure 1.3 - Hank Rosso's Concentric Circles suggest your best prospects are in the middle of the target, and you should plan to work from the centre to the outside.

Unfortunately many organizations find this concentric circle model does not always work: board members don't give much, if at all; clients or members may be too poor to give much; and they have not acquired major donors yet. They need other sources of prospects.

So where do you start when prospecting for new donors? Organizations have been successful with the following methods, although no model works equally well for every organization:

- Ask board members to identify personal and business contacts. While they may not feel

---

2 Rosso, Henry A. (Hank) (1991). *Achieving Excellence in Fund Raising*, Jossey Bass.

they know (or can reveal) contacts with people of great wealth, gentle probing may unearth connections to people the board members could ask for contributions that might be significant in achieving your organization's mission.

- Consider approaching the people who use your services, such as members and their families. Include people who contact your organization for information. Plan to capture the contact information of as many people as you can. Note that this may work well for a symphony orchestra, but would be inappropriate for a women's shelter where confidentiality is a life-and-death issue.

- Alumni is the term used at schools, but the same could apply to former clients and members who may no longer need your organization but are willing to support it. In the health care world these are often referred to as "grateful patients."

- Contact people who will give less (at least at first) with methods such as direct marketing through mail, the Internet, telephone, media, or door-to-door and street-based campaigns. Capture their names and build them into your prospecting data base.

- Invite people with less intense interest to donate by holding events or raffles. Even if they don't care deeply about your cause, they give because they want a nice party or the chance to win a prize. Keep their names and addresses on file for future events and lotteries. Note that relatively few people in this category respond to cause-based direct marketing campaigns. The conversion rate is sadly low. However they may continue to come to your events or gamble on your draws for years to come, if you continue to invite them.

- Exchange mail lists with similar organizations. This is one of the most effective ways to find people pre-disposed to give to charities. This can be handled in an ethically appropriate way. While some donors may ask you to put them on the "Do Not Trade" list, most charities gain more supporters than they lose. Despite the fears of inexperienced leaders, this is ethical and highly effective. In most cases you gain far more

donors than you lose. The cost is much lower than renting lists. For a handful of charities dealing with controversial and confidential information, such as an AIDS clinic, this may not be ethically appropriate, but for most it is a wise move.

- If you work in a geographically concentrated area or a smaller community, a little research can quickly reveal the names of those who give generously. Look for names on donation walls, theatre and concert programs, and in annual reports. Visit locations such as:

  - Hospitals, theatres, universities, colleges
  - Arenas, ball parks, rinks and other athletic facilities
  - United Way and other campaigns
  - Churches, Synagogues, Mosques, Temples, etc.
  - Local news media

- Hold networking/webbing sessions[3] with board members and special friends to discover who you know you didn't know you knew. If you ask leaders to name potential donors they often freeze, and say they don't know anyone. Plan to nudge their memories by reminding them of who gives the most. This may unlock their connections.

- One study asked the Canadian government to examine tax returns to determine which occupational groups gave the largest portion of their taxable income to charities[4] The results may not only surprise you, they should form part of your prospecting plan:

  - Accountants 1.98% of income (income lower than doctors, dentists or lawyers)
  - Farmers 1.83%
  - Doctors 1.45%
  - Lawyers 1.37%

3 For more on webbing sessions, see *Face to Face: How to Get Bigger Donations from Very Generous People*, by Ken Wyman.
4 Arlett, A., Bell, P. and Thompson, R.W. *Canada Gives: Trends and Attitudes Towards Charitable Giving and Volunteerism*, (The Canadian Centre for Philanthropy, now renamed Imagine Canada).

- Dentists   1.36%
- Average   0.66%

Please do not just rip the list of accountants or doctors out of the phone book and send them all a letter, or rent mailing lists of all the farmers in your area. That may work, but will not be nearly as effective as finding personal connections and making face-to-face visits.

Demographics also play a part in planning your prospecting. Donor surveys repeatedly reveal that many charities get the most support from four key groups. You should plan on doing your own donor surveys each year. Determine whether your donors match this pattern:

- Older people give more than younger

- Religious people give more to both religious and secular charities

- Women give more than men

- More highly educated people give more than those with less schooling

In shrinking communities that export people, include your diaspora of émigrés who have gone away but left their hearts behind. Those who have living family or deeply rooted ancestral ties in your community are among the best bets. This can include the inevitable parade of short-term professionals such as teachers, police officers, and health care workers. Their remittances to their hometown may add substantial revenue.

Much more can be written about prospect research. The point here is simply to make sure your plan includes resources to discover your best prospects and to reach out to those most likely to give.

Prospecting or donor-acquisition, as this phase is called, is usually expensive. This is an investment that is repaid if (and only if) the donors give again and again. If you add up the total of all the donations an average donor gives over all the years they support a charity, this is referred to as Long Term Value (or sometimes Life Time Value or LTV). Most charities find that average donors give for about five years, although those who enrol in monthly giving programs continue their support for ten years or more.

What is a reasonable LTV? The average donor contributed almost $100 to charity, according to a study

by Cornerstone.[5] Based on five years of data from 2005 to 2009, international relief charities had the highest LTV at $138.26, followed by city hospitals at $133.61, provincial heath care groups at $95.99, national health care at $71.57.

You may lose money or barely break-even during donor acquisition. In many campaigns, only one in a hundred may give to you immediately. This does not mean you have a 99% failure rate. Many who did not give immediately may become more aware of the charity's work, and may respond in the future. Still, the fact that only a tiny portion typically give may seem daunting. Compare this to the investment businesses make in advertising. Thousands of people may see an ad but not respond immediately. What counts is the portion that does take action.

This is short-term pain for long-term gain. Losing money to acquire new donors is completely justifiable if their LTV exceeds the cost of asking for donations. This is just as much an investment as building a solid foundation on a house. It may not seem glamorous, but it is essential.

A good fundraising plan includes an investment in the future through donor prospecting, even though this does not immediately improve the bottom-line. In business, this kind of customer development often involves loss-leaders and other investments that produce a negative return today for a better tomorrow.

FIRST GIFT

Prospecting only makes sense if you get more money at less cost later, that is, if the donors' LTV far exceeds the cost of acquiring them and asking again. You can think of donor acquisition as *friendraising*, not fundraising.

A good fundraising plan includes two elements at this stage:

- Get contact details from all supporters so you can ask them to give again. Get each donor's name and at least one way to contact them (address, phone, or email) for everyone you encounter. Under privacy laws you may also need to get their permission to contact them again. Enter this information into a database

5   Note that this is based on 32 charities, many of them of national importance. Retrieved from *http://csearch.ca/mc/GFA/download.aspx* (pp. 22-29, 53-54)

so it is easy to contact them again, and track when they give, how much they give, and what motivates them.

- Always leave donors feeling good about supporting your group so that they are willing to respond positively when you ask again.

RENEWAL

Tragically, only 40-60% of those who support an organization once ever support it again.

The average donor renewal rate has declined from 54.7% in 2005 to 51.4% in 2009, according to Cornerstone's Global File Audit[6] of a sample of Canadian charities. This includes both long-term and new donors. Worse yet, first-time donors to those charities had even lower renewal rates, dropping from 37.4% renewing in 2005 to 31.1% in 2009, the Cornerstone study shows.

A glimmer of good news is that multi-year donors are renewing in increasing numbers. In 2005 the study shows:

- 60.3% of multi-year donors who had not signed up as monthly contributors renewed, inreasing to 62.9% by 2009.

- Long-term repeat donors perform even better, with 71.4% renewing in 2009.

- Monthly donors were the most loyal, with 84.5% renewing in 2009.

The numbers can be frightening. This study looked at 621,928 people who had made their first gift to one or more of the 32 charities in the study, during 2005. Some of them gave more than once that year. They made a total of 724,955 gifts, worth $32,425,158.

Just one year later, only 31.58% of those donors (196,420 people) gave again in 2006, contributing $10,099,928 in total.

By 2009 only 14.03% of the original donors were still contributing. These 87,244 people gave $5,247,213.

This Canadian study breaks charities into five categories. It showed the highest renewal rates for provincial health charities, followed by city hospitals, and national health charities. International relief came last.

6   Retrieved from *http://csearch.ca/mc/GFA/download.aspx* (pp. 22-29. 53-54).

More data is needed to determine variations based on region, demographics or cause.

WHY ARE RENEWAL RATES SO LOW?

The most common answer from donor surveys is that the donors were never asked to give again. The charity either did not collect their contact information, or never contacted them.

The next most common answer is that the donors were annoyed because they were asked too often, and not thanked enough in a meaningful way. Far too few charities have a proper plan to retain new donors. Plan on investing in software to organize your donor list. Even more importantly, plan on investing in developing a team of people who will input the data quickly and accurately. Addresses that contain mistakes may mean your messages are never delivered. Names spelled wrong annoy donors. Data entered slowly makes donors feel you don't care about them, and did not really need their money.

Plan on thanking donors quickly. Research shows that thanking donors within 48 hours of their gift increases subsequent donations dramatically. (See *Donor-Centered Fundraising* by Penelope Burk http://www.cygresearch.com.)

Plan on thanking donors warmly. Thank you letters that let the donors know their gifts were immediately put to good use produce better results than form letters with no emotion or connection to the reason for the appeal. (See samples at http://www.raisersharpe.com/)

Ideally, you should plan on developing a special "welcome package" that you send to donors who are supporting you for the first time. (Your donor database should tell you who they are.) This welcome package has several functions, it will:

- Warmly thank the donor for the gift, and show that their support will change someone's life right away. Donors want to hear about the *impact* their gift has on someone's life. Did they save a hungry child? Make a dying senior more comfortable in their last moments? Provide art that brightened a student's day? Focus on *outcomes*: the work you set out to do. Do not get bogged down on *inputs* (such as hiring more staff or buying a new van or building a new clinic) or on *outputs* (such as teaching classes, printing brochures, or giving medicine). Donors need to know in their hearts that their last donation has transformed at least one life before they will give again.

- Increase their trust in your organization by showing them your past accomplishments and the names and abilities of your board and senior staff, and offering them additional information, including your annual report and audited statements.

- Discover the donor's individual preferences, usually through a short survey. Ask questions such as these:

  - Do you prefer to hear from us whenever there is news or only once a year?

  - Are you interested in all the different ways you can help, or do you have special preferences?

  - How do you prefer to be contacted? (Check all that apply.)

    □ Mail

    □ Email

    □ Phone

    □ In-person visits

Honour the donor's personal preferences to custom fit your approaches to their wishes.

Donor retention is very important. You must have a plan to convert one-time donors to "family members" who give several times a year. It is far less expensive to renew a donor than to acquire a first-time donor.

Return on investment (R.O.I.) is not just a concept for businesses. Charities need to carefully measure the results of each expenditure to produce maximum efficiency. It also requires calculating non-financial returns on investments, such as: new donors acquired, current donors retained, and lapsed donors renewed. Investment expenditures may also come in forms other than cash, such as staff and volunteer time, and goodwill.

Sending appeals to donors who will not respond is expensive. Worse yet, it annoys them and can result in bad publicity.

REGULAR GIVING

Renewing the donor's support to get a second gift is a crucial stage in moving up the donor pyramid. After that, you need a plan to get the donor to support your work at least once a year, and preferably more than once each year.

The next element of the plan surprises many people: *Asking often produces more money.* Not everyone responds with a donation the first time they are asked.

You must ask *at least* three times a year to get the majority of donors to give once.

Many charities and non-profit groups ask for support only once or twice a year, if that often. They are afraid of alienating donors who complain about being bothered too much. While it is certainly true that some donors prefer to be asked only once a year, and will tell you so in no uncertain terms, the majority do not mind more frequent communications.

"Donor fatigue" also known as "compassion exhaustion" is a real issue. People do get tired of repeated demands, or as the childhood chant puts it, "Gimme, gimme never gets."

However, donor fatigue can be cured by providing proof that problems are being solved and progress is being made. Donors must receive messages about positive results at least as often as they get asked.

One Canadian hospital which must remain unnamed reported that they mailed appeals to their donors four times a year. They did a donor survey that showed the majority of respondents thought this was too often. The next year they doubled the frequency of mailings to eight, alternating *uplifting newsletters* (with a *soft ask*) and appeal *letters* (with a *hard ask*). The donor survey showed the respondents thought this increased communication was "just right."

Email messages can also convey good news to donors in a cost-effective way. However email does not usually produce significant revenue (yet).

When asking often, vary the appeal to different aspects of your work. Novices feel they must tell the donors everything their organization does in every letter. The result is that there is not enough space to stimulate the donors about any one aspect. For example, when I worked at Oxfam-Canada, the international development charity, we wrote to our supporters seven times a year. This could have been overwhelming for the supporters if it was repetitious. Instead, each mailing emphasized a different aspect of the work, such as:

- Africa
- Women's projects
- Food
- Latin America
- Children
- Health care
- Water

This approach resulted in donations tripling. One donor wrote "I had no idea how often I had given to Oxfam until I added up all my tax receipts at the end of the year." She had given to the people helped, not the organization, and did not feel donor fatigue at all.

Other charities have found it cost-effective to write donors twelve times a year or more.

You'll need to evaluate your own donors to find out the right frequency for your organization. Plan for frequent communication, research the results, and adjust accordingly.

About 75-80% of your donors will give your group a donation once a year, if you ask properly. Some will give more than once a year, if your appeals strike them right.

Some attrition is inevitable. Donors die. They lose interest. They move. Your goal is to maximize retention – always remembering that it costs far more to acquire a new donor than to renew an existing donor.

Just keeping track of your current donors can be a challenge. Over 40% of Canadians changed addresses between 2001 and 2006, according to Statistics Canada.[7] Some people, particularly those in their early twenties, may move more than once a year.

Although not everyone who moves notifies Canada Post, their figures show that more than 12% of people - approximately 1.2 million households - file a change of address notification with Canada Post[8] each year, out of the total of 10,603,283 residences[9] across the country.

Few people send change-of-address cards to even their most favoured charities. Frequent mailings make

it more likely that your message will reach your donors and get a response so you don't lose a supporter.

MONTHLY GIVING

As your donors begin to give regularly, your next goal is to try and get them to give monthly. Donors are increasingly willing to sign up for monthly giving programs. Many will become monthly donors right from the start, for certain causes. You'll find much more on this system in Chapter 8.

For the moment, keep in mind to plan on including monthly giving options. In many charities 15% to 30% of donors are willing to enroll, and they often give more than half the total income that comes from individuals.

Monthly donors usually give more, and stay longer. Planning to encourage supporters to donate monthly is an essential step toward becoming a sustainable organization, and research has shown a strong correlation between donors who are monthly givers, and those donors predisposed to leaving a planned gift.

GIVING CLUBS

Upgrading donors can be the easiest source of new money. Some will give more if they are invited to join a "Giving Club." University alumni associations are among the masters of this art. These different levels often have names such as Sustainers, Benefactors, and Patrons.

The University of Toronto, for example, has *The Presidents' Circle* with approximately 4,000 Presidents' Circle members. These are people who give "an annual combined donation totalling at least $1,827 for individuals, and $10,000 or more for corporations, foundations and other organizations.[10] If $1,827 seems like an odd amount, consider that it is the year U of T was founded, and therefore an evocative number.

The University of Waterloo's *Chancellor's Circle* is for individual gifts of $5,000.

At the University of Victoria there are three levels:

- Annual Supporters: Donors $1,000+ to $24,999
- Benefactors' Circle: Donors $25,000 to $99,999

7   Over 12 million Canadians out of a total population of 29 million in 2006.
     http://www40.statcan.ca/l01/cst01/demo56a-eng.htm
8   http://www.canadapost.ca/cpo/mc/business/productsservices/atoz/ncoa.jsf
9   http://www.canadapost.ca/cpc2/addrm/hh/current/details/cdCAuALL-e.asp

10   http://give.utoronto.ca/recognition/presidents-circle/

• President's Circle: Donors $100,000+

Plan to offer low-cost incentives to encourage people to move up. Examples: plaques, artwork, books, private parties with prestigious people, nostalgic memorabilia, tours of your facilities, souvenirs, and trees planted in the donor's honour to name just a few.

These tokens of appreciation need not be expensive to have deep emotional value. What's more, Canada Revenue Agency rules prohibit charities from spending 20% or more of the donor's gift on rewards.[11]

The University of Victoria, for example, says:

"The stewardship office ensures that all donors who contribute over $1,000 are thanked by the university and receive a welcome package and VIP pass to selected campus facilities for new donors. Donors can also expect a student thank you letter for donors to awards; an optional listing in the donor honour roll, and an invitation to a special event on campus.

Recent events for our donors have included garden parties at the homes of other supporters or our own Finnerty Gardens, an advance preview of the Michael Williams collection at the Legacy Art Gallery and Café a spring concert with student performers in the Don Wright Symphonic Winds and campus lectures and receptions to meet some of student beneficiaries as well as hear from some of the world's top researchers and change agents".[12]

MAJOR ANNUAL GIFTS

Near the top of the pyramid are those very generous people who have the means and the will to give much more than others. These leadership contributions usually result from personal visits or phone calls, not from letters.

Typically 80-90% of the donations come from the top 10-20% of the donors.

Unfortunately many organizations are so busy running special events, sending email and direct mail, and other methods appropriate for the bottom levels of the pyramid that they never find the time to focus on these special few people.

MULTI-YEAR PLEDGES

Donors who are deeply committed may not be able to give as much as they would like all at once. For them, a commitment to giving over three to five years is an appropriate way to make a substantial donation.

Not everyone who pledges fulfills their commitment. On average, 70-90% of multi-year pledges are completed, although some achieve not only 100% compliance but increase donations to 110% or more.

Estimates of the pledge fulfillment rates vary. "Very, very few multiyear pledges are not being fulfilled," according to Guy Mallabone in Alberta. About "97% of campaign pledges are collected and a 3% figure is the norm for not being collected," according to Sandy MacKenzie, Philanthropic Architect and Partner of the Canadian campaign consulting firm Inspire.

Pledge redemption rates vary depending on the economy, the location, the type of cause and campaign, and how you approach the donor. For example, in telephone campaigns "generally, about 50-60% of those who say they'll send a contribution actually do."[13] In the USA "84-89% fulfillment rate on pledges is considered high in the world of [US] public television."[14]

"Pledge default rates go up in bad times," according to veteran US consultant Bob Pierpont in a presentation at "Fund Raising Day" in New York in June 2010.[15] Pierpont commented that capital campaign pledge payments may be cancelled, reduced or postponed in the face of stock market "crashes" or recessions such as was experienced in 2008 and 2009.

Recently Pierpoint cited examples from a US organization with a goal of $140 million that is basically stalled at $80 million:

• one pledge cancelled by a donor who had invested with Madoff

• one who has missed a pledge payment

---

11 Retrieved from *http://www.cra-arc.gc.ca/E/pub/tg/p113/p113-e.html#P99_6372*
12 Retrieved from *http://web.uvic.ca/givingtouvic/donorRelations.php#limitations*

13 Retrieved from *http://www.charityvillage.com/cv/research/rfrm29.html*
14 Retrieved from *http://www.allbusiness.com/specialty-businesses/non-profit-businesses/1045122-1.html*
15 Retrieved from *http://www.afpnyc.afpnet.org/atf/cf/%7B784ddc21-601f-4131-9d70-58d94d9affd6%7D/FUNDRAISING_DAY_IN_NEW_YORK_KARLIN_AMEND_PIERPONT.PDF*

- two delays in signing gift agreements after orally committing to substantial pledges
- another has fallen $200,000 behind on a one million dollar signed pledge
- another with a $2.5 million pledge has cited serious cash flow problems as a reason he is not meeting the agreed-to payment schedule
- a foundation that had offered a $3 million grant has reported it will not be made
- still another $1 million is doubtful because the donor says he is no longer making pledges
- one other multi-million donor has suspended payments for two years

A number of these were "booked" as pledges on the basis of a handshake with the CEO. This point is of interest because not all campaigns count pledges until a written commitment is received. In sum, approximately 11-12% of the $80 million that was reported as raised to-date looks weak and may never be received.

Apropos counting pledges, Pierpoint added that another campaign with a $100 million goal has been very conservative, booking only written pledges. Nevertheless, they have been impacted by the economy and stock market:

- they have had three pledges in the $250,000 to $500,000 restructured
- the economy's impact on their campaign was evident when they had to extend the solicitation schedule by 12 months because good prospects with whom they were having positive conversations or favorable negotiations were reluctant to commit.

The extra 12 months, ending December 2010, provided time to reorient their solicitations. With $90.5 of $100 million raised, they are confident they will succeed in raising the $15 million still needed.

While the Canadian economy has not been affected as badly as the USA, Pierpoint offers these lessons learned:

1. Counting pledges only when signed commitments are in hand is the conservative approach.

2. Gifts and pledge payments fall off in the face of stock market declines. The most recent *Giving USA* report confirms this.

Your plan must include investing time each year after the donors makes pledges to re-affirm their willingness to give. You must also send pledge reminders – delicately worded but essential – and not assume they will spontaneously remember to send the cheques. You may also need to renegotiate the payment period, amount and recognition, as their personal circumstances change.

LIFE-CHANGING GIFTS

Near the peak of the pyramid are donors who will be so excited by your work that they will make remarkable donations. These are also called transformational gifts. They come not out of their chequing accounts but their assets.

Depending on the size of your non-profit group, a large gift could be life changing for your organization, too. "Large" is, of course a relative term. Major universities might find that gifts of seven, eight or nine figures transform their futures, while smaller charities might be thrilled to get gifts of six, five, or even four figures on a regular basis.

Small organizations have found that large gifts change the way they operate. They can hire staff for the first time, or move to a more professional management structure. New programs can mean new buildings or land for an environmental group or art for a gallery that moves them into a new league. Funds put into an endowment can be invested, providing reliable annual income, so that an organization moves from being in constant danger of bankruptcy or living hand to mouth, to a sustainable long-term vision.

Receiving very large gifts can have negative consequences too. Fundraising campaigns can dry up if other donors feel their smaller financial support is no longer needed once the organization is on sound financial footing or is seen to have a wealthy patron. A sudden influx of cash can also lead to angry divisions among insiders who are suddenly competing for their share of the pie.

Giving a transformational gift can be life-changing for the donor too. Surprisingly this is not so much about suddenly having less money, and more about their self-image. After a lifetime accumulating wealth (or an inheritance or lottery win) they can change their personal goals to fulfill their vision for a better world. They may become happier, but they can also be depressed at how difficult it is to achieve social change. They may discover that friends and strangers now see them as "walking wallets" not as complete human beings. As one wealthy Canadian put it, asking that her identity be guarded after too many parties where people treated her "as an ABM machine with legs." Some donors find the attention of fundraisers so upsetting that they give only anonymously, or through an intermediary to protect their personal and family privacy and safety.

Multi-million dollar contributions may come from extremely wealthy donors who are still fabulously rich after they give. Michael DeGroote's gift of $105 million to support education, research and clinical service in medicine at McMaster University, for example, is the largest single gift given in Canada to date.[16]

In many cases, life-changing gifts come from ordinary people. I know of at least three donors who took mortgages on their homes so they could help an organization in a time of urgent need.

WILLS

Right at the apex of the pyramid are the ultimate gifts: donations by wills, bequests, life insurance and other planned gifts from estates. They are literally the "ultimate gift" because the word means "last."

These are often among the largest donations that an individual may give, and an organization receives.

Many professional fundraisers use the larger term "planned gifts" for these contributions. This category includes not only wills and bequests but also gifts of stocks and bonds, land, buildings, cultural artefacts and more. However I have not used that catch-all phrase here because donors may give with these methods for gifts at other levels of the pyramid.

A word of caution on the use of the term "planned giving." This short-hand term has become meaningful to fundraisers. However most donors, except a very few who are schooled in financial management, will

not find it a familiar term. Keep this as internal jargon, and talk to donors in plain and simple language.

Talking to donors about a planned gift can be risky. In training fundraising staff from *Ducks Unlimited* I encouraged the team to bravely raise the delicate subject of wills. One of the staff reported that he knew a long-time supporter was in the hospital, and likely at death's door. Would approaching him be exploitive? "I'm very nervous about this. I've never done anything like this before. I don't want to offend or upset him. What would I say?"

Since the donor was of a sound mind. I urged him to visit the donor immediately and say "I'm very nervous about this. I've never done anything like this before. I don't want to offend or upset you, but I've been urged to talk with you about your will."

A few days later the young staff person reported back. "The donor was overjoyed. He grabbed my hand and said 'my family refuses to talk with me about this, but I know that I'm dying and I want to make arrangements.'" The visit was productive and even pastoral, to use a term from the world of the clergy.

While this is hardly the ideal approach, it worked. The family might have been upset, and claimed the fundraiser had exerted undue influence, but they did not.

Plan now to offer simple brochures about planned giving to any donor that wants one. You can adapt from brochures already created by health organizations and religious centres. Consider providing free workshops on estate planning for your supporters. Enlist volunteers who have already remembered you in their wills to go and talk to the donors who have supported you the longest.

This is too important to neglect. If you don't get started soon, your best donors may leave this life – and leave their assets to other charities – while you are still planning on planned giving. See Chapter 12 by Val Hoey for more details.

AFTER-LIFE

While most classic versions of the pyramid end with the donor's death, I've added a halo for those donors whose commitment sets such an example that their friends, families, colleagues and business associates

---

16 Retrieved from *http://fhs.mcmaster.ca/main/documents/DeGroote_Gift.pdf*

decide to give significantly in their honour once they are gone.

Your fundraising plan might include discerning who is so beloved that this is an option. Discuss the potential with them before they die, and with their families after the fact. Anniversary reminders can keep such funds growing for years.

Figure 1.4 illustrates the lessons of climbing the pyramid:

Lessons of Climbing the Pyramid

1. Your most important task is to move donors up.

2. You must have a long-term plan to:

   • recruit

   • retain

   • renew

   • revitalize

   • reward

3. The best measurement of fundraising success is not how much money you make from one special event or a letter, or a campaign.

4. Building strong relationships is critical to fundraising success in the long-term. A short-sighted focus on maximizing immediate revenue and minimizing costs may undercut your ability to develop the warm relationships that last a donor's lifetime and beyond.

5. You must plan to develop donors not just donations. Fundraising success is all about "friendraising."

Figure 1.4

Now, the thing about the Pyramid, is it can be turned upside down. Figure 1.5 shows why it is important to spend more time with the donors at the top of the pyramid. That's where the biggest return on investment can be found. Don't neglect to replenish the donor base, feeding the roots to harvest the bounty.

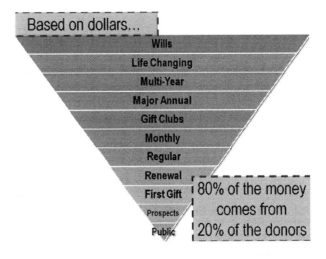

Figure 1.5

THE SPIRAL PATH TO THE TOP

To constantly move donors upwards to higher levels of commitment, combine the pyramid model with the donor cycle. You might envision this as a spiral path moving from the base of the pyramid to the top.

The donor cycle model is also referred to as the *fundraising continuum*. It works through five steps (See Figure 1.6).

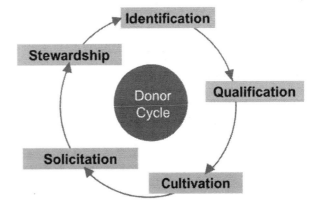

Figure 1.6

1. **Identification** - Identifying a potential donor is the start. At the base of the pyramid this may be a mass audience. Higher up it is an individual.

2. **Qualification** - Qualifying your lead is next. Prospect research helps you discover what part of your work interests them most, who should ask them, and how much to ask them to give.

3. **Cultivation** - Cultivating the donor is the next step. Warming up the relationship before asking for support is essential in most cases. Let the prospect know what the problem is and why it is important. Show that you have a solution that will work effectively. Capture the donor's heart.

4. **Solicitation** - Soliciting the donor is the essential next step. Actually asking for a gift can be frightening, and must be done carefully. At the bottom of the pyramid too many fundraising letters never have a *call to action* that clearly lets the donors know how much you hope they will contribute while urging them to "give now." Too many charity websites miss this step and do not have a prominent "Give Now" button for donors to click. Near the top of the pyramid, where face-to-face appeals are the norm, a *closer* must be prepared to ask the donor to give.

5. **Stewardship** - Stewardship is the process of thanking the donors, showing that their gifts have been used well, and making them feel so good about giving that they are ready to give again, and give more.

The spiral then comes back around to identify who can move up to the next level.

Figure 1.7 shows the iCycle. This is my own variation on the donor cycle, which may be easier to remember. I've adapted it from work that came to me originally from Alan Arlett, a leading Canadian fundraiser who was the founder of the Canadian Centre for Philanthropy (now Imagine Canada).[17]

The iCycle has seven stages, although the order in which they are done may shift, particularly for stages 2, 3, and 4, depending on the donor:

1. **Identify** - Focus on the people who are most likely to give. Find out as much as possible about them.

2. **Inform** - Give them the information they need to make an intelligent, intellect-driven decision.

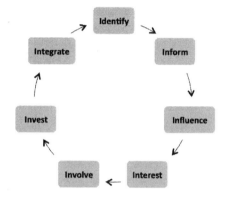

Figure 1.7 - Wyman iCycle

3. **Influence** - Since intellect is not the only driver, and perhaps not even the primary factor in decisions, consider what might capture their hearts. Often this means thinking about who the appeal is coming from, as who asks may be more important than what they say. At the mass-market level near the bottom of the pyramid this means who signs the letter, and who appears in the list of patrons. At the top levels of asking it includes the volunteer and staff leadership who visit the donor.[18]

4. **Interest** - Asking questions is the best way to get people interested. Move from seeing your organization as a good idea for others, to something that serves their self-interests.

5. **Involve** - A wise old saying in fundraising is "If you want money, ask for advice. If you want advice, ask for money."[19] At the base of the pyramid you ask donors to complete surveys, sign petitions, or add comments

---

17 Retrieved from *http://www.charityvillage.com/cv/archive/afundqa/afundqa10/afundqa1004.asp*

18 For much more on the science of influence, see *The Influential Fundraiser* by Bernard Ross and Clare Segal (published by Jossey-Bass) and *Influence: The Psychology of Persuasion* by Robert B. Cialdini.

19 I learned this from Joyce Young. See *Fundraising for Non-profit Groups* by Young, Wyman and Swaigen.

online. At the top you take donors on tours, ask them to be guest speakers, or involve them in committees or boards.

6. **Invest** - Now (and not before) is the time to ask. If you rush in too soon you may get a token donation. When the donors are deeply committed they make an investment of their wealth, and themselves.

7. **Integrate** - In this context stewardship is more than just thanking the donors; it is making them feel like part of the inner circle, like family-members, with a life-long commitment.

As this is a spiral, your plan now comes back around to identifying who can move still further up the pyramid.

BEYOND THE DONOR PYRAMID

This section invites you to base your plan on solid evidence. The three key questions are:

1. What resources does your organization have to invest? Input affects output!
2. What results have you had in the past? This can be a powerful predictor of the future.
3. What are the predictable outcomes of various tactics? Others have used most every fundraising tactic before, and their experience should influence your expectations.

Gathering this information is referred to as a "fundraising audit" or "diagnostic." You can find more on this in *The Fundraising Audit handbook: What you need to know to evaluate and improve performance*, by Guy Mallabone and Ken Balmer, Civil Sector Press 2010.

Armed with the results from an audit or diagnostic, we can proceed with building a plan. Figure 1.8 lists five key steps needed to begin building your plan. What follows are the core questions you must ask to develop your plan. This is much like visiting a doctor. Your medical history is essential before a treatment plan can be determined.

Five Key Steps in Building Your Plan

1. Assess your needs carefully

2. Assess your culture carefully

3. Review your fundraising history

4. Investment capital

5. Assessing the competition

Figure 1.8

These questions should give you a good start at a quick self-examination. Of course no book can substitute for an experienced practitioner adapting the questions and interpreting the answers based on your unique situation.

Not all these steps will apply to every organization. A group that is just starting up will have less data than an organization that has been in existence for years, for example.

A group offering aid in the midst of a crisis, such as an earthquake, flood, fire or Tsunami may be tempted to rush into action without doing a diagnostic first. Some people feel that planning is a luxury in those situations, taking too much precious time, even lacking in compassion. This can be a costly mistake. Without a plan you may waste time and money duplicating projects that already exist, or are unrealistic. It is true that the proper time to develop a plan is long before an emergency, not in the midst of panic.

STEP 1: ASSESS YOUR NEEDS CAREFULLY

Donors will support you only if they see that you are dealing with problems that are important to them, and have realistic solutions to offer. This is part of the creation of an essential tool called the *case for support* or *case statement*. Think of the case, as it is called for short, as a virtual bookcase where you can file binders containing all the information you need to create any kind of winning communication. You might prefer the image of a tool case, with all the equipment you need to construct a bridge between your donor and the person her donation will help. You'll find more on the *case for support* in Chapter 3 by Pearl Veenema. Start with questions like these:

What is your mission? Plan to invest time in answering the deceptively simple question: "What's the money for?" Focus first on problems external to your organization. Donors may not care that your organization needs funding for staff salaries; the question is what good do the staff achieve? Some organizations get bogged down in a needlessly complicated process of lengthy meetings where complex discussions are boiled down into a densely phrased motto that may not be meaningful to people who were not in the room when the decision was made. Simply state how the world will better if you succeed.

What proof is there that these problems are important? Give the statistics and stories that make your issues come alive. Plan to gather testimonials showing support from outside experts to add credibility.

What projects are essential to achieve your organizational goals? Develop action plans to show that you have believable ways to fix the problems.

What proves these solutions are wanted? Plan to show community support from the clients. Funders have seen too many projects fail because they were imposed by well-intentioned outsiders without confirming that the people they were trying to help were willing to cooperate.

What will it cost to implement these projects? Plan your budget to include an appropriate share of the unloved overhead costs in each project.

How rapidly do you need the funds? Urgent needs require different fundraising plans than situations where you can build patiently. If your need is urgent, plan to focus on major individual donors because they can give immediate contributions with no bureaucracy, while grants from corporations, foundations, and government can take three to six months or longer. If you have a list of donors, plan on a phone or email campaign, which can begin overnight, while letters and events take longer.

STEP 2: ASSESS YOUR CULTURE CAREFULLY

You can only plan to use fundraising methods that fit your organizations culture. Decide which of these issues affect your choice of tactics.

- Would you pay fundraisers a commission? This is prohibited in the code of ethics of the Association of Fundraising Professionals and many similar organizations. See http://www.afpnet. org/ethics/.

- Are there any corporations or other organizations whose support would be inappropriate for your work? corporate social reasonability is a growing issue.

- Do you have concerns about revenue that comes from gambling?

- Do you have concerns about events that include the consumption of alcohol?

- Does your organization have moral standards that would influence fundraising methods? For example, some charities might be troubled by The Brazilian Ball, a multi-million dollar charity event in Toronto that features scantily clad models. Some religious groups have prohibitions against credit cards because their interest rates are considered usury. A charity helping feed starving people might find a gourmet banquet inappropriate. An organization helping people with mobility challenges must make sure the venue for their event is accessible. Environmental organizations are troubled by the amount of paper wasted in direct mail.

- Do you have concerns about recognition offered to donors? Some point out that a poor person may give a larger portion of their limited resources than the wealthy person whose name appears on a plaque. Students may protest corporate influence on academic freedom.

STEP 3: REVIEW YOUR FUNDRAISING HISTORY

Reviewing the fundraising history of your organization is a critical step. If you are starting a new organization, consider these guidelines for the data you need to track from now on for an annual review of your fundraising plan.

Donor database:

How many donors do you have? Ideally you should break this into each category of the pyramid. You can combine several categories for your convenience.

- If you have very few supporters, you should probably plan for donor acquisition, but keep in mind this may not produce much revenue (and may even lose money) in the short run.

- If you have supporters at the lowest levels of the pyramid, but few at the top, your plan should probably focus on major gifts. You may find willing supporters who are giving much less than they could because you have never approached them personally to ask for more. They may be wondering why you have not asked at the appropriate level yet.

How many donors increased their gift from last year? Again this would be best broken out by each type of donor. If you do not have it in place already, your plan should probably include intentionally encouraging donors to give more than they did in the past.

How many donors did you lose and add? Calculate attrition based on those who gave two years ago who did not give last year. Too often the influx of new donors masks the loss of supporters. Most organizations need a plan to replace donors every year – often about 20% of the list – even before they can grow. What did it cost you to acquire the new donors?

How much do you expect donors to give over their long-term association with your organization? This *Long Term Value* (LTV) is often calculated as five years for typical donors. Your plan for investment in donor acquisition depends on knowing the payback.

How many lapsed donors gave again? Donors who have not given in a year or two are very likely to give again. A good fundraising plan has a series of letters to renew their support. Model this after the letters a magazine sends to renew subscriptions. Lapsed donors are more likely to give than those who have never supported you before. Many charities calculate that it is worth the cost to send them up to seven special letters to get them to give again. Even after that they include them in an annual prospect list

Fundraising tactics:

Return on investment (ROI). Before you develop a plan for the road ahead, look at the path so far. For each fundraising method you use (such as events, mail, personal visits, grant applications, etc.) determine the following:

- **Gross income:** All the revenue from each fundraising method. What specific steps could you do to increase income?

- **Direct costs:** This includes bills paid to outside suppliers, such as printers or caterers. What could you do to cut costs?

- **Net income:** Gross income minus direct costs gives the net income. When comparing your costs to other organizations, most only include direct costs. However all the factors below are real and should be included to determine true revenue (or losses).

- **In-Kind donations:** Inexperienced fundraisers do not include gifts of goods or services in their budgets. This might include free printing, or a donation of wine for an event. However ignoring these can lead to confusion when the gifts in-kind come in some years and not in others. Plan to show this as both an expense and a donation in all budgets. This is sometimes also referred to as *Gifts-in-Kind* (GIK).

- **Direct staff costs:** Plan to track the time fundraising staff invest in the work.

- **Indirect staff costs:** Plan for the real time other staff spend on fundraising, including managers, bookkeepers, secretaries, and, in some cases, project staff who are supposed to be caring for clients but instead are dragged away from regular duties to run an event or stuff envelopes.

- **Indirect costs:** Plan to honestly account for supplies used up, such as hundreds of sheets of letterhead and envelopes.

- **Volunteer time:** Plan to track the hours that volunteers work, and convert this to dollars. The easy way is to count everyone's time at minimum wage. A more accurate accounting would be based on the services people perform; for example a $300 an hour lawyer stuffing envelopes would be counted at minimum wage, while the same person providing legal advice would be counted at market value.

- **True net revenue:** Although this figure is often depressing, it needs to be honestly considered, at least for internal planning.

METHOD	Average Cost per $	Our organization's Cost per $
Direct mail acquisition	90¢ to $1.25	
Special events	50¢	
Product sales	35¢	
Telephone solicitation	32¢	
Planned Giving	25¢	
Gaming* (bingo, lotteries, raffles)	23¢	
Direct mail renewal	20¢	
Corporations/ Foundations	20¢	
Capital campaigns/ Major Gifts	10¢ to 20¢	
Workplace giving	7¢	
Average CTRAD	**26¢**	

* "One in four such games have fund-raising costs exceeding 40 per cent. More than five per cent lose money." *Globe and Mail*

Figure 1.9

Cost to raise a dollar (CTRAD):

Government and media are pressuring charities to spend less to raise more. While it is always good to eliminate waste, the reality is that fundraising costs vary widely, depending on factors such as the size of the charity, the popularity of the cause, the local economic climate, and many other factors. That said, surveys[20] have revealed average costs, and these can be useful benchmarks. How do your direct costs compare to the numbers in Figure 1.9? If you spend more, plan to explain why. If you spend less, plan to investigate whether spending more might produce more revenue.

The precise figures in this chart may vary from year to year. They'll also change for different types of campaigns; for example some special events are low budget and others require a high overhead. An organization just starting out or with a cause that is not in the media may spend more, while a popular cause could spend less.

The key message is not to put all your eggs in one basket (or as one punster, now mercifully unknown, said, "don't put all your begs in one ask-it").

A good plan uses a variety of tactics, which support each other. This is referred to as an "integrated fund development program." A direct mail campaign, for example, could be integrated with your website to provide more information, a related video and an interactive survey. A news release could be timed to go out just before the direct mail campaign is dropped, as a timely tactic to increase awareness and willingness to give.

The thank-you letter could invite donors to a special event, sponsored by a company, where an auction would be designed to upgrade the donors' gift levels. Planning for fund development means not thinking of any one tactic as free-standing, but looking at how they integrate so that the sum is greater than the parts.

Results:

Fundraising methods can produce a variety of outcomes. Money is not the only one, and not always the most important. Figure 1.10 asks you to

20 Association for Healthcare Philanthropy (AHP) Librarian Erica Heftmann, reported in *Canadian Fundraiser*, July 31, 1996 and Canada West Foundation survey of 1,516 charities (excluding religious groups and private foundations) reported in *Globe and Mail* 27 Aug. 1996.

Results	Previous Year 20__	Previous Year 20__	Last Year 20__	Current year 20__	Next year 20__	Future year 20__	Future year 20__
Gross revenue							
# new donors							
# new volunteers							
# new members / clients / other growth							
# previous donors renewed							
Media coverage or other quantifiable awareness							
Other							

Figure 1.10

assess the results you have achieved in the last year, and preferably several years. Also look to the future and project what you need to achieve in the next year to three years.

STEP 4: INVESTMENT CAPITAL

"It takes money to make money," as the old saying goes. In reality, it may take more than money - in the shape of other resources. Honestly estimate the answers to these questions:

Financial resources:

- How much could you spend on fundraising in the next year, with the understanding that you would get it all back, at worst, and likely have surplus income? If you have limited capital, plan to focus on low cost methods such as personal contact with major donors.

- How much risk capital would you be willing to spend on methods that might not pay back cash but would build strengths in other ways, such as acquiring new donors at a loss for long-term gain? If you can afford to invest, plan to acquire new donors. If you cannot, plan on upgrading.

- How much risk capital would you spend experimenting on tactics that might or might not produce good results for you? If you cannot take risks, plan on using the most predictably reliable tactics, such as direct mail. Special events are notoriously risky.

Figure 1.11 allows you to evaluate your success factors based on history and expectations.

	SCORE
This is the organization's first attempt at fundraising and we have unrealistic expectations for results. In addition, we have a tiny donor list, no budget or long-term plans for follow up, and have no time or willingness to learn.	**-1**
This is the organization's first attempt at fundraising, and we have unrealistic expectations for results. In addition, we have a tiny donor list, no budget or long-term plans for follow up, but have time and willingness to learn.	**0**
This is the organization's first attempt at fundraising but we have realistic expectations for results. We have only a small donor list, a small budget and limited plans for follow-up.	**1**
This is one of the organization's first attempts at fundraising, but we have realistic expectations for results. We have an adequate budget and realistic plans for follow up. However, we are not comfortable with standard practices such as list-trading or frequent mailings.	**2**
This is the one of the organization's first attempts at fundraising, but we have realistic expectations for results. We have a substantial investment budget and realistic plans for follow-up. We are comfortable with practices such as list-trading and frequent mailings.	**3**
The organization has a track record of fundraising campaigns but need changes to our systems, such as faster thank-you letters, introduction of monthly giving, list segmentation, new database software, etc.	**4**
The organization has been doing effective fundraising campaigns several times a year, and has good database software. We use all the techniques for upgrading effectively.	**5**

Figure 1.11

Human capital:

Fundraising is a people-to-people process. An honest assessment of your resources may tell you where you need to invest or how to plan.

- **Staff**: If staff resources are very limited, your plan may be best focused on tactics that can easily be delegated to outside companies, such as direct mail.

  - How many staff do you have dedicated to fundraising?
  - What experience in fundraising do they have?
  - What skills and talents does each contribute?
  - How many other staff could be involved in fundraising as needed?.

- Include your senior staff person, often called the executive director or president, because many donors want to meet senior staff. At Canadian universities and colleges, the senior staff person typically spends 40-60% her time on fundraising. Other staff can provide flexibility during busy times. If they are not available, you may need to plan to recruit part-time staff or volunteers to process donations quickly during peak periods, or help run labour-intense methods such as special events.

  - What experience in fundraising do they have?
  - What skills and talents does each contribute?

- **Volunteers**: Volunteers can be more important than staff for fundraising. Donors prefer to be approached by volunteers, because of their dedication. Fundraising costs are lower when labour is unpaid.

  - How many board members are, or could be, involved in fundraising? If the board is

Media Coverage	SCORE
Other major crises dominate the news so completely that your issue seems trivial or even inappropriate to raise at this moment.	-1
The issue is not in the news.	0
The issue was in the news more than six months ago.	1
The issue was in the news in the last six months, but is now fading.	2
The issue is in the news now, but not prominently featured.	3
The issue is prominent in the news, appearing on page one or the first ten minutes (or so) of the TV news.	4
The issue has been prominent in the news for several days. People who receive your appeals already know it is urgent.	5
Brand Recognition	
Your organization is brand new, has a name that is an acronym or not easily understood, and no budget for promotion.	-1
The organization's name is not familiar to most people, or it is an acronym not easily understood, or has recently been renamed, (particularly if the new name is not familiar). E.g.: CARE, Oxfam, the Munck Centre, Southlake Hospital	0
The organization's name may not be familiar to most people, but the name is self-explanatory. Examples: the Canadian Foundation for Cystic Fibrosis, Prostate Cancer Research.	1
The organization's name is familiar to the target audience, but not necessarily to outsiders. Examples: Rethink, McGill, Humber Institute of Technology and Advanced Learning.	2
The organization's name is familiar to many people, but there can be misunderstanding about the mission or roots of the group or negative connections. Examples: Ronald McDonald House, MADD, Jews for Judaism.	3
The name is familiar from media coverage, marketing or connections to others or the organization will invest in making it a household word. Examples: The David Suzuki Foundation, The Raptors Foundation	4
The name is familiar to almost everyone, and most people understand what they do. Examples: the Red Cross, UNICEF, Sick Kids Hospital, the Roman Catholic Church, The Canadian Cancer Society, Harvard.	5

Figure 1.12

not willing or able to actively contact people they know for donations, (particularly major donors) it may be time to plan on recruiting additional board members or a special committee (often called the *campaign cabinet*).

□ What experience in fundraising do they have?

□ What skills and talents does each contribute?

□ What contacts do they now (or might in future) share with potential donors?

□ Are they are willing to ask others to donate?

□ Do they donate themselves?

• How many other volunteers are/or could be involved in fundraising?

□ What experience in fundraising do they have?

□ What skills and talents does each contribute?

□ What contacts do they now (or might in future) share with potential donors?

□ Are they are willing to ask others to donate?

□ Do they donate themselves?

Reputation:

• The better known an organization is, and the more popular the cause, the better the chances of getting support. Use Figure 1.12 to score your organization. If you do not score well on this chart, either plan on lowering your expectations for results, or on investing in building your profile with your key donors.

Tactics:

• No tactic is sacred. Just because you have used it before, does not mean you should use it again. The fact that you have not used it in the past does not mean you should not start in the future. If you did try it and had a bad result, try testing with a different methodology. Use Figure 1.13 for each method you have used, and plot it against the following criteria:

Tactic	Not tested but could be of interest	Tested, results not promising	Tested, strong growth potential, needs work	Ready to roll out	In full bloom – will continue to use	Wilting. May be able to refresh but may be on the way out	Phase this out soon. It is past the best-before date	Re-testing this – we've done it and may be able to bring it back in future	Tried and died – will not do again (or not appropriate for us)
Direct mail									
Email									
Monthly giving									
Website									
Social media									
Door to door									
Street based									
Telephone									

Tactic	Not tested but could be of interest	Tested, results not promising	Tested, strong growth potential, needs work	Ready to roll out	In full bloom – will continue to use	Wilting. May be able to refresh but may be on the way out	Phase this out soon. It is past the *best-before date*	Re-testing this – we've done it and may be able to bring it back in future	Tried and died – will not do again (or not appropriate for us)
Other mass marketing									
Grants from corporations									
Grants from foundations									
Grants from government									
Other grants									
Corporate sponsorship									
Gala events									
Concerts									
Athletic events									
Lotteries & gaming									
Other events									
Major individual donors									
Memorial / celebration gifts									
Planned giving									
Earned income									
Other									

Figure 1.13

STEP 5: ASSESSING THE COMPETITION

Guides to developing a business plan for a small business often recommend starting here.[21]

The fundraising world is much less competitive than the business world. We are all out to do good. However, you may find that other organizations are approaching the same donors for support. This confuses the donors.

For example, there are at least 189 Canadian charities with the word "cancer" in their names (according to CRA). You can find 56 Canadian charities with the word "Haiti" in their titles, and 92 disaster funds, and that does not count all of the international development charities, or non-profit groups that are not registered charities. In the US the IRS shows 773 charities that include the word "Haiti" and 2,559 using "cancer."

Here are a few research tips to get you started on this segment.

- What other non-profit groups do work like yours?
  - You can find a searchable list of registered Canadian charities at the Canadian government website www.cra.gc.ca. For US charities, see http://www.irs.gov/app/pub-78/
    - □ If there are other charities like yours, exactly how is yours different?
    - □ Is another charity needed, or would it be more efficient to raise funds that an existing charity can administer?
- How much do other groups raise?
  - Each registered charity must file a report every year. The overview is available at the CRA website. In addition many charities produce annual reports detailing their income and expenses. These may be published on their website or print copies may be available on request.
- What makes you think you can raise more than they do?
- How will your fundraising be different?
- Where do they get support?

21 For samples guidelines on business plans, see *http://sbinfocanada.about. com/cs/businessplans/a/bizplanoutline.htm*

- Many non-profit groups list their major donors, sponsors and volunteers on their websites, in their annual reports, on plaques on their walls, or in booklets given to guests at special events.
- Would these same donors support you? We are not suggesting you steal their donor lists. We are recommending you look for patterns. If a company, foundation, government department, or individual supports several similar organizations, they may support you too.

THE PLANNING PROCESS

Developing your unique plan requires time and thought. This section recommends effective tools for planning itself.

Who is involved?

Ideally, the board should be involved in the early stages of developing the plan, to sketch in the big picture. They answer questions such as these:

1. Is the goal rapid growth, moderate growth, to maintain status quo, respond to a crisis such as the loss of a major revenue stream, or downsize in a managed way?
2. Is the focus short-term or long-term?
3. What resources are available to invest in the strategy?
4. What risk level can they tolerate?
5. What constraints affect the plan, such as aversion to direct mail or gambling revenue, or a bias toward special events?

With those parameters, a small team can go away to develop the plan. At least one board member should be on this team, so that they maintain ownership of the process.

Staff must be represented so that they can speak to the operational issues. Outside experts may provide missing knowledge, either as volunteers or consultants. Members, clients, patients or whatever you call the people you serve should also be represented, to make sure the plan does not unintentionally damage their wider interests while raising funds. For example, people with disabilities have rebelled against any campaigns that depict them as helpless, just to gain sympathy.

The team develops the specifics. They look forward three to five years, as well as looking at history over the same period.

Since there are so many unknowns when looking to the future, all estimates of expenses and income should include at least two scenarios: one based on a pessimistic view and one that is more optimistic. The plan must include options and variant scenarios depending on a range of possible developments.

Responsibility for the plan must be widespread, according to consultant Lynda Lysakowski:[22]

- Each department develops their own action plan, which includes timelines, budgets and responsibilities. The plan will be meaningless if it doesn't include the factors to implement the plan. How much will it cost? When will it be done? Who is responsible for implementing this strategy?

- The plan also needs to include a process for evaluation and must be measured at least quarterly to track progress. The best plan in the world doesn't work if it sits in a drawer. It must be dynamic and flexible.

- A system to monitor your plan is critical. A key person, often the vice president of the board, must be assigned to monitoring the plan on a regular basis, holding accountable all those who are involved in the implementation of the plan, and being prepared to make adjustments to the plan when necessary.

The recommended plan should be widely circulated for feedback. The planning process is not just to create a document, but to build widespread support for it, among all the players. For example, one organization found their plan worked in theory, but in practice was blocked by the actions of one employee – the receptionist – who was in charge of sending the thank you letters but did not like the wording, so she did not send them out. Although she had not been consulted on the plan, in reality she had all the power. Firing her was not an option. The plan was re-negotiated.

Finally, the plan should go back to the board for approval. While the board should not get involved in the operating details, they are legally responsible for the direction of the organization. They must accept

the plan or send it back for revisions. This means the planning process must allow for several months to complete.

Once a decision has been made, try not to change the plan more than once every quarter, unless there is a crisis. At the same time, be sure to update the plan at least once a year so that you are always looking three to five years into the future, and always make appropriate modifications based on what you learn along the way.

This is like Kaizen, the Japanese process of continuous improvement. Set goals, measure progress, then adjust either the means or the goals.

Use the goals in Figure 1.14 to help determine which goals need to be determined and measured.

CONCLUSION

Moving from random acts of kindness to sustainable support systems requires planning.

Your plans should be based on solid evidence, not wishful thinking. While fundraising is still evolving from art and gradually becoming a more exact science, the techniques and information here should help you move forward in an intelligent way, not depending on magical thinking.

---

22 *http://www.cvfundraising.com/resources/tutorials/does-planning-really-matter*

Goal	Previous benchmark (e.g. 3 years ago)	Current measure	Goal for next year	Actual after one year	Goal for 3 years into the future
Gross dollars raised					
Net dollars raised					
Cost per dollar					
Number of donors					
Cost to add a donor					
Donors renewed					
Cost to renew a donor					
Donors upgraded					
Cost to upgrade a donor					
Number of monthly donors					
Cost to convert a donor to monthly					
Number of major donors					
Cost of major donors					
Amount of media coverage					
Cost of media coverage					
Long-term Value of Donors					

Figure 1.14

ADDITIONAL RESOURCES

Books

▶ ALLEN, J. (2008). *Event Planning: The Ultimate Guide*, Second Edition, John Wiley & Sons Inc., Toronto.

▶ ALLISON, M & KAYE, J. (2005). *Strategic Planning for Nonprofit Organizations*, John Wiley & Sons Inc.

▶ BALMER, K & MALLABONE G. (2010). *The Fundraising Audit handbook: What you need to know to evaluate and improve performance*, Civil Sector Press.

▶ BURK, P. (2003). *Donor-Centered Fundraising*, Cygnus Applied Research Inc.

▶ CIALDINI, ROBERT B. (1984). *Influence: The Psychology of Persuasion*, William Morrow.

▶ HITCHCOCK, S. & WARWICK, M. (2001). *Ten Steps to Fundraising Success: Choosing the Right Strategy for Your Organization*, Jossey-Bass.

▶ KLEIN, K. (2000). *Fundraising for the Long Haul*, Chardon Press.

▶ ROSS, B. & SEGAL, C. (2008). *The Influential Fundraiser*, Jossey-Bass.

▶ ROSSO, HENRY A. (HANK) (1991). *Achieving Excellence in Fund Raising*, Jossey-Bass.

▶ SWAIGEN, J., YOUNG, J. & WYMAN, K. *Fundraising for Nonprofit Groups*, Self Counsel Press.

▶ WYMAN, K. (1993). *Face to Face: How to Get Bigger Donations from Very Generous People*, Ken Wyman & Associates Inc.

▶ WYMAN, K. *Planning Successful Fundraising Programs*, Ken Wyman & Associates Inc.

Online documents

▶ ARLETT, A., BELL, P. AND THOMPSON, R.W. *Canada Gives: Trends and Attitudes Towards Charitable Giving and Voluntarism* (The Cana-dian Centre for Philanthropy, now renamed Imagine Canada). Retrieved from http://www.givingandvolunteering.ca/files/giving/en/csgvp_highlights_2004_en.pdf

▶ *CASE Reporting Standards & Management Guidelines for Educational Fundraising* http://www.case.org/Publications_and_Products/CASE_Store/CASE_Reporting_Standards_and_Management_Guidelines_for_Educational_Fundraising.html

▶ *CMA Fundraiser's Handbook* http://www.the-cma.org/?WCE=C=47%7CK=225580

▶ CORNERSTONE CANADA 3rd Annual Global File Audit Report (2005-2009). http://csearch.ca/mc/GFA/download.aspx

URLs

▶ http://fhs.mcmaster.ca/main/documents/DeGroote_Gift.pdf

▶ http://give.utoronto.ca/recognition/presidents-circle/

▶ http://majorgivingnow.org/

▶ http://sbinfocanada.about.com/cs/businessplans/a/bizplanoutline.htm

▶ http://web.uvic.ca/givingtouvic/donorRelations.php#limitations

▶ http://www.afpnet.org/ethics/

▶ http://www.allbusiness.com/specialty-businesses/non-profit-businesses/1045122-1.html

▶ http://www.canadapost.ca/cpo/mc/business/productsservices/atoz/ncoa.jsf

▶ http://www.charityvillage.com/cv/research/rfrm29.html

▶ http://www.cra-arc.gc.ca/E/pub/tg/p113/p113-e.html#P99_6372

▶ http://www.irs.gov/app/pub-78/

▶ http://www.kwalliance.org/Portals/3/Writing%20
Your%20Fundraising%20Plan%20Final%20
Shanda.pdf

▶ http://www.raisersharpe.com/

▶ http://www.supportingadvancement.com/

▶ http://www40.statcan.ca/l01/cst01/demo56a-
eng.htm

ABOUT THE AUTHOR

Ken Wyman, CFRE

For more than 35 years Ken has invented and adapted techniques to help non-profit groups learn the secrets of growth. He has helped hundreds of organizations raise millions of dollars. Ken is professor and program coordinator in the Fundraising and Volunteer Management postgraduate program at Humber in Toronto.

Ken is a trainer, academic, and author, and has published seven books. Ken was the host and creative consultant of the educational TV series The Fund Raising Game. The eight half-hour episodes are available on video tape, with a 270-page workbook. Ken has been named Outstanding Fundraiser of the Year by AFP Toronto chapter.

Ken's voluntary service is extensive and includes Imagine-Canada's Development Committee, and the MetaSoft Client Advisory Board. He was a founding board member of The Change Canada Charitable Foundation and of the Canada Advancing Philanthropy Board, and a member of the Social Planning and Allocation Committee of the Jewish Federation of Toronto as well as the board of Family Day Care Services, and Information London, to name just a few.

Earlier, as a journalist and photographer, Ken filed stories from across Canada, Europe, South America and the Middle East. He has reported for magazines, newspapers, CBC radio and TV news.

CHAPTER 2

ETHICS AND THE BASIS FOR ETHICAL STANDARDS
DIANNE LISTER, CFRE

Never let your sense of morals prevent you from doing what is right.

- Isaac Asimov

read more...

Defining ethics is complicated.[1] Some philosophers have attempted to make ethics objective and universal, while others claim moral decision making is a lonely, intuitive, and wholly individual business of making fundamental choices. Some anchor ethics in religion; others believe morality is an odd mixture of received tradition and personal opinion. For the purposes of this chapter, I am using the definition from Michael Josephson of the Josephson Institute of Ethics:

Ethics is a code of conduct, based on moral duties and obligations, which indicates how we should behave. Ethics deals with the ability to distinguish right from wrong and with the commitment to do right.

Simply stated, ethics refers to standards of behaviour that tell us how human beings ought to act in the many situations in which they find themselves – as friends, parents, children, citizens, business people, governments, organizations, and so on. It is helpful to identify what ethics is not:

- Ethics is not the same as feelings – feelings may provide important information for our ethical choices; sometimes our feelings will tell us it is uncomfortable to do the right thing.

- Ethics is not religion – many people are not religious; most religions do advocate high ethical standards, but sometimes do not address all of the types of problems we face.

- Ethics is not following the law – a good legal system does incorporate many ethical standards, but law can deviate from what is ethical; law can be ethically corrupt (as some totalitarian regimes have made it); law can be a function of power alone.

- Ethics is not following culturally accepted norms – some cultures are ethical, but others become corrupt or blind to certain ethical concerns (consider the Truth and Reconciliation Commission and Canada's colonization of aboriginal communities).

- Ethics is not science – social and natural science can provide important data to help us make

better ethical choices, but science alone cannot tell us what we ought to do.

If our ethics are not based on feelings, religion, law, accepted social practice, or science, what are they based on? See Figure 2.1 for what philosophers and ethicists suggest are five different sources of ethical standards.

Five Sources of Ethical Standards

1. Utilitarian Approach

2. Rights Approach

3. Fairness/Justice Approach

4. Common Good Approach

5. Virtue Approach

Figure 2.1

The Utilitarian Approach
In this approach, ethics produces the greatest balance of good over harm. The utilitarian approach deals with consequences; it tries to both increase the good done and to reduce the harm done.

The Rights Approach
This approach starts with the belief that humans have a dignity based on their human nature *per se* and on the ability to choose freely what they do with their lives. On the basis of such dignity, they have the right to be treated as ends and not merely as means to other ends. Rights imply duties – in particular, the duty to respect others' rights.

The Fairness or Justice Approach
The essence of this approach is that all equals should be treated equally. If people are treated unequally, then such treatment should be fairly based on some standard that is defensible. For example, differences in salaries can often create a huge disparity, and many ask if such disparity is based on a defensible standard, or whether it is the result of an imbalance of power and is therefore unfair.

---

1   Much of the content of this section is drawn from Santa Clara University's Markhula Centre for Applied Ethics (*www.scu.edu/ethics/practicing/framework. html*.)

The Common Good Approach

Greek philosophies contributed to the notion that life in community is a good in itself and our actions should contribute to that life, This approach suggests that the interlocking relationships of society are the basis for ethical decision making and calls attention to the common conditions that are important to the welfare of everyone.

The Virtue Approach

A very ancient approach is that ethical action ought to be consistent with certain ideal virtues that provide for the full development of our humanity. Such virtues are habits and dispositions that enable us to act to the highest potential of our character and on behalf of values like truth and beauty. Such virtues include honesty, courage, compassion, generosity, tolerance, fidelity, integrity and prudence.

Later in this chapter, we explore how to heighten our ethical antennae through the use of an ethical decision-making framework.

UNDERSTANDING ETHICS AS IMPORTANT TO THE PHILANTHROPIC PROCESS

The impulse to give, community building and volunteering are traits built into our DNA.

Charity used to be seen as intimate, grass roots, neighbourly and personal, often reflecting an altruistic, if not faith-based, perspective. With the growth of charitable and non-profit organizations, professionalized staff and bureaucratic systems, we have moved from direct acts of charity to the business of philanthropy. In this 'business' model, a donor's funds are entrusted to third parties whose organizations' missions reflect the donor's values and personal charitable goals. The professional philanthropic fundraiser is now the honest broker, the go-between, the keeper of promises; the organization is the trustee of the funds, the steward of resources and the entity which ensures the donor's goals and wishes are executed, and in some cases, protected and enforced in perpetuity.

It is this intermediary function performed by professional staff who work for charities and non-profits

that creates a special duty of care to protect the public trust.

William Schambra argues that there is a crisis in public trust in the non-profit sector and it is exacerbated by a profound distrust of large institutions.[2] While his comments are centred on the United States of America, I believe they also apply within the Canadian context. No matter where found – in government, the economy, or the culture – large institutions sooner or later come to be seen as remote, bureaucratic, inflexible, unresponsive and undemocratic. Until recent times, the non-profit sector was largely immune from this reaction.

"Its local civic institutions – neighbourhoods, churches, ethnic and voluntary associations – were not run by distant, arrogant bureaucrats but by friends and neighbours. No arcane professional experience was required to be part of civil society; it was enough to bring amateur personal idealism, compassion and small gifts of time and energy. There was no radical division between the organization's "expert" and the subordinate "client." In a system of mutual self-help, today's provider was likely to be tomorrow's receiver. The failure of the sector to live up to this myth contributes to the erosion of public confidence in it."

In today's context, both individual philanthropic fundraisers and charitable and non-profit organizations require an understanding of the role of ethics in earning and maintaining the public's trust. A significant contribution to the field was made by the Independent Sector (IS) in 2004.

The Board of Directors of IS approved its *Statement of Values and Code of Ethics for Non-profit and Philanthropic Organizations* which was designed not only to guide its own organization, but to act as a model code for its members and for the sector as a whole. The "independent sector" includes private, family, operating, community and corporate foundations, and organizations whose primary purpose is advocacy. The introduction to the Code states:

"As a matter of fundamental principle, the non-profit and philanthropic community should adhere to the highest ethical standards because it is the right thing to do. As a matter of pragmatic self-interest, the community should

---

2   Schambra, William. (2008). *Restoring Public Confidence in the Nonprofit Sector.* In Janice Gow Petty (ed.), *Ethical Fundraising: A Guide for Nonprofit Boards and Fundraisers* (pp. 223-232). John Wiley & Sons.

do so because public trust in our performance is the bedrock of our legitimacy. Donors and volunteers support charitable organizations because they trust them to carry out their missions, be good stewards of their resources, and uphold rigorous standards of conduct."

The IS Code also notes:

"Adherence to the law is the minimum standard of expected behaviour. Non-profit and philanthropic organizations must do more, however, than simply obey the law. We must embrace the spirit of the law, often going beyond legal requirements and making sure that what we do is matched by what the public understands about what we do. Transparency, openness and responsiveness to public concerns must be integral to our behaviour."

The Association of Fundraising Professionals (AFP) has the longest standing and most robust Code of Ethical Principles and Standards in the world, binding over 35,000 members world-wide. Its enforcement process and sanctions move the Code from being aspirational and theoretical to being a practical guide in the complex arena of philanthropy. First developed in 1964, the primary message has remained constant:

"AFP members, both individual and business, aspire to practice their profession with integrity, honesty, truthfulness and adherence to the absolute obligation to safeguard the public trust. "

These Codes relate the place of privilege that charities and non-profits play in furthering the goals of donors with the fact that "ethics is good business." Conversely, once a charitable organization's reputation is damaged – even by actions which have a mere appearance of impropriety – donor and community support will drop dramatically.

THE ROLE OF ETHICS IN SELF-REGULATION

"Obedience to the unenforceable is the extent to which the individuals composing the na-

tion can be trusted to obey self-imposed law."
- John Fletcher Mouton

Mouton's concept, (an English mathematician, barrister and judge) provides an interesting lens through which to view the action of people who participate in the philanthropic process – board members, fundraising volunteers, professional fundraising executives, and leaders in the non-profit and charitable sectors.

Andrew Watt, President and CEO, of AFP discusses the topic of self-regulation and differing approaches to self-regulation among international fundraising associations in his chapter in *Ethical Fundraising: A Guide for Non-profit Boards and Fundraisers.*

He notes that it often takes a series of scandals, public scrutiny and the threat of direct regulation to affect a significant change in attitude within the non-profit sector, allowing organizations to begin to collaborate and discuss the tools that are necessary to improve transparency and accountability.

Figure 2.2 shows that the concepts behind these tools are not complex, and include:

Transparency and Accountability Tools

1. Standardized reporting and accounting

2. Clearly agreed-upon definitions of fundraising activities

3. Templates for Board reports

4. Sector benchmarking to provide internal comparative analysis

5. Web platforms for presenting statutory reports

6. A credible structure to underpin self-regulation (such as *A Donor Bill of Rights* or *Imagine Canada's Ethical Code* program)

Figure 2.2

Well-established structures for the regulation of non-profit activity exist in Canada, as well as the United States and England. It is not a coincidence that it is in these environments that effective self-regulation of fundraising activity has been firmly established as well.

Responsibility for the regulation of charities in Canada sits primarily with the Canada Revenue Agency, Charities Directorate. Legislation also exists at provincial level and territorial levels, and the common law concept of "parens patri" is carried out under the auspices of the various provincial offices of the Public Guardian and Trustee. For example, in Ontario, the role of the Office of the Public Guardian and Trustee is to protect the public interest and will undertake investigations based on complaints about the misuse of charitable property.

SHARPENING OUR ETHICAL ANTENNAE: ETHICAL DECISION MAKING

In order to support the position that fundraisers and those involved in the business of philanthropy ought to be self-regulating, it is critical to have a trained sensitivity to ethical issues and a practiced method for exploring the ethical aspects of a decision.

The following framework has been developed by the Markhula Centre for Applied Ethics at Santa Clara University, and has been abbreviated for the purpose of this chapter.

Markhula Ethical Decision Making Framework

1. Recognize an ethical issue

2. Get the facts

3. Evaluate the alternatives

4. Make a decision and test

5. Act and reflect on the outcome

Figure 2.3

Recognize an ethical issue
- Could this decision or situation be damaging to someone or to some group?

- Does this decision involve a choice between a good and bad alternative, or perhaps between two 'goods' and two 'bads'?

- Is the issue about more than what is legal or what is most efficient?

Get the facts
- What are the relevant facts?

- What facts are not known?

- Do I know enough to make a decision?

- What individuals and groups have an important stake in the outcome?

- Are some concerns more important? Why?

- What are the options for acting?

- Have all the relevant persons and groups been consulted?

Evaluate the alternatives
- Which option will produce the most good and do the least harm?

- Which option best respects the rights of all who have a stake?

- Which option treats people equally or proportionately?

- Which option best serves the community as a whole, and not just some members?

- Which option leads me to act as the sort of person I want to be (or, if an organization, leads it to be in alignment with its values?)

Make a decision and test it
- Considering all these approaches, which option best addresses the situation?

- If I told someone I respect – or a television audience – which option I have chosen, what would they say? (sometimes, this is also called the "child on the shoulder test")

Act and reflect on the outcome
- How can my decision be implemented with the greatest care and attention to the concern of all of the stakeholders?

- How did my decision turn out and what have I learned from this specific situation?

Professional fundraisers and leaders in non-profits require time and focus to practice ethical-decision making, and the case study methodology proves very popular in workshops. Ethics training materials and sample case studies are available through associations such as the Association of Fundraising Professionals, and the Canadian Association of Gift Planners.

HISTORY OF ETHICAL CODES IN CANADA

Ethical fundraising is essential for building the public trust on which philanthropy rests. There are two types of ethical codes: codes which are ascribed to by individual practitioners, and organizational codes which bind the Boards of Directors.

Canada has over 80,000 registered charities, and a growing cadre of professional philanthropic fundraisers. Within AFP there are over 3,000 members in Canada and the AFP Toronto chapter is the largest in the world, with over 1,100 members. The history of the development of ethical codes in Canada parallels the evolution of AFP's Code of Ethics. In the last two decades, Canadian leadership in the area of ethical fundraising has also been demonstrated through other organizations such as Association of Healthcare Philanthropy (Canada Regional Cabinet), and the Canadian Association of Gift Planners.

A key goal of AFP is to advance and foster the highest ethical standards in the fundraising profession. The fundamental purpose of the *AFP Code of Ethical Principles and Standards* and enforcement procedures is to eliminate unethical behaviour, not to impose punishment. The top ethics priority today is educating members, non-profit executives, lawmakers, regulators, donors, journalists and the public at large about ethical practices in non-profit fundraising.

The need for a professional code of ethics was one of the original driving forces behind the formation of the National Society of Fund Raisers (NSFRE - the precursor to AFP) and the code remains an essential core element of the organization today.

The original code was adopted by the Board of NSFR in 1965. It contained most of the core principles found in the current code and served NSFR and NSFRE until the early 1990's.

One of the most important incidents regarding the code occurred in 1987. The NSFRE Board was considering revoking the membership of a member accused of accepting percentage-based compensation, but legal counsel advised that taking such action would put NSFRE at risk of a legal suit or a restraint-of-trade sanction by the Federal Trade Commission. After much discussion, the Board voted to suspend the code's prohibition against percentage-based compensation. To deal with the shortcomings of the Code, a distinguished committee of senior fundraisers was created – this group took four years to revise the Code and develop formal enforcement procedures which could withstand potential challenges under administrative law concepts.

Key revisions of the Code include the following:

- November 1991 - an "aspirational" *Code of Ethical Principles* was adopted by the NSFRE Board

- November 1992 - *Standards of Professional Practice* and guidelines for interpreting the standards which, among other things, restored the prohibition against commissions and percentage-based compensation, was adopted by the NSFRE Board

- November 1993 - enforcement procedures were completed and adopted by the NSFRE Board

- November 2007 – seven new standards were adopted by the AFP Board to govern ethical practices of AFP business members and their employees, and the name was changed to the *AFP Code of Ethical Principles and Standards*

Currently the Code applies to anyone who has sworn to uphold the Code, which means members of AFP, employees of AFP business members and persons who hold an AFP-sanctioned professional credential.

The ethics enforcement process permits any individual to report an alleged violation of the code by an AFP member or other person subject to the Code, by means of an ethics query or formal complaint. A query is a means for inquiring whether or not a practice warrants filing a complaint, and to request assistance from the Ethics Committee to resolve an issue or practice of concern. The process allows for the protection of the rights of the complaining party and the accused.

Any individual, whether an AFP member or not, may file a formal complaint alleging ethical misconduct by a person subject to the code. The complaint must be in writing and signed by the complainant, using a form provided by AFP.

After a complaint is filed, the Ethics Committee will investigate the complaint to determine whether there is enough factual evidence to warrant a hearing. The committee will hold a hearing if necessary, at which the parties may be represented by legal counsel, and then will adjudicate the case. The enforcement procedures permit a variety of sanctions, the most severe of which is revocation of the CFRE credential and permanent expulsion from the AFP. Expulsions are published in AFP and trade periodicals and listed on the AFP website.

The AFP's Ethics program extends beyond merely enforcing the code. In 1993, NSFRE, AHP, CASE and AAFRC issued *A Donor Bill of Rights,* which spells out principles that donors should expect from charities and is now used and cited around the world.

AFP also helped propose and draft the *International Statement of Ethical Principles in Fundraising,* which organizations in 24 countries endorsed in 2006. Advocated by AFP, the Fundraising Institute of the United Kingdom, and the Fundraising Institute of Australia – and four years in the making – the statement is, in essence, a universal code for fundraisers regardless of where they work. The statement recognizes that the fundraisers are subject to many different jurisdictions, and that they must observe the law of the jurisdiction in which they work. The statement addresses five universal principles:

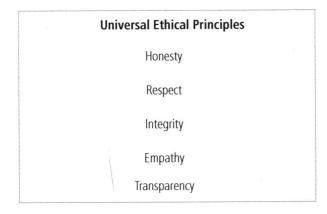

Universal Ethical Principles

Honesty

Respect

Integrity

Empathy

Transparency

Figure 2.4

Honesty – Fundraisers shall at all times act honestly and truthfully so that the public trust

is protected and donors are beneficiaries are not misled.

Respect – Fundraisers shall at all times act with respect for the dignity of their profession and their organization and with respect for the dignity of donors and beneficiaries.

Integrity – Fundraisers will act openly and with regard to their responsibility for public trust. They shall disclose all actual or potential conflicts of interest and avoid any appearance of personal or professional misconduct.

Empathy – Fundraisers will work in a way that promotes their purpose and encourage others to use the same professional standards and engagement. They shall value individual privacy, freedom of choice and diversity in all forms.

Transparency – Fundraisers stimulate clear reports about the work they do, the way donations are managed and disbursed and costs and expenses, in an accurate and comprehensible way.

Canadian charities wishing to make a public commitment to ethical fundraising and financial accountability may apply to join Imagine Canada's Ethical Code program. Imagine Canada describes its *Ethical Fundraising and Financial Accountability Code* as being owned and operated by the charitable sector. It was created through a series of Canada-wide sector consultations spanning groups from the social services, sports, arts and environmental sectors. It relies upon participating charities to promote its objects and uphold its integrity. Imagine Canada acts as the secretariat. The volunteer Ethical Code Committee comprising fundraising and finance experts is an arms-length body that can informally review practices and answer questions to the Code in addition to reviewing complaints from donors and members of the public, donors and stakeholders.

The program was endorsed by AFP, launched in 2007 and revised in 2008. Currently over 300 charities across Canada have applied for membership, and have the right to use the logo or trust mark. For donors and community members, this trust mark acts as a seal of approval, indicating that the charity is in full compliance with the Code, and assures donors that the charity will manage donations responsibility so that gifts can have the largest impact possible.

Sample of ethical codes used in Canada

Canada has a vibrant philanthropic sector, and all major associations which provide services to various members within the sector have Code of Ethics and related training materials:

- Association of Fundraising Professionals (AFP) – AFP Code of Ethical Principles and Standards (revised 2007)

- Association for Healthcare Philanthropy (AHP) Statement of Professional Standards and Conduct

- Canadian Association of Gift Planners (CAGP-ACPDP) – Code of Ethics (revised 2009)

- Council for Advancement and Support of Education (CASE) – CASE Statement of Ethics; CASE Reporting Standards & Management Guidelines (revised 2009)

- Imagine Canada – Ethical Fundraising and Financial Accountability Code (revised 2008)

In addition, several national and international non-profit and charitable organizations with operations in Canada have adopted Codes of Ethics, contain ethical statements in their core values and offer resources which assist professional staff, volunteers and governing bodies in protecting the public trust.

Examples include:

- The Salvation Army

- United Way of Canada

- Community Foundations of Canada

A soon-to-be-released AFP Ethics Assessment Inventory (EAI) is an online survey providing fundraisers and organizations with the following:

- A snapshot of their ethical performance;

- A comparison of themselves with peers from across AFP; and

- A way to assess and strengthen ethical dimensions of their practice.

The following tips for ethical best practice can be implemented by fundraising professionals in their organization.

Best Practice Tips

☐ Fundraisers ought to subscribe to a Code of Ethics and be encouraged to seek certification as a Certified Fundraising Executive (CFRE)

☐ Non-profit leaders ought to be committed to a reflective practice which allows time for case study and training in ethical decision-making

☐ Non-profit organizations ought to adopt an organizational creed of ethical practices

☐ Ethical audits or self-evaluations should be conducted annually

☐ Infuse the ethical decision-making process into the culture of the total organization

☐ Create a page on your organization's website titled "Ethics and Accountability" and post your organization's Code of Ethics, endorsement of *A Donor Bill of Rights* or your organization's trust mark as a member of Imagine Canada's Ethical Code Program

☐ Host community-based workshops or panel discussions on the topic of ethics – include donors, business leaders, volunteers

---

Figure 2.5

Issues within the Canadian context

Ethical dilemmas present themselves without regard to geography. But sometimes, practicing fundraising in Canada can present its own challenges.

The sector is still relatively small in comparison to the United States, and while there are over 80,000 registered charities, it is estimated that less than 25% have paid professional staff. This means that we often know the leaders at the national level (as do the professional recruiters), and we certainly know our peers within our own communities.

We also know that there is a fair amount of "churn" within the philanthropic and not-for-profit sector, with the average length of employment being 24-26 months. The combination of these factors means that over a decade, one professional fundraiser could be working for three to four charities in the same city or regional community.

Sharpening our Canadian ethical antennae, we should be vigilant about the following scenarios:

- *Monitoring* when donors or volunteers become friends, and how we set parameters regarding our personal and professional lives (especially within a smaller community).

- *Ensuring our behaviour* outside of the workplace, but in the eye of the public, does not create the appearance of impropriety.

- *Being clear with employers and donors*, that donor information resides with our employer and does not move with the fundraiser to the new job.

- *Offering training* and developing protocol guidelines for use within our own institutions that ensure the confidentiality of donor information and compliance with privacy legislation.

AFP CODE OF ETHICAL PRINCIPLES AND STANDARDS OF PROFESSIONAL PRACTICE

Adopted 1964; amended Sept. 2007

AFP is the world's largest organization representing professional fundraisers. It exists to foster the development and growth of fundraising professionals and the profession, to promote high ethical behavior in the fundraising profession and to preserve and enhance philanthropy and volunteerism. It's members are motivated by an inner drive to improve the quality of life through the causes they serve. They serve the ideal of philanthropy, are committed to the preservation and enhancement of volunteerism; and hold stewardship of these concepts as the overriding direction of their professional life. They recognize their responsibility to ensure that needed resources are vigorously and ethically sought and that the intent of the donor is honestly fulfilled. To these ends, AFP members, both individual and

business, embrace certain values that they strive to uphold in performing their responsibilities for generating philanthropic support. AFP business members strive to promote and protect the work and mission of their client organizations. AFP members, both individual and business, aspire to:

- practice their profession with integrity, honesty, truthfulness and adherence to the absolute obligation to safeguard the public trust

- act according to the highest goals and visions of their organizations, professions, clients and consciences

- put philanthropic mission above personal gain

- inspire others through their own sense of dedication and high purpose

- improve their professional knowledge and skills, so that their performance will better serve others

- demonstrate concern for the interests and well-being of individuals affected by their actions

- value the privacy, freedom of choice and interests of all those affected by their actions

- foster cultural diversity and pluralistic values and treat all people with dignity and respect

- affirm, through personal giving, a commitment to philanthropy and its role in society

- adhere to the spirit as well as the letter of all applicable laws and regulations

- advocate within their organizations adherence to all applicable laws and regulations

- avoid even the appearance of any criminal offense or professional misconduct

- bring credit to the fundraising profession by their public demeanor

- encourage colleagues to embrace and practice these ethical principles and standards

- be aware of the codes of ethics promulgated by other professional organizations that serve philanthropy

Ethical Standards

While striving to act according to the above values, AFP members, both individual and business, agree to abide (and to ensure, to the best of their ability, that all members of their staff abide) by the AFP standards. Violation of the standards may subject the member to disciplinary sanctions, including expulsion, as provided in the AFP Ethics Enforcement Procedures.

Member Obligations

1. Members shall not engage in activities that harm the members' organizations, clients or profession.

2. Members shall not engage in activities that conflict with their fiduciary, ethical and legal obligations to their organizations, clients or profession.

3. Members shall effectively disclose all potential and actual conflicts of interest; such disclosure does not preclude or imply ethical impropriety.

4. Members shall not exploit any relationship with a donor, prospect, volunteer, client or employee for the benefit of the members or the members' organizations.

5. Members shall comply with all applicable local, state, provincial and federal civil and criminal laws.

6. Members recognize their individual boundaries of competence and are forthcoming and truthful about their professional experience and qualifications and will represent their achievements accurately and without exaggeration.

7. Members shall present and supply products and/or services honestly and without misrepresentation and will clearly identify the details of those products, such as availability of the products and/or services and other factors that may affect the suitability of the products and/or services for donors, clients or non-profit organizations.

8. Members shall establish the nature and purpose of any contractual relationship at the outset and will be responsive and available to organizations and their employing organizations before, during and after any sale of materials and/or services. Members will comply with all fair and reasonable obligations created by the contract.

9. Members shall refrain from knowingly infringing the intellectual property rights of other parties at all times. Members shall address and rectify any inadvertent infringement that may occur.

10. Members shall protect the confidentiality of all privileged information relating to the provider/client relationships.

11. Members shall refrain from any activity designed to disparage competitors untruthfully.

Solicitation and Use of Philanthropic Funds

12. Members shall take care to ensure that all solicitation and communication materials are accurate and correctly reflect their organizations' mission and use of solicited funds.

13. Members shall take care to ensure that donors receive informed, accurate and ethical advice about the value and tax implications of contributions.

14. Members shall take care to ensure that contributions are used in accordance with donors' intentions.

15. Members shall take care to ensure proper stewardship of all revenue sources, including timely reports on the use and management of such funds.

16. Members shall obtain explicit consent by donors before altering the conditions of financial transactions.

Presentation of Information

17. Members shall not disclose privileged or confidential information to unauthorized parties.

18. Members shall adhere to the principle that all donor and prospect information created by, or on behalf of, an organization or a client is the property of that organization or client and shall not be transferred or utilized except on behalf of that organization or client.

19. Members shall give donors and clients the opportunity to have their names removed from lists that are sold to, rented to or exchanged with other organizations.

20. Members shall, when stating fundraising results, use accurate and consistent accounting methods that conform to the appropriate guidelines adopted by the American Institute of Certified Public Accountants (AICPA)* for the type of organization involved. (*In countries outside of the United States, comparable authority should be utilized).

Compensation and Contracts

21. Members shall not accept compensation or enter into a contract that is based on a percentage of contributions; nor shall members accept finder's fees or contingent fees. Business members must refrain from receiving compensation from third parties derived from products or services for a client without disclosing that third-party compensation to the client (for example, volume rebates from vendors to business members).

22. Members may accept performance-based compensation, such as bonuses, provided such bonuses are in accord with prevailing practices within the members' own organizations and are not based on a percentage of contributions.

23. Members shall neither offer nor accept payments or special considerations for the purpose of influencing the selection of products or services.

24. Members shall not pay finder's fees, commissions or percentage compensation based on contributions, and shall take care to discourage their organizations from making such payments.

25. Any member receiving funds on behalf of a donor or client must meet the legal requirements for the disbursement of those funds. Any interest or income earned on the funds should be fully disclosed.

SAMPLE ETHICAL CASES

In October 2009, AFP released 20 sample cases for ethical education. Further information on these cases can be obtained by contacting AFP International http://www.afpnet.org.

The following three cases will provide you with an opportunity to test your ethical decision making skills.

Case 1: Helping the Needy

You are director of an international emergency relief program in Ottawa. Within one month, three large scale disasters occur — an earthquake in Mexico, a hurricane in the Pacific, and a flood in Manitoba. Because of the severity of the disasters and the thorough, constant media coverage, donations have been pouring in. Most gifts are designated to either the earthquake or the hurricane victims; however, many people in Manitoba have lost their homes in the flood and are in desperate need of help.

As time passes, you see that the relief needs of the hurricane and earthquake victims will be easily met by 60% of the relief money coming in, but more than 95% of the money is designated by the donors for the hurricane and earthquake, leaving you with insufficient funds to meet the needs in Canada.

Would it be a violation of the AFP Code to use some of the donations designated for the earthquake or hurricane victims to assist victims of the Manitoba flood?

1. Yes   2. No   3. It depends   4. Don't know

Answer: Yes. This would be a violation of Standard #14 — Members shall take care to ensure that contributions are used in accordance with donors' intentions.

To comply with the Code, should you return the donations that were not needed in the areas for which they were designated?

1. Yes   2. No   3. It depends   4. Don't know

Answer: It depends. A member could contact a donor, explain the circumstances and request permission to use the funds for a different disaster (Standard #16). If permission is not provided, donations should be returned in order to comply with the Code.

Figure 2.6

Case 2: Bonus Points

You are the director of development of a biomedical research organization in Edmonton. The organization's Board decides to establish a bonus plan for all senior managers, based on performance of responsibilities. Your bonus is to be 10% of your annual salary if you bring in 10 new corporate sponsorships and another 10% of your annual salary if you bring in at least 10 major gifts of $10,000 or more.

Would this bonus plan be acceptable under the AFP Code of Ethical Principles?

1. Yes   **2. No**   **3. It depends**   **4. Don't know**

Answer: Yes. The AFP Code provides that members may accept performance-based compensation, such as bonuses, provided such bonuses are *not* based on a percentage of contributions (Standard #22). In this case, the bonus is a fixed amount and it is based upon the number of sponsorships and major gifts that you bring in, not a percentage of the amount of the contributions.

Suppose that instead of the plan above, the size of the bonus was based on your performance in three areas: (i) Number of new volunteers recruited; (ii) Number of new major gifts received; and (iii) Exceeding the amount raised the previous year in the organization's annual fund.

Could such a bonus plan be acceptable under the AFP Code?

1. Yes   **2. No**   **3. It depends**   **4. Don't know**

Answer: Yes, as there is no violation of Standard #22. This is an example of a performance-based compensation plan that provides financial and non-financial indicators that are acceptable under the Code.

Suppose that the bonus was a fixed amount (5% of your base salary) and was based on achieving three performance targets: (i) Recruiting 50 new volunteers; (ii) Successfully soliciting 10 new major gifts; and (iii) Growing the organization's annual fund receipts from the previous year.

Would this bonus plan pass muster under the AFP Code?

1. Yes   **2. No**   **3. It depends**   **4. Don't know**

Answer: Yes. There is no violation of the Code (Standard #22), and the criteria are not based on a percentage of contributions.

Figure 2.7

Case 3: Share and Share Alike

Two small arts organizations in Halifax each have struggled to generate sufficient public awareness for a community-wide annual fund campaign. The director of development of one organization suggests that if the organizations pool their resources, they can maximize their visibility in the community, minimize their individual costs, and increase their chances for a successful campaign.

If the two organizations worked from their own donor lists, would this arrangement be acceptable under the AFP Code of Ethical Principles?

1. Yes   2. No   3. It depends   4. Don't know

Answer: Yes. Two organizations may have a joint campaign and solicit from their own lists as long as each organization has the same clearly defined regulations, guidelines, policies, and procedures.

If the two organizations pooled their lists and hired a telemarketing firm to conduct a joint campaign, would this arrangement be acceptable under the AFP Code of Ethical Principles?

1. Yes   2. No   3. It depends   4. Don't know

Answer: It depends. It is the responsibility of the member organizations to "respect the wishes and needs of the constituents, and do nothing that would negatively impact their social, professional or economic well-being" (Guideline 1.c), so the organizations must approach the joint campaign with caution. They must "effectively disclose all potential and actual conflicts of interest" (Standard #3). Therefore, the Code would allow this joint campaign as long as the constituents are clearly informed about the relationship between the two organizations.

If the two organizations each solicited from their own lists in a joint campaign, would this arrangement be acceptable under the AFP Code of Ethical Principles?

1. Yes   2. No   3. It depends   4. Don't know

Answer: Yes. The donor must also be clearly informed about the destination of the gift. According to Standard #12, the organizations must "take care to ensure that all solicitation and communication materials are accurate and correctly reflect their organization's mission and use of solicited funds." This is particularly important in a joint campaign, because constituents need to understand the nature of the campaign and which organization they are supporting. Standard #14 further reinforces this principle: "Members shall take care to ensure that contributions are used in accordance with donors' intentions." The organizations also should follow Standard #15 guidelines regarding written policies for endowment funds, annual reporting, planned gifts, donor recognition, investments, and administration of restricted funds.

Figure 2.8

CONCLUSION

This chapter offers an overview of ethics and the five different sources of ethical standards. It illustrates why an understanding of ethics is central to the practice of philanthropic fundraising, and that incorporating an ethical decision-making orientation is not only the "right thing to do" but also works to our pragmatic (and competitive) best interests. Donors and volunteers support those organizations that they trust – trust to carry out their missions, respect the wishes of donors, steward the resources well and uphold and exemplify rigorous standards of practice.

Paul Pribbenow, Ph.D., President of Augsburg College and the current Chair of AFP's Ethics Committee, characterizes philanthropy as a public practice in a healthy democracy.[3] Our work is first and foremost possible because it serves the public trust, public needs and public goods.

ADDITIONAL RESOURCES

▶ FISCHER, M. (2000). *Ethical Decision-Making in Fund Raising*, John Wiley & Sons, Inc.

▶ GARRETT, C. & ROBINSON, D. (2000). *Introducing Ethics*, Icon Books Ltd.

▶ GOW PETTEY, J. (ED.) (2008). *Ethical Fundraising: A Guide for Nonprofit Boards and Fundraisers*, John Wiley & Sons, Inc.

▶ MORGAN, P. & REYNOLDS, G. (1997). *The Appearance of Impropriety: How the Ethics Wars have Undermined American Government, Business and Society*, The Free Press.

▶ TICHY, N. & McGILL, A. (2003). *Michigan Business School Guide to the Ethical Challenge*, Jossey-Boss.

---

3   Pribbenow, Paul. (2008). *Between the Real and the Ideal: A Meditation on the Future of Ethical Reflection for Philanthropic Fundraisers.* In Janice Gow Petty (ed.), *Ethical Fundraising: A Guide for Nonprofit Boards and Fundraisers* (p. -217). John Wiley & Sons.

ABOUT THE AUTHOR

Dianne Lister, LL.B., CFRE

Dianne Lister is a lawyer and has held senior roles in Canada's charitable sector since 1986. Currently the President and Executive Director of the ROM (Royal Ontario Museum) Governors, Dianne is responsible for all philanthropic, sponsorship and stewardship programmes, and governance of the public foundation. Prior to her appointment at ROM, Dianne was the Vice President, External Relations and Advancement for Trent University and President and CEO of SickKids Hospital Foundation

Dianne has served as a volunteer with the Association of Fundraising Professionals (AFP), holding positions as president of the Toronto Chapter, Chair of the AFP Canada Council, Chair of AFP Government Relations, and more recently, served as a member of the international AFP Ethics Committee for 9 years (holding the position of Chair in 2007-2009). Dianne has also served on corporate boards. She is currently a member of the Boards of the Community Foundation of Greater Peterborough, and of the Citizens' Alliance United for a Sustainable Environment (CAUSE).

CHAPTER 3

Case For Support
PEARL VEENEMA, CFRE

I began my development career with board direction to launch a *capital campaign*. My learned colleagues told me that it all starts with the case for support. Why? Because the case for support and the process by which you create the case is a document that clearly articulates the cause for which fund development is being undertaken. The document itself ensures alignment amongst all stakeholders as to the "scope" of the project. This can include the rationale for the funds; both factual and emotional. *read more...*

The stages of research, writing and gaining approval for the case are great guideposts in the fund development process. In today's highly competitive environment there is a strong need to capture not just the minds but also the hearts of key stakeholders, including the Board and ultimately potential donors. While a well-written stand-alone document can be very effective, some form of multimedia communication plan should be considered when taking the case from an internal document to the outside world.

Regardless of what kind of organization you work for, or which non-profit sector you operate within (health care, post-secondary education, social services, arts, etc), a case for support is a basic and necessary component of fund development. This is because the case for support is used for a variety of reasons - the most critical being to ensure alignment, through the research and writing phases, around the fundraising objective amongst the development team and other stakeholders such as the Board or staff.

The case can be in the form of key messages and images that tell the story in a way that creates awareness, understanding and interest in the specific cause. The finished case can be used to directly support: the fundraising effort, volunteer engagement, and recruitment of development staff.

Traditionally we think about the case for support within the context of a campaign. But a case for support is advisable for all elements of an integrated fund development program, including annual fundraising, major/campaign programs and planned giving.

The case becomes your story — and today the ways in which we need to tell our story are many. What will the case of tomorrow look like? What kind of checklist will be needed? What kind of format will the case take on in the growing digital environment? For me, today and into the future, the case will always begin with a conversation about the **who**, **what**, **why**, **when**, **where**, **h**ow and for **wh**om?

CLASSIC DEFINITION OF A CASE

Harold J. Seymour's landmark book on Philanthropy, *Designs for Fundraising*, offers the following definition:

"The case statement tells all that needs to be told, answers all the important questions, re-

views the arguments for support, explains the proposed plan for raising the money, and shows how gifts may be made and who the people are who vouch for the project and will give it leadership and direction… It should aim high, provide perspective, arouse a sense of history and continuity, convey a feeling of importance, relevance, and urgency, and have whatever stuff is needed to warm the heart and stir the mind."

The core principles as highlighted in this classic definition are consistent in all of the case for support examples referenced in this chapter.

The annual case for support

When creating a case for support for annual giving, consider what two experts in the field have to say:

Steven Thomas (Chairman and Executive Creative Director, Steven Thomas) stated that for his clients, "the mission and vision of the organization governs what they do. By its very nature, annual giving focuses on the work of the organization and projects; programs and equipment are featured as examples to facilitate support for all that the organization does. As such, no specific annual case for support is consistently available." So while there is no consistency in practice, a case can help an organization focus on the key priorities for its annual giving program. A case that would be built around the fundamental elements of the organizational objectives can help drive a more strategic effort and more tangible results.

Peter Blakely (President, Blakely & Associates) advocates for a case for annual giving. In his experience few organizations develop a formal case for annual giving. A strategy that the Blakely team uses with clients is to facilitate a brainstorming session on the annual goals. This process then leads to identification of the stories and case specifics to demonstrate need for investment in important and urgent initiatives. In some instances, a catalogue of items featuring equipment, facility and program needs are provided. From this, the Blakely team develops the annual case for support for direct response and other fundraising tactics.

Planned giving

The case for support for planned giving is told through the stories of generous donors. They inspire, educate and help individuals and their families to think about the lasting impact of a future gift. On the "Leave a Legacy Canada" website www.leavealegacy.ca four reasons to give are listed: *[handwritten: planned giving]*

- To enrich people and lives
- To provide support
- To leave a memory
- To make a contribution for the future.

Powerful, personal stories are provided to bring those reasons to life. You will find more details on the process for developing and marketing the case for support for planned giving in Chapter 12 by Val Hoey.

Philanthropy

The general case for philanthropy as proposed by Tom Ahern in his book, *Seeing through a Donor's Eyes* recommends articulating your organization's promise, your organization's proof and how the donor fits into your world. He proposes that it should be brief and fewer than 100 words.

Using my current organization as an example, the following represents an overall or general case for support.

Hamilton Health Sciences Foundation enhances the quality of patient care throughout life's journey (the organization's promise) by raising funds to enable; capital redevelopment programs, the purchase of medical equipment and technology, and the investment into medical research for disease causes, treatments and cures (the organization's proof). By generously supporting (how the donor fits into our world) the family of Hamilton Health Sciences' hospitals and the cancer centre, donors to Hamilton Health Sciences Foundation enable the investments needed to accomplish our goal of Health Care, Transformed for the residents of South-central Ontario.

The discipline of developing the responses to these key concepts is beneficial to any organization when presented with an opportunity to succinctly address who you are, and how you serve and fulfill human and community needs.

THE MARKETING BRIEF

Also in his book, Tom Ahern advocates for an internal case that serves as the marketing brief. He proposes that the brief answer the following questions:

- Why is your organization uniquely effective at delivering results?
- What are the reasons that gifts are so urgent?
- How can we show that the mission's/vision's success depends on philanthropic support?

These are the critical questions that donors ask every day. As the number of charitable organizations increase, donors have choices and it is our role to assist in the presentation of compelling opportunities that inspires their investment. As development professionals, it is essential that we have clarity ourselves in order to provide a clear presentation of compelling opportunities, and as such an internal case/brief serves an important function.

For illustrative purposes, I offer a marketing brief for Hamilton Health Sciences Foundation.

Major Gifts Today Guarantee Health Care, Transformed Tomorrow.

Hamilton Health Sciences Foundation needs to diversify its revenue base to insure its long-term sustainability. Donations support close to 100% of the costs to upgrade and purchase new medical equipment and fund programs for our hospitals. With such a heavy reliance on donations to support the quality of patient care throughout Hamilton Health Sciences, the current donation mix heavily weighted (approximately 65%) towards annual giving are important however tend to be smaller and fluctuate based on economic cycles.

To develop a more sustainable base there is a strong need to cultivate a major gift program. These gifts provide a more stable base of funding for The Foundation, reduce the average cost per dollar raised, and allow the highest fundraising priorities to be accomplished. Major gifts also provide the greatest opportunities for donor recognition. A strong program for major gifts significantly enhances the impact The

Foundation can ultimately have on the quality of patient care for residents of the Greater Hamilton area and South-central Ontario.

Specifically, through the generosity of our donors we will be better equipped to accomplish our goal of Health Care, Transformed. The rapidly aging and diverse socio- economic profile of the community are putting increased demands on the health care system. The cost of technology and programs to support patients and their families is also increasing rapidly. Philanthropy enhances the quality of patient care.

Through a strong, comprehensive major gift program we can better support patient care, research and education. This stable base of funding provides the means to allow for: the purchase of state-of-the art diagnostic and treatment equipment; the development of treatment spaces that align with current medical thinking; research into the causes, treatments and cures for a range of diseases; and ongoing education for the staff that enables more effective and appropriate care for the complete range of patient populations served by the hospitals and cancer centre of Hamilton Health Sciences.

Hamilton Health Sciences, and consequently The Foundation, support a complex range of medical care for patients at all stages of Life's Journey. With Hamilton Health Sciences' Centres of Excellence, patients throughout South-central Ontario have access to specialized programs and treatment that donations have enabled.

Campaign/Major Gift

Developing the case for support for campaign/major gifts begins with taking inventory of what is available on the project, determining what research and fact finding needs to be undertaken and who you need to interview to gather further insights and information.

I also recommend developing a system to catalogue the information gathered: photographs, letters, renderings, electronic and written materials. Most importantly, before you start collecting, decisions on nomenclature, version control and documenting your sources of information is essential. Information changes without a disciplined and consistent approach, will lead to wasted time verifying the accuracy of a dynamic case.

Case Filing Catalogue

Lay out in a traditional album to select those most suitable to the case. Remember that the ideal image illustrates what hundreds of words would attempt to convey. (If possible have a contact sheet at the front of the album either hardcopy or electronic.)

Lay out on foam core boards to aid in visualizing the elements that should be used.

Documents, brochures and other print materials.

Folders for interview information, facts and figures, videos, film clips, budget details and any others that help with the ease of finding information.

Figure 3.1

THE ESSENTIAL QUESTIONS

While reading a variety of published materials on writing a case for support, there is one consistent recommendation: The case should address the five "W's" – Who, What, Why, When and for Whom, along with How?

The Who and the Why

As you write about your organization and the people leading the initiative, it is necessary to provide supporting information on why your organization is best suited to launch such a project. Typically, this is the place to highlight historical records, facts and figures on the "largest, unique, national, global, first, top three" aspects of the project incorporating specific examples.

You also want to address why/would/should a prospective donor support this campaign as well as why the organization is compelled to pursue fundraising in support of this particular cause in the context of broader societal issues surrounding the issue.

Part of the "who" should include those who will be invited and inspired to participate - individuals, foundations (private and public), corporations and service groups (such as Rotary). When profiling leadership, obtain biographical notes and testimonials/quotes. This is also the place to profile your organization's leadership, mission, vision and values. The ultimate purpose is to ask and answer the questions that donors usually have – how is this service, program, capital infrastructure different or unique when compared with an organization and campaign with a similar purpose.

The What

Whether a school or hospital expansion, new service program or building, endowment campaign or equipment, framing the project involves the following:

- Gathering renderings and functional plans if a building project – this also helps in identifying naming opportunities for print and web applications

- Identifying funding sources – is 100% needed from the donor base or are there "own funds", matching gifts and grants from government agencies

- Identifying whether the project is part of a phased project and addressing what is the planned time horizon for future parts

- Budget details – capital, equipment, furnishings, technology needs, people, ongoing funding for sustainability

- The fundraising goal and how much is required at specific stages of the project

- Detailing how funds will be raised – face to face, online, events, general invitation through direct response and/or other multi-channel approaches

- Include the benefits of gifts pledged over time which raises the sights for a best possible gift commitment

The When

Donors expect to know all about the timelines - the milestones from start date to completion. You also need to address potential barriers to maintaining the schedule. Simple timeline charts are useful, and if placed in a text box can be easily updated. Some donors write milestones for payments into gift agreements. For example, pledge payments based on progress in a building campaign, or recruitment of an academic chair.

For Whom

Highlighting for whom the project is being undertaken and what the tangible benefits are for that group(s) is one of the most exciting parts of a case. This is where the case intersects with the organization's mission and vision, a donor's interests and motivations, and a beneficiary. The storytelling comes alive. Graphs and maps can show geographic reach and numbers of people, resources and communities impacted. In essence, the "for whom" conveys the emotional appeal augmented by facts.

How

The magic of philanthropy is enabling a donor to fully engage in a cause or effort where they can see themselves as part of the promise or solution. The cause needs to address how an organization intends to put donor dollars to work in support of the aims of the fundraising initiative, but most importantly how the donor can make a personal difference. Examples of how to accomplish this include:

- Painting the picture of children discovering and learning through interactive displays can convey the creativity and lasting impact that the experience can have on the child's development for a new exhibit in a children's museum.

- By supporting an academic chair or scholarship, a case can address critical research to advance a cure or prepare medical students for future practice.

- If supporting well-baby programs for young mothers, the donor can appreciate being part of the team working to ensure healthier children.

Capital campaigns and working with consultants

Organizations that engage fundraising consultants to support staff with a feasibility study prior to the launch of a capital campaign begin that engagement with the writing of a case statement.

The process often begins with drafting a preliminary case for support, or prospectus, and then seeking input from donors, potential donors and volunteer leaders. There are significant benefits to this process as it is the opportunity to:

- assess donor interest in the overall initiative
- address the questions/issues of potential donors
- gauge interest in specific components
- validate impact as presented
- identify leadership interest in being an ambassador for the project as a volunteer, spokesperson and/or fundraising ambassador

There are two primary benefits of a consultant-led process for case development. The first relates to efficiency. The consultant engagement has built-in time limits which help greatly since the process can take significant time. Also a consultant can bring additional personnel to augment staff resources both in time and skill set.

Secondly, in my experience the engagement of a consultant provides the opportunity for an objective voice to focus on donor interests versus an organization's sense of what will be important to a potential donor investor.

For more information on the role of a consultant please refer to Chapter 20 by Pat Hardy.

HIGHS AND LOWS OF A REVIEW

It is often a good idea to seek independent evaluation of a draft case statement. The advantage of objective feedback on the content and wording of what has been written is immeasurable. Care should always be taken to avoid trying to create "art by committee," where you end up settling for the lowest common denominator in order to obtain consensus.

But having recognized this risk, there is also a significant benefit to having a group review the draft case and provide their feedback.

Gather a group of development professionals together and the process for review and merits of a case development committee, can vary in many ways. Karen Willson, Senior Vice President with KCI Canada, shared that key individuals can be invited to participate in a facilitated brainstorming session to confirm key messages. This would be the forum for gathering consensus on the facts and intended impact. With that information, there would be no need to submit multiple drafts that would generate different editorial styles, leading to writing that contains many voices.

When asked about the involvement of a committee, Nicholas Offord, President, The Offord Group, advocated positively for the purposes of "making decisions about the campaign priorities and for project scoping." This view recognizes that the success of a fundraising initiative depends on the availability of the donor base – those currently giving as well as new donors who are to be inspired by the initiative and the human/service needs being met.

If a committee format for case development and review is expected in your organization, I would recommend no more than seven individuals. Ideally, this committee would include the institutional leader or designate who can make decisions, lead volunteer and development professionals, a donor, a potential beneficiary, project/content experts and the case writer. Most importantly, pre-determine the process for responsibility of final sign-off; I recommend one individual from the institution and one from the development team.

PACKAGING THE CASE

Once you have completed the research and writing, decisions are needed on the format presentation. Ideally, present the case in all mediums - print and electronic. Print includes booklets, brochures and electronic can be digital storytelling, videos, audio clips and more. How you present your case depends on your budgetary resources, the culture of your organization and your audiences.

Ultimately it is important to remember that the case for support is a communication tool that serves to support the conversations that development professionals and volunteers have with donors and prospective donors. Today, donors expect design simplicity and a minimum of expenditure but with high impact from a content perspective allowing for funds to be invested in important projects to meet real needs.

In regards to the ideal length for a case statement, Tom Ahern in *Seeing through a Donor's Eyes* recommends an average of 2200 words, however he has written cases that range from under 1000 to more than 4500 words. In *Making the Case,* Jerry Panas offers that a case should be as long as it needs to be to tell your story!

Regardless of length, an executive summary is needed. This summary should include a concise and clear description of the project(s) – the opportunity, the issue that you need to address and for what purpose or for whose benefit. A defensible explanation and support for why your organization is the right organization when compared to others with a similar purpose also serves to sharpen key messages. Jerry Panas proposes eight essential elements (Figure 3.2) that are most effective.

Eight Essential Elements – Jerry Panas

1. The title

2. Introductory paragraph

3. The urgent need

4. Your unique position

5. Strength of our organization and mission

6. Reinforcing urgency for action

7. Stating what we will be required financially to fund the dream

8. Closure and final commitment to achieving results together

---

Figure 3.2

Inspiring images and simple graphics

Once the tables, graphs, charts and illustrations are created they can be utilized to augment the case elements, facts and figures. Visually they not only break up the text, but serve to highlight key facts in an easy to remember format, while adding impact.

Photographs and digital stories are powerful. With photography, a common mistake is to pack in many small photos rather than choosing a select few that can be substantially larger. Today and into the future, the power of digital stories enable wider distribution of your case in a more cost-effective manner. Remember, that people give to people, so choosing photos that focus on putting people "into the proposed solution" can work well.

Personal interests aside, many of us are faced with experiential and skill limitations in utilizing technology to advance a case for support. Tamara Pope, Vice President Marketing and Communications, Hamilton Health Sciences Foundation, claims:

"Technology offers fundraisers the opportunity to generate more interest, have a much stronger and more sustainable emotional impact to a broader audience than was previously available.

Video productions – either informally done or professionally produced – offer an extremely cost effective means to bring alive the case for support. Once recorded, the images have the power to convey the emotions that motivate the case and the impact that success can have.

Once captured, the images can be used at events, or online (including YouTube or any of the social networking sites) thereby broadening the reach of your message.

The key to success is having a clear goal, a singular message supported by facts and compelling visuals that enable an emotional connection with the audience. Calls to action also need to be embedded as the spider web of networks today will take your visual case for support beyond your traditional channels. Looking into the future, I can only envision that there will be an ever increasing need to present the varied cases that all organizations will need in formats that contain powerful visuals and compelling calls to action that speak to an even more diverse group of donor communities."

Developing the theme

While a logo, positioning statement and theme are not sufficient on their own to drive donors to invest in your organization, they are very important elements to readily identify your project(s) in a highly competitive environment. Just as everyone is an "editor," everyone feels that they are a "marketer" and "designer." Investing in the expertise to develop the theme and expression of the campaign is not a luxury – it is a necessity to drive results.

An online search provides thousands of examples of campaign themes. Often it is the Campaign for (your organization or equipment or scholarships as examples), or it can be based on milestone years such as a centennial, or an emotional theme that is memorable.

Figure 3.3 shows several examples. At the Hamilton Health Sciences, the cancer centre utilized Hope Can't Wait (1) for the expression of a facility campaign. Previously, I framed an outcome with the goal such as mission:Possible (2). Trillium's addresses a challenge gift call to action (3).

Figure 3.3

Other examples of campaign themes include:

- Cornerstone of Care – a multi-site facility and equipment campaign for our family of hospitals at Hamilton Health Sciences.

- The Alexander Pavilion – when the facility has already been named

- One Day, One Centre, One Team – a promise upon which a breast assessment centre is to be built

- A favourite of mine is the combined call to action and the beneficiary- Be A SuperHero (4) -The Campaign for BC Children's Hospital.

The books on case writing at the end of this chapter have many other excellent examples that are worthy of review.

CREDIBILITY AND LEADERSHIP

The credibility of your case can be bolstered by identifying the members involved in the cabinet or committee. The leadership profiles of volunteer or campaign staff can have a significant impact, especially if done in a way that includes personal testimonials of why they are investing in the cause. This can serve to intrigue or entice an individual to join in support of your cause or ask to be included on a team.

In the case for support for annual fundraising and planned giving, grateful patients and their shared stories bring relevance and emotional texture to the case. For educational institutions, it can be alumni and for arts and culture your loyal patrons or artists.

For capital campaigns and significant special projects, the endorsement and involvement of community leaders gives credibility to your initiative; through leadership engagement, in terms of time and as an ambassador, and through personal financial support.

Written descriptions in addition to photographs (not formal portraits) that place the leaders within the context of the project are an excellent way to demonstrate community credibility and support.

THE LANGUAGE OF THE CASE

Once the details on the project, the facts and figures along with supporting photographs and images have been assembled, you might believe that the hardest part of preparing your case for support is over. But, "putting it all together" often requires an experienced communications specialist or case writer. In a small or large shop, this is a prudent investment to ensure that there is a consistent "voice" and key messages for the case.

A writer (preferably the individual also doing the key interviews) will develop the questions that will lead to a personal story unfolding and one where the reader sees themselves as a solution to the challenge or issue. Recently The Hamilton Health Sciences Centre received the support of a small number of friends and associates who raised $1 million for an MRI. The service needs, specialized pediatric features of the MRI and the talented medical leadership were all important, however it was the visualization of a brain tumour with and without the pediatric MRI application and the reality of what it meant for a child that inspired the donors, and moved them to immediate action. This resulted in the purchase of an MRI in the shortest time possible. Telling that story and unfolding each component in emotional terms helped each donor to feel intimately part of the solution to an urgent need.

Here are some additional "words of wisdom" from experts on case writing:

- write for the average grade 6 or 8 reader

- keep language free of jargon or provide a simple explanation if needed

- write to be able to move hearts and minds

- write about meeting human and service needs and not organizational needs.

Jerry Panas advocates stamping "DRAFT" on your case for support as you explore the importance, urgency and value for investment from the donor's perspective giving full permission to get constructive feedback. Another significant benefit will be in knowing what elements of your initiative appeals to a donor or volunteer.

The case is written – take a few steps back and assess for effectiveness

The most comprehensive evaluation tool or checklist that I have seen and used is the PanasLinzyCasEvaluator (Figure 3.4). It provides an objective assessment and assists with identifying the refinements that are needed. Also, if you need to have a committee review, the evaluation point system assists in assuring a comprehensive review and/or facilitates a constructive review.

Another "Case Effectiveness Checklist" by KCI Canada proposes five key questions centered on the presentation of emotional reasons for donor engagement:

1. Does it elicit confidence that the plan will be delivered?
2. Does it elicit emotional as well as rational reasons to give?
3. Does it emphasize opportunity instead of need?
4. Does it tell the donor how their gift will make a difference?
5. Does it tell a story about real people?

Regardless of the type of case, self-reflection and review becomes easier when an objective tool is utilized.

USING THE CASE FOR SUPPORT

Now that the case is complete, it becomes a very versatile communication tool. The end product is very gratifying. However, the internal conversations the writer and development team have on a donors potential interests and philanthropic aims are the most satisfying. It reminds me of a mystery. There are parts that we know and others that we must find out by developing a rapport and relationship. The internal and external uses have great similarities.

Internally, the case is the information source for the following:

- A strategic document for review with internal stakeholders to ensure that fundraising is focused on the highest priorities of the organization and those that would be of interest to donors and meet their needs for fulfilling a vision or dream. This should be an annual process. For campaigns it serves the timeframe of the project. Internal stakeholders in a hospital include the Chief Executive Officer, the Executive team inclusive of physician leaders and clinical or research experts depending on the case elements. For a university, it can involve the President and Faculty leadership among others.

The *CasEvaluator*©

There are many elements that must be included in a Case Statement. That's the mechanical and technical side of developing the material. But nothing takes the place of good writing. That's the creative side. You must prepare copy that sizzles—and states clearly and dramatically the need and urgency. Even a project that is unquestionably valid requires writing that has genius, magic, and power.

If the reader doesn't share your vision and isn't propelled to become a partner in your great cause—no matter how pressing the need, you haven't made the case. Period!

Don't be unduly concerned about the order. There are times that it's much more compelling to start with the vision. And sometimes, historical facts and details about current services can be handled best as exhibits in an Appendix. What counts is that you don't leave anything unanswered or open to challenge. And yes, one thing more—that you end up with a Case Statement that represents the Institution with style, grace, and integrity.

Use this *CasEvaluator*© to rate the twelve essential factors that determine the effectiveness of a successful Case Statement. Indicate the points for each item in the right hand column. Total the point to score your Case Statement. Note that the rating of *Poor* is scored as *minus two* (-2).

	Poor	Fair	Good	Very Good	Excellent	Points
	-2	4	6	8	10	
1. **Mission Is Stated or Interpreted for Easy Understanding**						
2. **Brief History** *explanation of why institution was founded and societal environment that existed at the time that impelled its creation*						
3. **How Institution Provides Its Services** *indication of constituencies served and statistics, and explanation of activities, programs, and leadership*						
4. **Institution's Vision For The Future** *clearly and dramatically stated*						
5. **Explanation Of The Proposed Project** *description and rational of the items to be covered in the program . . . and the cost*						
6. **Institution's Singular Role In Meeting The Need** *indication of how institution is uniquely positioned to meet the need through the proposed project*						
7. **Readability Of The Copy**						
Exciting, memorable title						
Compelling section headings						
Theme (title) is woven through material						
Reads easily						
Total (Page 1)						

Figure 3.4

	Poor	Fair	Good	Very Good	Excellent	Points
	-2	4	6	8	10	
Brief declarative sentences—mostly present and future tense						
Short paragraphs						
Strong, inviting opening statement						
Powerful close, a call for action, theme restated						
Emotional and dramatic copy						
8. A Clear Sense Of Urgency *the project must move forward—it is one minute 'til midnight, and time will not wait*						
9. Anecdotal Material *numbers and statistics have a place . . . but dramatic stories provide sizzle and make copy come alive*						
10. Emphasis On Those Who Receive Service *focus is on the need and those served . . . not on the institution*						
11. Focus On Reader *copy is reader-oriented . . . how the reader has a stake in the issue . . . and can help solve the problem*						
12. Reader Is Asked to Share In The Vision *invitation is extended to become a partner in the program*						
Total (This Page)						
Total (Page 1)						
TOTAL POINTS						

Scoring for the *CasEvaluator*©

165 - 200	You have an excellent Case Statement . . . compelling and urgent . . . clearly defined. You've made your case! Some fine tuning will make it perfect.
140 - 164	You're well on your way. There is still some work required to make it precisely the case you need . . . but you don't have much more yet to do.
120 - 139	It's good—but not good enough. You'll need to review all of the items where you scored poorly . . . and make necessary additions and revisions.
90 - 119	A *fair* Case Statement won't make the sale . . . you have major work to do to bring this up to high standards.
89 & Below	Unacceptable . . . at times, it's easier to start over than to attempt a major overhaul. Don't be discouraged . . . but your draft can't be used in its present form . . . you have work to do.

- During orientation of staff, volunteers and board members, it is best practice to include elements of the case (if not the entire case) to ensure an effective understanding of organizational priorities. The executive summary is most useful, as are one-page summaries of particular initiatives that may be featured in a case such as: a building campaign, major medical equipment needs, scholarships, and/or breakfast programs for children.

- Developing and supporting the suite of print and electronic materials to effectively reach all audiences and support programs. The case becomes the base for brochures, documentaries, web content, advertising, news releases, direct response programs, articles in newsletters, campaign supporting documents and for developing Q&A's on a project.

Externally the case is essential in garnering financial support and attracting ambassadors for your organization.

With an increasing number of worthwhile causes in the marketplace, it is incumbent on non-profit organizations to become storytelling experts. The human or societal need that needs to be addressed is highlighted throughout the case and as such, the case is used to introduce a potential donor or volunteer to your organization. The case is the basis for all information that inspires, informs and deepens the donor relationship so that an investment of time or funds is made.

From a practical perspective consider the following: You have the opportunity to meet with a highly sought after community leader, as the face and voice of your fundraising project. How will you and/or the team prepare to answer all of the potential questions that may be asked – internally and externally? Questions such as those listed below:

- Why will this project be important to those we are seeking support from?

- What is the time commitment?

- Who will be joining with me to lead the project?

- What support can I expect from staff and the internal leadership?

- What are the financial expectations for me and for donors and the community?

The answers to all of the above questions will be detailed in a well written case document.

From a donor's perspective, a common request prior to considering the investment in a gift, can be for a proposal or further background information. Perhaps the donor wishes to consult with family or an advisor or simply wishes to have a written document that would reflect the conversations that you have been having over time. The case is *the* source document providing the supporting facts and impactful images and testimonials from which you can extract the necessary information to prepare the backgrounder or proposal.

CASE DEVELOPMENT CHECKLIST

The fundraising project is determined by internal leadership who then delegate the task of writing a case for support. Here's where you begin:

☐ Gather information that is currently available. Prepare a brief on the project explanation to ensure that you have a clear understanding of it.

☐ Make a list of who to interview to augment and support available information. Include –

    a. Internal experts
    b. Former donors and external leaders
    c. Those who may benefit

☐ Develop a questionnaire that can be adapted for the above stakeholders.

    a. Why is this project important now?
    b. Who will be served and benefit? Is it local, national or international? Any specific demographic?
    c. How much funds will be needed and when – is it all upfront to begin the project or are there other financial resources available so gifts can be pledged over time?
    d. What will it cost to launch the project?
    e. How long will it take to raise the funds?
    f. Are there any external approvals needed? (i.e. building permits?)
    g. Who will provide leadership – internally and externally?
    h. What are the consequences of not launching this project?

i. How does this project line up with the organizations' mission and vision in the near and longer term?

j. Why we are best positioned to address this concern?

k. What will success look like?

☐ Inquire about the review process. Will there be a committee? Who will make final decisions?

☐ What support will be available for graphic and marketing needs – for the theme, and logo development, web writing and print material production, brochures, posters, stationery or other identity needs?

☐ Will there be budget for photography and in the case of a facility initiative, renderings to showcase the project?

☐ What recognition will be available for donors – new donor wall created, plaques and/or virtual and print recognition?

☐ Who will be the leaders? Plan for a biographical note, updated photography and a strong testimonial?

☐ The case is written and you now need to prepare yourself for the feedback. It will be most unusual that the first draft will be approved. Re-writing (especially for committee review) can be challenging. Aim for three to four versions. The fourth, if needed, should be for the final decision maker.

☐ The full case and executive summary are approved. Begin writing a series of Q&A's on the anticipated most frequently asked. These will likely match up to the questions list that you prepared.

☐ Develop a plan and process for updates as elements are achieved, new information becomes available (relevant statistics, new leaders on board, photos that show progress if facility related, testimonials etc.)

☐ The campaign is achieved and the case becomes part of the institution's archives – go back and ensure that all final materials in all formats are filed for future reference. It would not be unusual for the information to be needed for a second phase or expansion or to demonstrate a record of success.

CONCLUSION

As my professional experience grows, so does my belief that it is vitally important to take the time to research, write, validate and present a case for support for donor investment. While my initial frame of reference was centered on capital campaigns, it became evident that every element of the fund development process requires a thoughtful case.

For the development professional, a case for support encourages dialogue amongst stakeholders on priority, impact and return on investment. For the donor, it must inspire, create a personal sense of urgency to invest and be part of a solution. As the case unfolds, it becomes more about the journey of responding to the 5 "W's" and "the How," as well as the result - which can be viewed as the destination.

I leave you with these top ten tips (Figure 3.5) to help guide you.

Top 10 Tips

1. Make a list of all of the information and images you will need and people to interview.

2. Develop a detailed and realistic timeline.

3. Write to an audience of the few donors who will make the largest investment (for a capital campaign).

4. Decide upfront on the review and approval process.

5. Plan for the different applications and use of the case or case elements – print and electronic.

6. Dedicate time to develop the theme and the primary image and/or logo that will be the identification symbol for the project.

7. If creative, compelling and poetic writing is not your forte, invest in someone who can write the case.

8. Cases are dynamic documents so plan for regular review and updates – make it part of an annual cycle of review or when a project or program undergoes significant change.

9. As Jerry Panas reminds us all make the case bigger than your institution – he states, "make the case curiously inviting."

10. Keep the "marketing brief" as Tom Ahern proposes, current for each element of your fund development program – annual, major and planned giving.

Figure 3.5

ADDITIONAL RESOURCES

▶ AHERN, T. *Seeing through a Donor's Eyes*. Emerson & Church.

▶ PANAS, J. *Making the Case*. Institutions Press.

▶ SEYMOUR, HAROLD J. *Designs for Fund-Raising*. Reprinted by the Association for Healthcare Philanthropy.

Acknowledgment: The author wishes to thank Tamara Pope, Vice President Marketing and Communications, Hamilton Health Sciences Foundation for her contributions to the marketing brief and use of technology for presentation on the case for support.

ABOUT THE AUTHOR

Pearl F Veenema. CFRE, FAHP

Since August 2007, Pearl has been President & CEO of the Hamilton Health Sciences Foundation. The Foundation raises philanthropic gifts to support one of the most comprehensive healthcare systems in Canada, providing specialized services to patients from pre-conception through to aging adults.

Pearl began her healthcare career in nursing and has had extensive experience in healthcare administration, public affairs, marketing and as a patient representative. In 1999, Pearl decided to focus her career in healthcare development. She has held positions as a Chief

Development Officer for a small foundation, Managing Director of Campaigns for a $500 million campaign in Toronto and Vice President Advancement for a large foundation.

She is a Fellow of the Association for Healthcare Philanthropy (AHP) and a Certified Fund Raising Executive, CFRE International. In both organizations she has served as Chair. Currently Pearl is Chair, AHP University-based Programs (Madison Institute).

CHAPTER 4

PROSPECT RESEARCH
PETER MCKINLEY, MLIS

In Ersilia, to establish the relationships that sustain the city's life, the inhabitants stretch strings from the corners of the houses, white or black or gray or black-and-white according to whether they mark a relationship of blood, of trade, authority, agency. When the strings become so numerous that you can no longer pass among them, the inhabitants leave: the houses are dismantled; only the strings and their supports remain...

...Thus, when traveling in the territory of Ersilia, you come upon the ruins of abandoned cities, without the walls which do not last, without the bones of the dead which the wind rolls away: spider webs of intricate relationships seeking a form. *Trading Cities 4 From Invisible Cities by Italo Calvino. read more...*

Fitzgerald: The rich are different than you and me.

Hemingway: Yes, they have more money.

– Apocryphal

INTRODUCTION

In fundraising, we often deal with *"spider webs of intricate relationships:" this* professor taught *that* student, who married *this* fellow student, and was hired by *that* company; *this* doctor treated *that* patient; *this* counsellor helped *that* person in need; *this* wealthy board member has *these other* wealthy people in her network. And so on.

In serving the charitable organization that employs them, fundraisers provide the form those relationships are seeking: an instrument to identify and secure financial support by understanding, enhancing and leveraging the connections that already exist or may develop with stakeholders both real and aspirational.

At the same time, we can never lose sight of the fact that our responsibility as fundraisers is to secure financial support for our organizations. This financial support frequently addresses a critical need. It is important to openly acknowledge that this imperative dictates that the wealthier ("richer" to Fitzgerald, perhaps) members of our society will therefore receive a disproportionate amount of attention. They do indeed have more money.

Organizations that pursue major gift fundraising strategies are seeking contributions with greater value than the costs devoted to the activity of securing donations. Prospect research plays a critical role in that revenue generating activity by interacting with many other functional roles in a fundraising organization.

Prospect researchers are the development professionals most able to meet the growing information needs of the fundraising community. Using the Internet and other current technologies, prospect researchers collect, evaluate, analyze, organize, package and disseminate publicly available information in a way that maximizes its usefulness and enables accurate and educated decision-making.

Sometimes, in lieu of concrete, factual data, what the researcher needs to provide is enough information so that their partners in fundraising know that they are spending their time wisely meeting with a prospect – a meeting which in the end may produce the critical missing pieces of information that will allow for a more solid capacity assessment. Is enough known about a particular prospect to provide confidence that an introductory or discovery call can be justified?

Ethical and privacy considerations are a factor in handling prospect information. Researchers frequently belong to the Association of Professional Researchers for Advancement (APRA) and adhere to the APRA statement of ethics. This statement is reviewed and updated from time to time and is best reviewed directly in APRA materials.

As much as possible, scalable models and strategies will be presented in this chapter. For the numerous non-profits that are not in a position to adopt an "ideal" model approach, be assured that there are many ways that prospect research can make a significant, positive impact on your revenue generation capabilities.

PROSPECT IDENTIFICATION AND QUALIFICATION

A donation is the product of the capability to give, often expressed as "wealth" or "capacity" and the connection to the charity's mission, sometime characterized as "affinity." These will be discussed in turn.

Capacity
A fundamental place to begin is to define the group of stakeholders – existing or potential – who have the capability to provide philanthropic support to a charitable organization. This capability is frequently referred to as "capacity." Does the stakeholder in question actually have the ability to make a donation that will more than justify the investment of time and resources required to secure the gift?

There are important differences between individual and corporate/foundation prospects which will be discussed in the following section.

Individuals
Determining capacity relies on analysis of "wealth indicators" – pieces of information that indicate that

substantial wealth may be present. Figure 4.1 presents common wealth indicators for individual prospects. It is most useful to cross-reference a known group of stakeholders against these wealth indicators in order to identify the people most likely to be wealthy, and therefore, most likely to be capable of a major gift.

The Return on Investment (ROI) of prospect identification is reliant on a charity's ability to match

identified high capacity prospects with major gift development officers.

A typical full-time major gift officer should be able to manage a portfolio of prospects ranging from 100-150 in size, so fundraising administrators should evaluate whether a capacity analysis will result in a prospect pool that can be addressed in a timely manner.

Wealth Indicator	Basic	Intermediate	Advanced
Income	Word of mouth; mainstream/internet media	Online tools: Securities Regulatory reports; Public Sector Salary Disclosure; Vendors to the charitable sector	Data Analysis relying on Statistics Canada, census data, survey data
Real Estate	Advertisements of real estate listings	Online multiple listing resources	Data Analysis relying on Statistics Canada, census data, survey data
Donations*	Charity's own records; Word of mouth; mainstream/internet media	Vendors to the charitable sector; Imagine Canada; Canada Revenue Agency reporting	Data Analysis relying on Statistics Canada, census data, survey data, charity's own donation data
Investments	Word of mouth; mainstream/internet media	Online tools: Securities Regulatory entities reporting	Data Analysis relying on Statistics Canada, census data, survey data
Job Title/ Employer/ Profession	Charity's own records; Word of mouth; mainstream/internet media	Directories (electronic if available)	In-house data collection, management and analysis
Familial Relationships	Word of mouth; mainstream/internet media	Obituaries, Biographies	Obituaries, Biographies

*Donors frequently respond to the amount the requestor asks for, but rarely more than that ask amount. Therefore, past donations may simply indicate the lower end or "floor" level that the donor is capable of providing.

Figure 4.1 Wealth Indicators for individuals

Income

Income is an indicator familiar to most people. Here, it is defined as direct compensation for worked performed in an employment setting, as distinct from "investment income," discussed a little later on.

Knowledge of specific income levels is a seeming paradox, in that many people view salary information as private. At the same time, it is common that the higher an individual's income, the more likely it is to be made public either through forced disclosure by regulatory bodies or by the increasing call for transparency.

It is a useful coincidence that fundraisers are naturally more interested in the higher end of the income scale, making the inference that more compensation means a greater portion of income available for discretionary uses such as philanthropy. In reality though, it is often the case that individuals consume a similar proportion of their income, regardless of the raw amount of money earned.

As a "wealth indicator" however, income can be very useful in determining where fundraisers should devote limited time and energy. With respect to indicator strength, there is a very important distinction between income gained from employment in the public and private sectors: in the private sector, the concurrent acquisition of investment wealth is common, through equity ownership in the employing entity (the company).

This is not the case in the public sector, except in the rare case of privatization of publicly owned entities.

Information about income levels can come from a variety of sources, including the income earner themselves. Another source of useful information is found in the media; particularly newspapers and magazines. As in so many aspects of life, the development of the World Wide Web dramatically improved access to low cost public information about incomes. Online media (combined with news-tracking search engine tools) greatly enhance the fundraiser's ability to stay abreast of information about prospects.

Securities Commission documents, formerly available only via expensive subscriptions, are now available for no direct cost via the Internet on the System for Electronic Document Analysis and Retrieval (SEDAR) website managed by the Canadian Securities Administrators (CSA).

The CSA requirement for annual income disclosure of the top five income earners in each publicly traded company listed on a Canadian stock exchange in a document known as a *Proxy Circular* gives access to information on a smallish subset of the population. A subset that happens to be one that fundraisers are particularly focused on, as it aggregates factual information on the highest income earners in Canada. Data is available online from the 1997 reporting year forward. Companies must file these reports, and they are subject to audit, making the information quite reliable.

For public sector income earners,(a weaker indicator of wealth due to the inability of public sector employees to be compensated with equity) information resources such as Ontario's Public Sector Salary Disclosure website provides data on people earning more than $100,000 annually. Data is available starting from 1997 forward.

Income estimates are also available from information vendors focused on the charitable sector. Vendors will provide a statistically valid "screening" of a charity's stakeholder base, relying on (in Canada) data from Statistics Canada census gathering to determine average household income in a narrow geographic area. For this to be effective, the charity must have home address information for their stakeholders.

Most commonly, vendors will provide a one-time snapshot at a given point in time to their charitable clients. Relatively resource-rich charities with employees skilled in the analytical methodologies required may be able to purchase the household income data themselves and duplicate these results on an ongoing basis.

Real Estate

For the vast majority of people in Canada, home ownership is the single largest investment that they will experience in their lives. This is less true for the wealthiest people with the highest capacity to donate, but real estate value still can provide a good indicator of greater wealth – the same methodology can be employed for multiple properties owned. Property holdings will never be as completely reliable as income as a measure of capacity since it is difficult to know the degree to which real estate investment is facilitated through debt, but ownership of multi-million dollar properties incurring tens of thousands of dollars in annual upkeep and taxes can provide a sense of the overall wealth an individual may have.

A simple way to begin to gauge the value of real estate is to cross reference real estate advertising with home addresses of stakeholders. Asking prices for real estate are frequently determined through reviewing the recent sales of similar properties in similar circumstances (e.g. similar neighbourhoods), so even if the exact home of a stakeholder is not listed, something similar that is listed will provide a reliable estimate of property value.

As with data screening, this methodology relies on having current home address information for prospects. Charities most frequently gain this information via issuance of charitable receipts and by maintaining mailing lists for the purpose of communicating with stakeholders about events, meetings and so on.

Realtors maintain online listing services that contain asking prices of many properties, often in a searchable database. The cross-referencing process is still largely a manual task, but the database of listings usually provides a much more useful cross section of properties in a particular category.

Using similar methodologies to income screening, whether through external vendors or via internal analysis, data from Statistics Canada can be employed to determine the average value of a property in a geographic area. This can be quite costly, and perhaps beyond the capabilities of many charities.

Geographic clusters of high-end retailers positioned near certain neighbourhoods and offering expensive luxury items to consumers may be a rough and ready way to gauge the relative wealth in close proximity to those retailers – the assumption being that those retailers have engaged in the analysis to understand where their likeliest (e.g. wealthiest) potential customers are living.

Donations

For many fundraisers it is a truism that the best indicator of a future donation by an individual is a past donation to the charity. Similarly, the amount of a past donation is often used as a benchmark to identify the amount of money a stakeholder is willing to donate.

Caution should be employed here as past donation levels may have been heavily influenced by the amount solicited by the fundraiser. Simple review of past do-

nations, whether to the fundraiser's own charity or to another organization, will not accurately identify the higher end of the range of a donor's capacity.

Other charities can also be a source of information about donors. Some donors with high capacity but who otherwise keep a low profile may only be identified in a press release or an annual report that recognizes and trumpets their contribution with the hope of motivating others to donate. Regular scanning of media can assist in staying abreast of donation news.

Directed internet search may also provide valuable information. More recently, vendors have started to assemble this information from publically available sources, aggregating it in searchable databases, usually on a subscription fee model. For those charities that can afford the cost, these resources shorten the time consumed by the search process, thereby allowing research staff to focus on other tasks, such as interpreting results rather than assembling data. Essentially, however, the source is the same website or websites that can be searched by anybody, so it is a task any charity with enough time and an Internet connection could perform for themselves.

Investments

Like income, investments are an indicator that becomes more available for public knowledge towards the higher end of the wealth scale.

With respect to publicly traded companies, Canada requires that any person or company that owns 10% or more of the shares or equity must report their level of ownership to regulatory authorities, reported through SEDAR. Similarly members of the Board of Directors and certain executive officers must also report their share ownership. This same group, plus senior employees deemed to be "insiders" by virtue of their ability to affect the direction of the company must also report share ownership through the System for Electronic Disclosure by Insiders (SEDI).

Why does this matter, and how is it useful? The answer: tax.

Thanks to significant lobbying efforts in Canada, tax treatment of donations of securities (i.e. shares in publicly traded companies) is now very favourable. Employees receiving shares, or equity, in addition to cash compensation, are potentially able to build tax-sheltered wealth until such time as they need to sell that equity. Donating some of those shares in addition to selling some can alleviate capital gains tax incurred.

Tracking wealthy shareholders who can benefit financially from donating some of their holdings can inform both the timing and amount of a solicitation. Unlike income, individuals often retain the value of investments until they are in the most tax friendly position available.

Job Title/Employer/Profession

Researchers frequently rely on inferences – pieces of information like the value of a house that allow for a reasonable assumption about the level of wealth of the occupant (who might or might not be the actual property owner).

The type of work an individual does or often who their employer is, can serve as a proxy for more concrete information such as income or even the possibility that they are building shareholding equity in the company that they work for.

Acquisition of more than one type of information is necessary in this category: it is important to build knowledge about which kinds of work rewards individuals the most; to apply that knowledge, it is necessary to gather information on exactly what type of work stakeholders are performing, and at what level in the organization that employs them.

Is the prospect in question a member of a profession known for higher than average compensation? Do they have a job title like Partner or Managing Director, that could imply that an equity stake accompanies that higher than average compensation? Is the stakeholder the CEO of their company? Is the individual an entrepreneur, the founder of their company – and if so what does that mean?

Compensation surveys are conducted and may be reported in the mainstream media or in professional publications. The value of an entrepreneur's company may be well known, once again through media reports, or perhaps in regulatory filings. A further inference about the value of the company may have to be made – whether through data such as company revenue or the value placed on it through a publicly reported takeover bid.

Once the value of a company can be established or inferred, the next challenge is to gain knowledge of where your stakeholder may be placed within that company. Here again the available information about job titles skews towards the most senior (and presumably, best compensated) employees. Search engines provide access to company websites containing such information. Directories that track companies in particular industries may provide pieces to the puzzle. Appointment notices (a regular feature of many publications, and often are the subject of press releases) can provide solid biographical information.

One simple methodology exists with respect to collecting employment information, and it is scalable to every size of fundraising organization: ask the prospect themselves what they do, what their title is, who their employer is, and so on. Large organizations may be able to invest in tools that allow for the ongoing collection and maintenance of such data in a very significant way, but the smallest organization can perform this task, even if the data is stored in the proverbial shoebox.

Familial Relationships

Inter-generational wealth is a fact across the planet. Sometimes the inheritors of wealth are extremely prominent, to the point of being the subject of so-called "reality" television shows. At other times these people may be incredibly obscure and private. The value of tracking and understanding relationships is covered later in this chapter, but the sources of these pieces of information mirrors many of the other categories already discussed: mainstream media; biographical directories and Who's Who publications can help to fill in the blanks.

Of course, it is nearly impossible to know for sure whether a member of a wealthy family has actually benefited financially from that relationship, but the knowledge that it is *possible* can then send researchers down a potentially fruitful path, by looking for the other indicators already presented here.

COMBINING FACTORS

Prospect researchers have much they can learn from market researchers who look for patterns in data using statistically valid analysis. This can range from the common sense practice of "putting two and two together" to full-blown statistical modeling and data mining.

The core data that is required to make analysis a productive activity with demonstrable ROI can be found in the preceding discussion of indicators: combing that data in useful ways can only happen if it is collected, verified and maintained over time. Commonly, this analysis is out-sourced to third party service providers, but the subsequent answers provided are usually only a one-time snapshot. The ideal scenario, admittedly one requiring a significant investment in technology and expertise, is to have that ability in-house, with the opportunity to repeat or tweak analysis as need dictates.

CORPORATIONS/FOUNDATIONS

As in the case of individual prospects, corporate and foundation prospects must also be assessed on their capability to give or "capacity."

Corporations

A simple assessment of the capacity of a corporate donor consists of reviewing the profitability of the corporation and then making judgements about the size of donation that might be available out of the profits. However, this approach understates the complexity of the situation in a very significant way.

Corporations typically have a contract with shareholders to maximize the value of the investment the shareholders have made; in other words, the profits belong to the shareholders. Shareholders may authorize the company to use the profits in certain ways, including donating to a charity,

Corporations are usually subject to tax, and for competitive reasons will seek opportunities to reduce the amount of tax that they have to pay. Corporations may also be motivated by public relations or marketing needs to align with a charity that matches the values of the company's client base: so, a restaurant business that seeks a family clientele may partner with or donate to a children's health charity in order to present a pleasing image. There are other strategies available to reduce tax owing, but a corporation may choose to donate to reduce tax owing, which would create more profit for shareholders. For this reason the financial capacity of a corporation to donate may be very difficult to determine from the outside.

To further complicate the assessment, corporations frequently spend on marketing and public relations activities outside of the donation context. This spending is intended to drive business rather than reduce costs, tax relief may be immaterial. It may be possible to determine if a corporation will incur tax by monitoring whether a large capital gain is looming; knowing what a company may be budgeting for marketing is likely to be much more difficult.

The distinction between corporate philanthropy and sponsorship also needs to be taken into account. Corporations may desire certain kinds of recognition or quid pro quo in financially supporting a charity, which can negate the charitable intent component required by the government to receive tax credit. Perhaps more than individuals or foundations, assessing the capacity of a corporate entity to give requires one on one interaction with company representatives – more of a task for the major gift development officer than the researcher.

A corporation may simply set and publicize their capacity through establishing a certain percentage of profits, or a particular percentage of a charity's campaign goal. Because the funds required may come from different sources within the company, this should be viewed as a starting point – there is no sense in artificially limiting the amount of funding that might be forthcoming.

Foundations

Essentially there are two types of foundations: one is a distinct entity originally set up by either a private citizen, group of people or corporate entity that operates as a separate body; the other is a wealth and tax management vehicle closely tied to a still active and involved individual.

The capacity of the first type is often simple to determine: the foundation will have set dispersal amounts and the total assets can be reviewed in the filings on the Canada Revenue Agency website or in the Imagine Canada Directory to Foundations. Further injections of funds into the foundation are rare, and a charity can do simple math to determine capacity.

For a foundation that is connected to an individual or family that is still active, capacity assessment is more complex, the possibility for an injection of funds is real. Additionally, the opportunity to solicit the founder as well as the foundation may arise, in which case assessing the wealth of the individual will be called for, as described earlier in the chapter.

CAPACITY RATINGS

The process of evaluating indicators can lead naturally to the development of a capacity rating system. This can take the form of a scale (1-10; 1-100), or a concrete rating based on dollars, reflecting the presumed gift a prospect could make. Either allows for prioritization; the benefit of a dollar-based rating is that projections about fundraising programs can be made, once an agreeable discount rate (probability of actually getting a donation) is established.

TIP

Even at the most basic level, regular scanning of media and staying in tune with "word of mouth" sources of information can provide a very important foundation for understanding prospects' capability and willingness to donate.

Most analysis is a "snapshot" - presenting a picture of the facts at a particular point in time, with particular and static inputs, whereas wealth is dynamic.

Regular review of media reports is a way of staying abreast of changes in the world that will allow for adjustments of wealth and affinity assessments "on the fly."

Figure 4.2

AFFINITY

Individuals
Affinity or the degree of strength of the relationship an individual has with a charity is subjective. There is nothing inherently wrong with relying on subjective evaluations if the judgement of the person or people making the assessment is sound. This can come from one on one contact with the prospect. It can be derived by tracking involvement with a charity, whether through donating, volunteering, attending events, or advocating for the organization. It can be ascertained simply by asking.

Affinity measurement can be as simplistic or as complex as can be imagined. It can be a scale of one through ten; it can be an algorithm with weighted components. The most important thing is to engage in it, so that comparative analysis is possible. It will help enormously with prioritization of development officer efforts.

Just as with capacity, affinity has indicators. In the case of education, markers of affinity that correlate with willingness to donate include: the existence of a mentor relationship or the formation of a lifelong relationship during the school experience; willingness to recommend the school to others; or volunteering. Other types of charities will have their own markers of affinity.

Corporations
A corporation cannot have an emotional response that might generate affinity; the decision-makers within a corporation however, can. The public relations or marketing needs of a company might be a good match with the mission of a charity; the values and actions of that corporation may or may not be a similar, good match.

This is the dance that many charities do. The question of affinity is almost moot in this circumstance. The researcher needs to gain a sense of what either meets the marketing goals of the company in question, or is a good match with the values and interests of chief influencers of the company on a personal level.

The process for those two options differs. Understanding the company's interests is a business-to-business research task; what can be understood about the goals of the company?

Understanding the decision-makers in the company - the people, is again a process of understanding what motivates an individual.

Foundations
Identifying affinity with respect to foundations is not that much different than in the case of individuals, with an exception: the *Imagine Canada Directory of*

Foundations, the single best research tool in terms of understanding donor intent. In the directory, foundations are categorized by their declared philanthropic interests, and those interests are searchable.

For the foundation that has become an established entity independent of the founders, this directory gives guidance on how to match the needs of the charity to the interests of the foundation, so that a successful application can be submitted.

Much more exciting, is the insight that for foundations that are largely a wealth management vehicle of still active people, the directory points to the charitable interests of philanthropists and those interests are searchable.

In essence, the process of determining affinity, which can be a time consuming task requiring repeated interactions with a prospect can be significantly compressed. One database search can replace repeated qualification efforts conducted in personal encounters. The bonus is that once an interest match is made, the prospect that is identified may have more resources than are declared in the foundations assets. Personal cultivation of the foundation funder may be possible once identified and researched as an individual, as described earlier in the chapter.

Relationships

The spider webs of connections from the very beginning of this discussion are another component of the overall picture of a prospect that the researcher can illuminate. As already discussed, relationships can serve as indicators of capacity: employment, familial and so on. Knowledge of relationships and their inherent nature can facilitate the cultivation and solicitation process as well. Family members, friends or business associates may be willing to leverage those relationships in order to initiate a discussion between a charity and a potential donor, or they may be willing to reinforce a solicitation. Who knows the prospect, and how can they help?

The sources of information about relationships mirror those of the capacity discussion to a significant degree. Word of mouth information can be invaluable in understanding the interpersonal connections. Media reports often detail relationships, and common elements of newspapers such as appointment notices, obituaries and other announcements provide use-

ful data. Regulatory filings require the reporting of connections between people and companies, and by extension, connections between people sharing a relationship to the company. Even the reporting required by the Canada Revenue Agency detailing the directors of charities can be incredibly useful.

More than most other components of prospect research, resources and available tools make a significant impact on the fundraising organization's opportunity to leverage relationships. Very quickly, it can be quite difficult to keep track of the matrix of multiple relationships that an individual or organization can have. Modern relational databases offer significant advantages over more rudimentary tools in this case. It is possible to track relationships in a manual fashion, but the time commitment to review manual files may be prohibitive to many organizations.

THE PROSPECT PROFILE

In the fundraising world, the prospect profile, a comprehensive document detailing all of the elements described in this chapter, is where much emphasis is placed. There can be no denying the utility of the profile, which is really a biographical picture of a prospect. However, it should not be where prospect research begins and ends.

In assembling the profile it is necessary to review and detail the capacity, affinity, and relationships the prospect has, in addition to summarizing the specific interactions with the charity. If the resources of an organization dictate that all that can be managed is the creation of a static document containing those elements, then that is what must be done.

In an age where technology can assist in so many ways, the opportunity to rethink how a profile gets created arises. It can be so much more than a product of word processing software, saved in static form in a computer hard drive. Most of the components of a standard profile have a place in a database: prospect name and other biographical data, nature of their relationship to the charity, past giving and other interactions, capacity, affinity, relationships – they all can be stored in a computer. In this scenario, the profile becomes a database report. And the individual components become available for further analysis in statistical modelling and data mining.

Establishing the database as the central repository of all useful data is a crucial step in the development of a fundraising organization.

MANAGING THE PROSPECT POOL

Prioritizing research subjects is one of the most important steps an organization can take in ensuring that ROI can be derived from the researcher. Figure 4.3 paints a picture of a pool of identified prospects about which some information is known, but not enough information to conduct a successful solicitation. Plotting prospects based on wealth (capacity) on the vertical, and relationship strength (affinity) on the horizontal maps the prospect pool into a standard two-by-two diagram. A very simple mapping can place the entire prospect pool somewhere on this grid.

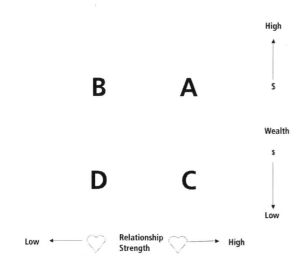

Figure 4.3
Wealth and strength of relationship – qualified prospects

In Figure 4.3, a model of an identified prospect pool is depicted. All members of the pool are accounted for in one of the four quadrants A, B, C and D.

Quadrant A

Prospects landing in quadrant "A" have high capacity and high affinity. These are likely to be the best donors that a charity already has. The research requirement of this group may be surprisingly low: they have already given a significant amount, and they are close enough to the organization that they may have already passed along most of the useful information about themselves that there is to find. That is not to say that they should be ignored, but the researcher may end up spending a lot of time acquiring information that is already known.

Quadrant B

Prospects in quadrant "B" have high capacity but lower affinity. Fundraisers rarely can do anything about a prospect's capacity, but experience dictates that a good fundraiser can enhance the affinity a prospect has with a charity. Researching the prospects that initially fall into quadrant B has the potential for the highest ROI – these are the prospects that if properly cultivated and informed about the activities of the charity, can provide the greatest amount of financial support.

Quadrant C

Prospects in quadrant "C" may have great affinity, but also have lower capacity. They shouldn't be ignored, because they may have such a strong connection with the charity that they give everything they are capable of giving. At the same time though, their wealth is probably not very liquid or disposable: they are probably living in their largest asset, and most probably will need that residence as long as they are alive. Quadrant "C" are great planned giving prospects – they may not be capable of giving to a charity right now, but once they don't need their assets (wealth) any longer, they may be quite happy to transfer them as a donation. Very little research is warranted.

Quadrant D

Quadrant "D" prospects have low affinity and low capacity. It is important to identify them if only to be able to ensure that scarce resources are not spent in attempting to build relationships or solicit them. Lowest cost fundraising strategies are warranted. No research is required.

CONCLUSION

Information management and analysis is the beating heart of many modern organizations. Fundraising organizations are no different, with the prospect researcher as the fundraising professional best positioned to provide the decision-support necessary for success. ***Capacity*** assessment ensures that cultivation occurs with prospects capable of making an impact once the relationship evolves to a successful solicitation. ***Affinity*** assessment ensures that the likelihood of a prospect becoming a donor is sufficient to embark on the cultivation process.

Prospect research is scalable; at the core, techniques useful for constituency-bases of hundreds of thousands can also be applied to prospect pools numbering in the hundreds. The challenges are similar as well – it is most productive to devote the majority of the finite amount of time available to perform research, to refining the picture of prospects that aren't well-known but who are suspected to be of high capacity. Managing the research process is as important as mastering the specific techniques in order to contribute to optimal fundraising efforts.

ADDITIONAL RESOURCES

Books
▶ HOGAN, CECILIA AND LAMB, D. (2003). *Prospect Research: A Primer for Growing Nonprofits*. Jones & Bartlett Publishers.

Online Documents
▶ IMAGINE CANADA. Canadian Directory to Foundations & Corporations. *Retrieved from http://www.imaginecanada.ca.*

URLs
▶ CANADA REVENUE AGENCY Charities Listings *http://www.cra-arc.gc.ca/chrts-gvng/lstngs/menu-eng.html*

▶ SEDAR (System for Electronic Document Analysis and Retrieval) *www.sedar.com*

▶ SEDI (System for Electronic Disclosure by Insiders) *www.sedi.ca* provide the equivalent regulatory documents to EDGAR from the United States: information on shareholding and compensation required to be filed by public companies to Canadian Securities Regulatory entities.

ABOUT THE AUTHOR

Peter McKinley, MLIS

In May, 2004 Peter introduced a pioneering graduate-level prospect research course in the Masters of Library and Information Science program at the University of Western Ontario. Currently, Peter serves at Director of Development and Donor Relations at Brock University.

In the various roles of manager, consultant, teacher and researcher, Peter has consistently pursued the goal of increasing knowledge about donor capacity and philanthropic intent in the non-profit sector. Peter has successfully transferred this knowledge through presentations to professional associations, and in workshops for non-profit organizations.

Peter has a BA (Honours History) and a Masters of Library and Information Science, both from the University of Western Ontario, and has completed the Finance for non-Financial Managers executive program at the Ivey Business School, and the Applied Research Methods program of the American Marketing Association.

CHAPTER 5

Annual Fundraising
NICK JAFFER, BCOMM

I've been thinking about renovating my kitchen. Well, actually, my partner has been thinking about renovating our kitchen. But, as many of you will know, that's pretty much the same thing: *I'm* thinking about renovating our kitchen. This, in fact, has its origins in a friend's kitchen. My partner was so impressed with what this friend had done with his kitchen that this naturally led to talk of us "needing" to renovate ours (she clearly missed the part of the conversation about living in a dust-strewn environment and surviving on take-out for an extended period!). *read more...*

I tried to put up the usual arguments: kitchen renovations could mean the death of a relationship ... the green cupboards and counters weren't really that bad and, besides, I thought they were grey anyway (a benefit of being colour-blind) ... couldn't we just put a wine fridge in the garage? ... this could take months and I wasn't that keen on KFC or MacDonald's for that long ... and, um, how *much* was this going to cost?

It's not that I am particularly attached to our kitchen, though the green/grey counters do always seem to look clean. No, I was much more concerned about how we were going to afford this given that we already have payments to the bank each month for the house and cars, not to mention the electricity, gas and water bills. It just didn't seem particularly do-able to me, especially given that we'd have to hire an architect to map out the configurations of the new layout then also fork out for a builder or carpenter, electricians, plumbers and a gasfitter. And, I haven't mentioned buying that wine fridge!

She figured that we'd just use some of the money from our savings account to pay for it all. We wouldn't even have to worry about stretching our paycheques or drawing from our chequing accounts.

So, why am I telling you all this? The point of this entire story is to get to the core of what annual fundraising is all about.

I was reminded of the kitchen analogy to fundraising – which I first heard about fifteen years ago at a fundraising conference in Banff – when we started to discuss financing the renovation. That is, my kitchen renovation is similar to a capital campaign; both take place over a finite time period and achieving the goal will be almost wholly funded by money from savings or assets, in other words, the equivalent of major gifts.

On the other hand, the monthly house and car bills are like the needs around my annual giving program; regardless of what other capital or special projects I decide to do now or in the future, I will still need to pay for these bills on a monthly and ongoing basis – just as an organization will need to fund its operational costs on an ongoing basis. Taking care of these bills or operational costs will be funded entirely out of my chequing account or my discretionary income as we know it.

So, in the big picture, the purpose of annual fundraising is to leverage discretionary income to take care of the house and the car bills – those core organizational costs that happen week after week, month after month, year after year in order for a non-profit to continue to exist so that it can continue to do what it needs to do to achieve its mission and purpose.

Of course, if you delve deeper than that, you'll know that there's more. Hank Rosso, in his book *Achieving Excellence in Fundraising*, described annual fundraising as "the cornerstone and the key to success for all aspects of the fund raising program." In doing so, he outlined a number of objectives for annual fundraising, or the annual fund, as shown in Figure 5.1.

Rosso's Objectives of the Annual Fund

- To solicit and secure a new gift, repeat the gift, and upgrade the gift

- To build and develop a base of donors

- To establish habits and patterns of giving by regular solicitation

- To seek to expand the donor base by soliciting gifts from new prospects

- To raise annual unrestricted and restricted money

- To inform, involve, and bond the constituency to the organization

- To use the donor base as a vital source of information to identify potential large donors

- To promote giving habits that encourage the contributor to make capital and planned gifts

- To remain fully accountable to the constituency through annual reports

---

Figure 5.1

Rosso was correct, of course, there is a lot more to annual fundraising and, in fact, it is worth exploring some of these concepts further later in this chapter. But, in the end, we must recognize that Rosso's points are stepping stones to the same final destination. The purpose of annual fundraising is to look after core ongoing costs to enable an organization to do what it needs to do to achieve its mission and purpose, week after week, month after month, year after year.

ESTABLISHING A STRATEGIC FRAMEWORK AND A CASE FOR SUPPORT

The definition of annual fundraising connotes a long-term horizon but also short-term funding concerns. This goes to the heart of annual fundraising and its fit within an organization's strategic framework.

Within this framework, an organization's annual fundraising program may strive to be either or both, efficient *and* effective. To be *efficient*, annual fundraising appeals need to be focused on individuals who have expressed continuing interest in the organization as these individuals are the most likely to respond positively with a donation. To be *effective*, annual fundraising appeals should seek to maximize participation through high renewal rates (people contributing every year) and identification of major gift and planned giving prospects.

Inherently then, to be efficient and/or effective requires some understanding of your constituency and a measure of segmentation in implementing your annual fundraising program. Adrian Sargeant et al[1] elaborate upon the rationale for this:

1. By segmenting markets, organizations develop a better understanding of the needs of their donors. They understand what motivates them to give, how they like to be approached, the messages they prefer, the outcomes they want to see, how they like to have their gifts acknowledged, and so on. This understanding can then be used to enhance the quality of fundraising activity.

2. All non-profits have limited resources. To target the whole market is therefore unrealistic for all but the largest organizations. The effectiveness of fundraising can be greatly improved when it is more narrowly focused on a specific group of donors.

3. Segmentation allows a non-profit to tailor its approach to reflect the needs of the individuals or organizations it is addressing. This is not only a more respectful approach (treating donors as individuals), but it also makes good economic sense, because donors approached with a tailored solicitation that reflects their genuine concerns and interests are significantly more likely to respond, to derive satisfaction from their giving, and to give loyally over time.

Sargeant raises a vexing issue for most organizations: how much to spend on annual fundraising? Budgets are generally limited and organizations naturally face short-term financial pressures which often dictate strategy rather than having strategy dictate budgets. In the area of annual fundraising, this often translates to communicating with selected segments that, as stated earlier, have the greatest propensity to respond favourably. In the short-term, a budgetary framework may require an organization to invest an amount that will cover the costs of reaching the target audience, and in the initial years, either be prepared to accept a loss or simply seek only to recover the cost of the appeals while measuring success less in dollars but more in numbers of donors. We'll pick up this discussion again later, but it's worth considering when working to establish the framework for new annual fundraising programs in particular.

Towards the aim of being effective, we alluded to segmenting the potential audience by donors and non-donors. This, of course, is very common among non-profits as is having a segment of lapsed donors though organizations may differ in how they define lapsed (i.e. gave last year but not this year (LYBUNT), gave some year but not this year (SYBUNT). But, segmentation can be far more in-depth than this. Sargeant also outlines the following methods of segmentation for individuals:

- Geographic location
- Demographics
  - age
  - generation
  - gender
  - family life cycle
  - income and occupation

---

1   Sargeant, A., & Shang, J. (2010). *Fundraising Principles and Practice*. John Wiley and Sons, Inc.

- race and ethnicity
- geo-demographics
- Psychographic segmentation
- Behavioural segmentation

The list is not exhaustive. For instance, universities may segment by degree or faculty, year of graduation, number of degrees held, etc. and approaches will vary from institution to institution. Therefore, segmentation needs to be specific to the circumstances and constituencies of a particular organization rather than a one-size-fits-all approach. Each level of segmentation is likely to have an impact on the cost of an annual fundraising program and an organization needs to strive to find its most optimum balance between segmentation to achieve a level of personalization yet which maximizes its return on investment.

Underpinning the personalization in communication is the development of an appropriate case for support which Harold J. Seymour defined as "an expression of the cause, or a clear compelling statement of all of the reasons why anyone should consider making a contribution in support of or to advance the cause."[2]

Consistent with the purpose of annual fundraising and the strategic framework which supports it, the case for support needs to pursue a long term outcome but acknowledge short term funding concerns.

To illustrate, let's consider a small, young charity in Surrey, BC. The *"Caring Hearts for Underprivileged Children Society"* received official charity status in May 2011. As found on the "Caring Hearts" website, their purpose is "dedicated to providing (hand crafted), warm clothing and blankets, directly to... BC's children in need." To achieve this, the organization is seeking not only financial donations but the following non-cash items:

- Yarn
- Crochet hooks and knitting needles
- Quilting fabric (cotton) and batting
- Fabric suitable for children's clothing (fleece, flannelette, denim, corduroy, t-shirt knits)

As outlined earlier, at its most basic, an organization's annual fundraising program should aim to support core ongoing costs which enable it to achieve its long-term vision and mission. The important aspect to this is an alignment of annual priorities to that vision and mission so that fundraising outcomes are not diluted by efforts to raise money for projects which are not core to the strategic direction of the organization as a whole or which require the organization to make up the funding gap if an initiative is not *wholly* externally funded as this would further stretch the operational budget. Towards this end, keep in mind that annual fundraising is not about funding *new* add-on initiatives or programs but rather funding those basic, nucleus programs.

For a young, grassroots charity such as "Caring Hearts," the need for these contributions is critical to its short term activities as well as the achievement of its long term purpose. Indeed, this simple message is highlighted in the following acknowledgment letter from "Caring Hearts":

"With your support and Lululemon's funding program proceeds we will be temporarily alleviated from fundraising proposals and will be able to focus on distributing the wonderfully crafted items to the children in need."

Annual fundraising, perhaps even more so than project or campaign fundraising, needs to consistently reflect the *end-goal* of the organization. And, by this, I don't mean the funding *outputs* of an organization – things commonly promoted in annual appeals like programs, services, research, scholarships or, in the above case, sweaters and blankets – but, rather, the funding *outcomes* that could be achieved with support.

The reason for this, of course, is that it is much more compelling and inspiring to a potential donor if he or she can help discover a cure to a disease, give a start to someone in need or save a life rather than help to fund equipment purchases, pay the salary to recruit a researcher or cover fuel costs so that a plane can deliver goods to a third world country. For "Caring Hearts," it's not so much about providing blankets, but providing warmth, security and safety to children in need.

Back to Rosso for a moment. In his book, he suggested "People do not give to people. They give to people with causes."[3] I don't think this is entirely true. After all, there are lots of people asking for a lot of

---

2   Seymour, Harold J., (1966). *Designs for Fundraising: Principles. Patterns. Techniques.* Mcgraw-Hill.

3   Rosso, Hank. (2003) *Achieving Excellence in Fundraising,* John Wiley & Sons, Inc.

causes, with the common misperception of volunteers being that if people understood how important the cause was, they would give. No, I would argue that people give to people with *solutions* for causes, or at least opportunities for solutions. And the need to articulate this solution or the opportunity of it is fundamental to good annual fundraising practice.

This may sound intuitive but for every example that carefully articulates the outcomes that could be achieved, I have seen another dozen that weakly state their needs or glorify their organization and the activities that it is performing. Picture reading a message like this: "We are marvelous … we do tremendous work … our people are fantastic … we have a great reputation … we are *really* marvelous … only we can do what we do … we are really, bloody marvelous … give us your money." Is this really motivational? The part that has been forgotten is "why is this *meaningful* for the recipient of the message?"

In the case of "Caring Hearts," their case for support for helping clothe children expands to the impact on the community:

"This is where your charitable contributions have the greatest social effect. Since a child's self-esteem and sense of worth ultimately effects (sic) their social attitudes, giving them both pride and comfort, can produce enormous long-term rewards for our community and society at large."

It may need polishing but the message is this: providing a gift of a blanket or clothing will ultimately impact you and me, not just the child who receives the warm clothing or blanket.

Not to be overlooked is the added benefit that focusing on the end-goal means consistency of message and better integration of fundraising programs. That is, if an organization is strongly communicating its outcomes, which one would expect are derived from its mission and purpose, then this lessens the worry about a potential recipient wondering why the organization is going to such efforts to launch a capital campaign for new research facilities but continuing to advocate the unwavering need for hiring new staff. Why hire new staff when you don't have the facilities for them? Building a message around the end-goal immediately helps tie in the annual giving program to the commu-

nications around major gift conversations or capital campaign efforts both of which, naturally, should be also articulating the benefit the community will derive from a potential donor's support.

DONOR CENTRISM: RESTRICTED AND UNRESTRICTED ANNUAL FUNDRAISING

I attended an annual fund conference in Las Vegas in the mid-1990s. As the Manager of the Annual Fund at the University of Alberta, if the idea of an annual fund conference wasn't motivating enough, then certainly the idea of escaping a frigid Canadian winter for a week to the hot climes of Las Vegas was!

At the time, I was relatively new to annual fundraising only having been doing it for a couple of years so I was excited about the opportunity to learn from more seasoned professionals who had been practicing it for years in the U.S. It was at this conference that I gained a huge insight into the difference in the practice of annual fundraising north of the 49th parallel versus south of the border. This had nothing to do with segmentation, the number of appeals per year or the use of calling programs to raise money from potential donors. In fact, much of what we practiced in Canada at the time was very similar to our American counterparts so, while there was some learning to be gained for me, it was more in refining my existing knowledge rather than learning entirely new concepts.

No, the big learning experience was that what the Americans defined and practiced as annual fundraising was really annual *unrestricted* fundraising while the more common Canadian practice included both unrestricted and restricted which, otherwise stated, might be "How can we help you give each year?" Let's explore this concept of unrestricted and restricted fundraising for the annual fundraising program a bit further.

Most fundraising professionals and certainly every seasoned fundraising practitioner will understand the difference between restricted and unrestricted funds. Restricted funds are funds allocated to specific purposes within an organization and must be used for those purposes. The level of restriction may vary, for instance, monies given for dental equipment within a dental school may be used for any piece of dental equipment but cannot be used for, say, salaries. Conversely, restricted monies specified to a dental school within a university can be used by the dental school in any manner but those funds cannot be used by another school or faculty within the university. The less-restricted nature of the second example moves further towards the middle of restricted/unrestricted continuum. Unrestricted funds, at its highest degree, are donations which a nonprofit may use for any purpose – consistent, of course, with the attainment of its mission and vision.

Because of the flexibility in use that it offers, unrestricted funds are highly valued by nonprofits. Historically, annual fundraising – certainly in America – focused on the raising of these unrestricted funds whereas restricted funds were primarily sought through major gift efforts. This was certainly the anecdotal evidence at the Las Vegas conference.

Generally speaking, the pursuit of unrestricted funds dictates that an organization's annual fundraising program must focus on the outcomes of an organization, which we previously indicated was a positive thing. The reason for this is quite intuitive: donating funds for general or operational use requires a belief by a donor that these funds will be used appropriately in the purpose and work of the charity. As highlighted before, it's much less inspiring to contribute to a salary than to a salary of someone finding a cure for a disease.

The great paradox within this for annual fundraising professionals is how to adopt a donor-centered approach. By the very nature of its mass communications and in comparison to major gifts, it's recognized that annual fundraising is more institutionally-centred than donor focused – and this is amplified in annual unrestricted fundraising because donors lack choice about where they may direct their funds. Instead, a charity selects the message it wants to convey and asks donors to trust their judgment in investing those monies.

This provides greater flexibility to the charity but it doesn't take into account the individual passions and interests of individual donors which likely negatively impacts their overall contribution levels. And, as we have seen with the rising sophistication of donors, a maturing culture of philanthropy and a growing base of younger contributors, donors are becoming increasingly selective in where they give their monies and how these monies are used. Quite simply, they want to decide where it should go.

Consequently, it's incumbent upon annual fundraising professionals to find that point on the restricted/unrestricted continuum that achieves a more optimum balance between offering donors some say in their investment and simply deciding for them. It's for this reason that (dare I say) I thought our Canadian approach was more sophisticated at that conference in Las Vegas and, as a result, it wasn't so much me doing the learning but our American colleagues gaining a newfound perspective.

Achieving a donor-centric balance necessitates appropriate segmentation and a focus on core funding priorities rather than new opportunities, which we discussed earlier. These core priorities are not limited to simply salaries and overhead costs but could include programs, services and other ongoing costs to the charity. The notion is that these core priorities are continually relevant to achieving the outcomes of the organization and therefore must be looked after this year and every year. Monies raised this year are meant to be used this year.

A second and sometimes overlooked notion is that these costs are likely being funded by a charity out of its operational budget and, in that way, are effectively internally restricted funds. But, by providing donors with the ability to contribute to those same core programs, it provides the charity with the flexibility and leverage to reallocate its own funds elsewhere to other ongoing programs or to *new* initiatives.

In essence, by moving away from the farthest point of unrestricted annual fundraising to a more donor centric approach, an organization can help donors to feel more connected and to increase their giving yet *still* achieve financial flexibility.

FUNDRAISING METHODS

The methodology behind annual fundraising is principally built around communications to larger audiences or segments. Most, if not all, tools of the trade are elaborated on in great depth in the chapters on Direct Marketing, Special Events, Monthly Giving and Internet Fundraising. As a result, other than recognizing that these various vehicles form the basis of the overwhelming majority of annual fundraising programs and that the use of technology is playing an increasingly important role in the delivery, reach and timing of annual fundraising messages, I'll leave it to my learned colleagues to delve into the specifics of each.

One area, however, that I do believe it's worth commenting on is the idea of integration of annual fundraising methodologies within an organization's broader fundraising and communication program.

First, it's important to recognize that annual fundraising does not exist in a silo. It's true that annual fundraising solicitations are sometimes the only interaction that some organizations have with their donor (and potential donor) constituencies but better annual fundraising programs skillfully integrate their messages within a wider communications program. This more holistic approach enables a charity to nurture deeper relationships encompassing cultivation, solicitation and stewardship. This recognizes that the annual fundraising program is not just a letter or call for support but a continual myriad of communications designed to more effectively generate support on a repetitive basis.

With this repetition of giving and the deepening of relationships may come the growth of annual contributions and possibly significant major gift support. In considering annual fundraising methodology, it's precisely in these instances where a charity should also consider not solely relying on mass communication vehicles (regardless of how tailored they may be) and, instead, use personal, one-to-one, face-to-face communication.

Of course, personal face-to-face solicitation can't be done for everyone in the annual fundraising program. But, it can be used astutely with high performing annual donors to grow their support, (particularly if they have hit a plateau) or in instances of transition where opportunities to support a campaign or special project at a major gift level are presented but where continuation of the annual gift is also imperative.

The advantage to personal solicitation in these cases, as with an integrated communications approach, is that it facilitates a deeper relationship with the donor; helping to build a greater understanding of their support to the charity. This makes it harder for a donor to say no to the opportunity and makes it easier for a charity to retain the donor at a higher level.

PYRAMIDS AND PIPELINES: ANNUAL FUNDRAISING, MAJOR GIFTS AND CAMPAIGNS

It's been said that annual fundraising serves as the gateway to more significant giving and the previous personal solicitation scenario alludes to the role of annual fundraising vis-a-vis major gifts and campaigns.

Certainly, we're all familiar with the fundraising pyramid highlighting the evolution of a potential donor initially as part of a "universe of prospects" through to a "first time donor," then "repeat donor" and so on to a position of leadership giving. There are few concepts in the area of annual fundraising as important as this one.

Lawrence Henze, Managing Director of Target Analytics, describes it this way:

> **Major donors with the greatest staying power are those that develop through the annual giving program. There is significant statistical evidence for that conclusion and absolutely no foreseeable reason that individuals originally acquired through online giving vehicles will mature any differently in the future. For example, research shows that $1,000 gifts to organizations occur most frequently when that donor has already been giving to the organization for about 7 years. Many years of research with successful nonprofits also shows that those very same donors are approximately 900% more likely to make a major gift in their lifetime than individuals without that progressive history.[4]**

Drawing on my own experience at the University of Alberta, I recall the story of a donor to the Faculty of Engineering who initially gave a gift of $1000 to the annual fund. It was a respectable gift, generous but not a standout by any means. With the appropriate acknowledgement, this support quickly grew to a gift of $10,000 again to the annual fund. This immediately got our attention. Further acknowledgement and stewardship turned this into a gift of $25,000 and then $100,000 all within a relatively short time span. The donor later said to the Dean that he wanted to know that his support made a difference before he

---

4   Henze, Lawrence. *Is the Fundraising Pyramid really a Lie?* Retrieved January, 2010 from http://www.nptrends.com/nonprofit-trends/is-the-fundraising-pyramid-really-a-lie.htm

was prepared to contribute any more. To make a long story short, after further cultivation over a period of approximately 15 months, the donor agreed to a multimillion dollar gift.

There are many more stories like this, not just at the University of Alberta, but at numerous institutions and charities across Canada. They highlight the ability of annual fundraising to initially engage supporters, to nurture trust and confidence in the charity, and to grow the level of support, thus moving donors through the pipeline for major gift fundraising and, ultimately, planned gifts.

However, achieving this goal does require some effort and time, however. As Henze (2010) states,

> **"The fundraising pyramid is not a lie; rather, it is an unfulfilled promise. The creation of a 'complete' fundraising pyramid requires time and patience."**

It also requires recognition that an annual gift or donor is not a product and, similarly, major gifts and planned gifts are not products to be managed or sold by different fundraising professionals who may specialize in each. Instead, it requires deeper integration and a removal of silos with an understanding that fundraising is about *managing relationships* with people and providing them with opportunities to engage across a range of giving vehicles. Andrew Olsen, CFRE, reinforces this thought:

> **"Rather than fostering collaboration and an atmosphere that promotes fully engaging donors to accomplish your organization's mission, this compartmentalization instead fosters an environment of competition that often results in one group or another hoarding donors (and income)."**

These internal conflicts result in lost opportunities.

Donors lose out on the opportunity to make more significant impacts on a cause they're passionate about. Your clients lose out on the opportunities that would have otherwise been created by greater donor investment. And your organization loses out because you're working against each other to accomplish individual performance objectives rather than working together

to maximize the impact you can have in your community.[5]

In short, taking a holistic approach in which you are focused on the relationship with your donor will not only help to maximize support for the charity but it will create a much more rewarding outcome for the donor, too.

Measuring success

"Show me the money!" Tom Cruise made those words famous when he shouted them into the phone in the movie *Jerry Maguire* but as fundraising professionals we hear those words regularly in one guise or another from board members, CEOs and even colleagues. Naturally, at the end of the day, our job as fundraisers comes down to money, that is, how much are we bringing in? But, to use the amount of money raised in a day or even a year as the only measure of performance can be both misleading and short-sighted.

Perhaps in recognition of this – or perhaps in spite of this – board members, volunteers and CEOs, fuelled by the media, have paid increasing attention to the cost per dollar raised or the return on investment (ROI). But this, too, can be misleading and short-sighted. And, for the annual fundraising professional, the attention to dollars raised or ROI can present a particularly precarious and demanding tightrope to walk. The reasons for this are many and complex.

To begin with, not every organization or cause or fundraising operation is the same. For newer organizations or fundraising operations, annual fundraising efforts are typically not "cash cows" and won't be for a long time. A newer organization like "Caring Hearts," which was mentioned earlier in this chapter, might have fewer donors and more non-donors compared to a mature organization like the Heart and Stroke Foundation whose ratio of donors to non-donors may be more favourable. As experience has taught us that acquiring a donor is more difficult and costly than renewing a donor, it stands to reason that measuring dollars raised and ROI would likely provide less positive results for Caring Hearts.

Some causes may have smaller audiences because of their geographic focus (e.g. Iqaluit versus Vancouver versus Ontario) or simply because of the cause they

5   Olsen, Andrew. *"Daddy, Where do Major Donors Come From?"* Retrieved July 21, 2010 from *http://fundraisingfundamentals.wordpress.com/2010/07/21/daddy-where-do-major-donors-come-from/*

represent. As an example of the latter, according to Health Canada, diabetes is now recognized as a major health issue with an estimated 60,000 new cases diagnosed each year in the country. Not to be insensitive but, with this, comes a greater potential pool of donors and funding. In comparison, how many have even heard of 'paroxysmal nocturnal hemoglobinuria' or PNH as it is alternatively known? It's a disease in which a mutation in bone-marrow stem cells causes red blood cells to pop or break open. As a rare disease, the potential donor base for this is significantly smaller than diabetes so drawing comparisons in monies raised would be unfair.

Then there are issues regarding the methods used in the annual fundraising program. For instance, as a developing new field, how should online and electronic fundraising be measured in annual fundraising? What costs of an organization's website, social media, or online strategy should be attributed to the annual fundraising program compared to its marketing and communications area or the development program as a whole? Should the amount of monies raised be the chief measure or should it be the level of un-subscribers?

What these questions and issues illustrate is that measuring success in annual fundraising is dynamic and poses a number of challenges. And, while differences between annual fundraising and major gifts may skew comparative measures of short- term efficiency for annual giving, they don't negate the need for a charity to examine how to be more efficient and, more importantly, effective.

To do it well, however, charities must acknowledge that annual fundraising *is* different. Analysis and measurement of success needs to consider acquisition of donors differently than or separately from the retention or renewal of donors. And measuring success must be framed within a much longer context, correlated to the fundraising pyramid and major gift pipeline outlined earlier. In other words, if annual fundraising is ultimately designed to build a culture of private support and identify potential major gift donors and planned giving prospects, then the measure of annual fundraising programs must also take into account these achievements.

To truly measure the long term success of annual fundraising, then, an organization needs to commit to measuring the Lifetime Value (LTV) of a donor

through the program. This is not as simple as measuring returns in one calendar year but it adds far greater understanding of the contribution of the annual fundraising program to the organization. Dirk Rinker, President of Campbell Rinker, an American marketing research firm elaborates:

> **"Most non-profits that pursue fundraising through mass media rely on basic analysis to measure the effectiveness of acquisition programs. Straightforward ROI computations (e.g. cost per dollar raised, cost per new donor, etc.) might be compared to a Corolla—not flashy, but reliable. Such measures as Lifetime Donor Value (LTDV) analysis are like a Prius hybrid—taking you farther, but with a higher initial investment."**

Quite simply, LTDV compares lifetime income with long-term costs, before you know what the lifetime income will actually be. Where ROI can only provide an immediate assessment of whether an acquisition or renewal effort makes money, LTDV offers a more complete picture of the donor's potential lifetime value. It accounts for such impacts as the cost to acquire a donor, the cost to maintain the relationship, and even inflation—forecasting two, five, and even ten-year lifetime values.

With the intense struggle for donor dollars, the need to identify the best acquisition sources is even more vital to success.[6]

Rinker goes on:

> **"Donor loyalty experts Adrian Sargeant and Elaine Jay write in *Building Donor Loyalty* (published by JosseyBass) that lifetime value can help nonprofits know which media deliver higher-value donors, identify donors for relationship, calculate how much the organization may profitably spend, and determine the level of care extended to donors in different value classes."**

Given the bottom-line difference that major and planned giving donors have on the fundraising balance sheet, and considering the impact of previous giving on generating a major gift as Henze noted earlier, realistic measurement of the annual fundraising program needs

6   Rinker, Dirk. *Is Lifetime Donor Value Still Relevant?* In Mal Warwick's *Newsletter*, Number 80, July 2006.

to not only reflect what activities are efficient in the short-term but what long-term value they have on an organization's ability to achieve its mission and vision.

CONCLUSION

- Annual fundraising doesn't or shouldn't exist in a silo, distinct from other parts of an organization's fundraising program; maximizing annual fundraising requires an integrated approach with prospect research, major gifts, planned gifts and capital campaign efforts.

- Ultimately, the purpose of annual fundraising is to look after core ongoing costs to enable an organization to do what it needs to do to achieve its mission and purpose, week after week, month after month, year after year.

- A donor-centric approach has greater likelihood to increase individual response rates and contributions. In keeping with this, annual fundraising can be used to raise funds for restricted purposes in addition to unrestricted purposes as long as the funds raised are for core, ongoing costs rather than new initiatives.

- People give to people with *solutions* for causes therefore the messaging in annual fundraising needs to prioritize the long-term end-goals of the organization or cause; that is, the outcomes being pursued rather than the outputs which may help to achieve those outcomes.

- Annual fundraising must be driven by long-term goals of effectiveness rather than efficiency.

- Annual fundraising is not limited to mass solicitations but, instead, should focus on integrated, continual communications designed to nurture deeper relationships with stakeholders. As part of this, personal solicitation can play a vital part of the mix in growing and retaining support.

- Annual fundraising plays a fundamental role as a gateway to giving but, more importantly for the long-term, for feeding the pipeline of major donors with committed and sustainable supporters.

- For this reason, measuring success in annual fundraising would be best to incorporate long-term outcomes and the lifetime value of donors rather than simply short-term goals such as monies raised or the return on investment.

ABOUT THE AUTHOR

Nick Jaffer, BComm

Nick is a leading fundraising professional with 22 years of international experience in education, health and community-based organizations. He has broad and diverse experiences in relationship development and management, capital campaigns, major and planned gifts, annual giving, special and signature event fund raising, and volunteer and project management.

Transplanted from Edmonton, Alberta, Nick moved to Australia to serve as Director of Development at the University of Sydney, overseeing their integrated fundraising program. Prior to this, Nick served as the

Director of Annual Giving at the University of Alberta, and also worked with the Leukaemia Foundation, the Alberta Lung Association, and the Aga Khan Foundation.

Nick currently serves as Senior Consultant with Global Philanthropic, where he heads up the Sydney, Australia operations, and is a popular speaker at Australasian fundraising conferences.

Nick has been recognised for his work by CASE and the Edmonton Chapter of AFP.

CHAPTER 6

Direct Response Fundraising
STEVE THOMAS, CFRE

Direct response fundraising is a subset of direct marketing. Direct marketing differs from above the line advertising in that it is completely measurable. I spent x, I received y and (hopefully) I netted z. In other words, we make an offer to a group of people and we do (or don't) receive a response in the form of a donation. *read more...*

Using the mail to ask for money has been around since at least Confederation. Canadian churches sent letters to adherents asking for money. In the 1920s the Canadian Tuberculosis Society began to mail unaddressed householders with Christmas seals. In the 1940s Easter Seals, created to fight polio, began mailing unaddressed householders at Easter. After the Second World War, War Amps mailed their car key fobs to Canadians.

However, it wasn't until the early 1980s that some Canadian charities, notably Oxfam and Amnesty International, began scientific direct mail programs modelled on what was happening south of the border.

In this chapter we will deal with eleven channels or media that can carry our offers to a group of people plus campaigns that integrate two or more of these channels. As some of the channels didn't exist 20 years ago we can predict with confidence that new channels will likely emerge in the future to enrich our direct response fundraising.

In direct response fundraising we have a number of offers. The oldest offer is a "one off" gift. But we also offer recurrent, committed or monthly giving (see Chapter 8), planned gifts (Chapter 12) or a special event sponsorship (Chapter 7). Creative fundraisers the world over are constantly trying to find yet more offers.

In direct response fundraising, we carry out acquisition or prospect campaigns to find new donors and renewal campaigns to secure additional donations from existing donors. In the UK they use the terms "cold" and "warm" campaign.

Acquisition is an investment. Break-even results are the best case scenario. Making money on acquisition is inefficient since renewal is so very profitable. It is better to find as many new donors as possible at an acceptable price and then harvest nets in renewal campaigns. A good renewal direct mail program, for instance, should be able to spend less than 20 ¢ to raise each dollar. Acquisition costs vary widely but $1.25 to raise $1.00 might be a rule of thumb.

Not all channels are useful for both acquisition and renewal. Figure 6.1 shows this for eleven different channels.

The Channels We Use

	Acquisition	Renewal
Direct Mail	√	√
E-Mail	√	√
Face to Face	√	-
Insert	√	-
Print Ad	√	-
Radio	√	-
Special Event	√	√
SMS Text Messaging	√	√
Telephone	√	√
Television	√	-
Web Site	√	√

Figure 6.1

Most direct response fundraising programs in Canada define their donors using the calendar year into current, active, and lapsed. Figure 6.2 lays out generally agreed upon donor file segments based on year of last gift.

2011 - Current	First Time 1x
	Reactivated
	Repeat 2x
2010 - Active	Loyal 3x or more
Lapsed 2009	
Lapsed 2008	
Etc.	

Figure 6.2

Each year the task is to turn active donors, (those who gave at least once in the preceding year) into current donors (those who have given this year).

If we don't succeed in getting another donation over the whole year from active donors, they become lapsed in the next year.

Three words are supreme in direct response fundraising: **recency**, **frequency** and **amount**.

Recency means when the donor last gave. Frequency is how often he/she has given and amount is how much she/he has given. Using these three indices one can chop and dice any donor file into a multitude of segments.

A very good segment would be $1,000 and higher donors who gave last month, and all of which have given every year for a decade. A very poor segment would be one-off $10 donors who last gave five years ago.

A good direct response fundraising program will attempt to move its donors through a *lifecycle*. One such lifecycle is illustrated in Figure 6.3.

have net. This is the money available for the organization's mission. If there isn't a net, your Board might well wonder why you're doing direct response fundraising!

Most of the large Canadian charity direct mail programs were created in the eighties or nineties when an investment could be paid back within months. Now

Donor Lifecycle

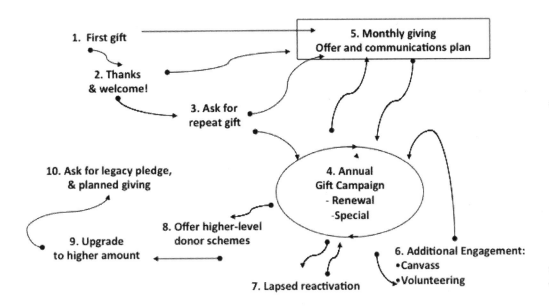

1. First gift
2. Thanks & welcome!
3. Ask for repeat gift
5. Monthly giving Offer and communications plan
4. Annual Gift Campaign - Renewal -Special
10. Ask for legacy pledge, & planned giving
9. Upgrade to higher amount
8. Offer higher-level donor schemes
7. Lapsed reactivation
6. Additional Engagement: •Canvass •Volunteering

Figure 6.3

Finally, a word about costs. Most Canadian non-profits work to Net. A campaign or a program can be judged and compared with others on a net basis, that is gross income minus direct expenses such as, in direct mail; printing, postage, art, imaging (laser printing), and letter shop (insertion and mailing services).

If an agency has been used, the agency fees should be subtracted from the total annual program net to arrive at a net. Why? To ascribe agency costs to an acquisition campaign will be much different than absorbing them in a successful renewal campaign. Above all else, direct response fundraising is about program. Agency costs should be subtracted from the net for the whole years' program.

Finally, there are in-house costs – caging, receipting, staff time, overhead, etc. When these are taken away, we

it takes a year or two but programs can still be built, witness Children's Wish Foundation which started with no donors in 2006 and by 2010 had over 30,000 donors and was making good money.

THE CHANNELS

Direct mail

The golden decade of Canadian direct mail fundraising was the 1980s. The channel was new, exciting and there was little competition from other channels. Amnesty International grew its file from 2,000 to 80,000+ during the decade and there were many other success stories. Although direct mail today isn't what it was then, it's far from dead. It is an important part of the fundraising mix for many Canadian charities.

Most direct mail fundraising in Canada follows a *Modified Annual Renewal Program*. Figure 6.4 outlines a typical program. Donors who have given to you before are your House File, prior year donors (actives) are solicited in House 1 for an annual gift. House 2, 3 and 4 are reminders to non-responders.

The House renewal series usually features the entire work of the charity. House specials typically focus on one aspect of the non-profit's work (Women's Programs, research, Uganda, the wolf for instance) or feature premiums (address labels, cards, pens) or special offers like a *sweepstakes*.

A careful reading of Figure 6.4 will show that a donor who responds to House 1 will receive four appeals in the year. One who doesn't make a donation will receive eight during the year. If he/she doesn't respond to any of these eight appeals, then he/she becomes a lapsed donor the next year.

Different times of year work better than others for each charity's acquisition although September, October and November and January and February work for most. Figure 6.4 shows a six mailing acquisition schedule that would allow for testing new packages or elements, rolling out winners and minimizing the risk.

It's never good to put all your eggs in one basket of one or two acquisition mailings a year. A Christmastime Canada Post strike in the nineties played havoc with late fall acquisition as did 9/11 in September 2001, so spreading one's risk is important.

Modified Annual Renewal Program

	House Renewal	House Specials		House Lapses ● →	Acquisition
Jan	1				X
Feb					
March	2				X
April					
May	3				
June		X			
July	4				X
August	Phone	X			X
Sept					
Oct					
Nov		X			X
Dec					
Jan	1				X

Figure 6.4

Many organizations have tested the best way to reactivate *lapses*. Generally speaking, putting lapses into the acquisition program is more cost efficient then keeping them in your house mailings, sending them WHYFU (Why have you forsaken us) letters, or telemarketing.

The modified annual renewal program works for most donors. Intermediate donors (generally $100-$1,000 givers) can benefit from an augmented program and small donors, under $25, sometimes benefit from a more streamlined program, say four inexpensive mailings a year.

If donors ask for it, and only if they do ask for it, they can be put on a once a year program. A typical once a year program involves House 1, one special acknowledging that the donor is once a year but saying the subject matter is important and Special 3 as a reminder if needed. Renewal results are usually very good but those that don't renew should go back in the regular schedule.

First time donors should renew at 50% and longer time donors at 65% or 70%. Average gifts vary widely from $25 for a non-life threatening medical charity to over $100 for a United Way or a political party.

The modified annual renewal program is a program for individuals. When writing to businesses an annual appeal with one or two reminders is usually sufficient. Direct mail is also used in legacy marketing and in lotteries (provincially regulated) and sweepstakes (federally regulated).

The direct mail package

There should always be at least four parts to a direct mail package – an exterior envelope, a return envelope, a letter and a reply form. See Figure 6.5 – The Essential Direct Mail Package. Once these are in hand one should ask the question, "Is there anything else I can put in this package that will increase my *net* return?"

The purpose of the exterior envelope is to get the package opened. Your donors like you. A corner card (name, address, and logo on top left corner) may well be enough. For acquisition one has, generally, to be more creative. This does not always mean a teaser. A teaser is meant to draw you into the package. Many of the teasers in use today are feeble and do nothing but signal "junk" mail.

A couple of teasers that do work are: "Your cancer test results enclosed" and "Income Tax information enclosed." I've never run the first but the second was featured on the most successful New Democratic Party acquisition package in the eighties. It wasn't misleading. The letter inside talked of income tax policy.

Rather than a weak teaser, colour, design, shape, size, or even nothing on the envelope may serve to draw the recipient into the package. A first class commemorative stamp on the exterior will get the best response but is usually not cost-effective. Metering used to be our second choice, but Canada Post now demands a very unattractive meter that shouts "junk mail." Use a printed indicia, but realize that design (making it look like a stamp) and creating accompanying faux postmark art will achieve a more welcoming look.

The purpose of the reply envelope is to carry the donation back to your charity. Generally speaking a business reply envelope (BRE) is the most cost-effective. You pay first-class postage plus a set fee for each one used, not printed.

You will always get your best response by putting a live first class stamp on your return envelope, however it only pays to do this cost effectively on intermediate and major donation appeals.

What never works is the little message "Your stamp will help XYZ charity raise more money" on the BRE. This has been tested countless times in Canada, the US and the UK. It is always less cost-effective than a plain BRE. Perhaps it's because people put the little message BRE aside to find a stamp. Some never do and the donation isn't made.

The letter should be a letter. It should look like one. Years ago in school we were taught the difference between business letters (justified and signature black left) and personal letters (indented paragraphs and signature block right). Every fundraising letter should be a personal one. They are easier to read. Book paragraphs are indented for the same reason, to draw the eye into the paragraph.

Studies have proven that the eye travels from top left to bottom right so graphic elements should be at the top or on the bottom right, nowhere else, so as not to detract from the reading. In a like manner, one should use black ink on white paper only with no graphic elements underneath such as a watermark. You want to make your letter as legible as possible.

Many books have been written about direct mail copy. Read some of them. But basically it's simple. Tell your story and make your request moving logically from A to Z.

Figure 6.6 has two letters from the UK that illustrate how we have a tendency to slip into direct mail "speak." Read them both and you'll see what I mean. Keep it plain and simple.

The Essential Direct Mail Package

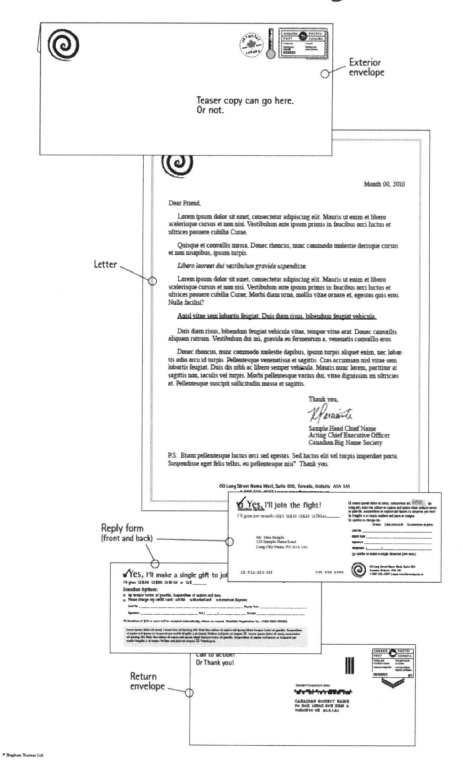

Figure 6.5

DEAR DAD, VERSION 1

Your kind gift of £700 has been safely received and is already at work in buying course text books and enabling me to enjoy a full part in the social life of the college. I cannot tell you how grateful I am for your continuing support.

I just cannot continue with my old computer.

A decent laptop is vital for today's student. When lessons are over, we typically go back to our rooms and write up our notes. Failure to do so can lead to poor marks, slippage in course work and – all too often – the derision of our fellows. 25 per cent of students fail to complete a degree here. The cause is often an inadequate computer.

I am one such student.

I labour nightly on a computer which is a positive impediment to my chances of academic success.

I ask you to imagine my machine. It is slow. Its printer is trouble-prone. It will not interface with any other known machine.

In short, I risk severe under-achieving. I have to tell you that I just cannot continue with this clapped-out computer.

Just £200 will make the difference!

Yes, a secondhand laptop of the required quality can be procured for just £200. Can you find it in your heart to make such a gift? You have proved yourself such a dutiful parent that I am sure you will want to make this extra investment in the academic future of your first-born. But, please give NOW… every day counts when it comes to vital word-processing.

I can only buy the computer with YOUR help.

Yours sincerely,

Adam

P.S. Why not phone through your response – the need is truly URGENT.

P.P.S. I cannot tell you how much this gift would mean to me!!!

DEAR DAD, VERSION 2

It was so good to hear you and mum over the phone. I've made a lot of new friends here at college and I'm not short of things to do. But I do miss home – especially Mum's cooking.

Can I come straight to the point? I need a new computer. The old machine has had its day. It's slow, it's not printing properly and I'm wasting hours shouting at the damned thing. More seriously, it's getting in the way of my course work – I've got a 10,000-word thesis on Jack Kerouac to turn in by the end of term and, at this rate, I'm not going to make it.

Worse, anything I produce on it looks crap compared with the professional-looking work that other students are producing. I know you've already spent a small fortune on getting me here- all I can say is that another couple of hundred quid will make a heck of a difference for the next three years.

I've seen a secondhand laptop advertised in the college magazine. It's not quite state of the art, but it does have the latest Windows and a decent printer and it's all I need to see me through to my finals. The bloke wants £300 and I think I can knock him down to £250 if I move fast. I think I can contribute £50 from what I've got in the bank.

So, I'm asking if you can spare another £200. I know it's a lot to ask and I think you know that I wouldn't ask unless it was genuinely important and urgent. If you can't afford it, then I'll shut up and soldier on with my current machine. But if you can, then it really is going to improve everything I do here. What do you say?

I really need to call this bloke before the weekend. (I'm sweating that nobody else has made him an offer in the meantime). So, if you could call me, or better still, just put a check for £200 in first-class post, then you'll make my week.

Sorry to be such a pest. All I can offer if you say yes is a beautifully presented, well-worded thesis on Kerouac that I'll happily show you at Christmas and which will make your paternal heart swell with pride.
I can't tell you how much I'm looking forward to Christmas. College is great, but there's nothing like family. So, give my love to Mum and to Jenny. Adam.

Figure 6.6

Lastly there is the reply form. The reply form belongs to the donor. It's how he/she tells you how they are answering your appeal. Some direct mail experts do the reply coupon first as it indicates the response you seek from your offer.

Great care should go into designing a user friendly reply form. If there are multiple requests of the donor (monthly and planned giving, for instance), you'll want to seriously consider a whole 8 ½ x 11" sheet of paper.

This then is the basic package; you must have these elements – the exterior envelope, the return envelope, the letter and the reply form. Now is the time to ask if any other piece would bring in more net dollars.

Your additional piece will almost never be a brochure. In most tests, brochures cut into your cost-effectiveness rather than improve it. Figure 6.7 has a list of some of the additional pieces that I've used over the last thirty years. But only because they brought in extra net funds.

Rather than a brochure

clipping	seals	poster
picture	press release	fridge art
schedule	fax	magnet
slip	ticket	candle
lift note	wallet card	confetti
publisher's note	extra envelope	card(s)
map	screw driver	bill
budget	mood strip	ice scraper
decal	Newsletter	toothbrush

Figure 6.7

Direct mail issues

An issue in direct mail is the use of up-front premiums, freemiums (address labels, pens, card sets) - included to boost response. (Backend premiums offer something free, a book for $125 for instance - to increase the average gift). A freemium package will almost always beat a mission package (one that talks only of the mission of the charity) in the number of respondents. It's called the theory of reciprocity - I give you something (address labels) and you give me something back (a donation).

My colleague, Neil Gallaiford, a not-for-profit data expert, has been studying freemium and mission donor behaviour for years. He believes that among those people who respond to your freemium acquisition appeal will be donors who truly care about your cause.

Best to think about the ones who are responding just because you sent them a freemium as subsidizing the cost of acquiring the true supporters. These aren't really "freemium-acquired donors," just people to whom you first sent a freemium. In the long run, they can be just as loyal as the donors who you first sent a mission package to.

Freemiums have taken a lot of the fun out of direct mail fundraising in the last decade.

Many organizations compete as to who can send the most elaborate gift; t-shirts, tote bags, wrapping paper sets, etc. Regrettably I believe freemiums are here to stay, although to be long-term productive your donors must become aware of, and supportive of, your mission.

Is direct mail dying? Direct mail donor files are over represented by those 60-90 years of age. Direct mail experts debate whether boomers will behave like their parents when they pass sixty. Will they become direct mail givers? Some say they will, but I doubt it. The mail and cheque book banking are less a part of their lives.

I see a gradual decline for direct mail although it will be a potent part of the fundraising mix for many years to come. In the end it may well become a niche medium for organizations that haven't other channels readily available or for specific intermediate proposals or club type offers. After all, television didn't kill radio and the movies, but it did change them.

Will direct mail work for every organization? No, Canadian university annual funds for instance, have a hard time making good money from direct mail. But they keep their programs as they are a constant source of intermediate donors and prospects for major or planned gifts. They should be emulated; your $500 donor might have the capacity to give much more if approached personally and that widow who gives you $35 year after year after year could be capable of a substantial legacy gift.

E-Mail

Direct mail is expensive and usually takes months to deploy. Emails are inexpensive and can be deployed quickly.

And the latter is the essence of the medium. Barack Obama's famous fundraising emails were almost instant reactions to the daily twists and turns of his 2008 Presidential election campaign. In every case several versions of an email were tested in the morning and the winner rolled out to millions in the afternoon.

Emails before or after a direct mail package (or both - a sandwich) will boost your response. In our experience, sending a post-DM email has elicited the best response, but you should still test to determine what works best for your unique email list.

Email can and should amplify direct mail, but it will be most useful to you in times of emergency, crisis or urgency. If you don't have any of these in your charity – then create them. "Two more days for a current year tax receipt," "ten days to access matching funds," "someone in your organization has won an award," "help us celebrate," etc. Do not create a modified annual renewal program using emails. It won't work, there's no urgency in it.

Creative is also really important in email. See Figures 6.8 and 6.9 Like direct mail, email is a form of personal one-to-one communication, and should be executed as such. Make your emails conversational in tone.

Pay specific attention to your subject lines – because, like a well-designed outer envelope, this is what gets it opened in the first place. Test subject lines with a small percentage of your list before you roll-out to your entire database. Experiment with the colour of your links, the position of your call-outs and images, including Johnson boxes and more. With the low-cost and instant response rates you get from email, there's no reason not to test every time you send an email.

An important issue in digital fundraising is spam. Although emails are quick and inexpensive, they are not as reliable as old-fashioned snail mail. If you send out a first class letter and it doesn't reach its intended recipient, you will receive it back. This is not the case for your emails.

Direct dialogue

Many practitioners, particularly those in Europe and Australasia, call it "Face to Face" (F2F). It uses the same principles as face-to-face in major giving. Person A personally asking person B for a gift but in this case person A is asking for a monthly commitment.

It was started by Greenpeace Austria in the mid-nineties, spread throughout continental Europe, the UK and Australia, New Zealand and on to Canada in the early 2000s.

Early adopters were the usual trend setters; World Vision, Sick Kids Hospital, Greenpeace and Amnesty International. Potential donors are approached on street corners, in malls or on their doorstep at home. The ask is a monthly donation by credit card or bank debit (pre-authorized chequing, PAC) with the latter being preferred. Peer to peer, i.e., young person to young person, usually works best.

Direct dialogue has revolutionized direct response fundraising around the world. Here in Canada it's a major part of the fundraising arsenal for World Vision, Plan, SickKids Hospital, Amnesty, Greenpeace and many more.

A monthly donor can have a long-term value (LTV) up to seven times that of a single one-off donor. Because of this, organizations are willing to pay a direct dialogue agency $200 or more to acquire a donor. There are a number of Canadian firms that specialize in this method of fundraising; you can't do it yourself.

And why haven't I talked about the United States in this section? As in so many other things, they are the world's greatest exception, not the rule. Because of their banking system, direct debit transactions, which they call Electronic Funds Transfer (EFT) are more

Generic email template

To: <first name, last name>
From: <first name, last name, organization name>
Subject line: <A compelling teaser that is 50 characters or less>

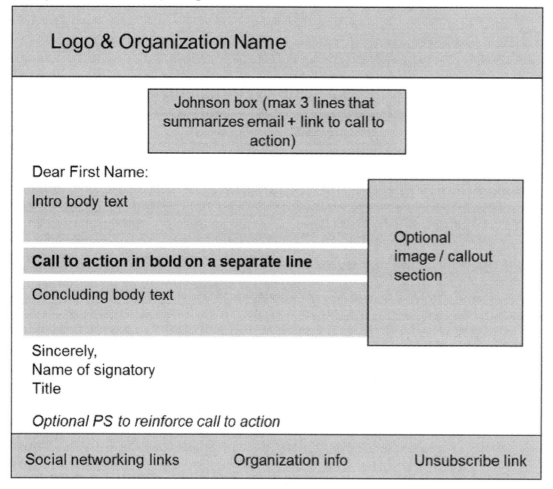

Figure 6.8

The Essential Direct Response Email Template

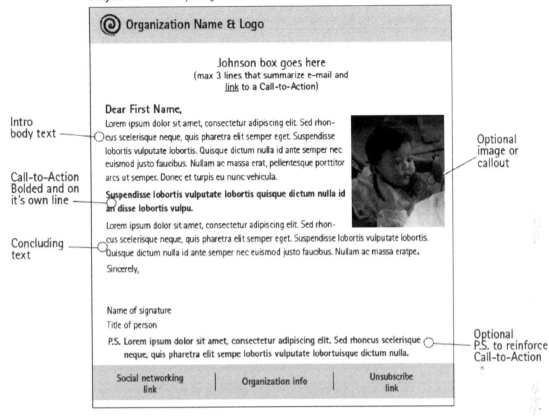

To: <first name, last name>
From: <first name, last name, organization name>
Subject line: <A compelling teaser that is 50 characters or less>

© Stephen Thomas Ltd.

Figure 6.9

difficult. Canadians use direct debits to pay all sorts of bills and support their charities. Americans traditionally haven't. The US is only starting to adopt direct dialogue. But when they do, and they will, they'll think they invented it!

An important issue in direct dialogue is initial attrition. Donors sign up to be monthly donors and then drop out after one, two, or even no gifts. A number of charities have developed telemarketing and digital solutions to keep these usually direct mail resistant donors on board.

Inserts

An insert is an all-in-one piece combining letter, reply form and return envelope. Magazine and newspaper inserts are not cost-effective for one-off donor acquisition. But the European experience has shown that inserts requesting monthly donations can work if judged by the same yardstick as direct dialogue, i.e., $200 or so to get a new donor. Canadian charities are only slowly moving into this medium, but we will see more of it. We know from data audits that a print origin monthly donor has a higher long-term value than a direct dialogue, telemarketing, or television sourced one. (see Figure 6.10).

The Essential Direct Response Insert

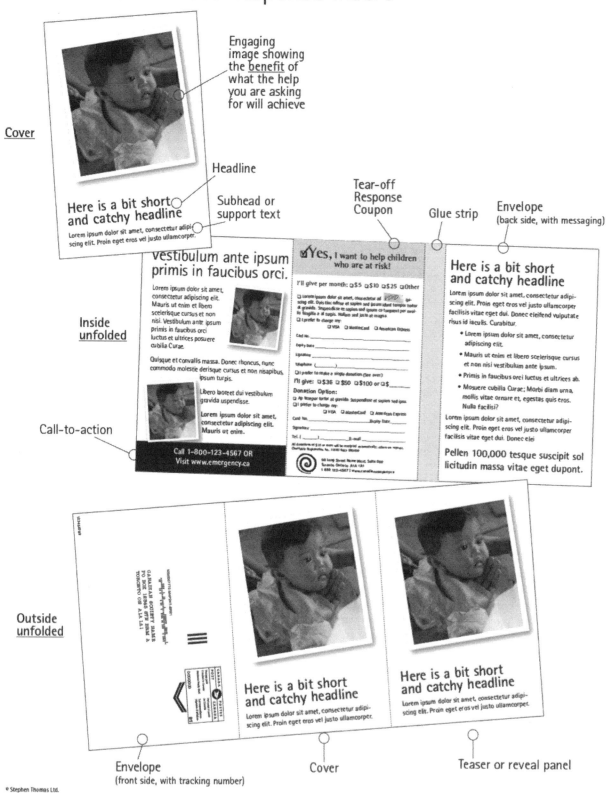

Figure 6.10

Print Ads

Print ads in newspapers and/or magazines are usually not cost effective. An exception is in times of emergency. Newspaper ads netted money for a number of international charities during the Tsunami (2004) and Haiti (2010) emergencies.

Print ads work when the crisis is front page news; when the emergency slips off the front page they no longer work. Organizations like World Vision and UNICEF have Canadian emergency plans that enable them to finalize ad design and place ads in newspapers within hours of a disaster. Such ads should always have a coupon on the bottom right of the page despite the fact that they push online or telephone giving. The coupon is useful for those who aren't comfortable with new media but it also signals loud and clear that a response is sought. (see Figure 6.11).

Radio

Radio ads are relatively inexpensive to produce and place. More and more charities are using radio commercials to drive monthly giving. Perhaps the best use of radio is the "radiothon." A radio station takes a day or number of days and involves the charity in all its programming. There are interviews and stories and all the announcers mention the charity and the goal. Sick Kids Hospital in Toronto has a radiothon every year that raises millions of dollars.

Special Events

Earlier in my career one was always warned against special events. They tended to take much trial and effort and netted little for most non-profits. They were often run for volunteer morale and community awareness, rather than net dollars.

Events like the Canadian Breast Cancer Foundation's CIBC Run for the Cure have changed the nature of many special events. Now using the web, participants sign up and recruit their friends and family as sponsors. Considerable net money is raised. There is ample evidence that donors in their twenties, thirties and forties like these participatory events. There seems to be an unlimited taste for them.

A woman of my acquaintance, in her mid-thirties, has participated in the MS Walk every year for the past decade. She is proud of the fact that she raises several thousands of dollars each year for *her* charity.

Please note that she isn't a monthly donor, she isn't a donor at all. This is how she helps. More and more the future of annual giving may involve people like her that fundraise, not give, annually as their parents and grandparents did.

SMS

Cell phones are used for fundraising in Europe and the developing world much more than they are in Canada. Brits will commonly receive a text message requesting a charitable gift of a small amount such as £5, most often at times of disaster or, at a large gathering, i.e., concerts and sporting events.

Cell phones are as important to Canadians as they are to Europeans. Millions of dollars were raised during the 2000 Haiti disaster, so SMS giving is beginning to catch on here too. Price has been a factor and the fact that fundraisers want not only the cash but also the name and address of the donor.

Asking for and collecting the cell numbers of your donors, and other contacts at all touchpoints now, will help you build a database, so that when SMS does take off, you're well positioned to take advantage of all it has to offer.

Micropayments processed through the telecommunications companies are a starting point, but we should look ahead and plan for robust mobile marketing campaigns combined with PayPal mobile and other mobile payment providers who process donations of any amount, and capture donor information.

Telemarketing

Telemarketing is expensive, but as it is a high-touch medium, it is much more effective than direct mail or emails.

There are five uses for the phone in fundraising: renewal, upgrade, emergency, acquisition and thank you calls.

About-to-lapse and lapsed donors can be renewed through the telephone when mail hasn't worked.

Telemarketing is a perfect tool in emergencies. Benefiting from their pre-existing emergency plans, good international organizations were on the phone to their donors within a day of the 2010 earthquake in Haiti.

The phone is also an excellent upgrading tool. Large monthly files like those of the Canadian Cancer Society, Ontario Division, have been built by phoning

The Essential Direct Response Print Ad

Headline

Subhead or support text

Engaging image showing the <u>benefit</u> of what your help will achieve

Call-to-action

Here is a bit short and catchy headline for an **EMERGENCY**

Lorem ipsum dolor sit amet, consectetur adipiscing elit. Proin eget eros vel justo ullamcorper facilisis vitae eget dui. Donec eleifend vulputate risus id iaculis. Curabitur.

Call 1-800-123-4567 OR Visit www.emergency.ca

✓Yes, I want to help children who are at risk!

I'll give: ❏ $36 ❏ $50 ❏ $100 or ❏ $_____
Donation Options:
❏ Ap tempor tortor at gravida abo suspendisse et sapien sed ipsu.
❏ Please charge my credit card: ❏ VISA ❏ MasterCard ❏ American Express

Card No. _____ Name on Card:_____ Expiry Date _____
Signature _____ Tel. (____) _____ E-mail _____
Address _____

All donations of $10 or more will be receipted automatically; others on request. Charitable Registration No. 13082 9850 RR0008

00 Long Street Name West, Suite 000, Toronto, Ontario A1A 1A1 | 1 888 123–4567 | www.canadiancompany.ca

Your Logo goes here

Response Coupon

© Stephen Thomas Ltd.

Figure 6.11

new and established donors and converting them to monthly giving.

Renewal, emergency, and upgrade calling is done by reputable telemarketing agencies of which there are a number in Canada. All these involve phoning prior donors, who, by and large, don't object to being called by one of "their charities."

Acquisition is a different matter. "Shotgun" telemarketing - phoning everyone in the telephone book from temporary "bucket shops" around the country – was popular in the late eighties, but although it generated large gross dollars, there was little net and many complaints.

"Rifle" telemarketing is a different matter. When donors of charity A, say an environmental organization, are phoned for charity B, also an environmental organization, there is much less anger and frequently satisfactory results. Although they work, such donor list exchanges happen infrequently as they are difficult to set up.

Volunteers do not make good telemarketers with one exception – thank you calls. Some United Ways have a volunteer phone-a-thon before their campaign kicks off. All the past year donors are phoned and thanked by volunteers. It is a win-win situation; excellent stewardship.

Television

Television is expensive, though it has garnered great results for organizations that have invested in it like World Vision, Plan and WWF. Canada makes the best long form direct response television (DRTV) – 30 min. and 60 min. – in the world. These shows are, in effect, infomercials that offer monthly giving with emotive stories and a sense of urgency. They are shown again and again in golden spots like Sunday afternoons and weekday mornings from 9-10am.

Short-form DRTV involves 30, 60, 90 or 120 second spots placed amongst traditional commercials. Christian Children's Fund has made good use of such spots during the Christmas season.

One-off telethons running over a number of hours or days and asking for single gifts have largely disappeared from our airwaves as they are not cost-effective.

Websites

I have divided digital fundraising into emails and websites. Emails are proactive and dynamic. Websites are neither, they are a digital pamphlet.

In case donors do find their way to your site, then you will want it to be as donor friendly as possible. Sometimes this is difficult as the website is under the control of communications or program staff at your non-profit. Some organizations have gotten around this by creating fundraising specific micro sites linked to the main sites.

OTHER CHANNELS

Direct response fundraisers are constantly on the lookout for new channels that will enable them to reach donors and prospective donors. Social media may well be such an emerging channel.

WHAT CHANNELS SHOULD YOU USE?

This is largely a dollars and cents proposition. A key question to ask yourself is, "What will you receive back in Long Term Value (5 years+) for any particular channel spend?"

Figure 6.12 contains some rough long-term values based on a lifetime of experience. Though there might

be disagreement with some of the details, most senior Canadian direct response fundraisers would agree with the general directional notion of the chart.

Not all channels will be available to you. DRTV, for instance, is very expensive and depends on an emotive cause. Volume plays a role in your decisions too. Though monthly donors acquired through mail have the best long term value, they are impossible to acquire in large numbers, hence the popularity of DRTV and F2F.

The higher the long-term value the more you should be willing to spend to get a new donor. That is why charities are willing to spend $200 or more to acquire monthly donors. Because of the obsession with costs in the Canadian charitable world they are not usually willing to spend much more or wait more than two or three years for payback.

This can sometimes hurt their mission as I believe that charities should be judged on Net[3] funds they raise, not their costs.

INTEGRATED FUNDRAISING

The nirvana for direct response fundraisers is to integrate a number of channels. Mike McCormick, a Canadian ad man working on New York's Madison Avenue, speaks of "Controlling the message for consistency, tone, voice and imagery in all communications."

Long Term Values

1.	Monthly Mail Acquired	$1,700.00
2.	Monthly Print	$1,650.00
3.	Monthly Web	$1,600.00
4.	Monthly Phone	$1,550.00
5.	Monthly TV Long Form	$1,500.00
6.	Monthly TV Short Form	$1,000.00
7.	Monthly F2F	$900.00
8.	Direct Mail Once a Year	$500.00
9.	Direct Mail Addressed and Householder	$350.00
10.	Print	$300.00
11.	Inserts	$275.00
12.	Door to Door Professional Canvass	$250.00
13.	Telephone Rifle	$200.00
14.	Direct Mail Addressed Premium	$150.00
15.	Telephone Shotgun	$100.00
16.	Telethons	$75.00
17.	Door to Door Volunteer Canvass	$50.00

Figure 6.12

Although multi-channel fundraising is oft talked about it is still rather rare in Canada. This country's largest charity, World Vision has succeeded with their city campaigns like Vancouver 3000. A set number of sponsorships is the goal over a two or three month period. There are media partners; television and radio plus print, a dedicated micro site and other channels such as direct dialogue, mall direct dialogue, house-holders, addressed direct mail and/or telemarketing. Classic integrated campaigns, that have been very successful.

A monthly visit to the World Vision web site is a good way to keep up with what's new and exciting in Canadian direct response fundraising. The organization is, arguably, the best in Canada at this sort of fundraising.

CONCLUSION

There will be few fundraising programs that don't use one, or preferably more, integrated channels of direct response. They raise many small and intermediate size gifts and they create leads for planned and major giving. Direct response provides stewardship and keeps your donors aware and engaged in your work. Don't neglect this important piece of your development puzzle.

ADDITIONAL RESOURCES

Books

▶ BURNETT, KEN. (2002*). Relationship fundraising: a donor-based approach to the business of raising money.* Jossey-Bass.

▶ JOHNSTON, MICHAEL. (1998). *The fund raiser's guide to the Internet.* John Wiley and Sons Ltd.

▶ LAUTMAN, KAY PARTNEY. (2001). *Direct marketing for nonprofits: essential techniques for the new era.* Jones & Bartlett Learning.

▶ MCKINNON, HARVEY. (2002). *Hidden gold: how monthly giving will build donor loyalty, boost your organization's income, and increase financial stability.* Bonus Books.

▶ WARWICK, MAL. (2008). *How to Write Successful Fundraising Letters, 2nd Edition.* Jossey Bass.

URL's

▶ *THE AGITATOR*, a blog with fundraising and advocacy strategy. Trends, tips… with an edge' is produced five times a week by old pros Tom Belford and Roger Craver. I read it religiously. It's free at editors@theagitator.net

ABOUT THE AUTHOR

Steve Thomas, MA, CFRE

Steve Thomas has been described as both the "Guru" and the "Godfather" of Canadian direct response fundraising. Though he started off life as a historical geographer and a teacher, he has been a fundraiser for well over 30 years.

Steve's career has included working with Oxfam Canada as development director, and in 1980 he founded Stephen Thomas Limited, Canada's first direct response fundraising agency working exclusively in the not-for-profit sector.

Steve was recognized by the Canadian (Direct) Marketing Association with the

Directors' Choice Lifetime Achievement Award and by AFP Greater Toronto Chapter with the Outstanding Fundraising Executive Award. In 2006, Steve was honoured by Amnesty International for 25 years of service.

A gifted speaker and presenter, Steve has lectured world-wide on the topics of marketing and fundraising. Steve is Chair of the Advisory Committee of the Humber College Fundraising Program.

In 2008 Steve was Fundraiser in Residence at York University. He is now chairman of the Amnesty International Human Rights House Campaign.

One of the original founders and past Chair of the Cana-

dian Fundraising Congress, Steve is past president of the AFP Greater Toronto Chapter. Steve has served as Chair of the International Fundraising Congress (Amsterdam) and is currently co-chair of the London based Resource Alliance

CHAPTER 7

SPECIAL EVENTS
HALA BISSADA, CFRE

In the not-for-profit world, special events can fall into one or a combination of the following categories:

- Fundraising (such as galas, golf tournaments or pledge-based events)

- Recognition (such as a donor or volunteer appreciation events)

- Launch (such as the start of a capital campaign)

- Celebration (such as anniversaries and scientific discoveries)

- Educational (such as planned giving seminars or lecture series)

In all cases, an event provides an opportunity to raise awareness for the organization. *read more...*

Events are used to achieve specific goals and objectives and can be an integral part of the overall annual fundraising plan of an organization. Events can be the first introduction a donor has to an organization. With proper identification and cultivation, event donors, volunteers and sponsors can potentially be leveraged to become major gift donors.

Events can be one of the least cost-effective methods to raise funds with as much as 50% or more of the gross revenue of the event going toward expenses. For this reason, it is imperative that an organization determine if they are "event ready" prior to launching a new *signature event*. They should ask themselves the following questions:

- Is there really a need for a new signature event?

- How does this new event fit into the organization's overall calendar of events and fundraising plan—in terms of timing, you ideally do not want multiple events to take place within a short period of time.

- Have you determined the objectives of the event?

- Do you have a history of executing successful events?

- Have they been cost-effective and worth the staff investment?

- Do you have the internal resources to execute an event? Executing successful events requires specific expertise. Hiring a consultant (common place in today's landscape) requires an organization to have financial resources.

- Does the organization have the financial resources to undertake an event, including up-front costs?

- Do you have a strong fundraising board and a solid corporate and individual donor base that you can access? This can dictate the size and scope of the event.

- Does your organization have a positive image in the community?

- Do you have adequate volunteer resources (i.e. resourceful and connected people) to chair the event or sit on an organizing committee with the main responsibility being "fundraising?"

- Have you completed a *competitive analysis* taking into consideration cause-related, audience-related, sponsor-related and event-related competition?

- Is your market saturated? Your concept must distinguish itself in the marketplace with a *Unique Selling Proposition* and a competitive advantage.

Once these questions are answered, and an organization determines that they want to move ahead with a new signature event, they should allow 6-18 months to plan and execute the event, depending on the size and scope. Next steps should include: developing the concept, conducting a feasibility study and preparing the strategic plan.

Despite the costs and the challenges, special events do have a place in the fundraising landscape. If executed successfully, the organization will reap many tangible and intangible benefits which include:

- significant non-designated funds

- acquisition of new corporate and individual donors

- acquisition of new volunteers

- increased public awareness

- an opportunity to upgrade existing donors

- a platform to educate the audience about the organization

This chapter will provide you with a level understanding of special event management. The topics are:

- Event concept development

- Enhancing an existing event/keeping it fresh

- The strategic plan

- Sponsorship/sales techniques

- On-Site fundraising vehicles

- Marketing

- Public relations

- Volunteer management

- Logistics

- Production

- Working with consultants

EVENT CONCEPT DEVELOPMENT

"Imagination is more important than knowledge."

- Albert Einstein

Developing a concept for a signature event can be a challenge given the level of saturation in today's marketplace. Depending on the organization's objectives it can range from an intimate, niche event for a limited group at a high ticket price to a huge endeavor with thousands of people raising pledges for your cause. In any case, for events to succeed they need to differentiate themselves with a unique selling proposition and a competitive advantage. A key philosophy is that there really is no such thing as a new event but rather an event that has been reinvented in some way to make it different.

For example, the Weekend to End Breast Cancer to benefit Princess Margaret Hospital in Toronto is a walk, but what make it successful and unique (in addition to being a heart-felt cause) is that they made it a bonding/sharing/life-changing experience. They provided participants with many tools, including; fundraising guides, training clinics, updates, meetings and online fundraising to name a few. They added fun elements to the event which included a "camping experience" by providing tents for the overnight stay, along with organizing meals and activities. In their first year, they had thousands of participants, over 150,000 donors and raised millions of dollars.

Being able to come up with fresh and new ideas is one thing, but turning them into something feasible is another. The event should be meaningful and enticing to your organization and the audience you want to attract. You do not necessarily need to reinvent the wheel, but rather participate in a creative brainstorming process that can help you put a fresh spin on an existing concept or idea, along with good planning and execution skills.

Eight steps to developing your concept:
1. Conduct an audit on your organization
2. Research/review the event landscape
3. Determine event parameters
4. Identify event considerations
5. Conduct your creative brainstorming session
6. Analyze and assess
7. Develop your initial concept
8. Conduct a feasibility study (some organizations do not facilitate this step until concept is approved)

1. Audit your organization
Some of the questions listed in the overview to determine if you are "event-ready" are duplicated here.

- Review your mission and your organization's goals and objectives. The event should fit with your mission and assist your organization in meeting its overall goals and objectives.

- Assess your organization's capacity which could dictate the size and scope of your event. Consider size of existing donor base (individual/corporate), board of directors (do you have a fundraising board or dedicated committee?), volunteer base (do you have strong key volunteers that can assist in fundraising and organizing your event), average gift size, *RFM* (recency-frequency-monetary amount) to determine how to leverage existing donors, and whether you have other events that can be leveraged for participation etc.

- Determine an audience you may want to access e.g. if you already have a high-end gala in your annual mix, you may want to think about a sporting event to reach a new audience.

- Your annual budget. Many events have up-front costs—do you have the financial resources?

- Do you have the internal staff resources or do you have the budget to hire an outside consultant? Consultants can be hired in the initial stages to do concept development and feasibility studies in addition to overall event management or various components of an event.

- Assess whether a special event should be incorporated into your fundraising mix. Sometimes special events are easy for boards/volunteers to conceptualize as a fundraising initiative, but they may not be in your organization's best interest.

- Do you have a strong case for support? Can you create a case for support that would marry well with an event?

- Does your charitable organization have high visibility in the marketplace?

Regardless of who the charity is, many events can be extremely successful in terms of participation, if it is unique and enticing to the participant. At the end of the day, your event has to be something they want to attend, the fact that it is benefiting a charity may be a secondary "feel-good" add-on.

2. Research/review the event landscape

- Do an assessment of the event landscape in your city, province and across Canada—you want to get a sense of what is already in the marketplace and who is your competition.

- Divide your events into categories i.e. golf tournaments, galas, sporting events etc.

- In your analysis, include the following information: location, date, years in existence, cost to participate, charity, registration methods, number of participants/attendees, a brief description of the event, sponsors, identify their unique selling proposition and their competitive advantage.

3. Determine event parameters

- Determine the purpose of the event (fundraiser, friend-raiser, brand-awareness etc.)

- What is your fundraising revenue target, if it is a fundraiser? This will impact the size and scope of your event.

- Identify your audience. For example, is this a high-end event to attract high wealth individuals?

- Consider the timing of the event (time of year, time of day, time of week, your other scheduled signature events etc.)

4. Event considerations

After setting your event parameters, you can begin to brainstorm. The following should be taken into consideration during this process:

- Your audience. Does it need to appeal to a niche or broad audience? What appeals to the audience (a sporting event, gala, fashion show)?

- What are the latest trends? Can you capitalize on something new? e.g. when step aerobics was popular, a variety of aerobic fitness events began to emerge

- Saturation level of the type of the event. Can your market bear another golf tournament, gala, walk, run etc.? If so, keep in mind, it will be important for you to differentiate yours from your competitors and think about ways to create a competitive advantage.

- Uniqueness. How can you make your event unique? What can become your unique selling proposition?

- Entertainment. Is it a fashion show, do you have a headliner, is it a magic show?

- Technical requirements. For more complex shows this could be very costly and could require extensive research in terms of finding suppliers that can facilitate your vision (i.e. building an ice rink in the middle of a ball room, cirque rigging, using a skateboard half pipe as a stage and incorporating BMX bikers and skateboarders into your show).

- Timing. Does it fit into your current calendar of events? Is it an outdoor event and is it required to take place at a certain time of year etc.?

- Sponsorship. What opportunities are there for sponsorship associated with this event? As you brainstorm you always want to be thinking about how you can create unique, interesting and lucrative sponsorship opportunities.

- On-site Fundraising. This can be a lucrative revenue stream for an event, so while brainstorming you should consider the type of on-site fundraising you may want to incorporate (i.e. raffles, silent and live auctions, balloon bursts).

- Volunteer Requirements. Keep in mind if your event is taking place outside the city, this becomes a crucial consideration in terms of recruitment and management.

- VIP/Celebrity involvement.

- Technology. This is becoming more and more an integral part of the event (i.e. online fundraising, utilizing smart phones, customized software programs).

- Theme/Décor.
- Venue.

5. Conduct your brainstorming session

Brainstorming is a technique which involves unrestrained creative thinking. It allows ideas to flow without critique or criticism so that the creative process can happen. Analysis and critique follow a brainstorming session, taking each idea and assessing its merit and potential.

Creative thinking is an ongoing process—you never stop. It doesn't start or stop because you are working on a specific project. It is something you do on a regular basis because you never know when something is going to spark an idea. Maintaining the events landscape will keep your creative mind working.

Conducting a productive brainstorming session is crucial to concept development. You may want to review Microsoft's methods for conducting a brainstorming session and implement for your session.

For your brainstorming session, you need to assemble what I call "Imagineers." You should select people who are creative, knowledgeable, clear thinkers, self-confident, have respect for others and have the ability to think "big." Imagineers could be members of your event team, board members, senior volunteers, creative thinkers from ad agencies, design firms, décor companies or experts in a particular field (choreographer, writer etc.).

The atmosphere you create should be spirited, enthusiastic, positive and tolerant. Competitiveness, threats, intimidation and fear have no place here.

The room where you hold the session should be quiet, devoid of intrusive and distracting elements, no cell phones or Blackberries should be allowed. You should have pads, paper, pens, refreshments, whiteboards/butcher paper available and comfortable seating. Incorporate breaks when timing is appropriate.

Your moderator or team leader should be someone the group will trust, has expert knowledge about events and the creative process. Their role is to guide the group, along positive, productive paths, away from negative or irrelevant tangents--someone who will not

manipulate the conversation, and guide without leading.

Figure 7.1 can be used as a tool to assist in the brainstorming session.

Special Event Brainstorming Worksheet
Parameters:

☐ Determine the purpose of the event (fundraiser, friend-raiser, brand-awareness etc.)

☐ Identify your fundraising revenue target (net goal) if it is a fundraiser. This will impact the size and scope of your event

☐ Identify your audience

☐ Consider the timing of the event (time of year, time of day, time of week, your other scheduled signature events etc.)

☐ Consider the venue

Event Considerations:

☐ Your audience—does it need to appeal to a broad audience, or a niche audience?

☐ What appeals to the audience (is it a sporting event, a gala, fashion show etc.)?

☐ The latest trends—can you capitalize on something new?

☐ Saturation level—is there room for another traditional event (i.e. golf tournament, gala etc.)?

☐ How can you make your event unique? (what can be your Unique Selling Points?)

☐ Venue

☐ Entertainment

☐ Event timing

☐ Technical requirements

☐ Resources required (ice rink, steps)—special rental needs?

☐ Sponsorship opportunities

☐ On-site fundraising methods

☐ Volunteer requirements

☐ VIP/Celebrity involvement

☐ Technology

☐ Theme and décor

Figure 7.1

6. Analyze and assess

Once you work through the process and have various ideas on the boards, the group should assess which ideas have merit. Some of your ideas may be based on what I call "adopt and adapt" tactic. Meaning you may adopt an existing idea that is out there already, but add your own twist on the concept.

7. Developing an initial concept

The output should then be refined and consolidated into a list of the top event ideas and the best elements. At this point, you may choose to do further research to flush out the concept, or you may decide to conduct a formal feasibility study.

8. The special event feasibility study

The *special event feasibility study* will determine the viability of the event and provide detailed information that will assist the organization in deciding whether they should move forward with the concept.

It will flush out the concept, identify the event's unique selling proposition and competitive position, the audience, the elements of the event, if it is an organizational fit, if it will be memorable, the competitive landscape and the projected budget among other things.

The elements of the feasibility study could include: an executive summary, a high level summary of the event elements (i.e. event at a glance), a situational analysis (SWOT, competitive analysis, USP's, goals and objectives), budget, legal considerations, marketing plan, venue analysis, critical path, sponsorship targets, volunteer requirements, and any special considerations such as technical requirements.

The feasibility study provides you with the blueprint for the event. However, an event is always fluid; things can change as you begin planning and implementation. The event coordinator/producer needs to be resourceful, adapting the concept of the event and its elements to take advantage of opportunities, deal with budgetary constraints and meet sponsorship requests among other things.

ENHANCING AN EXISTING EVENT

The best way to keep your event fresh and find ways to enhance it is to break it down into its basic components (from the moment the guest arrives until they leave and everything in between) and brainstorm around how to add to, enhance and/or change each component.

Use your creativity and involve others in helping you to brainstorm. Some simple suggestions are changing your venue, entertainment, event schedule, décor to meet the theme, the chef, Master of Ceremonies or the theme of the evening. You can also involve celebrities.

Working with a talented ad agency or design firm can assist with refreshing the brand, marketing collateral and advertising material. Often you can approach them to work on your project pro bono.

Keep up with technology to see how you can utilize it to enhance your event. For example, silent auctions are now able to utilize touch screen technology and Smartphones. Guests can see images and descriptions of the silent auction items on screens, place bids electronically and get updates on the status of their bid through notification emails to their Smartphones.

In terms of production, you can utilize lighting, special effects, unique staging, cirque rigging, dry ice, or ive remotes (a camera operator follows the host to the silent auction area to highlight great items in a unique way). This is a more entertaining way to advise guests of the interesting items available for auction. Visuals on screen help to tell your organization's story.

Small touches can really make a difference especially in regard to event themes. For example, if you have a Chinese theme, guests can leave with a "customized" fortune cookie that has a unique organizational message inside. If you are hosting a women's golf tournament, you can provide participants with a long stem rose as they leave, place slippers and toiletries in their lockers or have a make-up artist on hand for touch ups.

Here are a few other ideas:

- Look at unique ways to plate your food (e.g. if it is a winter wonderland theme serve your appetizer in an under-lit ice bowl).

- Dress your volunteers in the theme of the evening.

- If you have a chic bowling event, ask the guests to dress in black tie, at the entrance to the venue have a red carpet and marquee to welcome the guests.

- Dress up the washrooms and have washroom attendants.

- Consider a cocktail party to start the evening.

- Have an intermission with entertainment.

- Dress up the venue to look more like a ball-room. Think outside the box!

THE STRATEGIC PLAN

The event strategic plan is the blueprint for executing a special event. The elements of a strategic plan include: an event overview, fact sheet (with key details of who, what, where, when and why), budget, critical path, venue analysis (if required), goals and strategies and an evaluation procedure.

Budget

A budget is a list of all planned revenues and expenses of an event. It is important to track revenue and expenses as they come in to ensure you are on track.

Typical revenue for a special event include:

- Sponsorships (levels vary depending on the event and the categories created)

- Ticket sales

- Raffles

- Silent/live auctions

- Balloon bursts/mystery envelopes

- Gaming

- Registration fees

- Pledges

- Merchandise

- Expo/vendor booth

- Food & beverage

- Donations

Industry standard is that expenses should not exceed 50% of gross revenue. Typical expenses for a special event include:

- Venue, décor and signage

- Food/beverage

- Marketing & communications

- Production costs

- Prizes for patrons and gifting for volunteers

- Travel

- Courier/postage/shipping

- Long distance & supplies

- Photography

- Insurance & permits

- Raffle license

- Logistics (security/Police)

- Credit card processing fees

- Professional fees (eg. Consultants)

Figure 7.2 gives a sample budget for a typical golf tournament.

REVENUE	ACTUAL	BUDGET
FOURSOME REVENUE		
Venue	$104,000.00	$104,000.00
Total Foursome Revenue	**$104,000.00**	**$104,000.00**
OTHER REVENUE		
Donations	$6,284.35	$6,000.00
Kids Draw (06)/Million Dollar (07)	$2,100.00	$2,400.00
Reverse Draw	$12,800.00	$13,000.00
Silent Auction	$15,645.00	$15,000.00
Total Other Revenue	**$36,829.35**	**$36,400.00**
SPONSORSHIP REVENUE		
Presenting Sponsors (x2 @ $20K)	$40,000.00	$40,000.00
Augusta Packages (x6 @ $10K)	$60,000.00	$60,000.00
Total Sponsorship Revenue	**$100,000.00**	**$100,000.00**
Total Income	**$240,829.35**	**$240,400.00**

EXPENSES	ACTUAL	BUDGET
Courier and Postage	$1,643.96	$1,700.00
Gift Bags	$689.97	$700.00
Special Gifting	$23,662.13	$21,000.00
Golf Services	$5,045.55	$6,000.00
Miscellaneous	$5,857.46	$6,000.00
Office Supplies	$296.09	$350.00
Photography	$7,566.30	$8,000.00
Professional Services	$29,113.25	$31,800.00
Reverse Draw Prizing	$3,212.21	$3,200.00
Signage	$4,788.13	$5,000.00
Entertainment	$642.00	$700.00
Food/Beverage	$411.32	$500.00
Travel	$1,861.33	$1,800.00
Venue	$50,176.13	$51,500.00
Total Expenses	**$134,965.83**	**$138,250.00**
Net Revenue	**$105,863.52**	**$102,150.00**

Figure 7.2

Critical Path

The critical path is one of the most important planning elements of a special event. It outlines, in detail, all the tasks required to be done to successfully execute the event. A secondary critical path four weeks out from event will provide you with an opportunity to summarize the outstanding tasks and break them down into greater detail, so that nothing gets missed. Figure 7.3 gives a sample critical path for sponsorship activity.

The steps in writing the critical path are:

1. List the tasks and activities needed to be executed by category (i.e. logistics, marketing & communications, health & safety, volunteer management). Ensure your list is exhaustive and create an excel spreadsheet with each tab representing a different category. Your headers could include: Action to Be Taken (i.e. task), Assigned to, and Status.

2. Sequence the tasks in terms of timing. Keep in mind that some tasks cannot be started until others are completed, others will be done simultaneously.

3. Include timeframes and build in progress checkpoints for all tasks.

SALES & SPONSORSHIP			
Action	**Assigned to**	**Deadline**	**Status**
Develop prospect list			
Prepare and send out solicitation materials			
Follow up with prospects			
Confirm sponsors and foursomes and send out confirmation			
Coordinate sponsor approvals for collateral and other marketing material			
Obtain logos from sponsors			
Send out e-mail confirmations, reg forms, and invoices			
Follow up with registration forms			
Input registration forms into database			
Finalize list of guest names			
Call to thank all supporters in a timely manner			
Prepare and send thank you letters			
Prepare sponsor reports			
Select and order sponsor thank you gifts			

Figure 7.3 Critical Path for Sponsorship

Venue Analysis

Selecting the venue for your event is one of the most critical decisions you make. It can impact the look and feel of your event; be a key factor in terms of making your event unique; and could be one of your more expensive line items. In addition, the professionalism of the staff at the venue can greatly impact the successful execution of your event (assisting you with a smooth move in/move out, discounted charitable rates, or even how your guests are treated).

Some important venue considerations include: cost, location, date availability, size/layout of space, venue rating (i.e. 5 star), liability insurance required to host the event at their venue, amenities, uniqueness of venue, the ability to expand your event, security, parking, existing technical equipment/support and power. If the venue is union costs can increase substantially, especially if event is on a Sunday or holiday. Check the quality of food and beverage, the flexibility of the venue with special requests (such as beverage donations), overall cleanliness, proximity to hospitals & airports, storage, handicap accessibility, special services such as interpreters and translators and ease of the move in/move out areas.

Other things to think about: If your event is a destination event, is the infrastructure in the city you are hosting the event? Do they have the resources you require i.e. hospitals, local suppliers for tenting and barricading etc.? If your location is not a metropolitan city or in a remote location, you may have issues sourcing these items and it can become costly if you have to bring them in. Other considerations to keep in mind for a destination event is the climate, safety of your guests, economic conditions, proximity of local attractions, shopping, and restaurants.

Goals & Strategies

Goals and strategies state the desired results for an event and the strategies required to successfully achieve the goals. You can have both primary and secondary goals.

Goals should be specific, stated in terms of desired results, expressed in quantitative terms, so that actual results can be measured, and should be achievable within a specified period of time.

For example, a primary goal would be to raise $100,000 net. The strategy you put in place to achieve this goal would be to raise XX dollars in sponsorship, XX dollars in ticket sales, XX dollars in silent auction revenue, XX dollars in donations etc. while keeping expenses down. Specify how you will manage expenses and what the timeframe is to implement the strategy.

Evaluation Procedures

Event evaluation is the process of critically observing, monitoring and measuring the implementation and outcomes of the events to determine if objectives have been achieved. Evaluation is a critical step in successful event management and is often looked upon as an afterthought. It enables you to measure the success of the event, implement learned lessons in your event's next year planning process, continuously improve and refine the event. The evaluation process takes place throughout the life of the event and requires the commitment of time and resources. The results of your evaluation are only as good as the information obtained.

The steps in evaluating your event are:

1. Identify the objectives
2. Decide on the methods to evaluate
3. Analyze and interpret the data
4. Compile an event report, summarizing the results
5. Distribute to all key stakeholders

Evaluation methods include: direct observation by staff, volunteers and other key stakeholders; staff meetings & reports, where the progress of the event is monitored and controlled; administrative reports such as sales reports; postal code analysis; professional reports such as police crowd estimates; incident reports; traffic and parking statistics; debrief meetings; photographic documentation of the event; media coverage and reports; surveys; economic impact studies focus groups; one on one interviews with key stakeholders; and secret shoppers.

SPONSORSHIP

Sponsorship is the act of corporations and individuals providing financial or gift-in-kind support to an event in return for benefits and recognition. This is usually an important and lucrative revenue stream for events. You should plan to approach sponsors at least one year ahead to hit their budget cycles (depending on the corporation, they tend to start planning between July-November of the previous year, for the following year).

In terms of compiling your list of prospects, the best place is to start is to review your circles of influence (i.e. board members, volunteers, clients etc.). Who is already involved with your organization that would step-up to support you?

Mine your existing database to see who already supports you, to determine if you can broaden and leverage the relationship.

In addition, it is important to conduct research into corporations and individuals that would most likely support your organization. Many corporations have community investment policies regarding areas (i.e. health, education, children) they support. You can utilize prospect research online databases (i.e. iwave, bigonline Canada) to gain information on corporations and individuals, however keep in mind the annual fees can be expensive.

Take a close look at your event demographics and determine which corporations would benefit from showcasing their products and services to your guests/participants.

Compile your list of prospects and share with other members of your fundraising team to ensure there is no overlap and the corporation or individual is not being approached for something else philanthropically —although in some cases they may support more than one initiative.

Once you finalize your list of prospects, you need to develop an approach strategy. Gone are the days that you can submit a generic proposal and obtain a positive response. An effective sponsorship proposal means that you must understand and respond to sponsor's motivations, and then provide perceived value through the benefits and features inherent in the proposal. Often this means a process of research, application, customization and effective packaging of the proposal. Sometimes it means modification of the event design to provide a sponsor with the incentive to say "YES!"

It is still important to develop an overall sponsorship package that you can produce in hard and soft copies, as well as post online for easy access.

Key elements of your sponsorship package could include:

- Event overview
- Organization overview

- Event at a Glance—point form key details of the event (i.e. date, location, cost, key elements of the event, schedule etc.)
- Your unique selling proposition - why they should sponsor your event?
- Demographics of those attending the event
- List of sponsorship opportunities with corresponding benefits and recognition
- List of past supporters
- Board of Directors/Committee Members (if you feel they are influencers)
- Statistics/Photographs (visuals are important to make the package visually more enticing to read)
- Samples of past materials (for hard copy packages, or posted online)

Once the package is developed, it can be customized for your top level sponsor prospects. You need to excite them about your event, but at the same time demonstrate how you can showcase their product or service to your event audience (a desirable demographic for them). It takes careful research to understand their product/service and their marketing objectives. Experiential opportunities are huge for many corporations, as it gives them the opportunity to have people touch/feel and "play" with their products.

Typical benefits and recognition are as follows:

- Naming/titling
- Marketing/media benefits (i.e. logo recognition on collateral or advertising material, media releases, web-site recognition)
- On-site recognition (i.e. signage, booth, product placement, opportunity for senior executive to speak)
- Hospitality (tickets, access to VIP receptions or areas)
- First right of refusal

ON-SITE FUNDRAISING INITIATIVES

On-site fundraising initiatives are additional lucrative revenue streams for an event. These could include:

- Silent & live auctions
- Balloon bursts
- Raffles
- Gaming (Monte Carlos)
- Donation kiosks

Some of these initiatives can be extremely labour intensive. Ensure you have the resources, tools and the proper planning time to execute them. The following is a list of activities involved in executing on-site fundraising initiatives:

- Prepare prospect lists
- Prepare request letters and donors forms
- Prepare customized proposals as needed
- Develop budgets
- Follow-up with donors
- Track donor information in database
- Package items
- Write brochure copy
- Organize all display accessories such as mannequins
- Coordinate delivery and pick-up of items
- Obtain donor documentation for tax receipting purposes
- Hire décor personnel
- Prepare bid sheets, receipts and master logs
- Prepare raffle license applications and reports
- Prepare gaming applications and reports
- Produce all technical elements including live auction video, raffle reel if required etc.
- Coordinate all silent/live auction post-event follow-up/clean-up

MARKETING YOUR EVENT

The competition in today's event market is fierce, with new events being launched every year. It is getting harder to capture market share and the attention of your target audience. As a result, marketing your event successfully has become a paramount priority.

The key to a successful marketing campaign is developing an integrated marketing plan, that identifies the tools and channels you require to effectively communicate key messages to your audience.

The plan you develop should answer the following questions:

1. Where are you now? Get to know your competition by conducting a situational assessment (SWOT and Competitive Analysis).
2. Where would you like to be? (set marketing objectives)
3. What will you do to get there? (marketing activities)
4. How will you make sure you get there? (marketing management)
5. How will you know when you have arrived? (marketing evaluation)

Step 1: Where are you now? SWOT and Competitive Analysis

SWOT Analysis

A simple tool to get a quick overview of an event's strategic situation is to conduct a SWOT analysis. This consists of sizing up an event's internal strengths and weaknesses and its external opportunities and threats.

A strength can be a competitive asset, or an element of an event that puts it in a position of market advantage. What does your event have to offer? What is your unique selling proposition? From a strategy-making perspective, an event's strengths are significant because they can be the cornerstones of strategy and the basis on which to build a competitive advantage.

A weakness is something an event lacks or does poorly (in comparison to others) or a condition that puts it at a disadvantage. What are the issues you still need to work on? What are your areas of improvement? A weakness can be strategically important or not, depending on how much it matters in the competitive battle the organization is in.

Market opportunity is a big factor in shaping an organization's strategy. Not every organization is well positioned to pursue each opportunity that exists in the marketplace—some are always better situated then others and some organization's may be hopelessly out of contention (i.e. conducting a mega lottery). Why is your event going to be a success in the current marketplace?

Often, certain factors in an organization's external environment pose threats to its well-being. Threats can stem from the introduction of new or better products by rivals, new regulations that are burdensome, unfavorable demographic shifts. What are potential pitfalls for your event? What could happen that will affect the success of your event (outside your scope of influence)?

Competitive Situation Analysis

Evaluate your competition. Look at *Cause-Related Competition* (organizations that have similar mandates), *Audience-Related Competition* (targets a similar market audience), *Sponsor-Related Competition* (targets similar sponsors) and *Event-Related Competition* (similar event).

There are three areas to assess in terms of evaluating your competition:

1. Comparison: Directly compare your situation to that of your competitors. In particular, highlight your competitive strengths and weaknesses to avoid head-on competition with their strengths while capitalizing on their weaknesses.

2. Identification of USP: Your analysis should highlight your competitor's unique selling proposition—characteristics that make their event unique. These points are different from your competitors' strengths and characteristics which you do not possess but they do.

3. Opportunity Identification: Identify areas where your competitors are particularly successful (can you be successful too?). Pinpoint opportunities that your competitors have overlooked.

In addition to the preceding three areas; create a competitive analysis chart and track the following information for other events: location, annual date of event, type of event, years in existence, cost to participate, benefit to charity, number of participants, registration method, sponsors and sponsor levels.

Where you can, source "intelligence" on your competition include: annual reports, newsletters, web-sites, media coverage, marketing brochures, advertisements, media events, attend their events.

Step 2: Where would you like to be? (setting marketing objectives)

Once you understand your current position and your competition, you can set clear targets. You need to identify your market segments, rank them in priority and establish objectives for each of them.

Your market segments must be -

Measurable: You should be able to measure the size of your targeted market segment so that a reasonable estimate of potential market share can be attained; and

Accessible: You must be able to reach your target market segment through advertising, promotion, and social media. The target market must be able to reach you, too.

Depending on your market segments you need to customize your messaging and consider the appropriate channels for promotion to reach them. You can no longer run with a "general campaign."

Step 3: What will you do to get there? (marketing activities)

Now that you have identified your objectives and the specific targets you would like to reach, you will need to develop an effective communication strategy to reach your target audience. Part of your communication strategy could include branding the event, logo identification, messaging, and creative development (definitely if it is a first time event). These design/creative elements will be used to develop your advertising and collateral materials.

Your communication strategy needs to have succinct messages and showcase your unique selling points. Once you are clear on what you want to communicate you should determine your *marketing mix*. It is essential to communicate your messages through various channels. Repetition is important in disseminating your message. The quantity (i.e. size of your media buy), frequency and mediums used will depend on the budget you have for your event. Below are a list of possible and effective channels you can utilize to deliver your message:

- Print Ads
- Outdoor Billboards
- Radio Advertising
- One-Stop Media (Canada's largest portfolio of digital out-of-home advertising properties)

- Guerilla Marketing
- Television Commercials/PSA's
- Direct Mail
- Brochure Distribution
- Mini-Billboards (i.e. Zoom Media/New Ad)
- Social Marketing (Flicker, YouTube, Facebook, Linkedin, Blogs etc.)
- Event Web-site
- Captivate Network (Digital programming and advertising network targeting the business professionals at work)
- Wild Posting
- Viral Campaign
- Website calendars and links

Once you determine the channels, you will need to formulate the campaign calendar.

Step #4: How will you make sure you get there? (marketing management)

The marketing team leader plays a vital role in the marketing process. It is their responsibility to ensure that an effective communication strategy is developed and the right marketing activities are utilized to maximize results. They also need to involve other members of the team in setting objectives and developing, implementing and evaluating the marketing plan. By harnessing each team member's expertise and allowing them to provide input you, generate by-in from the team and hopefully it will lead to a successful campaign.

Step #5: How will you know when you have arrived? (marketing evaluation)

Each team member should prepare debriefing notes. It is important that the team have the opportunity to review all data, reports, etc. so that they can provide appropriate input.

Each element of the marketing plan and the campaign should be reviewed and discussed. What worked well? What didn't work well? Why? Which activities were worth the investment? What would you do differently next time?

A proper and thorough evaluation will afford you the opportunity to more effectively manage your mar-

keting campaigns, learn from previous mistakes and improve your future marketing efforts.

Marketing & Communications Execution

The following is a summary of tasks to execute the marketing and communication elements of an event:

Marketing Plan

- Prepare the marketing plan
- Recruit ad agency
- Work with agency to develop strategy and creative
- Determine advertising vehicles/facilitate media buy
- Negotiate advertising partnerships
- Guerilla marketing
- Coordinate material for advertising mediums
- Web development (mapping, content, e-commerce)

Collateral Materials

- Source printer and designer
- Write copy for all collateral material
- Obtain sponsor approvals
- Work with design firm to develop work-back schedules
- Liaise with design firm, printers and photographers to produce all collateral material including items posters, brochures, training guides, map books, volunteer books etc.

PUBLIC RELATIONS

Public relations (PR) includes activities that will educate the public about your organization and your event, as well as build a strong public image. It is often considered as one of the primary activities included in promotions.

Like marketing, effective public relations will often depend on developing and implementing an effective strategic plan. The plan often includes an overview of the event, touching on the role and objectives of public relations. Typical PR objectives would include:

- To generate maximum media coverage to educate the public around the organization and event.

- To establish/re-establish the event as the most unique, the largest, most exciting (whatever your event is) event in your market.

- Leverage celebrity participation (if applicable) to assist in generating a wider breadth of coverage.

- To generate maximum media coverage to showcase donors.

- To drive awareness of the event and the organization and encourage public participation.

- Assist with building profile for the purposes of donor recognition/solicitation.

The plan would also identify opportunities that can be capitalized on to create media interest. Usually these opportunities would be generated from the events unique selling proposition.

The plan identifies the audience, budget and strategy and tactics to gain media coverage. Other key considerations would be things like media partnerships, elements of concern, finding the right spokesperson etc.

When developing the strategy the following should be considered:

- Who are the stakeholders that you need to reach and how?

- What impressions do you want each of the stakeholders to have?

- What communications media do they see or prefer most?

- What media is most practical for you to use in terms of access and affordability?

- What messages are most appealing to each stakeholder group?

Public relations are conducted through various mediums including print, radio, television, social media and online. The communication tools prepared for the media are fact sheets, media releases and backgrounders. Other items you may include in your media kit are B-roll (footage from the event), photographs, samples of your collateral materials etc. There may also be an opportunity to create a media event that attracts coverage by mass media organizations, particularly television news and newspapers in both print and internet editions. Depending on your objectives you can plan when, where and what to stage. For example, if you plan a media event prior to your main event, it will assist in promotion and generating participation.

Unlike advertising, with publicity you have little control over the message in the media—reporters and writers decide what will be said.

You may have internal resources to assist you with your PR efforts. If not, and your budget permits you will want to outsource public relations. There are numerous firms to select from and there is an opportunity to secure their services pro bono if you can present an enticing proposal to them. If you hire an agency, your expectations of them should include: that they develop and execute an effective strategy, provide evaluation parameters including a comprehensive media report summarizing and valuating any coverage received.

The agency will expect you to provide all the appropriate information, a clear sense of expectations and spokespeople. Figure 7.4 gives you an outline of how to prepare an advertising and public relations brief if you decide to approach an agency.

VOLUNTEER MANAGEMENT

Volunteers are essential to the success of a fundraising event. They provide you with the staffing/labor required to execute the event while keeping your expenses down. Senior volunteers can be recruited to sit on committees to assist with organizing the event and soliciting sponsorship, silent/live auction and raffle items, among other things.

For volunteers who have agreed to sit on an organizing committee it is important to provide them with a committee terms of reference; a position guide for the sub-committee they are working on and an overall event organizational chart. This will provide them appropriate guidance on their role and what is expected of them.

Volunteer management is a continuous cycle involving planning, recruitment, orientation & training, supervision & evaluation and recognition. Please refer to Chapter 18 of this text for detailed information on volunteers.

How to Write an Advertising and Public Relations Brief

Purpose of the Brief

- To entice the agency to provide you with their services pro bono (if applicable)
- To provide a good understanding of the organization/event
- To provide the specifics about the event, including USP's, event schedule, etc.
- To provide intended objectives – i.e. is it to obtain pre-publicity to boost sales, event day media coverage, post-event media coverage, to raise awareness about the organization etc.
- To provide parameters such as intended audience
- To indicate the "challenge" i.e. to brand, to create collateral pieces, enticing ads etc
- To provide creative focus i.e.
  - What do they currently think?
  - What do we want them to think?
  - What is the most persuasive thing we can say to get them there?
  - Why should they believe it?
  - What personality or tone should the advertising have?
- To advise agency of confirmed media partners
- To advise of client/agency expectations
- To advise agency of scope of work, duration and fee

Elements of a Brief

- Organization overview
- Event overview
- Event schedule
- Unique selling proposition
- The challenge
- The creative focus
- Objectives
- Scope of work
- Project duration/fee
- Appendix (past coverage, samples)

Figure 7.4

LOGISTICS

Logistics for an event involves all the elements required to be executed to ensure the smooth operation of the event. Below is a list of typical action items for various types of events:

- Continually monitor event's progress against critical path.
- Determine signage requirements and produce signage.
- Develop seating plans/guest lists.
- Develop and implement registration and cash management systems.
- Liaise with venue on the following:

- Booking the space
- Work with key parties to determine floor plan and traffic flows
- Organize walk-throughs with key players
- Work with key parties to develop move-in/move-out schedules
- Develop menus
- Determine and organize room requirements, podiums, easels, tables, chairs, linens, power requirements, staging, security, coat check, risers, communication needs, room requirements, tastings etc.
- Obtain all required permits (i.e. special occasion permits, raffle licenses, liability insurance, hole-in-one insurance).
- Organize truck and all transportation of event materials to venue.
- Develop event schedules and scripts.
- Prepare truck lists, strike down lists
- Prepare on-site event binder (event manager's bible)
- Recruit and manage event photographers
- Solicit and manage all event day service providers
- Invitations to key parties to speak
- Recruit MC, auctioneers
- Develop crisis management plan
- Coordinate all necessary equipment (tenting, pylons, portolets, hand washing stations, Stanchions, tables, chairs, bins, bleachers, etc.)
- Coordinate required vehicles and storage containers if required
- Coordinate Road closures, crowd barriers/traffic management plan
- Coordinate on-site sponsor requirements
- Develop event overall communication plan
- Coordinate food and beverage requirements for the event
- Source possible health & safety firms

- Develop RFP's for various services, interview prospective companies and select company
- Develop health & safety and risk management plan
- Coordinate on-site services such as massage and physiotherapy

PRODUCTION

Production for an event includes coordinating the technical, décor and entertainment elements of an event. This can be a daunting task for those who are not experienced in it. It is extremely important to hire professional, experienced service providers with a proven track record. Speak to other colleagues to obtain recommendations. Ask for references; consult with special event associations for their recommendations such as ISES (International Special Events Society—many provinces have their own chapters), and access suppliers in special event resource guides (e.g. in Toronto Special Events (TSE) directory). Your event is only as good as the team you put together. Ensure all service providers are adequately insured.

Many venues also have in-house technical teams that you can work with. Keep in mind; many venues are union, which increases your costs substantially. Avoid hosting your event on a Sunday or a holiday or you will have to pay labor double time. In addition, work with your technical director to determine ways to structure your shift to save dollars.

In terms of hiring service providers: you should prepare a Request for Proposals (RFP). This is an invitation for suppliers, often through a bidding process, to submit a proposal on a specific service. Break down your event into the various elements, so you can determine what you require.

Elements of an RFP:

- Overview of the event/organization
- Scope of Work (technical requirements: staging, lighting, communication, audio/visual, monitors, labour etc.)
- Event schedule
- Venue specifications
- Budget (if available)

- Contract and term
- Selection criteria
- Proposal format
- Submission instructions and deadlines
- Special clauses (e.g. insurance requirements, termination, indemnification, right of negotiation etc.)

Production Activity Summary:

Concept Development

- Research entertainment segments
- Creative development of entertainment segments
- Determine consultants required to deliver entertainment segments (e.g. choreographer, fashion director, cirque producer, skateboard consultant etc.)
- Develop production critical path

Technical

- Hire key production team including technical director, executive producer, show director, scriptwriter, relevant consultants
- Develop detailed production budget
- Liaise with production firm on technical requirements including audio visual, staging, lighting, rigging, labour
- Work with executive producer to determine camera operator requirements
- Develop running order
- Prepare production script
- Prepare screen visuals (i.e. videos, logo graphics, sponsorship reel, lower thirds etc.)
- Develop floor plan
- Prepare move-in and move-out schedules
- Coordinate back of house requirements (i.e. mobile, production trailers, dressing and make-up rooms, mirrors, rolling racks etc.)
- Work with show director to acquire back of house stage management team

- Manage team on-site
- Prepare agendas and conduct production meetings

Entertainment

- Develop detailed budget
- Finalize entertainment segments
- Acquire talent for entertainment segments
- Develop rehearsal schedule
- Conduct rehearsals
- Determine make-up and costume requirements with relevant consultants
- Liaise with evening Master of Ceremonies
- Manage team on-site
- Provide content copy for program

Decor

- Break down your event into the various elements to determine what décor you require in each section of the room
- Work with design firm to develop budget and conceptual designs
- Finalize décor elements
- Manage team on-site

ADDITIONAL RESOURCES

Books

▶ BANGS. DAVID H. JR., (1998). *The Market Planning Guide.* USA: Upstart Publishing Company.

▶ RUTHERFORD, JULIA. (2004). *Professional Event Coordination.* New Jersey: John Wiley & Sons. Inc.

▶ SONDER, MARK. (2004). *Event Entertainment and Production.* New Jersey: John Wiley & Sons Inc.

▶ TARLOW, PETER E. (2002). *Event Risk Management and Safety.* New York: John Wiley & Sons Inc.

Associations

▶ INTERNATIONAL SPECIAL EVENTS SOCIETY (ISES)

▶ MEETING PROFESSIONALS INTERNATIONAL (MPI)

Magazines

▶ SPECIAL EVENTS MAGAZINE

▶ CANADIAN EVENT PERSPECTIVE MAGAZINE

▶ BIZBASH MAGAZINE

Resource Directories/URL's

▶ TORONTO SPECIAL EVENTS RESOURCE DIRECTORY

▶ MEETINGSCANADA.COM

▶ CANADAEVENTSCALENDAR.CA

ABOUT THE AUTHOR

Hala Bissada, BComm, CFRE

Hala Bissada is an international award-winning event-producer and, with 20 years of experience, one of Canada's foremost event fundraisers.

Prior to establishing Hala Events and Communications Inc., Hala spent 5 years with SickKids Foundation (the fundraising arm of one of the top three pediatric hospitals in the world) where she managed several complex events including: The 10th Annual Sick Kids Telethon, raising $5 million and the Wishing Well Lottery, the first mega-hospital lottery in Ontario, Canada netting $5.2 million. She also won her first national industry award (AHP Development Showcase Award) for her work on

Miracles in Motion (Canada's largest step-aerobathon) in 1995.

As Chief Development Officer for the Children's Aid Foundation from 1996-2004, Hala increased revenue from $500,000 net to $3.8 million net. As part of her portfolio, Hala executed the following high profile events: The Teddy Bear Affair, The Women's Golf Classic, The Golf Classic and the EZ Rock Radiothon.

Since establishing Hala Events & Communications Inc. in 2004, Hala has won 6 international awards, 4 national awards and 5 provincial awards for her innovative work.

Hala taught part-time at Humber School of Media Studies and Technology for four years, and is a part-time

faculty member at Ryerson University (both in Canada). She sat on the Board of the Association of Fund Raising Professionals for three years, chaired the 2003 Fundraising Day Conference, and is a much sought-after speaker. Hala will teach a new special event certificate program to be launched at Ryerson University in September 2012.

Hala holds a Bachelor of Commerce from Ryerson University and is a Certified Fund Raising Executive. In 2003, she was nominated for the Globe & Mail's "Top 40 Under 40" award and for the 2008 and 2010 Royal Bank of Canada's Women Entrepreneur of the Year. Hala was also selected as a recipient of the prestigious Ryerson Alumni Achievement Award in 2010.

CHAPTER 8

MONTHLY GIVING
HARVEY McKINNON, CFRE

If you want to acquire donors for life, monthly giving is the way to do it.
read more...

There are two core principles to successful fundraising. The first you know already - you "have to ask" (the right person, at the right time, with the right proposition).

The second principle is "make it easy." Making it easy is underrated. Have you ever logged off a website when you were trying to donate, or buy something, or left a long store line because you didn't want to waste time? Perhaps you couldn't donate at an event because you had no cash and they didn't take credit cards? If so, join the club of millions of people who opted out because it wasn't "easy."

The "ease factor" is one of the core reasons why monthly giving raises billions of dollars annually for non-profits worldwide. It's a beautiful thing.

Ultimately, monthly giving is a payment program whereby a donor has money deducted from their credit card, bank, or credit union account.

The channels you can use to recruit monthly donors are numerous, and later in this chapter I will outline some of the pros and cons of the different channels. Other chapters in this book should also give you a few useful ideas for converting single gift donors to long-term committed friends.

I joined my first monthly giving program in 1979. I'm in year 32 of giving every month. Including the extra single gifts I've made, I've made about 400 gifts in total. There are many more gifts to come for this non-profit. In fact, when I factor in my genes, my age, my excellent physical shape (once I start doing more exercise), I should be able to give another 432 gifts before I die. That's more than 800 gifts to just one charity.

I've upgraded four times. And, I've given a number of large single gifts as well.

All I had to do is put my signature on a piece of paper to sign up for…well…probably 66 years. I'm not alone.

Many non-profits have donors who will give for decades. And don't you think that these dedicated donors are the ultimate legacy prospects?

SEVEN GREAT REASONS WHY EVERY ORGANIZATION SHOULD RECRUIT MONTHLY DONORS.

1. It's convenient. It's easy for you and it's easy for the donor. Pre-authorized chequing (PAC) or credit cards allow deposits to be easily transferred into your bank account. And guess what's even more beautiful? For most non-profits monthly pledge income is un-earmarked.

2. You will increase your income dramatically on an annual basis. Donors generally give double or triple their annual gift average, once they sign up on a monthly donor program, and in many cases their annual giving is dramatically higher.

3. You build a better relationship with the donor. Monthly donor programs can help bring donors closer. Your communication becomes more about thanking them, and reporting on how their gifts are used, as opposed to just asking for more money.

4. Donors will stay with your organization longer. My long-term value studies show that monthly donors, especially those on pre-authorized chequing will be with you, on average for 5 to 10 years. A $15 monthly donor will give $180 a year or $1,260 over a seven year period. Upgrading will increase this amount. Many will give every month until they die.

5. Predictability. You have guaranteed income every month. This money will cover monthly overhead costs and help cash flow. This can be especially helpful for smaller non-profits.

6. Savings. You don't have to send monthly donors all your direct mail packages. Every organization we've worked with has lowered their administrative costs and increased their income through a monthly donor program. Your monthly donors will be one of the most profitable parts of your fundraising program, especially when you use automatic deductions from bank accounts or credit cards. (One of our clients has just one staff person who manages a program of 6,500 monthly donors

who give $2 million a year. That's cost effective.)

7. You are fighting for scarce resources. It's important to lose no time in starting or growing your program, and to act quickly before your competition recruits your donors to their monthly program.

PAYMENT OPTIONS FOR YOUR MONTHLY DONORS

1. PAC (pre-authorized chequing) also known as EFT (electronic fund transfer). This is your best option to collect gifts. To establish a PAC arrangement, a donor fills out a simple form indicating they will pre-authorize the monthly transfer of their money to you. They specify the monthly gift amount, sign the form and VOILA! You count the money and smile a lot.

2. Credit Cards – A number of our clients have a slightly higher average credit card monthly gift than PAC gift. However, there are small drawbacks to having donors give their monthly donation by credit card. The charge card company will take 2%-4% of the donation. Not a problem with a $10 monthly gift but pricey for a $1,000 monthly gift. Also, the donor has to renew their commitment when their card expires. Since this makes it easier for them to stop giving, they generally have a higher drop off rate than PAC donors. With people changing cards, losing cards, etc. you have a higher attrition rate. Plus it takes your organization more time, and therefore money, to guarantee that they continue to give.

SEVEN WAYS TO RECRUIT MONTHLY DONORS

1. Direct Response Television. Very expensive and successfully done by religious broadcasters, international aid and environmental agencies. Always costly when well done. Can be either long form (30-60 min), or short form (1-2 min). Then you must add the cost to buy TV airtime. This is an option only for a few major brands with powerful emotional stories. Over the years it has become more expensive. If you use a telethon, <u>always</u> promote monthly giving. If you are one of the rare organizations with a radiothon, make sure you focus on acquiring monthly sign-ups.

2. Telemarketing. Also expensive but can work well depending on your donor base. Some groups use this as their main method of recruitment. Others find letters more cost-effective. Successful programs generally call donors who were first acquired by direct mail. Telemarketing can also work especially well with new emergency donors, symbolic donors and petition signers.

3. Direct Mail. The most common and a highly successful way to build a monthly donor base. Direct mail acquired donors generally have the greatest lifetime value of all monthly donors. They are usually recruited to monthly giving by house mail letters, and sometimes through prospect mail letters. Converting direct mail donors to monthly giving is a longer-term process than either face-to-face or television, and doesn't produce the same rapid growth, but it is significantly cheaper.

4. Space Ads and Brochures. Many organizations recruit donors through these tools. While cost-effective, the numbers recruited are usually low.

5. Special events can be used to promote your program. Special events provide an opportunity to distribute flyers and use a highly motivating speaker (ideally a board member, person helped by the cause, etc.) to invite people to join.

6. Face-to-Face, Direct Dialogue, Door-to-Door. Essentially each of these methods is one individual asking another individual to sign up as a monthly donor while looking them in the face. This is obviously a very expensive method to acquire new donors because you are paying individuals to talk to potential donors one-on-one. However, for

a few well-known non-profits it can be cost effective. I've only seen it work for major brands. And as I write this chapter, the cost to acquire a donor has increased significantly from when the method was first introduced to Canada. In addition, the attrition rate seems to be getting higher, meaning the breakeven point is much further into the future. Very expensive upfront costs but can generate a lot of donors.

7. Online. E-mail conversion, social media, website promotion etc. are all good ways to promote your monthly program. Generally though, unless you have incredible traffic to your site, the number of conversions will be low (unless you have a child sponsorship program). Still, it's very cost-effective and attracts donors whose attrition rates are fairly low. Calling web donors to convert to monthly can work well.

WHAT IS THE "LIFETIME VALUE" OF THE TYPICAL MONTHLY DONOR?

- A $10 monthly donor will be worth $1,200 over 10 years.

- A $20 monthly donor will be worth $3,360 over 14 years.

- A $30 monthly donor will be worth $9,000 over 25 years.

"Lifetime value" is the core of why the monthly giving program is so important. The two factors that make a program lucrative are the regularity of receiving ongoing gifts each month, coupled with the fact that people have an extremely high annual renewal rate. Over time you will be able to determine the attrition rate of donors from each method of recruitment. You'll understand, thanks to your measurement and testing, how many monthly donors will upgrade each year.

Monthly giving is likely the most predictable source of income for any non-profit. Moreover, when you have a good estimate of the lifetime value of these donors, you know how much you can invest to recruit them. And since you are probably using a method like direct mail to recruit new donors, you know that if 10% of your newly acquired donors become monthly donors, that dramatically increases the long-term value of acquiring each new direct mail donor.

The lifetime value of a donor will vary depending on a number of factors. The most crucial one is the channel (or method of recruitment: direct mail, face-to-face, radiothon, etc.) through which they are recruited. The channel has the greatest impact on how long they are likely to continue giving.

METHOD OF RECRUITMENT MATTERS

Mail and Phone
Research shows that direct mail donors are the most loyal monthly donors. Donors recruited by telemarketing are pretty steadfast as well, because almost all of these gifts come from direct mail acquired donors. The biggest annual drop-off rates come from face-to-face recruitment and direct response television. That said, the drop-off rates vary quite widely. An important factor is how non-profits treat their donors. For example, they need to thank their donors promptly, keep them inspired about the cause and communicate effectively through their newsletters and websites.

Face-to-Face
The first major drawback is that many face-to-face campaigns have drop-off rates that are much higher than other methods of recruitment. For instance, attrition in the first year can range from 20%-35%. A further 15%-30% drop-off is common the second year. When donors have been giving for two years, the drop-off rate decreases. But organizations must track this carefully to ensure they are getting value. An extra 10% drop-off each year makes a phenomenally negative difference in lifetime value for the original group that was recruited. A good quality donor communication program will help to reduce the rate of attrition and make a big difference to the long-term value of the entire fundraising program.

New or undeveloped markets still have significant potential for face-to-face recruitment. If face-to-face is done well and the non-profit organization has a good communication program for the people they recruit, it is a worthwhile investment. Recognizable brand names have an enormous advantage in face-to-face recruitment. Some non-profits find door-to-door canvassing produces better long-term donors than face-to-face.

DRTV

Direct response television (DRTV) can also be an excellent way to recruit monthly donors, but there are many conditions that must be met: your organization needs a brand name, you need to make people cry, and you need to motivate them to pick up the phone. Also, you need great creative, the right time slot, and you require a lot of up-front investment money. Very few causes can afford to do DRTV in Canada.

Your website

The key to recruiting monthly donors through your website is to follow the basic rules of good communication: great copy, clean design and emotional and logical reasons to join your monthly giving program. Your website must be easy to read and navigate.

Recruitment through your website is highly dependent on traffic. You can have the best monthly giving proposition and the best website in the world, but if people can't find it, or don't come back for repeat visits you'll miss out on all of these potential monthly donors.

There are factors which you can control that will determine how many people on your programs will drop off:

- Quality of your projects, services.
- Stewardship of donors.
- The gift level.
- Are they on credit card or PAC?

The most important variable, however, is the channel of recruitment.

Will monthly donors also give single gifts, or upgrade their monthly gift?

Yes! They are among your most loyal donors. In emergency appeals they are especially generous. I've written letters that have pulled single gifts from as high as 40% of people already giving every month, and an average gift 50% above single gift donors. Most non-profits upgrade 5-20% of their monthly gift donors each year. These donors who upgrade usually increase their monthly pledge by 20-30%.

What are the average monthly gift ranges?

They range from $5 to $1000 but most are $10-$25. However, this depends on:

- The method of recruitment, or channel through which the donor was recruited i.e. mail, phone, face-to-face.
- Which donor segments you appeal to.
- The strength of your message.
- Whether you include a personal solicitation.
- The amount(s) you ask for.
- The length of time the program has been active. i.e. an organization with supporters who have been upgraded for a number of years should have a higher average.
- Premiums or benefits that you offer. This can increase the monthly pledge.

You want to get there first! And if not first - today!

Do you find that every time you look at the attrition level of your regular donor file you break into a cold sweat? Monthly giving is the solution to your problems.

Monthly donor plans are one of the best ways to reduce donor attrition and upgrade an individual's giving level. While most philanthropically-minded individuals will give gifts to four to ten charities a year, they rarely join more than two to five monthly donor clubs. And they do not necessarily choose their favourite causes. As with other types of fundraising, they will often join programs based on *who asks them first*.

When a donor joins a monthly donor club, there are consequences. They may even start reducing their single-gift donations to other non-profits – perhaps yours! – because they have committed a greater share of their charitable funds through monthly donor programs.

Let's consider a hypothetical donor, Cindy Williams, who regularly gives a total of $1,000 a year to ten charities, or $100 each. That's her limit. Then, she's successfully recruited by two of the charities into their $25/month donor programs. This means that she will give them $600 (or sixty per cent of her annual giving), leaving only $400 for the other eight charities. If Cindy splits the remaining money evenly, the charities will see their donations decline to one $50 gift each – a reduction of 50%.

The clear winners are those who recruited her to their monthly donor programs. Over time Cindy may even decide that she'll give $100 to four non-profits and stop giving to four others. She could even increase her total giving somewhat, but when the smoke has cleared, the odds are still very high that her average single-gift will have declined substantially from its original $100 level. She could choose a combination of any of the above scenarios. But whatever decision she makes, the non-profits who recruited her to join a monthly program did very well. They each upgraded Cindy's annual giving by 300%.

Even if – as is highly unlikely – a non-profit continues to receive a $100 annual donation from Cindy, it has lost. The other two organizations have dramatically increased their share of Cindy's annual giving, and she's now even less likely to join a third monthly giving club at the $25 a month level. That's why you need to approach your donors first and <u>before</u> your competitors do. Multiply the Cindy scenario by hundreds or thousands of individuals, and you see the loss of potential income for your non-profit.

To make matters still worse, Cindy is far more likely to lapse if she is giving annual gifts than if she is on a monthly donor program. What's more, there is a good chance that she did not select her two favourite charities, and join their monthly programs. Most likely, she responded to the two charities who asked her first. Donors have often told me they joined organizations that are not at the top of their priority list, but they continue to give because they have "made a commitment."

CHALLENGING THE MYTHS

Many non-profits are reluctant to launch monthly giving programs. Too often, they fall prey to the mythology that has grown up around monthly giving. There are at least seven widespread myths.

1. **We tested it and it didn't work.** If it doesn't work, the results could be because of the creative, the quality of the telemarketing script, the strategy, or a number of other factors. Monthly giving programs work around the world, and for non-profits in every sector.

2. **It won't work with our donor base.** A few years ago, a large European charity spent a fortune on a campaign to recruit monthly donors. It bombed. The organization concluded that its donors wouldn't respond to a monthly giving program. But, two years later, after developing an effective proposition and an integrated recruitment campaign, they now make more than 50% of their income from monthly donors – and the proportion grows every month. The organization learned from their original mistake that they needed to make sure they had the right proposition.

3. **Our donors are too old.** I have worked with a large U.S. non-profit where the % of monthly donors is in exact proportion to the number of 65 plus donors. The same seems to be true in Canada. Seniors are comfortable with automatic deductions since it makes their life easier. Basically, it is one less thing they have to remember.

4. **Our donors aren't loyal enough.** My experience is that any organization can make a significant amount of money from this program with committed and loyal donors. You won't know until you try.

5. **It's too much work.** A monthly donor program is easy to implement and very cost effective for the dollars raised even if you do not have a large in-house staff. Consider hiring a consultant to develop the strategy and creative. Your only extra work will be spending the actual income.

6. **It's a small amount of money.** I worked with a medium sized Australian non-profit that went from no monthly donors to 11,512 in about a decade, for an annual value of $3,492,381. This is in a country of only 22 million people. The success of your program will be based on many factors: the product, the offer, the benefits to the donor, the media you use, your budget and the copy or pitch. Your program will work if it's well executed.

7. **It costs a lot.** It will cost a lot more if you do TV or face to face. Better to start small

to see if your donors convert. Adding a "give monthly" section on a reply form costs you no extra money – you're already printing the form.

THINKING ABOUT YOUR MONTHLY DONOR PROGRAMS? QUESTIONS TO ASK IN ADVANCE

Before you start a monthly giving program, ask yourself these questions and jot down your responses to get an overview of what you know and don't know about your plans for a monthly donor program.

- Is the maximization of long-term income one of your organizational goals? Sometimes the focus has to be on raising money for the short-term. But if you only focus on short-term, your organization will never be financially stable.

- What methods will you test to recruit monthly donors?

  □ mail

  □ phone

  □ television

  □ door to door

  □ online

  □ e-mail

  □ newsletters

  □ volunteers

  □ special events

  □ face-to-face

  □ radiothon

  □ mobile

- Are you going to give individuals a choice of making a single gift in addition to a monthly commitment? Another area to test.

- What is your marketing proposition? What do you offer a prospect? Is it appealing to become a member of this club?

- What segments of your donor file will you approach to invite to join your club? Start with recent and new donors, donors who give more than 1 gift each, $25 + donors.

- Is there a staff person, dedicated volunteer or consultant who can devote time to this program? Someone needs to drive the growth.

- Do you have the ability to manage a pledge program with your current database? This is essential.

- Do you have a compelling reason for people to join a monthly program?

- Do you have committed donors who you feel would join a program given the opportunity?

- Have you considered testing other methods to build a program in addition to direct mail and telemarketing?

- Do you have the staff to create and direct the program, or do you need outside assistance? What are the costs if you need outside help?

- Will you offer credit cards as a payment option? You must.

- Will you offer pre-authorized chequing or electronic funds transfer? You must.

- What benefits will you give to donors? People will join without benefits but our extensive testing shows that premiums and benefits increase the sign up rate.

- Is there organizational support for the program?

- What overall resources do you have to devote to the program – financial, technical and human?

- Do similar organizations have monthly giving clubs? Have you researched their programs and promotions? Have you researched other programs?

- Have you done a survey to supporters that would help you tailor a monthly giving proposition that will attract them?

Your responses to these questions will give you a sense of how much planning you will need to do in order to initiate a program. Remember, however, even without being completely ready, you can start a program and increase your income and long-term stability.

LEGACY OPPORTUNITY

There is probably no other group on your donor file more likely to leave you money in their wills than your monthly donors - donors who have really bonded with your cause. They're willing to give you direct access to their personal bank account numbers, and to make an ongoing, multi-year commitment. Organizations that have long-running programs find that their monthly donors are among the most likely donors to leave a legacy.

Extensive research has shown that the people who leave bequests are not necessarily the wealthiest people on your donor file. In fact, legacy donors tend to be loyal, low-level donors who have given regularly for many years, exactly the kind of donor who joins your monthly donor program.

You should always keep in touch with lapsed monthly donors who have contributed for a number of years. When people retire, their annual giving often declines due to a decreased cash flow. This does not mean that their commitment has stopped – far from it. But it could mean your organization will need to wait a few years before the donor can make another gift – or the ultimate one. If you lose touch, they may decide to give part, or all, of their estate to other non-profits. Ask these individuals if they would like to continue receiving information, or simply send newsletters and other information as appropriate, to maintain the relationship and reinforce their importance as a member of your donor "family."

OBSTACLES TO STARTING MONTHLY GIVING

1. I don't have the financial resources to launch a monthly giving program.

- Start small! It's okay if you can't afford to develop a logo, letterhead, and special newsletter for a monthly giving program and provide valuable benefits to members. Ask people to join a monthly program, anyway.

- Explain the convenience and cost-savings of monthly giving in your communications to donors or members.

- In your appeals to donors, offer monthly giving as a special way to help.

- Include a box on the reply form for more information (or a section people can fill out to join immediately). Reinforce this option with a paragraph in your letter.

- Consider using volunteers to recruit members.

- Many donors will join a monthly giving program simply because you invite them to do so. One of my clients, with a large donor base, placed a small, 120-word promotional ad in its newsletter – and attracted 227 new monthly givers. The cost: almost nothing.

2. I don't have the authority to set up a monthly giving program and have to convince my superiors.

- Make a proposal to the decision-makers in your organization. Try starting your proposal with the following lead sentence: "Would you prefer that our donors give once or twice a year, or every month?"

- Propose survey research (with questions on monthly giving included in any donor survey you conduct).

- Propose a test. Select the segments of your donor file most likely to become monthly givers, and test an appeal to them. Analyze the Long-Term Value of the donors who enter the program, and determine if it's worthwhile to proceed.

3. I'm afraid a monthly giving program will take too much staff time.

- Jim Fleckenstein, of the Navy Memorial Foundation in Washington, DC, told me that when he started his monthly giving program, he was the only staff member responsible for development. He felt that he didn't have the time or resources to run a manual monthly billing program, so he decided he would only offer PAC to his donors. His supporters tend to be conservative older males, many of whom don't even have credit cards. Yet he managed in a short period to recruit many members from his donor base with only low-intensity efforts. This has significantly increased the income from these donors, while the investment in Jim's time was minimal.

4. Other staff members in our development department think a monthly giving club will "take money" from their programs.

- Smaller non-profits often have only one or two staff persons in the development department. Therefore, there is normally little concern about where money comes from. The concern usually is how to raise more money.

- In larger organizations, there may be competition for donors and income, especially if specialized-staff have particular targets to reach. Not surprisingly, a monthly giving program will reduce income from other areas of fundraising, principally direct mail, telemarketing, and special programs for "mid-level" donors ($250-$999 annually). So, even though the non-profit's income will increase, the new program may be threatening to staff members responsible for particular areas of the budget. (A similar situation could arise if you introduce a new telemarketing program and pull donors from direct mail, or launch a major donor program that pulls the best donors out of the mail program.)

- There are two ways to resolve this perceived problem: either (a) unwavering support from the decision-makers in your organization, or (b) setting a success measure of overall departmental income targets rather than for individual managers. Either way, the organization benefits because monthly giving revenue tends to be unrestricted revenue. And even if revenue is "lost" to another program, the organization can direct the unrestricted revenue to any area it chooses (including the one that decreased). Meanwhile, there is still a net benefit to the organization's programs.

USE DONOR RESEARCH TO BUILD THE CASE

Raising money – or creating a monthly donor program – without conducting research is like trying to build a house without blueprints. It is sometimes said that research is what you do before you spend a lot of money,

and testing is what you do afterwards. Good research will help you develop your most viable offer.

To a fundraiser, research means:

- **Understanding who your donors are.** When you know who they are, you'll know how to communicate effectively with them. You'll discover where they live (more than just an address), what they read, their religious affiliation, etc. You'll be able to compile demographic, psycho-graphic and behavioural pictures of your donors.

- **Understanding their giving patterns.** When you analyze how they give – dollar amount, date of most recent donation, and frequency – you'll be able to select the best prospects for a monthly giving club. You can also look at the types of appeal they respond to and tailor your monthly invitations accordingly.

- **Understanding why they give to your organization.** You can discover what motivates a single-gift donor versus a monthly donor, and you can shape future offers around this valuable information to convert more single-gift donors to monthly pledgers.

- **Finding which outside lists produce a higher proportion of monthly donors than others.** For instance, you may find that your local environmental activist organization is considered to be a marginal prospect list, but it provided a disproportionate number of individuals who later became monthly donors to your cause. Since these individuals have such a great Long-Term Value, you could decide to test other environmental lists, and continue using what originally seemed to be a marginal list.

Research comes in two flavours: primary and secondary.

1. Primary research may be either qualitative or quantitative. Qualitative research (including one-on-one interviews and focus groups) always involves smaller numbers and more in-depth information gathering. Quantitative research (larger numbers) may be done by mail or phone, and most likely these days, it will be done online.

2. Secondary research involves sifting through information that has been compiled, analyzed, or published elsewhere. It may be found in publications such as academic journals or in published government research and statistics. Also, some direct marketing and fundraising periodicals provide valuable second-hand research. Another form of secondary research, collecting direct mail samples, can be invaluable, because packages that are successful are mailed again and again. Also, these successful packages are used as "control packs" when looking to test another creative or proposition for an organization.

Both primary and secondary research is useful when launching a monthly giving program. You must "know" your audience before you invite them to make such a big commitment: their gender, age, income, giving history, and any other relevant information you can obtain about them. The more you know about the demographics and psycho-graphics of your target audience, the higher your response rate is likely to be.

In designing a monthly giving program, you'll probably find that it's useful to gather the following information and analyze it closely:

- samples of all the organization's mailings from the previous three years

- information on the segments mailed

- what kind of statistical results they yielded

This way, you can determine which themes or projects did well and which did poorly. You can recognize patterns and identify the elements that seemed to have the most powerful impact on your donors. On the basis of these observations – and of other, solid research findings – you can design a monthly giving program calculated to be compelling to your prospects.

WHAT'S WORKED FOR ME

It's hard to generalize about what works, because every organization's donor list is somewhat unique. Here, though, are some elements I've tested that seem to pay off for most organizations.

- Offers with premiums tend to pull in more monthly donors; premiums are cost-effective.

- Giving premiums for joining at a higher entry-level increases the average gift per month.

- Donors who make several gifts a year are more likely to become monthly donors than those who give once a year, regardless of gift.

- Personalization pays off in invitation letters.

- Using live stamps on outer envelopes and reply envelopes increases response rates and is cost-effective.

- A subtle ask for a monthly pledge in a prospect mail package pays off, so long as it isn't the primary focus of the appeal. But test this for your cause.

- People who drop out of a program are good prospects to sign up again. (Unless they are dead, but don't give up on them completely, you never know - they could be a zombie.)

Lapsing PAC donors are best renewed by paying attention to why they lapsed; they will usually volunteer a reason why they stopped giving. If they drop out because they lost a job, go back to them in six, or nine, or twelve months. The best time to re-approach them depends on why they lapsed, but many tests show this is a very good segment because they have a donation history with the organization.

A WORD OF CAUTION

For some non-profits, the opposite will be true. Not EVERY donor base is the same. For instance, live stamps may decrease the response rate to an invitation package, or they may make the package less cost-effective. Always test, and always be careful to test what's important. Your donors may not react in the same way as supporters of other causes do.

Even if your organization doesn't have a monthly donor program yet, almost certainly you already have single gift donors who are just waiting to be asked to make a greater commitment. People give for emotional reasons. Inspire emotion and people will make a commitment.

The number one reason people don't donate to a cause is: they haven't been asked. The number one reason people why people neglect to join a monthly program is the same: they haven't been asked.

Many non-profit staff and board members fear change, even if the change is clearly beneficial. Those who are particularly risk-adverse will miss out on wonderful opportunities and may even endanger the long-term stability of their organization.

"WHAT WILL MY MONTHLY GIFT DO?"

Can your organization tie a monthly amount to an appealing area? For example, the greatest proposition in monthly giving programs is child sponsorship. Organizations that offer child sponsorships make people feel like they are directly connected to the children. There's nothing more appealing than that.

Animal charities also attract an enormous number of monthly donors. Children and animals have a remarkable way of evoking deep emotional responses, which compel a lot of people to make a regular commitment. If people feel inspired they will, in fact, give you more money.

ROI

It is critically important to analyze your return on investment (ROI) for all fundraising initiatives, particularly monthly giving. You need to evaluate ROI by source (e.g. direct mail vs. telemarketing). This will tell you how much it is worth investing to acquire a new donor.

The method or channel of recruitment is a key factor in determining a donor's lifetime value, and therefore your anticipated return on investment.

CONCLUSION

You will dramatically increase the value of a donor when you convert them to monthly giving. I urge you to make this a focus of your work and am confident you will reap great rewards from the effort. You will leave a legacy to your non-profit long after you are gone - the monthly donor you recruited could give for decades.

ABOUT THE AUTHOR

Harvey McKinnon, BA, CFRE

Harvey McKinnon is recognized as one of North America's leading fundraising experts. He has authored the only books on monthly giving: Hidden Gold, and Tiny Essentials of Monthly Committed Giving. He is the co-author of the international bestseller, The Power of Giving, and Winner of the Nautilus Gold Award for books on social change

His latest book, The 11 Questions Every Donor Asks has received rave reviews. Fundraising guru Jerold Panas calls it, "a beautifully polished gem." The UK's Management Centre says it is one of top six must-read fundraising books.

An award-winning copywriter, Harvey has written for numerous publications including Grassroots Fundraising Journal, Contributions, Mal Warwick's newsletter Successful Direct Mail, Telephone and Online Fundraising, The Globe and Mail, Toronto Star and many others.

Harvey is a highly-rated speaker who is regularly invited to present at AFP regional and international conferences, CCAE, AHP national and international events, and the IFC (Netherlands). He has been a member of many non-profit and business boards, including the Resource Alliance (North America).

His company, Harvey McKinnon Associates, has offices in Vancouver and Toronto, and it works with many of Canada's leading non-profits.

CHAPTER 9

MAJOR GIFTS
GUY MALLABONE, CFRE

My own experience in major gifts began in the 1980's when I was working as Director of Fund Development at the Canadian Red Cross Society, Alberta-NWT Division. One morning I opened an envelope and found a cheque inside for $1,000 – an unsolicited donation. What could possibly motivate someone to write such a large amount on a cheque, and send it off unsolicited? I did a little research on the mystery donor, and found out that she had made numerous donations to the Red Cross, but there was no special connection between her and the organization. No one knew her, and no one knew what her connection or interest was in the Red Cross. *read more...*

I couldn't imagine sitting at my desk and writing a cheque for such a large amount (back in the 1980's), and wondered what motivated her to do this. Then I began to ask myself – if this person is motivated to write a cheque for $1,000, what would she consider donating if we spent time to build a proper relationship with her, presenting tailored opportunities to fund? Now my mind was racing. I had caught the major gift bug.

Fast-forward to 1999, and my arrival at the Southern Alberta Institute of Technology (SAIT) as their newly-minted Vice President of External Relations. In the eighty plus year history of this institution, the largest gift they had ever received from an individual donor was $140,000. After 15 months of organizing and applying a major gift methodology and philosophy at SAIT, SAIT was able to secure their first 7-digit gift, a $1 million gift from Mr. Clayton Carroll, a local business man who graduated from the institution in 1940. Five years after Clayton's watershed gift, SAIT secured their first 8-digit gift, a $10 million gift from Keith MacPhail, a 1980 graduate from SAIT and a prairie-boy-does-good success story from Medicine Hat. SAIT has gone on to secure numerous other major gifts, including a $15 million donation from John Aldred, which still stands as the largest individual gift made to a College in Canadian history.

The SAIT example demonstrates what can take place if time is taken to build a major gift program with engaged leadership, a strong methodology, and a supportive culture in place. SAIT is not your typical 4-year university institution, it is a two-year college, with trades/apprenticeship training offered. In the past, alumni had very little connection with or communication from the College after they graduated, and the institution wasn't valuing relationships with their alumni enough to warrant keeping up-to-date addresses on them. No one had given thought to the importance of managing existing relationships with former students.

Organizations that get the "major gift bug" rarely turn-back to old practice. In the case of Vertigo Theatre, a small and visionary theatre group operating in Calgary, the Board and Executive staff asked themselves the same series of questions that I asked myself when I was at the Red Cross. What would people consider do-

nating if we spent time to build proper relationships, and present them with opportunities to fund?

Vertigo had undertaken a significant fundraising goal and challenged itself to shift gears into major gift fundraising and was having significant success moving from an organization that primarily raised small annual gifts, to one that could build relationships producing larger transforming gifts. General Manager Suzanne Mott stated, "I never thought it was possible, we're a small organization. But the beginnings of key relationships existed already, what we needed was a methodology to bring these to fruition. We'll never turn back from major gift fundraising now."

The examples of the Canadian Red Cross, Vertigo Theatre, and SAIT Polytechnic all demonstrate that major gift fundraising can have a profound effect on an organization – not just in raising larger gifts, but in serving as a change agent for the organization.

Major gift fundraising is not only a methodology, but a cultural force within the organization. Mott at Vertigo Theatre went on to point out that their Board was recently interviewing candidates for an Artistic Director, and they used their new fundraising cultural perspective to assist them in determining which candidates were suitable for their major gift culture. Cleary not all Artistic Directors are created equal, and for Vertigo, the need for the Artistic Director to mesh with this new culture is important. Clearly, they had seen the value of a major gifts culture.

FEWER GIVE MORE

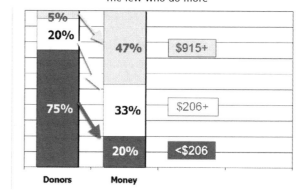

Figure 9.1

Major gift fundraising represents a natural evolution in fundraising best-practice in an organization. As organization's mature and develop more and more relationships, they are well positioned to undertake a major gift approach to fundraising.

As Ken Wyman pointed out in Chapter 1, in Canada, almost half of all donations made from Canadian individuals come from the 5% of the population who claim charitable tax credits (see Figure 9.1). The reality is, a few donors give most of the money in Canada. If an organization wants to become more effective in its fundraising, taking the next natural step in its evolution to major gift fundraising is important.

In today's landscape where competition for grants and new donors is increasing while operating budgets are decreasing, non-profits are wondering how to get more with less. The idea of implementing or improving an existing major gifts program might sound appealing to most Boards. An interesting characteristic about major gifts programs is that many of the elements that can make it successful are often already in existence even before the program is created – such as passionate staff members, a worthwhile organizational mission, and untapped donor assets such as goodwill and existing donors.

Major gift fundraising – or leadership giving, principal gifts, or other titles that an organization might apply – cultivate and solicit individuals and/or organizations who have the capacity and inclination to make contributions that are both substantial in size and transforming in nature. It's not the title of "major gifts" that makes the practice, it's the practice that delivers the result. For the purposes of this chapter, we shall use the words "major gifts" to be all encompassing.

Providing prospective donors with the opportunity to make meaningful gifts to an organization, or as James Hodge calls them … "Gifts of Significance,"[1] is one of the most challenging opportunities available to a fundraiser. According to Hodge, "…the Hank Rosso model of total development depends on personal solicitation of major gifts to complete the donor pyramid." As with so many other areas of fundraising, success in major gift fundraising is dependent upon the development of effective donor relationships.

Gifts of immense size and purpose leave many Canadian fundraisers, and organizations, fascinated and overwhelmed. Major gifts, such as the top eleven Canadian gifts made by Canadians listed in Figure 9.2, provides a unique glimpse into the depths of a benefactor's soul because they are, by definition, a contribution of a large share of one's life's work to a given purpose. Major gifts often complete a benefactor's life, and in so doing become dramatic public testimony to the foundation upon which that life has been built.

DEFINING MAJOR GIFTS

Defining major gifts by only their size is inconclusive alone. While there is no minimum or maximum gift size that qualifies a gift to be termed "major," the common characteristic is that all major gifts are solicited face-to-face or over the phone and the amounts given tend to reflect that personal approach.

In Europe and Australasia, major gift fundraising is referred to as "major donor fundraising." An interesting choice of emphasis on the word "donor" instead of the word 'gift' as used in Canada. Some might argue that the Canadian (and US) emphasis reinforces our attention to the priority of landing the gift over landing the relationship. Others scoff at this interpretation and point out that gifts only come from major relationships and the wording is semantics only.

However you interpret the language, know that you will be referring to major "donor" fundraising when travelling in other parts of the worlds … a subtle but important distinction.

---

1   Hodge, James M. (2003). Gifts of Significance, In H. Rosso (Ed.), *Achieving Excellence in Fundraising*, by Hank Rosso, (p.89). John Wiley & Sons Inc.

Top Eleven Canadian Major Gift Donations	
Gift Amount	**Benefactor**
$105 Million	Michael DeGroote In 2003, Michael DeGroote, the former CEO of Laidlaw Transport Ltd. donated an eye opening $105 million to the medical school at McMaster University, transforming it into one of the best-endowed in North America. Degroote's gift was the largest single cash donation in Canadian history and the school was renamed in his honour.
$100 Million	Seymour Schulich In 2011, mining magnate Seymour Schulich, donates $100 million to inaugurate the Schulich Leadership Scholarships, with hopes to be the Canadian equivalent of the Rhodes Scholarship. Noted Canadian philanthropist, Mr. Schulich's name already adorns schools of business, music, medicine and engineering.
$100 Million	Randy Moffat In 2001, communications mogul Randy Moffat gave Canada's second-largest charitable gift, a whopping $100 million, to the Winnipeg Community Foundation to help needy children and families.
$70 Million	Ken Thomson In 2002 Ken Thompson donated $70 million to the Art Gallery of Ontario. Along with this impressive endowment, the former chairman of Thomson Corp., who was Canada's richest man, also left the AGO with more than 2,000 pieces of artwork valued at more than $300 million.
$64 Million	Richard H. Tomlinson In 2000, Richard Tomlinson, founding director of Gennum Corp. (the world's largest maker of chips for hearing aids) donated $64-million to his alma mater, McGill University. Tomlinson received his PhD in chemistry from McGill in 1948.
$50 Million	Larry Tanenbaum In 2006, sports and construction magnate Larry Tanenbaum contributed $50-million to the endowment arm of the United Jewish Appeal Federation of Greater Toronto, the city's largest Jewish charitable organization. Tanenbaum, the chairman of Maple Leafs Sports and Entertainment Ltd., hoped the gift would "inspire" others to take advantage of new tax measures passed on donated stock.
$50 Million	Barry and Honey Sherman In 2002, Barry Sherman, the head and founder of pharmaceutical company Apotex Inc. and his wife Honey donated $50 million to the United Jewish Appeal Federation of Greater Toronto.
$50 Million	Dr. Stewart Blusson In 1998, Stewart Blusson's $50-million gift to the University of British Columbia, was at the time, the largest single donation ever made to a Canadian public institution. Dr. Blusson, who graduated from UBC with a Bachelor of Science in 1960, went on to become one of Canada's most acclaimed geologists and co-discovered the Ekati diamond mine in the Northwest Territories.
$50 Million	Joseph and Wolf Lebovic In 2006 Joseph and Wolf Lebovic donated $50 million to Mount Sinai Hospital in Toronto, adding to an earlier gift of $10 million. The brothers were born in Czechoslovakia and their family made its fortune in land development in the Toronto area. They have given to various causes, including a sizeable donation for the building of a Jewish community campus.

Top Eleven Canadian Major Gift Donations	
Gift Amount	**Benefactor**
$40 Million	Joyce Young In 2000, Joyce Young, a Hamilton-area investor, having made a windfall by investing in her nephew's high-tech business stock, donated $40 million to the Hamilton Community Foundation.
$37 Million	Peter Monk In 2006, Peter Munk, the founder of mining giant Barrick Gold, donated $37 million to the Toronto General Hospital. The largest direct donation of its kind directly to a Canadian hospital, the was used to fund and build new facilities in the Peter Munk Cardiac Centre at TGH.

Figure 9.2[2]

Consider these five key factors when examining a definition of major gifts:

1.   Major gifts are relative. What is major to one organization may not be major to another organization. For some organizations a major gift might be defined at $1000; for other non-profits, a major gift might start at $100,000 or more. Find the definition that fits your organization stage in its fundraising evolution. Don't feel you need to add "zeros" after your definition just because the organization down the street does so.

2.   Major gifts should be substantial. By substantial we mean those gifts that are extraordinary for both the donor and the organization. Because a typical gift can vary greatly from organization to organization, we need to look at defining "substantial" not on specific dollar size alone, but on its proportion to an average annual gift received by that same organization. For minimum definition purposes, the size of your major gift should be 100 times the size of your organization's usual annual gift. For example, at the Southern Alberta Institute of Technology, the average annual gift was approximately $80 dollars. Their definition of a major gift was $10,000 dollars.

3.   Major gifts should be transformative. They should create opportunities - endowing scholarships; permanently funding a research project; constructing a building – that have a permanent impact on the organizations future. Both concepts – relative substantial size and transforming nature are important to understand the definition of major gift.

4.   Major gifts are those which warrant one-on-one attention. Major gifts result from donor relationships. And donor relationships don't just happen by accident or overnight. They require time and attention to nurture and cultivate. A major gift definition should be set that reflects the need to provide one-on-one attention for cultivation and eventual solicitation.

5.   Major gifts depend on the maturity of the organization's development history. Major gift fundraising is very dependent upon prospective leads being identified and nurtured for solicitation. Many of these leads come from a strong annual fund that has been operating and which has built up a substantial donor base; upgrading donors by moving them up from gift level to gift level; and have recruited and trained staff and volunteers in effective major gift cultivation and solicitation.

What is your organization's major gift definition?

---

2   CBC News. Retrieved from *http://www.cbc.ca/news/background/wealth/charitable-donations.html*; National Post, October 14, 2011 (p.1).

Using a Fundraising Budget to Define Major Gift			
Total Annual Fundraising Income	Low	Middle	Major
Low = under $1 million	$1 - $499	$500 - $4,999	$5,000 and up
Middle = $1 million - $10 million	$1 - $9,999	$10,000 - $24,999	$25,000 and up
High = over $10 million	$1 - $14,999	$15,000 - $99,999	$100,000 and up

Figure 9.3

MAJOR GIFTS AND THE FUNDRAISING BUDGET

When looking to define a major gift for your organization, it's helpful to first review gifts made by individuals over the past five years. List the ten largest gifts and ask yourself the question, "Were these gifts typical and straightforward to obtain?" If so, you may want to define your "major gift" at this level. If you would rather challenge your organization and have the resources to expand your major gift program, then you may wish to set your definition at a higher level.

Remember, that the definition of a major gift is relative to your organization only.

Figure 9.3 provides a discussion for starting point to define major gift within your organization.

MAJOR GIFTS AND CAMPAIGNS

When looking at major gifts within the context of a campaign, we could say that major gifts are those gifts which play a major role in reaching the fund-raising goal. Using the rule of thumb that says the top gift is usually 10-15 % of a fundraising campaign goal, and the next four gifts are set to provide a further 10% of the goal, with the top 10 gifts equal to approximately 40-50% of the goal. Eighty percent of the goal will be provided by 20% of the donors.

Using the gift chart in Figure 9.4 (provided by Nicholas Offord in Chapter 11) we can see that one

way of defining major gifts is to look at their relative importance to the success of the campaign.

Number of gifts @ level	Total at this level	Cumulative Total
1 @ $1,500,000	$1,500,000	$1,500,000
1 @ $1,000,000	$1,000,000	$2,500,000
2 @ $500,000	$1,000,000	$3,500,000
4 @ $250,000	$1,000,000	$4,500,000
5 @ $200,000	$1,000,000	$5,500,000
6 @ $150,000	$900,000	$6,400,000
10 @ $100,000	$1,000,000	$7,400,000
15 @ $50,000	$750,000	$8,150,000
30 @ $25,000	$750,000	$8,900,000
50 @ $10,000	$500,000	$9,400,000
Many < $10,000	$600,000	**$10,000,000**

Figure 9.4

Campaign-for-one

When thinking about major gift and fundraising campaigns, it's helpful to think of the campaign as a series of individual campaigns-for-one. Each prospective donor has a campaign tailored for their own situation. Donor's comes in different shapes and sizes, each with their own motivations, inherent timelines, and unique obstacles and advantages. Each prospective major gift donor warrants their own "campaign plan" to ensure that the best opportunity is presented to them, at the best time, by the best person.

Building a major gift program

We can begin this conversation with the premise that every donor at one level of an organization's giving ladder is a prospective donor for a gift at the next higher level. You may not agree that this is likely for all donors, but as fundraising professionals, our job is to assume this is the case and to plan the steps that can lead the donor forward to their next gift.

Leaders in the fundraising profession have developed models that demonstrate this. Hank Rosso's "Ladder of Effectiveness" (Figure 9.5) shows that personal face-to-face visits are the most effective way to raise money. A face-to-face meeting is very effective when one person is knowledgeable about, and committed to the organization's mission and feels comfortable soliciting. The degree to which the person is committed and feels an "ownership position" with the organization can in many ways, pre-determine the outcome of the meeting.

Perhaps one of the best models is that proposed by David Dunlop (2000) where he classifies gifts as "annual," "special/capital," and "ultimate." In his work, major gifts are ten to twenty-five times larger than the annual gift: they are infrequently requested and require considerable thought on the part of the benefactor prior to making a commitment.

The Ladder of Effectiveness

1. Personal: face-to-face
Team of two
One person

2. Personal letter (on personal stationery)
With telephone follow-up
Without telephone follow-up

3. Personal telephone
With letter follow-up
Without letter follow-up

4. Personalized letter, Internet

5. Telephone solicitation, phone-a-thon

6. Impersonal letter, direct mail, e-mail

7. Impersonal telephone, telemarketing

9. Fund raising benefit, special event

9. Door-to-door

10. Media, advertising, Internet

Figure 9.5

Still another model (Figure 9.6) helpful in understanding and securing major gifts, is that proposed by G. T. Smith,[3] where the five key steps all being with an "I."

---

3   Smith, G.T. (1988). *Presidential and Trustee Leadership in Fund Raising*. San Francisco. CASE.

Five Steps in Securing Major Gifts

Identification:	Identify those who could be major gift supporters. Remember, the likelihood is that they are the ones closest to your institution.
Information:	Learn additional information about the potential donor. This is the "research" step, where information is identified about the person's tastes, values, and interests.
Interest:	Furthering the prospect's interests. Successful organizations offer donor's opportunities not only to meet the needs of others, but to find personal fulfillment at the same time.
Involvement:	Encouraging meaningful involvement. When the interests of the individual are creatively matched with the goals of the organization, meaningful involvement results. The greater the involvement, the greater the likelihood of increased gifts.
Investment:	Receiving added financial investment. If persons have been appropriately identified, informed, and involved in ways that are of interest to them, there is a good probability that they also will be willing to invest their financial resources generously. People tend to invest their most charitable dollars where they also invest their time and talent.

Figure 9.6

Most of these models focus on "why" major gifts are given, not "how" major gifts are given. Major gifts tend to be made to organizations that earn the trust and confidence of potential benefactors. It's the big ideas and transformative vision pieces that compel potential major gift donors to invest in, and partner with, worthy organizations.

Major gift fundraising models which are relationship-based require an "agent-of-change" to be involved – we tend to call them Development Officers. These individuals, working on behalf of the organization, participate in the articulation of the organization's mission, helping the prospective donor see the potential of what could be, and help create a deeper sense of the role of philanthropy in one's life.

LIA (Linkage, Interest and Ability) apply also in major gift fundraising evaluation. All models share the need for Development Officers to work with volunteers in determining the financial capacity of a prospective donor as well as their inclination to make a gift to the organization.

The Fund Raising School (2002) uses an eight-step model (see Figure 9.7) to describe solicitation of major gifts. As donors are further involved in the life of the non-profit organization, they continue to develop a sense of "ownership position" in the mission of the organization, and the good work that is delivered through the organization. As donors increase their "ownership position" in the organization they begin to see their personal values overlap with the values of the organization.

Major Gifts: The Eight Step Solicitation Process

1. Identification

2. Qualification

3. Development of Strategy

4. Cultivation

5. Solicitation and Negotiation

6. Acknowledgement

7. Stewardship

8. Renewal

Figure 9.7

So, if we see that donors are more apt to make major gift donations as they see their personal values overlapping with the values of the organization, then the obvious question becomes – how do development officers engage prospective major gift donors so that the values of each overlap?

Once prospective partners are discovered, and qualified, it is usually through active relationship building that the development officer can begin his/her work to mesh values and then promote major investments.

Asking donors to volunteer on important committees, raise funds, share their expertise, and serve on the governing board are some of the most common ways of building this sense of ownership. The key is not so much the technique but rather the spirit behind the technique that is important. The prospective donor needs to feel that the engagement is real, sincere, and natural.

The wealthy, like all of us, are tired of being manipulated – whether for their votes, their purchasing power, or their philanthropy. The proper position to take in relationship-based major gift fundraising is not to manipulate but rather to inspire. Involving major gift prospects in an organization will engage their ownership in the mission, and pull them towards making a major gift.

A MAJOR GIFT CULTURE

Successful major gift fundraising occurs in organizations that have evolved a culture supportive of major gift fundraising. Sounds obvious, but all the logic in the world won't ensure success in major gift fundraising if the organization's culture is not supportive of the activity. In the SAIT example, it was ultimately the creation of a major gift culture within that organization that allowed for major gifts to successfully "take root" and flourish.

Where is your organization's culture? What gaps exist, and where do you need to be in order to create a successful major gifts culture? Figure 9.8 provides a quick Ten-Point Quiz to provide an indication of the type of culture you have in your organization in relation to major gift fundraising.

Major Gift Cultural Assessment
Global Philanthropic Inc.

☐ All involved in our organization are proud to be associated with a charitable, non-profit organization.

☐ All Board, staff and volunteers understand that the ability to raise philanthropic support is directly related to the impressions and messages that each and every person delivers to constituency groups – and understand that each and every contact is an opportunity to build or diminish positive reputation.

☐ Our organization embraces the philosophy of cultivating prospective major gift donors one-on-one.

☐ Our organization promotes a development culture that fosters the building of meaningful individualized relationships.

☐ Our organization has a structure that will allow the tracking of initiatives with prospective donors, and accountability of staff.

☐ Everyone involved in our organization has the opportunity and feels the desire to become a donor.

☐ Our major gift donors are fully respected.

☐ Our Board and staff are aware of and engaged in coordinated major gift stewardship and cultivation strategies.

☐ Our organization understands the difference between fundraising and fund development, and resources (including staff) are available to work aggressively towards an integrated, relationship-based fund development program.

☐ Our organization has a clear structure for the assignment and management of major gift prospects/ donors.

Scoring: 0-4 No major gift culture presently - a long way to go; 5-6 A good start – keep up the evolution; 7-8 Excellent progress – above the Canadian average; 9-10 Best practice - well done.

Figure 9.8

MOTIVATING MAJOR GIFT DONORS

Paul Shervish states that, "what motivates the wealthy is very much what motivates someone at any point along the economic spectrum. Identify any motive that might inspire concern – from heartfelt empathy to self-promotion, from religious obligation to business networking, from passion to prestige, from political philosophy to tax incentives – and some millionaires will make it the cornerstone of their giving."[4]

While completely true, Shervish's words aren't particularly helpful in getting us to understand what might motivate a major gift donor to support our mission.

In what has become a fundraising classic, Russ Alan Prince and Karen Maru File, outline their *Seven Faces of Philanthropy*. Their work segments wealthy donors into one of seven motivational types:

1. The Communitarians - This is the largest segment (26%). Communitarians give because it makes sense to do so. They believe in actively supporting local non-profits as a way to help their own communities prosper.
2. The Devout – (21%). This group is motivated to give for religious reasons, and channel almost all of their giving to religious organizations.
3. The Investor – (15%). Investors organize their giving to take advantage of tax and estate benefits. They are most likely to support "umbrella" non-profits and donate to a wide range of causes.
4. The Socialite – (11%). Members of local social networks who find social functions benefitting non-profits an especially appealing way to help make a better world and have a good time doing it. They tend to support the arts, education and religious groups.
5. The Altruist – (9%). Altruists embody the perception of the selfless donor – the donor who gives out of generosity and empathy to urgent causes and often modestly wishes to remain anonymous. Altruists tend to give to

social causes and tend not to want active roles in the groups they support.

6. The Repayer – (10%). A typical repayer has personally benefitted from some institutions, and now supports that institution from a feeling of loyalty or obligation.
7. The Dynast – (8%). For these donors doing good is a family tradition. Giving is something their family has stood for and they believe it is expected of them to support non-profits.

In 2000, a large Canadian study was undertaken by myself and Tony Myers to examine motivational factors for Canadians making the "ultimate" gift – defined as the largest gift a donor could make in their lifetime (i.e. major gift).

Over 1,200 Canadian donors took part in the survey, making it the largest survey of donors presently conducted in the English-speaking world. The statistical validity of the survey was +/- 3.5% 19 times out of 20. The results for the question of, "What motivates you to make the ultimate philanthropic gift?" are listed in Figure 9.9.

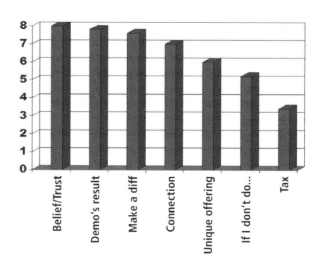

Figure 9.9

The motivational factor of belief/trust was the number one motivational factor inspiring people to make a major gift. Followed closely by (the charity) "demonstrating results" and "I can make a difference," and "I have a connection with the charity." The remaining key factors included the charity "having a unique offering" and the belief that "if the donor didn't make

4 Schervish, P.G. (1997). *Inclination, Obligation and Association: What We Know and What We Need to Learn about Donor Motivation*, in D.F. Burlingame (ed.) *Critical issues in Fund Raising*. Wiley NY (pp.67-71).

the gift, the work wouldn't get done." Finally rounding out the field was "tax" as a motivational factor.

Understanding what motivates a donor to make a major gift can assist organizations in planning how to segment and communicate with their donor base. For example, knowing that Canadians are motivated by charities that "demonstrate results" and which "make a difference" should allow organizations to plan their communication strategy to existing donors to ensure they are made well aware of the impact of existing giving and how that is bringing about key outcomes in the community. It will also give a clue to major gift officers as to how to conduct a conversation with a prospect major gift donor – knowing that they are looking for evidence of results and how the organization has made a difference.

The number one motivational factor, "belief/trust" speaks to the need for donors to believe in the mission of the work being done by the organization, and trust in the leadership of the governors and executive in charge of delivering that mission. To demonstrate this to potential donors, organizations must look for ways to involve potential major gift donors in the organization so that they can see first-hand how the mission of the organization overlaps with the personal life mission of the donor. Where these values overlap (Figure 9.10) represents the degree of opportunity for major gift development.

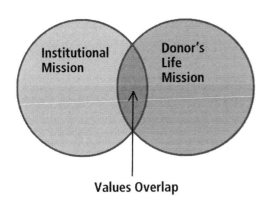

Values Overlap

Figure 9.10

MOVES MANAGEMENT

Before I discuss moves management and major gift relationship-based fundraising, it's important that I share my philosophy around relationship-based fundraising, and declare my bias. I begin with the premise that donor-centered relationships are the key to raising major gifts for our organizations – an obvious place to begin when talking about major gifts.

I also believe that those who practice major gift fundraising without appreciating the importance of donor-centered relationships are, in my opinion, poor stewards of philanthropy. Perhaps a little harsh, but it's the truth. Relationships are core to major gift fundraising and philanthropy is strengthened and organizations benefit when fundraisers understand the importance of relationship building to the process.

But the reverse is *even more true* – those who *talk* about donor-centered relationships without mastering the techniques of major gift fundraising, through methodologies like moves management (including effective solicitation), do a disservice to themselves, their organizations, and philanthropy overall.

What I mean by this is that relationship building, while important and vital to the process of major gift fundraising, and provides many benefits to the organization beyond money – is not the "end game" for fundraisers. Fundraising professionals operate at their peril if they develop relationships as the end objective, rather than as a stepping-stone to soliciting major gifts. At the end of the day, if you have a portfolio of great relationships, but no money raised, you haven't done a very good job as a major gift fundraiser.

In other words, recognizing that donor-centered relationships are fundamental to success in major gift fundraising is only half the battle – understanding and putting-into-action effective operational methodology to leverage those relationships is equally important.

In my career, I have come to recognize a fundamental truth about major gift fundraising: people give their money to things in their life that they are *closest* to. This includes themselves, their children, parents, school, community, the disease that took their parents life, etc. If you believe in this fundamental truth in life, then our job as major gift fundraisers become focused on one key thing … bringing people closer to your organization.

Moves management allows for this systematic bringing of people closer to us and our organizations.

Mallabone's Fundamental Fundraising Truth

People give their money to things in their life that they are *closest* to.

If you believe in this fundamental truth then your primary fundraising responsibility is to ...

BRING PEOPLE CLOSER TO YOUR ORGANIZATION

Figure 9.11

In the early 1960's, G.T. "Buck" Smith was Vice President of the College of Wooster in Wooster, Ohio. He started his career at Cornell University. I suspect that while Buck was travelling the back roads of Ohio visiting alumni and friends of Wooster, he observed this fundamental truth, and developed ideas that have become known as the cultivation cycle and moves management system.

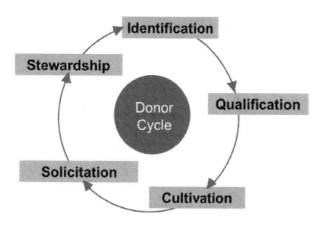

Figure 9.12

Smith's cultivation cycle (Figure 9.12), sometimes called the fundraising continuum, is a model of how relationships develop for all of us. It follows that in securing major gifts we need to be concerned primarily with caring and nurturing a strong relationship with our donors, and be less concerned with securing an immediate commitment. This is the cultivation part of the cycle.

Moves management theory came out of the idea of the cultivation cycle; it puts into place a system of planned initiatives to "move" an individual through the cycle, furthering their relationship with the organization to the point of philanthropic investment.

A "move" is not, as some have thought, making manipulative actions to get a person to make a commitment. Moves emphasize nurturing and fostering passion in an individual to *want* to make a significant difference in an institution, program, or cause that can bring the potential donor joy and satisfaction. They build upon the natural desire in people to want to become closer to things that are important to them.

Definition of a move

A move is a planned call (i.e. consciousness penetration with the prospective donor) with a predetermined and specific objective and fixed action, that brings the prospect/donor closer to the organization.

A move is significant enough of a contact that you would follow up by submitting a call report. It is accomplished by a letter, telephone or personal visit – the former almost always being the least preferable and beneficial, and the latter almost always being the most preferable and beneficial.

Who completes moves

Ultimately, a move can be completed by anyone working on behalf of the organization. However, to be most effective, a move should be completed by a staff development officer personally, or by another person (including volunteers) facilitated by the development officer.

Some organizations refer to the person managing/planning the moves as a Key Relationship Manager (KRM) or Account Manager (the former title highly preferred over the latter). Each KRM is responsible for managing a portfolio of relationships on behalf of the organization. In smaller organizations, the role of the KRM might be undertaken by a single fundraising officer or even the Executive Director, portioning some of their time to manage a major gift portfolio.

In larger organizations, entire departments exist to manage large numbers of relationships. Most major institutions have large teams of KRM's and KRM Managers to help focus resources and enhance effectiveness for the operation. At the University of British

Columbia the major gift unit has even hired its own full-time HR specialist to focus on recruitment and retention of the major gift specialists.

Responsibilities of the Key Relationship Manager (KRM)

The fundamental job of the KRM is to build and manage the implementation of a moves management plan for each relationship they are responsible for. The design of each moves management plan will be unique for each of the major gift prospects in the portfolio. Some plans may be short in length, and involve people interacting with the prospective donor. Other plans may be lengthy, detailed and sophisticated, involving many different volunteers, leaders of the organization, visits, and meetings.

Fundamentally however, each plan has the same objective - to move the prospective donor (through tailored moves and interactions) to the point where the prospective donor is ready to be presented with an ask.

Determining when to present the formal ask to the prospective donor, is a key responsibility of the KRM. Ideally, prior to presenting an ask, you should have answers to five key questions pertaining to the prospective donors. These five key questions are addressed in more detail by Tony Myers in Chapter 10 on Solicitation. The KRM's role is to find answers to these questions through planning and implementing moves.

It might help to consider these five questions as "five moons" (Figure 9.13) – and you are looking to get them into alignment before proceeding with an ask.

1. Amount
2. Timing
3. Project
4. Who's Asking
5. Who Should be Asked

Figure 9.13

While this paints a powerful picture and helps one remember the concept, I would only caution that it

is a rare thing that all "moons" can come into perfect alignment before it is the time to make an ask. It`s sometimes difficult to get full answers to all five key questions.

While we work towards getting answers to all five key questions, sometimes the time to make an ask is presented to us before the "moon's" have all aligned perfectly. This is what is sometimes referred to as the "art of fundraising" vs the "science of fundraising."

Trusting your inner voice, your instinct and experience is an important tool for the fundraising professional. Use the aligning moons as a guide. Prepare yourself adequately for the ask presentation by trying to get as complete as possible answers to the five key questions, but don't be too rigid in following it. Don't let opportunity pass you by while you are focused on aligning your moons. Five key questions:

1. What project should we present to the prospective donor for consideration?
2. How much is the gift that we are asking of the prospective donor?
3. What timing issues should we be aware of in presenting an ask to the prospective donor?
4. Who should be on the "ask team?"
5. Who should you ask?

Success in moves management is based on three factors: (1) the quality of your moves; (2) the frequency of your moves; and (3) the continuity of your moves.

It`s important that the moves organized and implemented are appropriate for the donor prospect (i.e. quality). What works as an appropriate move for one prospective donor might not work for another prospective donor – even within the same organization.

You are only limited by your imagination as to types of moves that you can plan and implement for prospective donors. Figure 9.14 shows examples of moves you might consider:

- write a personal note
- send a birthday card
- give a facility tour
- give a program tour
- give a behind the scenes tour
- invitation to internal event
- invite to community event
- introductions to Board members
- bring along to a conference
- ask for assistance/advice
- create a unique experience
- ask for a legacy review
- play a round of golf
- invite to a luncheon
- invite to a work party
- set up a home visit
- share information
- place a telephone call

Figure 9.14

Types of moves

There are essentially five types of moves that can be conducted:

1. Discovery move – An initial contact made without prior contact having been made to a prospect/donor within the past 24 months.
2. Cultivation move – A non-initial, pre-solicitation contact, for the purpose of engaging and maintaining the interest and involvement of a donor or prospective donor in the organizations people, programs, and plans.
3. Solicitation/ask move – The single predetermined act of presenting the ask (either verbal or written) for a gift.
4. Ask follow-up move – The ongoing process, or contacting the prospective donors, to reinforce, negotiate, solidify, and close the original ask.
5. Stewardship move – Ongoing contact whereby the organization seeks to be worthy of continued philanthropic support, including the acknowledgement of gifts, donors recognition, the honouring donor intent, prudent investment of gifts, and the effective and efficient use of funds to further the mission of the organization.

Process of implementing moves

Moves should be planned by the KRM and then implemented either by the KRM or by others (such as volunteers) organized by/through the KRM. There are six key steps to implement a moves management process:

1. Review the prospect/donor relationship with your organization. What has happened in the past? What milestones exist already? What is known about the donor so far? Take a look at which "moons" are already in alignment.
2. Plan the most beneficial next moves. Remember to be donor-centered. Knowing that your ultimate goal is to bring the donor prospect to a place closer to the organization, where they will be more receptive to making a gift, plan your next move accordingly. Should they be invited to see a new program launched (something you think might motivate them to get involved)?
3. Coordinate and check "moves" plans with others involved. In smaller organizations this is not as critical a step, but in larger organizations "traffic control" (the left hand knowing what the right hand is doing) can be very important. Also, in all sizes of organizations, making sure that all moves are coordinated will ensure that there are no misaligned initiatives taking place that are at cross-purposes with others happening within the organization. No loose cannons!
4. Execute the moves. Make it happen. If the KRM is implementing the move, then logistics are more simple than if the KRM is organizing others (volunteers and other staff members) to be involved in moves.
5. Evaluate what transpired. How did the donor prospect interact during the move? Were there key questions asked/answered? What new information was discovered that might help align the "moons?" Any next steps?

6. Report back to the individuals involved. It's important that all involved in the move for the organization's perspective be advised of the move implementation and outcome.

A WORD ABOUT VOLUNTEERS

An active and involved volunteer force is one of the most important elements of a major gift program. Boyd McBride will discuss volunteers in greater length in Chapter 18, but a few words here will reinforce the importance of this resource to a successful major gift program.

It's also important to understand that volunteers are among your most likely major gift donor prospects also.

We're already spoken about how people give to causes where organizational values overlap with their own, and because of this it is seldom the case that major gift fundraising can be done in a mechanized manner or without the involvement of enthusiastic and committed advocates for the organization's mission. The most successful major gift campaigns are those which have involved the people who are the organization's most effective boosters and partners – its volunteers.

The role of major gift volunteers

Your organization's major gift's campaign will need volunteers to serve in a variety of roles. Primarily, they can be involved as "chess pieces" for the "moves" that are being coordinated by the organization. Ideally, there should only be one "chess master" involved in planning and organizing the moves for a particular major gift prospect, however there may be many different "chess pieces," and volunteers are the best prospects for this role.

Volunteers can be involved in a variety of major gift roles, including: as case-makers; as prospectors of potential major gift donors; as qualifiers of major gift prospects; as cultivators; as door-openers; as note writers; as event attendees; as stewards; as advocates; as solicitors; and, as donors.

Volunteers also play a critical role as leaders for the cause including serving to validate and speak on behalf of the organization. Volunteers can play the role as "peer" in participating in approaches to donors

for gifts, and they serve to vouch for the organization in the community. Involving volunteers in major gift fundraising is a critical element to plan effectively.

CONCLUSION

Some general ideas about major gift work have been explored in this chapter, along with ways to approach and manage the major gift process, but when all is said and done, it is still the spirit behind the major gift process that determines its success.

Building relationships is the cornerstone of effective major gift fundraising. Without a relationship building culture, an organization will not be able to exploit the intersection of shared values between the prospective donor and the organization.

Just as important as the "relationships message" however, is the message about mastering a methodology that can move a prospective donor closer to the organization, to the point of presenting them with an invitation/opportunity to make a gift.

As Canadian non-profit organizations compete for perceived limited charitable dollars, care must be taken not to look like we are fighting ourselves for perceived limited donors. In major gift fundraising, it's important to stay focused on the long-term relationship and not the short-term gift.

With patience, comes reward. Care should be taken not to be distracted by immediate needs. Long-term success results from demonstrating to prospective donors how their personal life mission intersects with the organization's mission. As donors come to understand this connection, and then realize the connection, they become ready to make major gifts a reality in their life.

ADDITIONAL RESOURCES

Books

▶ CARNIE, CHRISTOPHER, GIGNAC, PAMELA M., GREENFIELD, JAMES M., & HART, TED. (2006). *Major donors: Finding Big Gifts in your Database and Online.* John Wiley & Sons, Inc.

▶ FREDRICKS, LAURA. (2006). *Developing Major Gifts: Turning Small Donors Into Big Contributors.* Jones and Barlett Publishers of Canada.

▶ INGRAHAM WALKER, JULIA. (2006). *Nonprofit Essentials: Major Gifts.* John Wiley & Sons, Inc.

▶ IRWIN-WELLS, SUZANNE. (2001). *Planning and Implementing Your Major Gifts Campaign.* The Fund Raising School at the Indiana University on Philanthropy.

▶ SARGEANT, A., & SHANG, JEN. (2010). *Fundraising Principles and Practice.* Jossey-Bass. USA.

ABOUT THE AUTHOR

Guy Mallabone, MA, CFRE

Guy is recognized internationally as one of the non-profit sector's most thoughtful and inspiring fundraising leaders. Since 1980 he has been providing exceptional advice and service to the non-profit sector.

Guy is currently President and CEO of Global Philanthropic, and has served as Vice-President of External Relations for SAIT Polytechnic and Chief Development Officer for the University of Alberta, as well as senior fundraising positions at the Canadian Red Cross Society and cultural non-profit organizations.

Guy is an active volunteer and has served as a former member of the International Board of Directors for AFP and CFRE International. He currently serves as Chair of Canada Advancing Philanthropy (a national advocacy group), and is currently an Adjunct Professor for the Master in Fundraising program at the University of Bologna, Italy.

Guy is a regular "heavy hitter" speaker and presenter on fund development at international conferences in Canada, the United States, Europe, South Africa and Australasia. Guy was recognized in 1999 by the Edmonton Chapter of AFP as the Outstanding Fundraising Professional, in 2009 by Alberta Venture Magazine as one of Alberta's most influential citizens, and by the Calgary Herald in 2009 as one of Calgary's 20 most compelling citizens. Most recently, AFP Calgary named Guy "Outstanding Fundraising Executive" for 2011.

CHAPTER 10

SOLICITATION
TONY MYERS, CFRE

When it comes to asking for money, there are three guiding principles that immediately come to mind.

- If you don't ask, you don't get
- Passion outdraws logic
- It's all about relationships – people give to people, peers give to peers

read more...

"If you don't ask, you don't get" is the crude equivalent of the biblical quote with the same message. When it comes to raising money, it seldom happens unless we ask. The challenge that many of us have is that asking for money can conjure up all sorts of emotions; especially fear.

"So, first of all, let me assert my firm belief that the only thing we have to fear is fear itself—nameless, unreasoning, unjustified terror which paralyzes needed efforts to convert retreat into advance."

- Franklin D. Roosevelt

When Franklin D. Roosevelt spoke those famous words his goal was to inspire a nation to move beyond the depression and to "advance" into the future. The expression "the only thing we have to fear is fear itself" is easy to say. It is a bit harder to act upon. My hope is that after you read this chapter, it will be easier to act.

PASSION OUTDRAWS LOGIC

One of the first workshops I ever attended on fundraising was given by a passionate fundraiser who told an amazing story of crawling across the floor of a bank shortly after an armed hold-up, to greet a donor she had been unable to meet after numerous earlier tries. She was passionate about her cause. This was her opportunity. She wasn't going to miss it. She greeted the donor, asked her if she was alright, comforted her with the knowledge the robber had left and police would arrive soon, and as one conversation led to another, they decided to meet at a later date and a gift eventually followed.

Passion outdraws logic. There are few things that engage a donor as much as passion for a cause.

IT IS ALL ABOUT RELATIONSHIPS

It sounds trite, but it is a fundamental principle upon which we ask for money. People give to people. Peers give to peers.

Think about when you were in public school and you came home with a fundraising project. Maybe you had a class trip you wanted to go on, or you decided

as a group you were going to raise money for the poor and the hungry. Whatever the project was, I would guess you went to those who you knew best. You probably started with your parents, aunts and uncles, and then moved on to ask your neighbours. And yes, I am assuming you had relationships with all these folks. In high school, college, university and beyond, when you had a cause you were passionate about and you wanted to raise money, you probably started with your peers and the people you know. The same basic principle applies to raising money for charities and non-profit organizations. People give to people, peers give to peers; it is all about relationships.

These three basic rules or principles are the foundation for the discussion in this chapter. Though there are numerous ways we can ask for money, this chapter focuses on face-to-face solicitation of major donors and high net-worth individuals. Please note, the principles and approaches to solicitation in major donor fundraising are highly adaptable to annual giving and planned giving.

We will begin by defining solicitation, place the activity in the context of the donor cycle and then outline various critical aspects of a solicitation process. The chapter explores the various elements of the process by connecting the person, with the opportunity and the motivation for giving. The anatomy of "the ask" will be followed by challenging you to develop an environment of success.

DEFINITIONS

Major donors are identified as those 10-20% who give the largest amount of money to a charity and who you generally solicit on a face-to-face basis. High net-worth individuals are major donors or prospects (potential major donors) who have ready access to one million dollars that they are able to invest or contribute.

Solicitation is the process involved in presenting an opportunity to a potential donor or prospect to make a financial contribution or to invest assets into the programs or activities of an organization. Sounds simple enough, doesn't it? Then why do we think so many people have difficulty with this activity?

Before we explore the details of how we can ask for money, it will be helpful to look at the psychology of "the ask" that will help put the challenges into perspective.

OVERCOMING FEAR

First of all, it is not about you. Many of us involved in this activity take this personally. I know I did when I first started asking for money. I thought it was up to me and me alone. I thought it was about me. I thought that if I asked someone for money that if they said yes or no, they would be saying yes or no to me. Then I realized it wasn't about me. It is not about me and it is not about you. What it is about is our ability - yours and mine, to represent a case for support to someone who has the ability to give to an organization, its programs or cause. We are facilitators. We present opportunities.

If we're working for the Girls and Boys Club, then we are representing the girls and boys who can't be in the room to ask for money. It is not about us. It is about the girls and the boys. What a privilege to represent girls and boys in need of a place to play, a safe place to gather or who need people to help supervise their activity. It is not about us. It is about those we represent. If we get a "yes," then we get a yes for the boys and the girls. And if we get a "no," normally it is not a "no" to us. It is a "no" to the boys and the girls.

Now I didn't say, it doesn't matter who asks for money. It does matter and more on that later in this chapter. The point here is that overcoming fear begins by not taking it personally. It begins by knowing it is not about you. It begins by knowing our role as a representative for those who can't be in the room to present an opportunity to give.

Second, it is not about the money. As Scott Decksheimer continually reminds me, we are not in the business of fundraising; we are in the business of program raising. We are not raising money for the sake of raising money. We are raising money to support programs that ultimately help people in some way.

Quite often people get nervous because they are asking for money. They get nervous because money is involved. Money tends to conjure up all kinds of emotions. The point is that money is not the object of the activity. Money is only a tool. It is only a resource intended to help an organization further its vision, mission, goals and objectives. There is no other reason to raise money. I find it easier to think of it as only one of the resources necessary to get the job done. The second way to overcome the fear is to realize that money is only a tool for the job. The job is to further the vision, mission and priorities of the charity.

Third, I think I'll embarrass people and make them feel bad if I ask for money. Continuous feedback received from workshops and seminars to the question of "How do you feel after being asked for money?" is as follows:

- "I felt important."
- "It actually felt good to know that I could make a difference."
- "I felt respected. Someone took the time to come and talk to me about the importance of their work and asked me to make a contribution."
- "I got excited about the opportunity."
- "I want to learn more about this."
- "This was a good experience for me. I don't know if I'll give, but I want to give it more thought."
- "I like the way I was treated. Nobody was pushy. I didn't feel pressured."

You can see from the responses that people can and do feel good about being asked. It is how people are asked and how they are treated in the process that will impact on how they feel. If you are embarrassed, they will be embarrassed. It you feel bad, they will feel bad. If you are excited they will see, feel and experience your excitement (remember passion outdraws logic). If you have done your homework, you'll feel more comfortable and more confident.

ATTITUDE IS EVERYTHING

Your talent determines what you can do. Your motivation determines how much you are willing to do. Your attitude determines how well you do it.

When we ask for money there are two kinds of people we want to focus on; the donor and the beneficiary.

The first kind of person we want to focus on is the person for whom the money is being raised—the beneficiary. When asking for money, we are only there to represent those who can't be there. If we are raising money for the poor, for cancer care, or for the hungry we are only there to ask on behalf of others. Remember the "boys and girls?" When asking for money, we need to focus on the people we are truly representing.

The second person we want to focus on is the donor. It is not about what *we* want. It is not even about what the *charity* wants (though of course we take that into consideration). The case for support built to guide our work, is only that. It is a guide that outlines the needs, and presents the arguments we "could" use to ask for money. The focus of the ask has to be on the donor. It has to focus on the donor's interests, on the donors values, on the donor's aspirations and on the donor's expectations.

It seems a bit evangelical to think that as a fundraiser, we can actually make a difference in the lives of beneficiaries and donors. I believe the greatest difference we can make in the work we do is by providing donors and high net-worth individuals an opportunity to give to something important to them, something consistent with their values. When we do this well, at the right time, with the right person, we can present opportunities that transform the lives of beneficiaries and donors alike.

Consider this quote from a high net-worth individual who gave a recent gift of $1M.

> "I passed the psychological barrier. I remember once my father saying to me ... 'it looks like your rice bowl isn't very full.' I was confused by what he said, so I asked him what he meant. He repeated it again. He said, 'Your rise bowl mustn't be very full. If it was, you would be willing to share some of it with others.'
>
> I remember five years ago, giving $10,000 was a lot of money and giving that amount of money was a difficult thing for me to decide to do. Then I gave $50,000. And then $100,000. So when (a non-profit) came to me and asked for $10 million, I gave them $1 million. And it wasn't as difficult for me as it would have been some years earlier because I had crossed the psychological barrier. You get to the point that the amount does not mean that much.

> I've had a five-year conspicuous education. I've gone from conspicuous giving to a new plane where self-actualization is the only thing left. It is now more about legacy giving."

Over a five-year period of relationship development and constant opportunities to make a difference, this donor's life has changed. And so have the lives of those who he has helped. The relationship between the donor and non-profit have gone from transactional (you ask for money, I give you money) to transformational (you ask me for money, I give you money, it changes my life and the lives of others and I feel different about myself).

Asking for money is only one of a whole set of skills—called fundraising. Preparing to ask for money is a discipline—called development. Asking for money – head-to-head, heart-to-heart, soul-to-soul – can be transformational and it is called philanthropy.

ASKING IS ONLY 5% OF THE WORK

We already mentioned solicitation is only a small fraction of all the work we do in raising money—particularly in major gifts. It is just one step in the process of raising money. It is only one of five steps along the path outlined in the donor cycle. Nonetheless, solicitation is an equal partner with all other five elements of the Donor Cycle (see Figure 10.1).

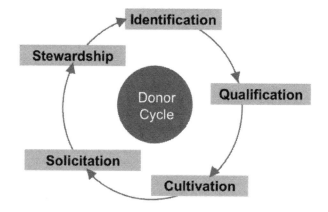

Figure 10.1

Regardless of what kind of fundraising we are involved in, we still need to guide donors through the five stages of the donor cycle. We need to identify people and organizations that are likely to give, qualify them in terms of their linkage to the charity, ability to give and their interest in the charity, cause, initiative or cause being proposed.

Cultivation is a process of bringing the donor closer to the charity and the charity closer to the donor so that an ask can be made. Once the ask is made, and the donor has given a gift, stewardship activities ensure that the money goes where it was supposed to go, that it is used for the purposes intended and that it gets the results expected. Stewardship is often described as the process of taking care of the money and taking care of the donor relationship. It is critical to take care of both, in order to get another gift.

The point to be made is this: asking people for money involves the least amount of time in the process. Asking for money involves only a fraction of the work that needs to be done. But it is important work. As we all know, "if you don't ask, you don't get."

METHOD OF THE ASK

There are many ways to go about asking for money. Figure 10.2 outlines just a few of the methods available to us.

Ways of Asking	
Method	Success Rate
Donor Acquisition – Mailing to Prospects	1% - 2%
Donor Renewal – Mailing to Donors	5% - 15%
Telephone – Prospects & Donors	25% - 20%
Face-to-Face – Prospects & Donors	70%-80%

Figure 10.2

Figure 10.2 highlights the success rate that we can anticipate when asking for a gift face-to-face, person-to-person. There is a sense that if someone is willing to see us and talk about a gift, then there is a good chance

that we will be able to facilitate a gift on behalf of a charity.

Keeping in mind the relative success of acquisition mailing, direct mail, telephone solicitation and person to person asking, I have a bias for combining a number of elements in the personal solicitation activities undertaken.

For example, I'm not likely to get an appointment to see a donor, unless I give them a call. There are exceptions to the rule of course. I may see a donor prospect at a special event and arrange to have coffee or lunch. But most often I will have to make a call. And of course, I'm using the telephone or in some cases e-mail.

I may ask for a gift verbally or I may put my ask in writing. I often use both methods simultaneously and will only limit an ask to a written proposal when it is the only way I can reach a donor. I always want to meet personally and present an ask face-to-face. Nothing can replace a personal ask.

People give to people. When we ask personally, we put a human face on the process. It is always more difficult to say no in person and in particular to a peer, than it is to say no to a letter or a proposal on paper.

How I go about the ask is only one of the questions I need to figure out before asking. There are several other questions I'll want to address before sitting down with a major donor or high-net worth individual.

THE FIVE W'S – WHAT I SHOULD KNOW BEFORE ASKING

What project or cause to ask for, how much to ask for, who to ask, when to ask and who will actually do the asking, are questions I want to answer before I make an ask. If I answer these questions I'm far more likely to be able to frame an ask in a manner that will result in a yes.

These five questions (introduced by Guy Mallabone in Chapter Nine), also known as the five W's or the five "right" questions, are the very questions that we seek to answer before we make an ask. The five W's are questions that we attempt to answer in the qualification and cultivation stages in the donor cycle. The five W's have always given me an automatic agenda for cultivation visits with major donors. When I go into a major donor meeting I want to be listening for the answers to the five questions.

Let's review each question in more detail, one at a time.

1. What is the right project/program?

Most charities have a number of projects or programs going on at the same time. Some will appeal to certain donors more than others. Our job as a fundraiser is to listen to a donor, watch for their responses, identify the key areas of interest and engage them in the areas of greatest interest. The reason is simple. Donors are more likely to give to areas of interest, and are more likely to give more to *their* area of interest than they are to give to *your* area of interest.

This does not mean I will ignore the program priorities of the charity I am representing. However, if I know and understand the donors bias, I'm far more likely to be able to facilitate an investment or contribution that meets the donors priorities and addresses the charities vision and mission

2. What is the right amount to ask for?

If you think it is difficult to determine how much to ask for, you are not alone. It is a tough question for all of us to answer. Finding the answer begins with prospect research (see Chapter 4) and continues with conversations with the donor about areas of interest and degree of interest. Prospect research can determine how much a donor has given to other causes or projects. By bringing together information about gifts given by a prospective donor to similar projects, their net worth or other indicators of wealth (i.e. property value, summary of stocks and bonds held, current employment and position, it is possible to make a "guesstimate" of what you might ask.

With guesstimate in hand, additional conversations with your CEO, Board members and professional colleagues in your organization, will give you an opportunity to narrow the scale and scope of your ask.

Think it through to the best of your ability. Consult with other people in your organization, and in particular those who may know the prospect, their financial position and their affiliation with your cause.

Finding an answer to this question is never easy. But if you do your homework, maximize input, weigh the value of the input you get, talk with your colleagues in

your own organization, my experience is that you will build a comfort level on how much to ask for.

One of the questions I'm often troubled by is do I go high, or do I go low in the ask I am about to make? In the majority of cases, once you've placed an ask on the table, you can seldom go higher. So when in doubt, increase the ask amount – but not too much. There is a balance here. Asking too little, can result in leaving money on the table. Asking too much indicates to the prospective donor that you are either greedy or that you have not done your homework.

Another guide I use in setting an ask amount is the donor's financial stage in life. Most of us go through three stages: wealth accumulation, wealth protection, wealth disbursement. And that doesn't mean I have to get access to their bank balance. You'll know from reading Chapter 4 that there is a great deal of information we can access from public sources that will tell us about an individual's financial position. I find that knowing where a donor is in the wealth cycle, adds another level of consideration and helps me to determine the amount of an ask.

3. Who is the right person to ask?

I will never forget the time a well-known charity identified the right project for the right person and had identified the right amount ($1 million) but took for granted "who" they would ask.

The donor was a very wealthy elderly gentleman who had worked all his life building a very successful company. The opportunity was there to name a significant sports facility in his name. As a sports fan himself and a former athlete, he was enamored with the idea. However, to complicate matters, the elderly gentleman was ill and there was a concern that if the ask was not made soon, he might not be around long enough to answer the request.

On the day of the ask, those involved, visited the home of the gentleman and asked him for the gift. His wife was ignored in the process. It wasn't that she was ruled out—she just wasn't included. You can imagine my colleagues' surprise when they found out that this gentleman had given power of attorney and control of all of his financial affairs to his wife. The person who had not been included in the process, was the very person who had the ultimate power to say yes. Ultimately the organization received a gift in excess of the original ask – however it took two years to recover from the mistake made. Lesson learned.

We must never take for granted who has the power to say yes. We must never take for granted who needs to be in the room during the ask. Whether working with an individual donor or a major corporation my habit is to continually seek the answer to the question, *who* can say yes? Who is it that can really make things happen?

4. Who is the right person to do the ask?

When we ask for money in support of a project or cause, the goal is to get a yes. If we understand that people give to people and that peers give to peers, then we want to find that right person, or the right combination of people, who can get a yes. The challenge is mixing and matching asking styles and personalities that will be effective. The other challenge is that the mixing and matching changes with every ask.

There is a common perception that raising money is about twisting arms; that we have to be tough; that we can only be successful if we are really persistent and insistent.

I would be lying if I said that style doesn't work sometimes. However I would not encourage you to take that approach. In a recent study I conducted on major donors and high net-worth individuals, one of the things that influenced their decision making was the manner in which they were treated. Treating a donor with respect, providing them with the information they need, and giving them the time to make the decision that is right for them, will get the best results.

The right person to do the ask is the one who:

- Has a relationship with the prospective donor
- Understands their motivations and values
- Knows the charity and its case for support
- Has already given a gift themselves
- Knows how to ask with confidence and certainty
- Demonstrates respect for the donor
- Does not possess an attitude of entitlement

The best person to ask has a relationship with the donor, is seen as a peer, and has a passion for the charity and the cause. It may take more than one person to get the characteristics you need in order to make the

ask. That's O.K. More on this later when we look at the anatomy of the ask.

5. When is the right time to ask?

Ideally the right time to ask is when you have answers to the "Five W's." Take some comfort in knowing that doesn't always happen. If we all waited for the "perfect" time to ask, we might never get around to it. So it is not about finding the "perfect" time to ask.

It is about listening for the kinds of things going on in a donor's life. For example, if they are a business owner have they just sold their business? If so, when does the deal close? Are they in the process of accumulating wealth or at the stage in life when they are considering allocating the wealth they have? If they are in business, how is business going? Are they buying assets or are they selling assets? Conversations about vacations may tell you whether they have a cottage or if they own a sailing boat or a yacht. Has there been a recent separation or divorce. Have their kids just started University and are they helping pay the way. These are all questions that will help me determine an appropriate time to ask.

For the sake of discussion, let's assume for the moment that you've come up with the answers to the five questions. What's next?

ANATOMY OF THE ASK

If you have asked for a major gift before, then you will be familiar with these steps and this will be a reminder for you. If you have not yet experienced the joy of asking for a major gift, the following information will act as a guide.

The golden rule in real estate is location, location, location. If you buy a home, in a good location, then it will maintain its value and when the time comes, it will be much easier to sell.

In major gift fundraising, the golden rule of asking is preparation, preparation, preparation. If you prepare for an ask, it allows you to do a good job of representing your organization. Preparation gives you a better chance of representing your cause, of putting forth a good case for support. Preparation builds alignment in the ask team. Preparation shows respect for the donor. Above all, preparation builds confidence and certainty.

Confidence and certainty builds trust. People are more likely to give money to people and organizations they trust.

If we don't take the time to prepare thoroughly, we reduce our chances of being successful.

Put it in writing

Writing is a discipline. It forces us to put our ideas and thoughts down in a logical and orderly manner. It forces us to consider how others will interpret the messages we send and the nature of the ask we are about to make. Writing forces clarity. If you can write it, then you have really thought it through. If you've thought it through, you are more likely to be able to deliver the ask verbally and with confidence. If you cannot write it down, then you probably have not taken the time you need and put in the effort required to successfully ask for a large sum of money.

Writing it down means putting the ask in the form of a letter to the donor (even if you never send it) or in the form of a proposal outlining the opportunity to give while identifying specifics regarding the ask. A letter or proposal answers questions about what the money is for, how it will be used, what benefits come from the investment and the difference it will make in the world. Writing it down shows respect for the donor because, it often forces you to think things through from the donor's perspective.

If you decide to hand over the written letter or proposal, it gives the donor a document to ponder and think about after you've left the meeting. It allows for a proper evaluation of the strengths and weaknesses in your case. And it helps them decide in your favour.

It will help you to be thoroughly prepared and helps you ensure others involved in the ask team are prepared as well.

The ask team

There are three roles we play when asking for money. Sometimes these roles can be exercised by one person, but more often than not, it takes more than one person to fill all three roles.

I. **The asker:** There needs to be someone in the room who can actually "ask" for the money. There needs to be someone in the room who can actually "mouth the words." This role should never be taken for granted. If we are heading out to ask a major donor for $1,000 or $100,000, there just has to be someone who can actually ask for the money. There just has to be someone who can say the words, "… based on all we've talked about today, we would like to ask you to consider a gift of $100,000." There is no substitute for what I call "mouthing the words."

II. **The influencer:** If we believe major gift fundraising is about relationships and if we believe that peer to peer asking results in the greatest success, then who is it that we can find who is considered a peer to the donor and at the same time has a relationship with the donor. Finding this person to join in the ask, or to do the ask (if it is the right person) may well increase the likelihood of success.

III. **The observer:** I remember asking a President of a large international corporation for a personal gift of $50,000. As soon as I asked for the money, he took his left hand and rubbed the back of his neck—a nonverbal gesture indicating defensiveness. I knew something was wrong. I adjusted the conversation accordingly.

I had asked for too much, not beyond what he may have been able to give, but too much for a first gift and too much considering where he was in the financial stage of his life. Asking for money can be a highly emotional, engaging and for some a private and sensitive interaction. We want to have an observer in the room watching and listening for verbal and nonverbal cues that let us know how it's going.

In some cases, and in the example provided, we play all three roles at the same time. In other cases we can have two or three people involved in the ask, each with a firm understanding of their specific role. I'm comfortable having two people ask one donor, however I avoid a three-on-one situation. Too many askers in the room with one donor can bring on an air of intimidation and as a result can be detrimental to the desired outcome.

Another role that needs to be accommodated for (at least in my experience) is the role of the "expert witness," the person who is best positioned to speak about the case or the project at hand. This might be the surgeon who can speak to the hospital's case; or the artistic director for the museum; or the President of the university, but someone needs to take on this mantle.

Regarding the number of people in the room, one is ok and can be appropriate. Two is appropriate and usual. Three is ok, but more rare. It's even more rare to have more than three. If you are asking an institution for a gift, you might have a person to take notes or work the computer - more of a formal presentation, but for individuals, three max!

While we have focused here on individuals, when preparing an ask for a corporation, you may wish to bring along several copies of your proposal.

THE ASK AGENDA

Draft an agenda. It is not overkill. You have upwards of three people heading into a meeting to ask for a significant amount of money. Coordinating the activity of three people is enhanced by the existence of an agenda. Write it out. Show it to the others who are going to ask for the money. However it is not necessary to have the agenda at the ask meeting.

Use the agenda to keep the parties involved in the ask, informed about the process, aligned with the order of activity and to allow for an orderly and seamless interaction with the donor. If you have an agenda, and something goes wrong, you're more likely to get back on track before the end of the meeting, than if you are winging it. See Figure 10.3 for a sample agenda.

WHEN IS NO ... A NO?

Even if the donor responds with an absolute "no" and you've determined that in "no way" will you get a gift this time, there is still work to be done following the ask. You'll want to keep a record of the meeting, make notes on the reaction of the donor, determine what follow-up may be possible such as sending out regular newsletters, providing updates on the progress of the plan or providing additional information as requested.

I may hear "no" in an ask meeting, but not "never" - there is a difference. Most often when I hear "no" I hear "no, not right now" or "no not at this time" or "no, I don't know enough about your organization yet." No seldom means, "No, I will never, ever give you

anything, for any reason, at any time for any cause." "No" is never a "no" until it's been qualified in terms of its scope and meaning.

Turning a "NO" into a "YES!"

Turning a "no" into a "yes" is actually not that complicated. it may be difficult or in some cases impossible, but it is not that complicated. Turning a no into a yes is a matter of finding out why a no was given in the first place. Finding out the reason for a no is a matter of asking the potential donor the right questions after you've received a no response. Then it is dependent on the donor's willingness to respond honestly and directly to your questions. Because "no" is never a "no" until it is qualified, then what are the questions we need to ask the donor to determine the scope and meaning of a "no" response. Our job is to continually explore the "no" until we hit a solid roadblock.

- Is it the charity / NGO?
- Is it the project?
- Is it the amount?
- Is it the timing?

To turn a no into a yes, we need to find out if there is something about the charity or NGO that doesn't appeal to the donor. If there is, then we need to determine if there is anything we can do about it. The same applies to the project. If there is something about the project then we need to determine if there is anything we can do about it.

If it is the timing, then changing the timing does not have to be a complicated matter. If the donor is willing to entertain an ask six months or a year later, then it is a matter of recording that fact, keeping the donor informed in the interim, and coming back at the time designated by the donor and making the ask again.

If it is a matter of the amount, then the key is to determine what amount would be suitable to the donor at this time in their life and in consideration of their financial circumstances.

AGENDA

Meeting location:

Name of Donor(s):

Name of Participants:

Project or Cause:

Ask Amount:

1. Introductions

2. Review of Donor's association with the charity and or the cause.

3. Review of the Donor's previous gifts and the benefits flowing from those gifts.

4. Indication of the current project and need, with reference to previous conversations regarding the same.

5. State your understanding of donor's commitment to charity and the cause.

6. The Ask.

7. Nothing. That is what you say after asking. You say absolutely nothing. Once we ask, we are absolutely silent until the donor responds.

8. Respond to questions, concerns, objections (a term that is used quite often is "obstacle" ... our job is to wait for the obstacles and then focus on removing them.

9. If Yes ... then

    a. Say Thank you. Reinforce the value of the gift and the outcome

    b. Pledge form – if the donor says yes invite the signing of a pledge form outlining how much will be given, when and how the payments will be made

    c. Gift Agreement – if the gift is large and complex there may be a requirement to draft a gift agreement outlining the purpose of the gift, the payment details and specifics and a detailed explanation and description of the allocation of the funds including reporting obligations of the charity / NGO

10. If No .... then

    a. Say thank you for their time and consideration

    b. Try to determine why a "no" was given

    c. See if there is follow-up or additional information that may change a no into a yes

11. Prepare to be grateful. Whether you get a yes or no, be prepared to show gratitude. Those who show gratitude will be welcomed back another day. Those who are not grateful may convey a message of entitlement, isolate potential donors and initiate a negative impression of their charity.

12. Determine next steps – never, ever leave a meeting without agreeing on next steps. If it is a yes, then it is the "beginning" of a new relationship. If it is a no, it is the beginning of a journey to a yes, and you'll want to agree on the steps to be taken.

Figure 10.3

If it is the amount, don't assume that you've asked for too much money. A colleague asked a wealthy woman for $100,000 annual gift in support of a university. After more than a dozen refusals, my colleague asked the woman why she had decided not to give to the university. The woman said the amount that she was asked was not enough to do what she wanted to do for the university. This donor wanted to build an architectural school in honour of her husband. Tens of millions of dollars later, the school was built. The ask that was made 14 times was too low. When asked at the right level, the donation was forthcoming. The lesson here is two-fold. Find out why a no is given, And if it is about the money, never automatically assume the ask has been too high.

There is one other reason why a donor may choose not to give. A donor may decide not to give, because the person asking is not the right person or the method and manner of the ask is not appropriate. We could ask a donor that question, but it is an awkward and potentially embarrassing thing to ask, both for the donor, the charity and the person asking. We can only hope that we can find the answer by asking the first four questions outlined above.

HOW WOULD YOU LIKE TO BE ASKED?

Arrogance breeds resistance. Entitlement breeds avoidance. Greed breeds rejection. There are rooms in which arrogance, entitlement and greed are present.

Listening is an act of humility. Kindness is an act of compassion. Honesty is an expression of trust. There are other rooms in which you will find humility, compassion, honesty and trust; rooms in which people have conversations and listen to each other.

If you were a donor which room would you want to be in?

As a fundraiser, our ultimate goal is to raise money. As a successful fundraiser we probably want to raise money in a room that has heart, in a room that a donor would want to visit a second time. A room that optimizes the potential of all involved in the process.

As fundraisers, we can influence the environment of the rooms in which we work. If we build rooms in which we are comfortable, we are likely to build rooms in which others will be comfortable as well.

- If you don't ask, you don't get.
- Passion outdraws logic.
- It is all about relationships. People give to people. Peers give to peers. Build rooms and create environments where people want to give.

If you do, you'll not only raise money, facilitate donor gifts, support the mission and vision of charities and NGOs, you will likely realize the incredible satisfaction of helping to make a difference in the world.

CONCLUSION

Major gifts make a difference in the world. They also have the potential to make a major difference in any fundraising initiative. The ability to make the difference depends on our ability to ask for a gift in a way that allows a donor to say yes. We will never have the power to get another person to say yes. Our only power and strength lies in our ability to present a strong, urgent and compelling case that resonates with the donor and is consistent with their values and priorities.

So are there some final suggestions I might be able to give?... Yes!

- Relax.
- Leave your ego at the door – it is not about "you" it is about the charity, the cause, the victims, or the clients you represent.
- Know that you are not asking for a handout, you are giving an opportunity for a donor to give, and in the process, to realize the satisfaction that comes from making a difference in the world.
- You're talking to someone that is already interested in what you are doing (or they wouldn't be talking to you).
- It is just a conversation that ends in a request for someone to give to a cause, an organization or a group of people you have been so privileged to represent.
- Asking for money is a noble and worthy activity. It is at it's core a philanthropic act and an expression of the love of humankind.

For me, asking for money is a joy, it is a privilege and it is fun. When I ask, I am grateful for the opportunity to represent those who for whatever reason, can't be there with me, those who may not have the skill, ability, time or know-how to go about the task. There are fewer greater satisfactions in life than asking for money for causes and people who are worthy.

Try it! If you approach it with a positive attitude, and a "can do" perspective, and have done your homework, not only will you be successful, but I really think you too will enjoy the process.

ADDITIONAL RESOURCES

▶ AHERN, TOM AND SIMONE JOYAUX. (2008). *Keep Your Donors: The Guide to Better Communications & Stronger Relationships.* New York: John Wiley and Sons, Inc.

▶ BURNETT, KEN. (2002). *Relationship Fundraising: A Donor Based Approach to the Business of Raising Money, 2nd ed.* San Francisco: Jossey-Bass.

▶ DOVE, KENT E., LINDAUER, JEFFREY A. & MADVIG, CAROLYN P. (2002). *Conducting a Major Gifts and Planned Giving Program.* San Francisco: Jossey-Bass.

▶ FREDRICKS, LAURA. (2006). *Developing Major Gifts: Turning Small Donors into Big Contributors.* Sudbury, MA: Jones and Bartlett Learning.

▶ GRACE, KAY SPRINKEL. (2005). *Beyond Fund Raising, 2nd ed.* New York: John Wiley and Sons, Inc.

▶ GREENFIELD, JAMES M. (1999). *Fund Raising: Evaluating and Managing the Fund Development Process, 2nd ed.* New York: John Wiley and Sons, Inc.

▶ HART, TED AND GREENFIELD, JAMES M., GIGNAC, PAMELA M. & CARNIE, C. (2006). *Major Donors: Finding Big Gifts in Your Database and Online.* New York: John Wiley and Sons, Inc.

▶ JOYAUX, SIMONE P. (2011). *Strategic Fund Development: Building Profitable Relationships That Last, 3rd ed.* Aspen Publishers.

▶ PANUS, JEROLD. (1984). *Mega Gifts: Who gives them, who gets them.* Chicago: Bonus Books Inc.

▶ PEACOCK, ROBERT IAN. (2007). *Face Time: Relationship Philanthropy. A Resource for Canadian Major Gift Fundraising.* Toronto: Civil Sector Press.

▶ PETTEY, JANICE GOW. (2008). *Ethical Fundraising: A Guide for Nonprofit Boards and Fundraisers.* New York: John Wiley and Sons, Inc.

▶ ROSSO, HENRY A & ASSOCIATES. (2003). Temple, Eugene R Editor. *Hank Rosso's Achieving Excellence in Fund Raising.* San Francisco: John Wiley & Sons Inc.

▶ SARGEANT, ADRIAN; SHANG, JEN AND ASSOCIATES. (2010). *Fundraising Principles and Practice.* San Francisco: John Wiley & Sons Inc.

▶ SKRYPNEK, MIKE (2010). *Philanthropy: An Inspired Process.* Calgary: Bound Publishing.

ABOUT THE AUTHOR

Tony Myers, PhD, CFRE

Tony is the founder, principal and senior fundraising council with Myers & Associates, an international fundraising consultancy based in Canada with offices in Calgary and Edmonton.

Tony has spoken and made presentations on philanthropy, development and fundraising on four continents.

He has participated in some of the largest and most successful fundraising campaigns in Canada. His work has been recognized through national and international awards. He has written articles for Canadian Fundraising & Philanthropy, local fundraising

publications, has recently completed a chapter for "Fundraising Feasibility Studies" and is currently working on a book on Philanthropy.

Tony just completed his PhD – a comparative study on primary influences on philanthropic decision-making in Canada and India.

Tony brings passion and commitment to his work in support of philanthropy.

CHAPTER 11

CAPITAL CAMPAIGNS
NICHOLAS OFFORD, BA

Why a capital campaign?

It can be said that fundraising and philanthropy are fundamental forms of social activism; the organization of people, resources and ideas to achieve significant objectives that will benefit the communities in which we live. In this regard the capital campaign – though in this day and age the word capital can be a misnomer as campaigns for significant operational investments beyond traditional bricks and mortar or endowment are becoming more common– represents the apex of well-planned and structured fundraising to raise funds at a much higher level than the normal infrastructure would be able to secure. *read more...*

For most charities a campaign is not just about addressing the needs of an organization, but more essentially about testing its relevance in the donor marketplace. Asking hard questions about whether or not people care enough about your goals - not merely to support them verbally but to go the next step and take action. Sometimes "action" (through giving or volunteering) can put charities under a microscope of external eyes that makes the organization uncomfortable. It is no longer good enough to "take the money and run," as campaigns often did in the latter half of the last century. Now campaigns will have donors, volunteers, and stakeholders, especially government, asking questions about impact, relevance, and sustainability.

Capacity building opportunities are often considered first when planning campaign. It provides a chance to raise the profile of the charity, to recruit new volunteers to the cause, to reach out and have conversations with new donors, and to build fundraising infrastructure and experience that will provide momentum for the future. Beyond the dollars raised, these are vital elements of raising the game for any organization to address their mission.

However, campaigns and campaign planning will surely expose a weak board, poor organizational leadership, ill-thought out plans, and management limitations. There is also the potential risk that people just won't care enough about you to identify and give you the resources you need. In that regard, the planning process for a campaign often serves as a wake-up call to an organization and will force change, or the campaign won't get to a public phase. Most campaigns fail at this early stage, while very few fail once launched publicly. This gives some board members the impression that "anyone can have a successful campaign" or that "if they can do it, we can too" without fully understanding the difficult and meticulous planning that goes into any successful campaign. As is often said, campaigns are like fine dining: what the customer experiences is only 10% of the time and effort put into bringing the meal to the table.

The goal with this chapter is not to provide a step-by-step guide to mounting a campaign, (though the reader should know what to expect through the process) but to encourage strategic thinking on where your organization stands in regards to mounting a campaign, while avoiding the crucial mistakes so many make.

INTEGRATED PROJECT PLANNING AND PRIORITY SETTING

Getting started the right way on the journey is vital. A clear agenda needs to be set with leadership from senior management and the CEO in particular, along with key players from the board. For any exercise in strategic planning, defining the scope and methodology of the planning work and ensuring discipline in execution is essential to get through (what can be) a difficult moment in the life of an organization. Why is it difficult? By necessity, strategic planning asks questions that should challenge the status quo of a charity. Are we achieving our mission? Do we have the right business model? How do we know we are successful? What tools do we need to have even greater impact? What do we continue to do that is no longer core to our mission? All such questions test the current structure of a charity. In some cases program leaders and employees will be nervous about the choices being made and about changes that will affect them directly.

Achieving balance in planning is particularly difficult. Striking the right tone between being adequately consultative while also being entrepreneurial and opportunistic is a delicate matter for all charitable leadership. Strategic planning, particularly in the institutional or major organizational setting, has become problematic. In part this is driven by a management psyche that is often geared toward stakeholders that aren't donors – government, students, patients, clients, other users, the public – and one that seeks to be at once risk-free and inclusive. The result is often mushy and meaningless vision and mission statements that fail to capture the imagination of key players inside and outside an organization.

The other key risk around planning is that projects will get too far advanced, even to the extent of receiving government funding, before the community hears about it. At this point it is usually too late to have a meaningful dialogue with a community of donors around the plan. This problem is particularly acute when a given leader has the command and authority to fulfill highly ambitious agendas for growth but fails to bring the rest of the community along for the ride. The risk is that plans become too ambitious and unsustainable and the community falls short of funding either the requisite capital amount or cannot sustain the operating costs that the expansion implies (assuming of course that there has been a realistic analysis of those costs).

Canada has had more than its fair share of government bailouts for stalled capital projects and operational infrastructure. And, while many may suggest that it is an appropriate role for government to play, it is becoming increasingly clear that governments are scrutinizing projects much more closely than ever before. Moreover, donors are especially interested in knowing that their funds will be used in the way they intend and that the project has a real and well planned way of coming to fruition.

Many capital campaign architects believe that including donors, even at the earliest stage of project planning, is absolutely vital. Some institutional leaders don't like this approach because they are anxious about providing others with an in-depth look at the difficult issues in a charity "warts and all." Some leaders focus solely on accentuating the positive. However, there is no question, that if the future of the organization is going to be dependent on substantially raising more funds, bringing potential donors in on the planning process will not only add the value of external perspectives, but will also increase ownership of the plan by the board and key donor stakeholders. They will feel they have had a say and it will be easier for the organization to recruit them as leaders and lead donors when the campaign launches.

Research on the topic also strongly indicates that people are much more likely to give when they "have a voice" in the organization. The strategic planning exercise is a wonderful opportunity to engage a donor, alumni, patient, or other community in a dialogue around what matters to them. Modern online (you are collecting those e-mail addresses aren't you?) research tools make market research available to the charitable sector in ways that were previously not affordable. These are powerful tools for testing the views of your community (in larger institutions, the internal community is particularly important) on your plans for the future. Having market research expertise to help plan and execute donor attitude studies is especially important for credibility purposes. You will need several hundred respondents to generate a statistically valid sample set.

Without question, such research empowers decision makers around the strategic plan to both promote projects that have broad appeal to donors and to reconsider the financing of certain projects that hold no appeal for those who might give.

Whether community engagement in strategic planning occurs through group consultation or active engagement in the planning process, the goal is to have the community that supports the charity own the project as much as those insiders who oversee and manage it.

GOAL SETTING AND PLANNING STUDIES

All campaigns are built around the need to fulfill five key elements for success:

1. Securing volunteer leadership that will provide you the requisite access to the donor community;
2. Having an interested and committed community of prospective donors that will be open to an approach for funding;
3. Having campaign projects packaged in a clearly articulated case for support and attendant communications strategy that will inspire philanthropic action;
4. Imposing the discipline of a campaign plan and timetable to ensure focus on achieving the goal in a timely way; and
5. Creating a management team that will provide the necessary energy and guidance to ensure success.

It may sound facetious, but all campaigns are achievable in the fullness of time. However, the key to goal setting is to find a number that is believable and can be fulfilled in a reasonable time frame. The primary reason for this is that many larger campaigns simply take too long. Volunteers, for the most part, aren't interested in being campaign leaders for a decade-long exercise. They want to accomplish something and measure their success. Charities should want that as well. Instead of rolling the kitchen sink into a long list of campaign priorities (40% won't get funded in a campaign that includes multiple priorities), it is better to go from success to success, and build a philanthropic culture.

Campaign themes and communications are also stronger and more focused with fewer specific objectives than broad philanthropic fields of opportunity. Campaigns are also closely associated with the vision of the charity's CEO so they should not commit to a campaign that cannot be accomplished before their term of office is concluded. This is unfair to successors at hospitals, universities and arts organizations who arrive in office with their own ideas but must first clean up fundraising priorities from their predecessor.

There are essentially two approaches organizations may take when planning a campaign: the first is to determine what you need in terms of a goal and then build a plan to achieve it, the second is to determine what you can raise and then prioritize your needs to fit this amount.

In the first instance, there is almost no reference to historic performance or the current state of the fundraising management and volunteer leadership cohort. This is a fairly common situation for clients considering their first campaign or is committed to a project that is far beyond their historic capabilities. This is the case where a museum needs a new building, or a welfare agency needs to build a new housing project, or where a theatre company wants to conduct an endowment initiative. In such cases, fundraising track records and other elements are largely not in place and so a planning study that outlines the steps an organization needs to take to become campaign-ready is a vital resource.

A planning study, usually conducted by a consulting firm, will look at the client's current fundraising operation and the kind of capacities it will require in order to raise a specific objective. Planning studies should include:

- An internal audit of resources, personnel, and corporate culture with a view to assessing the leadership and management commitment to the initiative and to identify gaps that will need to be filled.

- Interviews with 15-25 key external leaders, including selected board members, who may be either potential campaign leaders or leadership donors. The views of this group are disproportionately important for if they show weakness in their support and commitment to the project, this is a major red flag at the outset and cause

for concern (For those of us in the consulting world, the worst red flag occurs when the client fails to even secure such interviews!).

- A review of the current internal and external communications program and suppliers and proposed communications strategies to support the campaign.

- A donor database assessment. These take many different forms but the need to identify high-net worth individuals who might have the capacity to make a major gift is most important. More consultants are now moving toward sophisticated projected giving models that have shown reasonably robust predictive fundraising forecasts.

- A detailed plan. This will include a timetable for implementation, a staffing model, a volunteer model (with detailed job descriptions, a "Standards of Giving Chart" (showing the size and number of gifts that will be required for success) and, a budget that details the required size and time of investments to be made in the fundraising enterprise, and projected pledge and cash revenues.

In the second strategy, where a charity wants to know how much it can raise to tailor its needs to meet the capacity of the community, the methodology is more complicated. There are serious methodological concerns about traditional feasibility studies, which have claimed to answer the question "how much can we raise?" Feasibility studies typically depend upon 60 - 80 interviews with potential donors and volunteers to determine the campaign goal.

These have been a favorite of boards and chief fundraisers for half a century, yet, in addition to there being almost no independent methodological validity to such an exercise, the truth is that they are surrogate "asks" by a consultant at a premature stage in the exercise. While they might uncover the odd new donor or campaign volunteer, they do little to validate a campaign's full potential that inspired leadership and compelling communications might create. The core problem is that too often most of the interviewees have little or no in-depth knowledge of the charity and cannot adequately answer the questions that are posed. Moreover, in Canada there has been an unusual reliance on corporate respondents to these studies which further skews results. Many businesses and CEO's refuse to do such interviews unless they are intimately familiar with the organization.

For estimating campaign goals, predictive giving models that combine the capacity of your database with the effect of campaign activity are recommended. Such models depend upon analytics regarding the conversion rate of prospects to donors, average gift size, frequency of solicitation, and staffing complements. These are very useful tools to demonstrate the kind of work and resources that would need to be put in place to achieve certain gift ranges. As fundraising in Canada becomes more sophisticated it is likely that more and more organizations will be utilizing the power of predictive modeling to plan campaigns rather than old school feasibility studies.

There is one additional idea that should be noted with respect to goal setting. Board chairs and CEO's often ask consultants to put some parameters around the scope of the charity's ambitions during the planning exercise. In this regard a rule of thumb is suggested: the maximum goal for an organization to consider should be no greater than the average gift revenue (cash) of the charity for the last three years, times ten. In other words, if you have been raising $2 million on average for each of the last three years, a reasonable working goal for your campaign should be no greater than $20 million.

Some colleagues within the industry think that this may be encouraging some charities to be too ambitious, though experience suggests that most charities considering campaigns have no shortage of ambition!

THE ROLE OF THE BOARD

The question has been asked many times before - what is the most important committee of the board of directors? The surprising answer is the nominating and governance committee. Getting the right people on the board with the necessary capacity to reach out into key target markets is a cornerstone of high performance campaigning. Yet the work of the nominating committee in identifying and cultivating strong leaders for an organization is very much a secondary consideration for most boards and often left until the weeks before

the AGM. It's challenging work, and there are too many of us willing to go for the easy win, or to compromise on having the frank conversation with potential candidates about giving and fundraising. It's no wonder that a 2009 survey by Canadian Fundraising and Philanthropy identified the board as the top issue for charities as it pertains to fundraising. In truth, most boards like to talk much more about spending and accountability than they would about revenue generation. Too many want to delegate fundraising responsibility directly to management. This has resulted in unrealistic expectations of performance and is a contributing factor to the appalling level of turnover in the fundraising sector.

The work of board-building is not done overnight. It may take as many as four years of governance focus prior to the proposed campaign launch, to bring a cohort of power players to your board; those prepared to use their leverage to recruit campaign leaders and secure major gift donations. While at some level it would be good to see boards with all members contributing in some way to the fundraising of a charity, this is simply not practical for most organizations. Most charities use board consultants or borrow governance models from agencies that systematically downplay the importance of fundraising as a core mandate for charities. This is the fuzziest of thinking, and a major sector weakness.

The corollary to this has been added pressure placed on the CEO to be the best paid "fundraiser" for the organization and, while this is natural role for some leaders, for others it is a major burden and for many, they simply haven't had the preparation to fulfill this role effectively. This is especially so in the Canadian health care system, where growing accountability to the health ministry as a result of regionalization and program based funding, has turned most CEO's into glorified bureaucrats. Many hospitals these days don't even have CEO's, or Boards, and it is left to the affiliated foundations to stand up for quality health care in a given community. Many universities and museums also have boards appointed by government and this can be problematic in terms of building fundraising leadership. This close relationship between the public and the philanthropic sector is a dynamic tension in the Canadian context, and one that all fundraisers need to be particularly sensitive to.

When it comes to campaigns the board has a number of mission critical responsibilities:

- First and foremost is to develop and maintain a strong board of directors that has a cohort of leaders that can support the fundraising ambitions of the charity.

- Boards must hire and hold accountable a CEO with the capacity not only to run the organization but also with the passion and vision to represent the mission to the external community.

- The board must take responsibility for annual and multi-year financial goals. This will often mean formal approval of planning or feasibility studies and their findings and recommendations.

- Boards need to understand that campaigns will require an upfront, strategic investment in fundraising personnel, operations, and communications. It must make reasoned and informed decisions on those funds and expect discipline in their execution, as well as a concomitant return on investment in revenues – typically on an 18 - 24 month basis.

- It must assume responsibility for providing the initial leadership for the proposed campaign volunteer structure, with key players taking appropriate roles in the volunteer structure. Often this will begin with a committee of board members, for the express purpose of recruiting a campaign Chair (the Enlistment Committee).

- Each board member should be prepared to work with development staff on the identification, cultivation and, where appropriate, solicitation of major gift prospects for the campaign.

CAMPAIGN GIFT TABLES

The importance of leadership gifts in securing the campaign goal is one of the few realities of campaigns that does seem to transcend time. Lead gifts – the biggest gifts your campaign will get – still account for 10 - 15% of most campaign goals. The top 10 gifts account for about 40 - 50% of the goal and the top 30 - 50 gifts will get you to 80 - 90% of your goal. These statistics are arranged in a gift table or "Standards of Giving" chart that is a vital tool for planning a campaign.

Standards of Giving Chart

**Mont St. Hilaire Community Hospital
Giving from the Heart Campaign
Goal = $10 million**

Number of gifts @ level	Total at this level	Cumulative Total
Leadership Gifts		
1 @ $1,500,000	$1,500,000	$ 1,500,000
1 @ $1,000,000	$1,000,000	$ 2,500,000
2 @ $500,000	$1,000,000	$ 3,500,000
4 @ $250,000	$1,000,000	$ 4,500,000
5 @ $200,000	$1,000,000	$ 5,500,000
Major Gifts		
6 @ $150,000	$ 900,000	$ 6,400,000
10 @ $100,000	$1,000,000	$ 7,400,000
15 @ $50,000	$ 750,000	$ 8,150,000
30 @ $25,000	$ 750,000	$ 8,900,000
50 @ $10,000	$ 500,000	$ 9,400,000
Many under $10,000	$ 600,000	**$10,000,000**

Figure 11.1

Such charts are well understood by those with campaign experience, but are often a surprise to new volunteers whose initial reaction is that campaign goals should be averaged out among everybody in a given community. The experienced campaigner needs to point out the fuzziness of this thinking. Not everyone in a community has the same means, not all are going to be as interested as the next, and not all are inclined to philanthropy (some give less, some give elsewhere, and some just don't give at all).

These tables essentially define how the standard should be set relative to the capacity of the charitable community we are working with. Because it defines the number of gifts required, it will also tell us the number of prospects that must be identified and, derivative of that, how many volunteers and staff will be needed to manage the prospect pool. Figure 11.1 shows what a classic campaign might look like.

It needs to be emphasized that these numbers are averages and that in reality we see quite a good deal of variation in the actual size and numbers of giving. Some leadership gifts exceed 25%, while in others community giving (especially when annual funds and special event revenues are thrown into the campaign counting pot) can be as much as 30% of goal.

Yet while every campaign will have a unique chart that reflects both its prospect pool size and capacity to give, it will be impossible to win a campaign without sufficient focus on the leadership gifts that are required to make it successful.

Nelson C. Lees Senior Consultant Marts & Lundy Jan 08

Figure 11.2 Average Campaign Length By Goal for 246 Campaigns

In very large scale campaigns, where the goal is $50 million or more we do begin to see this formula breakdown, with larger volumes of major gifts required at various levels than the basic formula suggests. The planning for a billion-dollar campaign in the United States, classified gifts less than $1,000,000 as part of the "gifts below" section at the bottom of Figure 11.1. This isn't the case in Canada though, as very large campaigns here are still dependent upon the aggressive solicitation of everything from $5,000 and up. In fact, one concern is that an organization becomes so involved and obsessed with leadership gifts that they fail to organize and prepare adequately for solicitations

at the lower end of the campaign. The result is a campaign that quickly reaches 70 - 80% of its target and then struggles over many years to make its final goal.

For smaller campaigns, independent schools in particular, the success of the campaign may be limited to a group of the top 20 donors constituting 80% or more of the campaign total. Securing the requisite leadership gifts to justify whatever the overall campaign total will be is vital. Reaching too far into the prospect pool to get these gifts puts the goal at risk because smaller institutions and organizations will not have the capacity to expand their access into new prospect groups.

PLANNING THE CAMPAIGN TIMETABLE

How long does a campaign take? It's a pretty straightforward question, but is subject to significant variables. Figure 11.2 shows the length of campaign for various goals that was compiled by the US consulting firm Marts and Lundy. As the chart demonstrates, few campaigns are as short as most people think, and certainly longer than most volunteers are really ready for. Experience suggests that campaigns in Canada are 10 - 15% longer on average than the American experience for reasons suggested below.

There are a number of items that can skew the campaign timetable. Campaign length key variables include:

Planning and priority setting. Big institutions can take years to identify and set priorities. How long? As much as three years in some places. While many stakeholders will have a say in such an exercise, it won't add much to the kind of product that a six-month exercise might generate. Project creep is another major cause for delay as design parameters for buildings shift and costs escalate.

Securing government funding. While a great deal of campaign planning can occur in advance of a government decision, most donors won't even consider signing on for a campaign if a portion of the project that is to be funded by government is not cast in cement. Some charities have taken to securing leadership gifts in order to put pressure on governments to accelerate capital decision making, though the novelty of this strategy seems to be wearing off in the face of weakened financial forecasts for government largesse.

Recruiting the chair and cabinet. This crucial decision, one that often determines success or failure is not to be taken lightly. The Enlistment Committee for the campaign will often have to cultivate and engage a list of potential recruits to secure the right leadership with the appropriate skills and assets. It is worth taking the time to get it done right and can often take a year to eighteen months to ask and recruit the right person. The charity with a great leader who is ready to go as Campaign Chair certainly has the potential to take a year or more off their campaign timetable.

Putting the management team in place. The market in Canada for experienced professionals is impossibly tight, so recruiting good people who are mission-ready is still a major challenge. Even when you have a great person, it can take 3 - 6 months for new staff to become comfortably conversant and an expert in the charity.

Community fundraising. Every campaign is an opportunity to bring new donors into the charity and to turn annual givers into pledgers. This last portion can often represent the last 10 or 20 % of campaign revenue, but requires the most resources, volunteers, staff support, communications, and database utilization. Many campaigns once geared to major giving have a difficult time switching to lower-end fundraising. It's hard work and can take up to three years to execute properly.

Pro forma, the simplest form of campaign timetable looks something like Figure 11.3.

CULTIVATION AND AWARENESS PROGRAMS

For most organizations a campaign is a chance to test their sphere of influence within a defined community. However, what happens when the community shows no interest in your priorities? Or potentially worse, what if your priorities are compelling but you don't have a community to deliver it to? Ideally you have a campaign consultant who will tell you that your grasp exceeds your reach and will deliver the bad news to your board and leaders about the challenges they will face selling the campaign. It is surprising that so many charities at this critical juncture would rather proceed with a campaign with a lower goal than to engage in a well-organized exercise to have a dialogue with potential leaders and donors to sell them on the full vision.

A well-thought-out and executed cultivation and awareness program can last 12 - 18 months and can be run parallel with other aspects of campaign operations. If handled correctly, the potential increase in the readiness factor among major donors will offset the time spent on cultivation.

Such programs take advantage of existing board members and friends to host small receptions or dinners to introduce new prospects and friends to the charity. They often feature a frank and well-prepared talk from a charity leader and a subtle request to get involved. As indicated earlier, if this is done as part of a broader campaign planning exercise, asking everyone who participates to be interviewed and give their opinion, shortcuts the exercise, add prospects to your pool, and gives you fresh and honest feedback from those outside your inner circle.

VOLUNTEER LEADERSHIP

Campaigns are increasingly dependent upon the right combination of leadership from the senior management team and the voluntary leadership of the organization. While a few campaigns may be won with just voluntary leaders, and some may be won with just institutional leadership, increasingly the partnership between the executive team and the voluntary team is the foundation of success for the modern campaign. Too many charitable leaders, and some boards too, think that the recruitment of a campaign cabinet effectively delegates the fundraising to this body. This is a mistake that must be avoided at all costs, for when volunteers see that the board and leadership team aren't aggressively pursuing the fundraising objectives they in turn will be substantively discouraged, which can be a momentum killer for any campaign.

Mt. St. Hilaire Campaign

Phase	\	Year 1				Year 2				Year 3				Year 4 (Public Launch)				Year 5			
		Q1	Q2	Q3	Q4	Q1	Q2	Q3	Q4	Q1	Q2	Q3	Q4	Q1	Q2	Q3	Q4	Q1	Q2	Q3	Q4
Planning Phase		▓	▓	▓																	
Enlistment Phase						█	█	█													
Leadership Gifts Phase								▓	▓	▓	▓										
Major Gifts Phase													█	█	█	█	█				
Community Gifts Phase																▓	▓	▓	▓	▓	▓

Figure 11.3

For this reason the first committee of the campaign should be the enlistment committee which should include the Chair of the Board, the CEO, the Chief Development Officer (CDO) at least a couple of board members and select influencers, usually existing major donors to the cause. All must agree at the outset that they will take on a role within the campaign cabinet once the Chair is secured and they will form the base from which to build the rest of the team.

It is not enough to simply review names and make recommendations; this team should be engaged in a variety of active conversations to validate candidates' potential and interest and importantly, fit with the corporate culture of the charity.

A key decision at the outset of the campaign is whether to have a Chair or Co-Chairs. The preferred situation is to have a single Chair with primary authority over crucial campaign decisions and responsibility for campaign success. In Co-Chair situations, it is virtually impossible to share responsibilities equally and can result in blurred accountability. There are exceptions to this of course (notably the recent campaign for St. Michael's Hospital in Toronto, where the three co-chairs each agreed to chair one year of the campaign), but a campaign will test the trust and depth of any personal or professional relationship.

Another example worth citing is the Southern Alberta Institute of Technology Campaign run with two co-chairs. The campaign is regarded as highly successful in the college sector, landing the two largest individual gifts made to a Canadian College in Canadian history. Yet, despite these examples of success, rather than Co-Chairs it remains preferable for key leaders to take vice-chair titles and participate regularly in campaign meetings with their own specific mandate.

The following are aspects that make leaders say yes to a campaign leadership role:

- They find the head of the charity an inspirational partner with whom they have substantive personal chemistry;

- They see the active involvement of key board members in both campaign planning and execution;

- They have a chance to influence the way in which the project and campaign will take shape;

- They see a competent team of professionals and/or consultants to show them how to succeed and to manage their time for most effect;

- They see that key insiders, often board members, have shown their commitment through early leadership philanthropy;

- There is a carefully considered planning study that provides a reasonable platform for success;

- They see an organization with the communications expertise to adequately promote and support a campaign within the community; and

- There is a reasonable chance of delivering the core campaign within a three year timetable. Essentially, volunteers are reluctant to sign on for much more than three years, or at least remain active for more than that length of time.

The key soliciting body of any campaign is the Campaign Cabinet which, under the direction of the Campaign Chair should be up to a dozen of the most active and committed fundraisers for the campaign. The body should meet monthly throughout the course of the campaign and will have as the main agenda item the solicitation of the best prospects. Campaign administration should be kept to a minimum during these meetings. Fundraising is the focus and it's important for the Campaign Director to manage the meetings to ensure this is the case. At the end of the day, this body will determine campaign success, usually driven by 4 - 6 of the most active and able volunteers, with assists from the other members of cabinet.

But the cabinet is not the whole story. Many campaigns have the opportunity to bring in other volunteers into soliciting divisions. Generally, caution should be exercised in the creation of too many divisions as these require significant organizational resources and can feel like mini campaigns in and of themselves.

Each requires separate recruitment, training, prospect assignment and solicitation strategy for multiple prospects. Many campaigns still prefer to organize their sub-divisions by capacity to give, (usually leadership gifts, major gifts, and community gifts or variations thereof) representing the most simple and manageable form of campaign structure.

Increasingly, larger organizations are running campaign divisions organized by sub-case (essentially mini campaigns for faculties, medical specialties, diseases, etc.). Other institutions are also running geography-based sub-divisions, but this is mostly in the educational sector where there are concentrations of alumni in various cities.

Given that most good volunteer leadership campaigns have had some formative experience with the United Way-model of industry based sub-divisions, it is important to counsel against this structure as most campaigns simply will not be able to support such a large volunteer structure, nor will they have access to workplace solicitation which is the basis of this model.

The other committee of the campaign that should be carefully considered is the family campaign. This is the part of the campaign targeted at the internal constituency, beginning with the board, senior management team and staff. In the past, getting 100% participation from all these constituencies was seen as a critical endorsement of the Case for Support and a strong message to potential campaign leaders. In truth, potential leaders of campaigns are much more interested in the giving and fundraising strength of the board and senior management team than they are for the employees of an institution. The donors that ask this question are exceptionally few and far between, as they are primarily mission and project focused. Every charity that is planning a campaign should seriously measure the pros and cons of extending the family initiative to employees. They require extensive resources, much internal angst (especially where there are problematic labour negotiations) and the fundraising results may not be worth the investment.

PROSPECT PIPELINES AND TARGET MARKETS

While consultants try to make order of campaigns and synthesize such data, patterns are hard to discern because so much of what happens during the campaign is unpredictable and highly dependent on personalities and leadership dynamics which vary considerably from organization to organization. One can try to scientifically assess a database to predict what might happen during a campaign, but those predictions are still subject to the vagaries of execution and leadership.

One of the most interesting analytical aspects of campaigning that is rarely undertaken by organizations is a head-to-head comparison of the prospect databases before and after a campaign. While there are few absolutes, the general pattern suggests the following: one-third of gifts will come from well-qualified known prospects and existing donors to the organization, and another third of gifts will come from people already on the database either as suspects (people with the potential to be involved) or annual donors, who have yet to be qualified as having major gift capacity. The final third of donors will come during the course of the campaign: through the networks of donors, volunteers, staff, and often just those who hear about a good cause through community buzz.

It would be ideal at the onset of a campaign to have prospects properly qualified from both an interest and a capacity (i.e. they are rich enough) perspective. Unfortunately this is rarely the case. Most organizations have a limited cohort of donors with a demonstrated interest, that big list of Canadian companies from the business magazine, and a whole bunch of foundations that have the right guidelines, but no one has really spoken to them directly. For this reason, the campaign from start to finish is an exercise in prospect identification, review, qualification and discovery.

We can never be satisfied that this work is ever complete and the best practice in charity would be to have all major gifts staff continually held accountable for the sourcing of new prospects. (It is a cause of major frustration on the part of senior management that so many campaign/major gift fundraisers expect qualified major prospects to be spoon fed to them from above or from a research unit trolling the internet for signs of wealth). One of the most important questions fundraisers should ask everyone, all the time is: Do you know anyone else who might be interested in talking to me about this project? This is the missionary work of the business of fundraising, the serendipitous aspect of community networking and connections. It is also the one where fundraisers contribute most to the charity, as well as being one of the most satisfying aspects of the job.

Prospective donors can be identified in a number of different ways. Some include:

- Self-qualification: "I just sold my company."

- Electronic screening: usually done by third parties using high net worth indicators

- Peer screening: "I know Jack just sold his company."

- Research: in-house staff actively seeking out and qualifying suspects

- Database search: reviewing and scoring existing databases

Most charities simply have not done a good enough job identifying suitable prospects from natural constituencies: patients, parents, alumni, concert goers and the like. Charities really must be more proactive in knowing who is already in their database. In many cases, there is enormous wealth hidden among annual fund donors who write a cheque for $100 just because they got a letter in the mail asking for that amount.

Many Campaign Directors still believe in the rule of thirds around prospects: that you will need three prospects for every campaign gift. This model is fair enough when you have unqualified prospects, but when you have qualified prospects with both confirmed interest and capacity, the success rate on solicitations is usually much better than 50%.

Interestingly, some very advanced U.S. institutions are using a tiered conversion rate that matches degree of interest and wealth to determine their campaign potential. For top-ranked prospects, they expect a 100% conversion rate to a gift. In any event, throughout the course of the campaign there is a need to have a prospect list whose ratings add up to something in excess of twice the campaign goal.

CAMPAIGN COMMUNICATIONS AND MARKETING

Campaigns need to be about something in particular. There are only a few charities with sufficient brand recognition that they don't need specialized and supplementary campaign communications tools, or ones where donor confidence is so high that they will trust the charity to apply the gift to whatever priority they deem necessary. The unrestricted gift to an institution is a rare commodity. In a cluttered and noisy charitable marketplace most campaigns need a short, compelling, graphically driven story line that is digestible in just a few sound bites. Supporting the narrative is an array of materials that speak to the thoughtfulness and careful planning behind the initiative.

Communications tools in a campaign fall into two categories. Some materials support one-on-one conversations between campaign volunteers and prospects while others create an environment for such conversations to happen.

One-on-one conversations begin with a case for support: a carefully thought out, well-articulated argument for the campaign, what the project is and how it will advance the mission of the organization. In the early stages of a campaign a case may go through numerous iterations as projects unfold, as issues need to be addressed and as volunteers learn how to tell the story in the community. For this reason, and because the case is a vital tool for early stage conversations with potential donors and volunteers, it is important to develop a case that is at once well-written and graphically interesting, but also one that can be regularly updated to accommodate changes. Modern in-house publishing technology allows this to happen, though most charities would be wise to use internal or external communications management to arrive at a core product suitable for presentation. A well-presented case is a vital confidence builder for all involved.

Other tools may also be necessary to support donor and volunteer conversations. Detailed designs for buildings, comprehensive project lists, ways of giving, naming opportunities, the pledge form, and stationary are all fundamentals that must conform to the graphic look of the campaign and support the negotiation of gifts. Increasingly, sophisticated looking custom proposals that selectively include elements of the case and other support information can be prepared in-house to create an impressive package for the donor.

During the quiet phase of the campaign when early stage gifts are sought and secured, the personal solicitation tools may be all that is required, but as a campaign starts moving further afield it will need to be supported with a broader communications strategy that garners the attention of target audiences and creates a buzz in the donor community as much as possible. Such campaigns have traditionally relied on a combination of printed material in the form of brochures and paid media, particularly around the launch of the public phase of a campaign.

These tools should be leveraged against the organization's existing communications assets, especially magazines, newsletters, videos for special events, and increasingly the website, e-mail blasts and online social media forums (the latter has yet to translate into fundraising success, but there are encouraging signs it can

play a role). The decision around how much to spend on media and support communications is driven largely by how "public" a campaign needs to be, both from the viewpoint of establishing and legitimizing the importance of the charity in the marketplace, but also in terms of the penetration required to reach decision makers, particularly in the corporate sector. Another ancillary effect of marketing is the positive profile it provides to volunteers. Public acknowledgement of the leadership team reinforces their commitment to success and their personal accountability for achieving the goals.

Ultimately, the campaign cannot live in a communications vacuum from the rest of the organization. Internal and external publications must not only promote the campaign, leaders, and specific gifts, but it must give the charity optimism about the future of the organization. It is particularly important therefore to work closely with the institutional communications professionals to plan and coordinate the look, feel and content of campaign communications and to have a consolidated marketing and communications strategy, whether or not the campaign is working with an external agency on design and production.

MANAGING THE CAMPAIGN

With many books written about campaign management, there is time in this chapter only to emphasize several key areas that campaign planners will have to give significant thought to in order to be ready to go to the marketplace.

First will be the recruitment of someone to provide overall direction for the campaign. While some charities still like the idea of outsourcing this to a consulting firm, most charities are arriving at the notion that the campaign is the primary vehicle to build their program for the long term and that entrusting vital volunteer and donor relationships to a third party just doesn't make sense. However, recruiting the right leader is a particular challenge with so few experienced professionals available in the market. For this reason, some charities are choosing to re-position their top fundraiser as Campaign Director and are relieving them of administrative and other programmatic duties so that they can commit themselves to winning the campaign.

With the supplemental partnership of counsel this is an increasingly important way for charities to fill the management gap.

Supplementing the Campaign Director may include a team of Campaign Officers, (typically one per 100 prospects with a mandate to coordinate between 30 and 40 major gift asks in each year of active campaigning) Campaign Associates to manage the prospect research and administrative requirements of front line fundraisers and, in large campaigns, specialized Prospect Researchers and Proposal Writers. The size and structure of the campaign will determine the full size of the operation, but a useful rule of thumb would be about three staff per $10 million of the campaign goal.

From a budget perspective, the accepted percentage of cost to campaign goal is in the range of 12 to 15% although that number often fails to include resources from the rest of the organization that may be required such as space, technology, human resources support, and even the time of the CEO that will need to be allocated to fundraising. It is also axiomatic that many campaign costs are upfront investments in planning, outside counsel, communications and staffing. Boards need to understand the design and structure that is called for in the campaign planning study which should always include a budget. Often the decision to allocate sufficient start-up funds is the most difficult decision a board will make with respect to its commitment to entering into a campaign.

Related to this, of course, is the need for the charity, the Campaign Cabinet, and the board to have an agreed upon set of metrics by which they will judge the success of the campaign. Obviously raising funds is the key metric and this will usually be displayed in a time/money chart which tracks the campaign on a monthly or quarterly basis. Another key metric is to calculate proposals pending: this ensures there is due attention to filling the pipeline with well-structured asks to potential donors. Campaigns fail because people don't get asked, not because people say no. By year two of a campaign, about 20% of the goal should be in the pipeline at a given time. Also, critical for any building project, are cash flow projections that allow planners to stage the funding of a capital project appropriately. While a campaign may take five years to secure the pledges, it may take an additional five years for all the funds to be collected.

Key to any transparency around campaign metrics are early decisions about what will and will not be included in the campaign. Many charities still choose to include special government grants, municipal grants, and internal allocations in the total campaign numbers. The rationale for this is to maximize the scale of the project in the eyes of the donor and to reinforce the credibility of the project that government funding signifies to Canadians. Other important decisions include the degree to which cash revenues from bequests, annual gifts and special events add momentum to the campaign, though for many these funds will offset fundraising costs and ongoing operational grants for the charity. Another critical issue is whether or not to count gifts for projects that are not for stated campaign priorities. Most charities do count these while making the case that the campaign generates interest in the cause beyond that of regular fundraising.

Generally speaking, planned gifts have not been included in goals for campaigns in Canada though there is a case to be made about having a supplementary goal, particularly for those whose campaigns are designed to have a long-term impact through endowment building. Some might discount the nominal value of a bequest intention relative to the age of the donor, but most charities these days are finding that the establishment of special donor clubs encourages and promotes the opportunity for bequests and planned gifts in the long-term interests of the charity.

It is also necessary to have detailed information related to campaign activities kept in a reliable database. Too many charities have fundraising staff managing their work on personal spreadsheets. In an age of high turnover among staff, despite an ongoing commitment to fundraising by the charity, knowing who spoke to who about what, and when, is a vital resource for the sustainability of any program.

DONOR RECOGNITION

The old saying "In fundraising, example isn't the main thing, it is the only thing," remains as true today as ever before. While the media continue to take pot shots at institutions who promote major donor namings, in truth it has been this kind of donor acknowledgement that has caused an explosion in leadership giving in

Canada since the beginning of the new millennium. While some make the case that tax changes in 2005 (mostly related to the elimination of capital gains on gifted assets) were the primary driver of this giving, in reality major giving has been on a steady upswing since the mid 1990's. While tax changes certainly helped donors make larger gifts than they might otherwise have done, donors' motivation to support the mission remains paramount.

There is certainly a close correlation between a robust donor recognition environment and the growth of philanthropy. In the 1980's campuses across Canada were still naming new buildings for former presidents and deans. Now such opportunities are strictly preserved for leadership philanthropy. And it's not just for top donors any more: increasingly donor clubs, endowment naming, and donor walls figure prominently in the construction of campaign design, planning and budgets.

CONCLUSION

This chapter began by looking at campaigns as acts of social change. While the discussion is often focused on architecture, planning, organization and operations; one must never let go of this notion as a key driver of success. Authentic, passionate campaigns are almost always successful because people are attracted to causes that matter. Campaigns have the potential not just to raise money for an important initiative, they also have the power to transform an organization and build a philanthropic legacy for the future sustainability of vital revenues. Campaigns are never as easy as they look from the outside. But always, at the victory party or ribbon-cutting ceremony, the difficult parts of the campaign pale beside the sense of pride and accomplishment that accrue to staff, volunteers, and donors as they celebrate a great success.

ADDITIONAL RESOURCES

▶ INGRAHAM WALKER, JULIA. (2006). *Nonprofit Essentials: The Capital Campaign.* Wiley.

▶ LYSAKOWSKI, LINDA & SNYDER, JUDITH. (2005). *Getting Ready for a Capital Campaign.* John Wiley & Sons Inc.

▶ NOVOM, MARTIN L. (2007). *The Fundraising Feasibility Study: It's Not About the Money.* Wiley.

▶ WEINSTEIN, STANLEY. (2003). *Capital Campaigns from the Ground Up: How Nonprofits Can Have the Buildings of Their Dreams.* Jossey-Bass.

ABOUT THE AUTHOR

Nicholas Offord, BA

Nicholas Offord began in fundraising as a capital campaign consultant with KCI Canada in 1984. He went on to join the development office at McGill University and as Executive Director was recognized with the Gold Medal for "Best Development Program" from the Canadian Council for the Advancement of Education. Nicholas then moved on to become President of Mount Sinai Hospital Foundation and Vice-President, Resource and Development of Mount Sinai Hospital.

Nicholas is a well-known speaker across Canada on fundraising and community development. In 1999, the Toronto Chapter of AFP
awarded him "Outstanding Executive of the Year." In 2000, he was selected as one of "Canada's Top 40 Leaders Under 40" by Report on Business. He now leads The Offord Group, a national consulting firm to the charitable sector.

CHAPTER 12

Planned Giving
VAL HOEY, CFRE

At the intersection of integrity, authenticity, and passion

Many accomplished experts and professionals have contributed to the body of knowledge in the area of planned giving. Although the experts have spent endless hours gaining knowledge about tax law and ethical liability, while keeping abreast of changes in the sector, as a fundraiser, you may not have to know every technical aspect.

read more...

For example, you do not need an exhaustive understanding of tax credits being considered by Finance Canada and Canada Revenue Agency. Instead, ask yourself, where can the information you need be found, and how does planned giving affect your day-to-day work as a professional fundraiser? In this chapter, I will describe how planned giving should be an integral part of the offerings of every professional fundraiser.

For the inexperienced fundraiser, planned giving might seem to be a complex journey through tax law, legal offerings, and complicated gift agreements. In reality, the journey is through experience, knowledge, and relationship-building, in an environment of trust and good ethics. I encourage those that are new to planned giving to not get lost in the detail, do not lose sight that your primary role is as a relationship builder, between your charity, the donor and financial advisors.

Planned giving options can be crafted into every element of giving, whether it's an annual fund, a major gift campaign, or independently perched at the top of the "pyramid of giving" as outlined in previous chapters. Key to a successful program is to recognize the elements (Figure 12.1) of integrity, authenticity, and passion and your role representing your charity. In your work with donors and professional advisors, you will always need to balance these three elements as you create opportunities for giving.

Elements for a Successful Program
Integrity
Authenticity
Passion

Figure 12.1

In this chapter, you will learn about some of the tools that will ensure your success as a planned giving fundraising professional, and a roadmap to help determine your readiness for approaching prospective donors. You can also determine the readiness of your charity to begin its planned giving program, while discovering who might be your new best friends in the sector, and how to rely on experts for getting the knowledge you need. You will learn to recognize the role of donors in multi-tiered relationships, and what they can bring to the partnership.

Planned giving involves a number of key players (see Figure 12.2) including: the charity that creates the environment for successful planned giving, the planned giving fundraiser who understands the sector, and the professional advisor who has the knowledge of taxes and legal requirements for advising clients on the most sensible use of their personal portfolios.

Lastly, and most importantly, are the donors. They come prepared with their financial plans, visions for contributing to your charity, and a willingness to work with the charity, fundraising professional, financial legal counsel. All players bring with them their integrity, authenticity, and passion.

THE PLANNED GIVING FUNDRAISER

As a fundraiser, you need to first assess your personal readiness and the readiness of your charity to use planned giving, which can open many new doors for your charity. Planned gifts can provide sustainability for your organization, and they display confidence and support for your charity from the philanthropic community. The sheer willingness of philanthropists to create a lasting legacy with their assets can empower and sustain the mission and vision of your charity for decades.

At a personal level, do you have a good sense of your strengths and weaknesses? Do you have strong listening skills? Do you understand why you entered the field? Being aware of your motivations, do you understand your preferred style of communication? Speaking, and more importantly, listening are vital tools that can distinguish a good planned giving professional from an exceptional planned giving professional.

While many books can help you discover your personal style of communication, the key is to know how your communication style connects with your donor's style. Often, soft skills can make or break your success. If not an active listener, you run the risk of missing the signals from donors, missing out on opportunities, or failing to find the needed solutions.

In all organizations, the relationships between donor and institution must be well respected. Once at a University, I was invited by a distinguished faculty

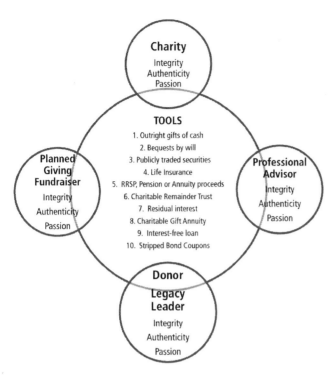

Charity
Integrity
Authenticity
Passion

Planned
Giving
Fundraiser
Integrity
Authenticity
Passion

TOOLS
1. Outright gifts of cash
2. Bequests by will
3. Publicly traded securities
4. Life Insurance
5. RRSP, Pension or Annuity proceeds
6. Charitable Remainder Trust
7. Residual interest
8. Charitable Gift Annuity
9. Interest-free loan
10. Stripped Bond Coupons

Professional
Advisor
Integrity
Authenticity
Passion

Donor
Legacy
Leader
Integrity
Authenticity
Passion

Figure 12.2

Dean to visit a donor of their faculty. As we entered the donor's home, I noticed an abundance of plaques on the wall recognizing the donor's many philanthropic gifts to other well respected charities. I gathered that the donor liked to be recognized, since all who entered the home would immediately see the celebratory wall, just inside the front door. As our meeting unfolded, I had the opportunity to talk about various gifting options that the donor might consider for our charity. At one point, the donor bluntly asked, "What makes you think that I would give to your charity?"

After a second to think, I realized that I could respond by supporting a gift to my charity or respond with information that the donor could use for a gift to any charity. In a split-second of reflection, I indicated to the donor, that the choice to support my charity was not mine to make. I gulped and said, "What I have said can be translated for any charity you wish to support."

The donor then replied, "Well then, tell me who should I support?"

I gulped once again, and remembered hearing the Dean take a large intake of air, before I went on, "You can give to any charity that you wish. The purpose of my being here today is to share with you the oppor-

tunities of giving that you have, and to let you know what we believe we can do with your gift at our charity. But truly, at the end of the day, it is completely up to you to determine the charity you wish to support."

You may have heard about the awkward silence that usually follows a major gift request. In that home, for a brief moment, the silence was deafening. Then, to my relief, the donor began to smile and laugh, saying, "There have been many fundraisers that have been to my home, but none have ever told me I could give to a charity other than theirs. This has been a first! And for that, I'm going to give to your charity, because of your honesty."

A collective sigh went around the room. At that moment, I suddenly realized that, yes, I was representing a charity, and yes, I have passion and loyalty. But at the end of the day, it was my professional integrity that came through. I had spoken to the donor in an authentic manner, and my genuine sincerity was rewarded. The three elements, Integrity, Authenticity, and Passion, are crucial when working with planned giving donors. Even if a donor has already made a decision, a genuine answer to a provoking question can make all the difference.

The one thing that we all have in common, as fundraisers, is that we will be interacting with individuals who believe in your charity. They believe in the mission and vision of your charity, or at least, recognize the personal financial benefits available from some of the planned giving instruments. Still, they will see you as the expert, or facilitator, to help guide them to make their wishes a reality. Although a heady responsibility, if managed properly, you can achieve a new understanding of the philanthropic process.

You can sharpen your ethical standards, and advocate for donors while building a trusting, respectful, and mutually beneficial relationship with a variety of players. Diplomacy and tact are developed along with knowledge and experience. Planned giving is not for fundraisers who only want a quick answer. It is for those who enjoy the process, who never lose sight of the request, and who always move toward the goal of creating a gifting opportunity that makes sense to all stakeholders.

CHARITY'S PERSPECTIVE

I would like you to visualize having the option of choosing between two types of planned giving vehicles for your charity: one is the limousine model, and the other is the family car model. Either model will allow you to reach your destination but the choice will be based primarily on what your charity can afford.

In the "limousine" model, the charity has the funds to invest time, capacity and dollars to build up and enhance a planned giving program. Such charities generally have larger infrastructures and excellent databases, are well-developed in all areas of philanthropic giving with a thriving annual fund, and a successful major gifts portfolio, and are supported by a strong prospect research capacity. In reality, however, not all charities have had enough time or depth of investment to build planned giving as a serious offering for donors.

The "family car" model would be a good fit for a small to mid-sized charity, that is exploring the idea of developing a planned giving program. You want to move forward and gain some understanding of the opportunities that donors consider when they make philanthropic contributions to your charity. At the same time, you may be somewhat afraid of the complexity that seems to be involved with a planned giving portfolio. In this chapter, I hope to alleviate those anxieties and help you envision the variety of options that you can offer prospective donors and that will work well within a limited budget.

When I first began my career in the mid-1980s, the only available resource in this area was Minton and Somers' *Planned Giving for Canadians*. I always kept the book close at hand, since it provided the tools for structuring an organization, designing policies, and creating blueprints for an effective planned giving department, replete with a planned giving committee. The book is still highly relevant for today. In addition, before running your planned giving program, you may wish to review a quick list of the key elements as outlined in the "check point audit" for a successful program.

In today's charitable sector, we can benefit by looking at other charities that have long and well-established planned giving programs. Technology and FOIPP (Freedom of Information and Protection of Privacy) has been beneficial to the sector in creating structures of transparency and accountability. Because of widespread online marketing, it is easy to examine the marketing tools used by other charities. By exploring the marketing messages, and the links to organization home pages, you can see the varied forms of giving that are available to donors. Most websites are rich in information and reveal a wide-range of programs and offerings.

Due to the ease of accessing website information, (especially publicly-funded organizations, like universities, colleges, and hospitals) you can quickly conduct your own best practice audit. Many websites also contain policies for gift acceptance, and for the types of gifting packages that can be accepted. In all cases, readers can find more information or contact an individual who will assist them in their next step. If you do not know of a person in your community who is respected and knowledgeable about planned giving, experts can be found online through well-established charities.

The experts are usually professionals like you, who have had the privilege and opportunity to hone their skills and build expertise in the area of planned gifts. Usually, they are well versed in current tax laws, know what may be coming around the corner, and have experience in crafting innovative gifting structures for donors. From my experience, experts will always take the time to mentor those who are seeking assistance, or direct you to your local chapter of the CAGP-ACPDP (Canadian Association of Gift Planners) for further training.

Robert F. Sharpe Sr., in *Planned Giving Simplified*, provides an excellent outline on what needs to be in place within an organization, in terms of leadership and structure[1]. The author identifies the Board and the Chief Executive Officer (CEO) as key players, because of their understanding of the financial investment and the management skills that are needed to build and deliver a successful planned giving program. The culture of your charity is a key consideration towards the success of your planned giving program, the support and understanding of the leadership of your charity can make or break your program, an investment of funds towards your program is critical, along with an investment of political will to allow your program to grow and to develop. When your charity decides that it

---

1 Sharpe, Robert F. Sr. (1999). *Planned Giving Simplified*. New York: John Wiley & Sons, Inc. (pp.141-161).

has the capacity to invest in a strong and fully-funded planned giving program, with support and buy-in from its leadership you will be ready to embark on a rewarding new journey.

You may have already been offering gift options from the four pillars (see Figure 12.3) of a planned giving program: cash, bequests, securities, and life insurance, and find yourself ready to go one step further after having secured the financial and political investment necessary to begin a fully-funded, integrated planned giving program.

Four pillars of a planned giving program

1. Cash

2. Bequests

3. Securities

4. Life Insurance

Figure 12.3

You can now offer the next six elements (Figure 12.4) to your philanthropic community: RRSP's, pension or annuity proceeds, charitable remainder trusts, residual interest, charitable gift annuities, interest-free loans, and acceptance of stripped bond coupons.

Next six elements of a planned giving program

1. RRSP, Pension/Annuity Proceeds

2. Charitable Remainder Trusts

3. Residual Interest

4. Charitable Gift Annuities

5. Interest Free Loans

6. Stripped Bond Coupons

Figure 12.4

Many charities establish a variety of giving clubs, whether for an annual fund, major gifts, or planned giving. Generally, the type of gifts that qualify for membership in a planned giving society consist of the ten items identified in Figures 12.3 and 12.4. Regardless of the product mix in any planned giving program, wills and bequests are always at the center of any planned giving club. Don't forget it!

If you are working at a small charity, with a small infrastructure, you can certainly design a successful program around the first four pillars of the planned giving portfolio. Don't get lost in the technical product side of planned giving. Numerous publications discuss the elements of planned gifts, though they may provide details that are beyond the scope of this chapter.

PROFESSIONAL ADVISOR

Professional advisors play important roles in assisting charities with their planned giving programs. Typically, the advisors include lawyers, who specialize in estate planning and tax law; accountants, private bankers, and trust officers; insurance agents; and investment advisors and financial planners. Frequently, advisors are from the real estate profession. All advisors must follow their professional ethical standards and principals and should adhere to the CAGP code of ethics.

Many advisors work closely with the charitable sector and can become known for their knowledge, ethics, and expertise in planned giving. They serve as experts in crafting gifts that are matched with a donor's intent (as would a lawyer, when drafting a will, obtaining probate, or assisting in bequest management). Financial planners and accountants can have unique knowledge of their clients' affairs, and a profound understanding of their assets and goals.

The advisors usually have opportunities for reminding donors about the taxable benefits of donating certain types of marketable securities that appreciate in value. Professional advisors typically have close personal connections to individuals who may be interested in philanthropy, and can be useful allies as you build your program. They can help you avoid mistakes and may be important when you craft a gift with a donor. As you build your program, you need to also build your network of advisors, perhaps through your involvement in a local CAGP committee or roundtable where you can learn from the experts.

Some charities develop planned giving committees with members that represent a variety of professions. In this way, the advisors can be brought closer to your charity to assist you in the delivery of your planned giving program. You may want to ask your advisors to provide lectures for groups of prospective donors on topics such as tax laws for estate planning, or a workshop on how to construct a will. As your program becomes more complicated, you may ask an advisor on your planned giving committee for general advice, or retain an advisor for discrete tasks on a professional basis.

Many Canadian charities find that 80-90% of funds raised by planned gifts come from bequests and wills. Planned giving officers who work for a charity are not permitted to prepare wills for potential donors nor provide advice on estate law. Thus, strong relationships with professionals in those areas should be built to promote effective collaborations.

DONOR – THE LEGACY LEADER

Donors, with their insight, passion, and desire to make a difference, are pivotal for planned giving fundraisers. They are at every transaction, and like the fundraisers, wish to make good things happen. They recognize the need for a relationship with your charity, possibly involving their own professional advisors or the advisors you may have introduced to them.

Donors play the most critical role in all gifting opportunities, and often motivate fundraisers to find innovative ways to construct the gift. The passion of donors to contribute and make a difference often initiates our conversations with professional advisors. Some donors have already considered what they would like to do, have addressed their family plan, and have even created a legacy plan that fits with their family values. They may have done their homework on your charity, and when they meet with you, they may already be aware of what is needed and how to provide the solution. For those donors that have *not* entertained the concept of designing a planned giving portfolio you can gently direct the conversation by sharing stories of how the simple act of creating a clause in a will has the capacity to leave a lifetime legacy.

Before looking at the main tools in planned giving, a checkpoint audit could be useful at this stage. The audit is a reminder of the four key players in planned giving and can reveal your charity's readiness to operate a planned giving program.

The three elements (Integrity, Authenticity, and Passion) should be assessed for their presence in you (as the practitioner), your charity, the professional advisors that may assist you and, of course, the donors. When all of the elements are in place, you will have an extremely successful planned giving program.

Sample Will Clauses
Specific Bequests

To pay the sum of _____ Dollars to the Charity of choice for its own use absolutely.

To pay the sum of _____ dollars to the Charity of choice, to be used for_____(specific purpose) provided, however, that if circumstances make the specified use of this bequest impractical or undesirable, the Board of the Charity is authorized to apply this bequest to other purposes; such purposes, however, to conform as much as possible to the spirit and intent of this bequest.

To pay the sum equivalent to_____% Percent of the fair market value of all Registered Retirement Income Funds and/or Registered Retirement Savings Funds owned by me at the time of my death to the Charity of choice, to be administers as _____ (named fund) in accordance with the …

Figure 12.5

CHECK POINT AUDIT

Do you have all of the elements in place for running a planned giving program? The following checkpoint audit (Figure 12.6) can help you decide whether or not you are ready to move ahead.

	Integrity	Authenticity	Passion
The Planned Giving Fundraiser	☐ Committed to honesty and transparency ☐ Respectful of individuals ☐ Key knowledge of donor motivations ☐ Understand individual reasons for giving ☐ Aware of tax law and gifting instruments ☐ Member of AFP ☐ Member of CAGP	☐ Is genuine ☐ Ability to freely associate disparate bits of information gleaned from conversation ☐ Exceptional listening skills to move discourse forward in a meaningful way ☐ Remembers that individuals have innate antennae to detect phoniness! ☐ Follows through with actions that support your work	☐ Passionate about your charity. ☐ Knowledgeable of the key facts of your charity ☐ Equipped to convincingly build on the two-sentence elevator speech, with examples ☐ Intricate knowledge of the charity's mission
The Charity	☐ Policies in place and governed to protect Donors Rights ☐ Gift acceptance policies in place for receipt of all planned giving contributions ☐ Annual reports that include financial statements ☐ CRA guidelines are followed and adhered to	☐ The charity is well-established and has a long future ☐ Mission and programs clearly articulated ☐ The charity can state the progress it has made from charitable contributions ☐ The programs make sense ☐ The Board and senior leadership of the charity understand and support the role planned giving plays, to ensuring long-term growth and stability	☐ Short-term and long-term goals are defined and measured – good charities relish this – they know what they are working towards ☐ Marketing tools are designed outlining gifting opportunities and are written with passion and knowledge

	Integrity	Authenticity	Passion
The Professional Advisor	☐ Membership in a professional body that adheres to ethics and standards of practice ☐ Follows CRA guidelines ☐ Puts the needs of the donor first ☐ Is a trusted advisor	☐ Knowledge of planned giving ☐ Ability to construct a gift; e.g., write a will, sell a life insurance policy, counsel on tax law	☐ Willing to voluntarily assist your charity ☐ Knows and is passionate about your vsion and mission
The Donor (Legacy Leader)	☐ Shared their plan with their family	☐ Has a financial legacy plan ☐ Involved in their community – possibly your charity ☐ Aware of the needs of your charity ☐ Is clear on whether they are philanthropic or tax motivated	☐ Clear values ☐ Vision of what they want to change in world ☐ Their values and the Mission and Vision of your charity merge well

Figure 12.6

TOOLS AND OFFERINGS

Current gifts of cash need little explanation, while bequests, publicly traded securities and gifts of stock (the foundation of a solid planned giving program) need to be thoughtfully marketed and understood.

Technology can become an ally in promoting your planned giving program along with being a great investigative tool to discover what other charities are promoting. Most charities have websites that can be designed with a planned giving link to outline the kinds of gifts your charity can receive. Online newsletters can also tell your prospective donors about new opportunities for giving. Some charities also use direct mail appeals, inviting prospective donors to come forward. As your charity moves into a planned giving community, you will find an array of educational opportunities for collaboration with professional advisors.

1. Current and outright gifts
Gifts of assets, such as cash, stock, real estate, or tangible personal property, even though given for the current use and enjoyment of a charity, qualify as a planned gift by virtue of their dollar value and the fact that they are combined with other assets.

2. Bequests
Bequests are the backbone of all planned giving programs, and without doubt, one of the most effective and popular planned giving tools used by donors. Bequests are easy to understand, and more importantly, do not require a donor to part with any assets during their life time. Bequests may be of three types:

a. Specific bequests are from donors who state exactly what they wish to bequeath to the charity; such as a specified dollar amount, a gift of property, or a specific piece of artwork, in terms clearly stated and easily understood.

b. Residual bequests are from donors who typically use this type of bequest after taking care of family, individuals, charities, and institutions that are most important to them. A residual bequest can be likened to the residue of the estate, it is not an afterthought, but is placed towards the bottom on the list of priorities, from the donor's perspective. The donor wants to ensure that all of the higher priorities in the will are taken care of financially, and after all debts, taxes, and administrative expenses have been paid, any residue is to be disbursed to your charity.

c. Contingent bequests, which are least desirable, have a low probability of being realized. A contingent bequest would only take effect if none of the donor's primary intentions can be met. For example, Minton and Somers indicate that a contingent bequest might only be possible when the primary beneficiary does not survive the donor.

3. Publicly traded securities

Publicly traded securities, sometimes known as appreciated stock, represent the most common type of non-cash gift to a charity. Publicly traded securities include shares, mutual funds, and bonds that are traded on the Canadian stock exchange. These are wonderful gifts for your charity, as they are highly liquid and can be sold immediately by way of a brokerage firm. Donors would have a significant benefit in giving this type of gift, since any tax payable on the capital gain is eliminated.

4. Life Insurance

These gifts are usually made jointly by spouses and involve significant contemplation and planning, unlike annual fund gifts, which are usually spontaneous responses to a mail appeal.

Recently, a trend within the sector is to include a line on an annual appeal card that gives prospective donors an opportunity to indicate whether or not they have included the charity in their will or estate plan. In some cases, a call to action might be included, targeting prospective donors and allowing them to ask for more information about planned giving opportunities. This is a good way for organizations with a limited marketing budget to place messages about planned giving in front of their current and prospective donor base.

The life insurance gift allows donors to make a lasting and significant gift to a charity with a nominal investment of cash or income. An insurance policy can be used in two ways: first, the charity can be made the beneficiary of the policy, and upon death, the charity will receive the value of the policy. The second way is to make the charity the beneficiary and the owner of a new or existing policy. This would entitle the donor to receive an immediate charitable tax receipt for the cash value of the policy (if it has some) and for all premiums paid to the policy.

5. RRSP, RRIF, Pension or Annuity Proceeds

These tools are often the foundation of an individual's retirement plan and may have been purchased on the premise of deferring tax. Nevertheless, on death, the total value of these funds must be reported as income and, at that time, they are fully taxable to the owner's estate. If, however, the owner named the charity as a beneficiary on any of these instruments, the donor's estate will be issued a charitable tax receipt for the value of the donation, which can then be applied to the final income tax return. This is a popular tool for some donors who are able to leverage the taxable advantage by naming a charity as a beneficiary.

6. Charitable Remainder Trust

A charitable remainder trust is established by an individual as a trust and an irrevocable gift of the remainder interest is made to the charity. This type of gift can be funded with cash, real estate, or securities. The immediate benefit to the donor is that they receive a charitable tax receipt for the present valuation of the remainder interest, which may result in immediate tax savings. The income generated by the asset placed in trust generally never decreases in value.

7. Residual Interest

Gifts of residual interest are made by a donor irrevocably when real estate or personal property is given to a charity while the right to use the property is retained for life or for a term of years. The donor retains the right to use the property with no impact on the donor's lifestyle. The option exists to put a term (i.e., ten years) on gifts of this nature. If the donor has provided a gift of residual interest (i.e., on a family cottage), the donor has the right to reside in the cottage for the next ten years before it is legally transferred to the charity.

No taxable capital gain is involved when a donor gifts a principal residence and the valuation of the gift is conducted at the time the gift is made. Donors need to understand that residual interest gifts are irrevocable; the donor cannot regain title of the property, the property will have been removed from the donor's estate and will not pass to other beneficiaries.

8. Charitable Gift Annuity

A charitable gift annuity is an arrangement when a donor transfers a lump sum to a charity in exchange for fixed, guaranteed payments for the life of a donor and/or another person for a term of years.

Generally, a substantial portion of the annuity payments will be tax-free. This type of gift needs to be constructed by a life insurance professional, and annuities can be established with modest amounts of capital (generally, they start with $10,000 or more).

This gifting tool is of interest to donors who are 65 years of age or older, and especially for those who are 75-90 years of age. The benefit to donors is that they have the security of guaranteed payments. This gift is also irrevocable; donors cannot get their contribution back and have no control over how it is invested. Donors should be advised to seek qualified legal and accounting advice for gifts of this nature.

9. Interest-Free Loans

Donors, who are in a financial position that allows them to forgo the interest from a capital asset for a period, but who do not want to lose the asset, may consider making an interest-free loan to your charity.

The charity cannot issue a charitable receipt for either the interest earned or for the principal received, but can use the money generated in interest for any project or program. This type of gift has a few benefits to donors. Donors have a sense of assisting the charity, but can demand the principal back at any time should they need to become liquid quickly. In effect, the gift is a demand loan, which is repayable at any time. The loan can be forgiven should the client wish to, in which case, the charity will issue a charitable receipt to the donor for the value of the loan. The major benefit to donors is that they do not have to pay tax on the interest earned on this capital asset throughout the duration that the loan is outstanding.

10. Strip Bond Coupons

A strip bond enables donors to immediately make a larger gift on a discounted basis. The donor will receive a charitable receipt for the market value of the bond at the time it is transferred to the charity, and the charity benefits from receiving either the market value of the strip bond immediately, or the redemption value at a later date. A strip bond is sometimes viewed as an alternative to a gift of life insurance, when securing a policy is not desired or possible.

CONCLUSION

This chapter is in not intended to be a comprehensive study in planned giving, rather it provides you with some easily accessible tools, allows you to look at options that are currently at your disposal and (hopefully) demystify the complexity of planned giving. I encourage you to explore planned giving and to incorporate the tools appropriately.

As you continue your journey as a fundraising professional I suspect you will frequently find yourself at the intersection of integrity, authenticity and passion and trust that your professional ethics and training will guide you with the necessary wisdom and knowledge to know when and how to take your next step. Enjoy your journey!

ADDITIONAL RESOURCES

Books

▶ MINTON, DR. FRANK & SOMERS, LORNA. (1998). *Planned Giving for Canadians.* Somersmith.

▶ SHARPE, ROBERT F. (1998). *Planned Giving Simplified.* AFP/Wiley Fund Development Series.

Organizations

Canada Revenue Agency (CRA): Administers tax laws for the Government of Canada and for most provinces and territories; and various social and economic benefits and incentive programs delivered through the tax system. The agency has a *Summary Policy* specific for planned giving, which states that planned giving is a fundraising program that involves arranging donations to serve the interests of a registered charity, and is suitable for the personal, financial, and tax situation of an individual donor.

Through a planned giving program, registered charities can seek to attract significant gifts by identifying potential donors and helping them with information and advice. Retrieved from http://www.cra-arc.gc.ca/chrts-gving/chrts/plcy/csp/csp-p01-eng.html.

ABOUT THE AUTHOR

Val Hoey, MA, CFRE

Valerie has over 30 years of experience in the non-profit sector beginning with an international development organization – CUSO, working in Papua New Guinea, Solomon Islands and Vanuatu along with being the Regional Director for Alberta. As CUSO's first Major Gift Officer in Western Canada, Val was responsible for all fundraising in Alberta, Manitoba, Saskatchewan and the Territories.

Valerie served as the Director of Planned Giving and Associate Director of Development at the University of Alberta, and then relocated to Calgary where she is currently the Associate Vice President of College Advancement at Bow Valley College.

Valerie has a long history of volunteer involvement with the Association of Fundraising Professionals, as an inaugural member of the Edmonton Chapter and holding various roles (including President) for the Calgary Chapter. Val has presented at numerous workshops on topics such as Planned Giving, Major Giving, Ethics, Fundraising Fundamentals and most recently for Centre Point in Calgary on the role of brand promise in fundraising.

CHAPTER 13

Corporate Giving & Sponsorships

RICHARD WALKER, BSC

While a smaller sub-set of fund development, smaller than the amounts contributed by individuals or major donors, participation by Canadian corporations in fundraising initiatives can produce significant financial rewards for non-profits that know how to plan their approach. While it varies from year to year, corporate participation in the fund development arena is generally 10-15% of the volume of gifts from individuals. The key to successful corporate involvement in your annual fundraising or campaign is to understand the motivation and the expectations of the corporation and to ensure that you have completed your research before you prepare your proposal. *read more...*

Approaching corporations in Canada for charitable gifts and financial support is a common fundraising strategy among non-profits, however the way corporations contribute and the expectations of non-profits are often mismatched. Non-profit organizations should acquaint themselves with the "*Canadian Survey of Business Contributions to Community*"[1] a broad based study of corporate contributions and the more focused work, "*Corporate Community Investment Practices, Motivations and Challenges.*"[2] Both reports reveal anomalies in generally held beliefs regarding philanthropic, sponsorship and cause related marketing activities of companies in Canada. They also provide an excellent snapshot of where corporate support is headed.

In general, corporate contributions are shifting from what has historically been referred to as "cheque book philanthropy"[3] to a more strategic and focused effort. Corporate philanthropy now comes in many forms, not just cash, and fund development professionals should explore all avenues when seeking corporate support.

Mary Ann Blackman, Community Relations Director for the Bow Project, Encana's new 58 story skyscraper in Calgary was quoted in Corporate Community Investment Practices, Motivations and Challenges as saying that "Large companies are stepping up to the plate and devoting a wider range of their assets and resources in the name of building healthy communities, and they are doing it in unique and diverse ways."

When asked, companies suggest that their engagement with non-profits help them build stronger communities. While this may be true, they also use these relationships to forge better business relationships with the community and broaden their corporate audience - all of which is good for business. More than half of the companies interviewed reported activities that are associated with sponsorship and cause related marketing, which affirms the observation that relationships with non-profits that aid the bottom line are more desirable than previously thought. Think "win – win"

– win" where the corporation benefits as much as the non-profit and the community/society.

While Canada Revenue Agency[4] numbers suggest that corporate donations exceed sponsorships, the line between donations and sponsorships gets increasingly blurred as corporations seek more and more recognition, return on investment and community awareness for their "gifts." The days of a contribution being given with no expectation of return are fading in the rear view mirror.

While less than a third of corporations report[5] using any form of measurement with respect to the impact of their charitable contributions, an increasing number of shareholders and government agencies are seeking clarity and accountability with respect to the decisions made by senior management. In addition, more than a third of companies in Canada[6] report frustration with duplicate causes and charities that solicit funds for similar if not identical programs. It behooves a non-profit manager to get ahead of the rush toward clarity, metrics and accountability and begin to entrench solid measurable benefits into the corporate solicitation program. Being able to rationalize why your program is unique, compelling and important to a corporation in terms that they can understand can only be a benefit.

As a rule, you should resist the urge to seek out the largest office tower in town and head there with your empty briefcase. In Canada, the largest corporations give less than their smaller cousins, as a percentage of their pre-tax revenues. In addition, large corporations generally gravitate toward larger, well-established and more commonly known charities, leaving the smaller, local or emerging non-profits on the outside looking in.[7] In Canada the small business sector is the engine behind the economy and in reality is a better place to seek corporate support than head-office towers.

If you apply the thinking put forth in *The Long Tail*[8] and focus your efforts on a good number of moderately sized gifts rather than a few huge contributions,

1   Demczur, Jacqueline M. & Thomas, Paula J. Business Contributions to Canadian Communities: Recent Survey Results. *Charity Law Bulletin.* (No. 112) Imagine Canada.

2   Hall, Michael H. (2008). *Corporate community investment practices, motivations and challenges: findings from the Canada Survey of Business Contributions to Community.* Toronto: Imagine Canada.

3   Ibid.

4   Canadian Revenue Agency (2009) *Financial Data and Charitable Donations Record.* (number: 4106). Retrieved from http://www.statcan.gc.ca/start-debut-eng.html. For a listing of CRA definitions see: cra-arc.gc.ca/chrts-gvng/chrts/glssry-eng.html

5   Ibid.

6   Ibid.

7   Hall, Michael H. (2008). *Corporate community investment practices, motivations and challenges: findings from the Canada Survey of Business Contributions to Community.* Toronto: Imagine Canada.

8   Anderson, Chris. (2008). *The Long Tail: Why the Future of Business is Selling Less of More.* Hyperion Books.

you will enjoy more frequent success and have a better chance of meaningful and lasting relationships with your corporate supporters. While this involves a larger number of prospects, more cultivation and a greater emphasis on the use of volunteers and champions, your fund development program will be more sustainable in the long run. In corporate sponsorship as in the natural environment, diversity and a multitude of contributors is always better than a single "mono culture" where all of your revenue is dependent on one or two sources.

In a 2010 report prepared for Canadian Fundraising and Philanthropy[9] researchers at the Innovative Research Group analysed the Canadian non-profit sector and reported on recent and projected fund development trends. Of interest is the analysis of the corporate sector involvement. Innovative Research Group suggests that fully 70% of respondents reported that corporate donations were the most commonly sourced support with government revenue close behind. This same group reported declines in sponsorships and significant growth potential for cause related marketing as a means to partner with corporations. The report goes on to analyse the return on investment for non-profits and all three corporate engagement methods rank as medium or high in efficiency. This indicates that when compared to special events, mailings or door to door promotions, a non-profit is wise to focus more attention on relationships with corporate Canada and work at establishing a solid, diversified corporate development program.

As more companies migrate to strategic giving, (finding non-profits that align with their corporate values and/or entering into contribution agreements which provide a strategic market advantage to the company), you need to be equally strategic in the way you position your cause, identify you prospects and formulate your case.

So, what have we learned so far:

- Corporate gifts and sponsorships represent a smaller portion of overall charitable activity in Canada, but can be a valuable part of your campaign or annual giving program.

- You need to know what motivates a corporation to make a gift or enter into a sponsorship. Research exists that can help you understand the nature of corporate philanthropy in Canada. Get it and read it.

- Companies are interested in many different forms of contributions. Don't just focus on cash. You may be able to cultivate gifts of equipment, staff time, program assistance or training for your volunteers. Be creative.

- Companies not only want to do good things, they want to be seen doing good things in the community. Plan your media and recognition activities carefully so that you highlight the company and your organization equally.

- Start thinking about how you will measure the impact of a company's involvement and build these metrics into your program. Executives need to report to a Board or shareholders and having real numbers always helps.

- Think "inclusive" rather than "exclusive." By making your case attractive to multiple organizations you spread costs out over a larger number of partners, reducing the risk associated with a single source funder.

- Cause related marketing can be an effective and efficient method to engage corporations in your cause. A solid CRM program can be a win-win situation for both the corporation and your organization.

DEFINITIONS

In order to facilitate better understanding and to navigate through a myriad of conflicting terminology, the following definitions will serve as the baseline for this discussion.

Corporate giving

Whether it is called corporate philanthropy, corporate gifts, community investment, social partnering or some other term - the act of a corporation donating funds, material or services to a recipient non-profit organization can generally be referred to as corporate

9   Innovative Research Group for Canadian Fundraising and Philanthropy. *Economic Pulse of the Non-Profit Sector 2010.* Retrieved from *www.innovativeresearch.ca/Economic_Pulse_Aug2010.pdf.*

giving regardless of the size of the business/corporation. These are philanthropic activities entered into by corporations with no expectation for return. Often a charitable tax receipt is issued and little if any recognition takes place. While common in the 1980's and 1990s' the corporate giving budgets in industry have shrunk significantly and many are focused on employee "matching programs" or specific areas of executive or shareholder interest.

During a university campaign that I worked on recently I was greeted with the frank and honest statement from a senior executive at one of the country's largest pipeline companies. "We really don't care about public recognition. The public –doesn't get to choose which pipeline moves their natural gas. We only contribute to projects in those towns and cities where we have a large employee base."

Understanding the motivation behind a corporation's giving is critical to effective and efficient fund development.

Corporate sponsorship

Corporations entertain sponsorship opportunities as part of their marketing, community investment or stakeholder engagement programs. They enter into sponsorships as a business transaction with a clear expectation of a return on their investment. Sponsorships came into vogue in the 1990's when sports and industry entered into a decade-long relationship. Originally measured by the advertising value (viewer impressions) sponsorship now is strategic, focused and very much centred on the return to the corporation and access to their target market.

After having arranged for a meeting with a large multinational oil and gas company, preparing documents to make a compelling case and bringing along two of our top volunteer "influencers," my first meeting with senior community investment officials started with their opening line, "Tell me how contributing to your cause will bring more people to our gas pumps." Being prepared to answer ROI questions is critical when seeking corporate sponsorships.

Corporate partnerships

Partnerships are an entirely different method of engaging a corporation. However, they represent a position on the continuum of corporate involvement and there-

fore deserve understanding. The term clearly indicates that the corporation is a partner not a supporter, sponsor or contributor and as such is, and expects to be, involved in the decision making, implementation and monitoring of the project, property or event. The implications for recipient organizations is that the partnering corporation will have clear and definite goals for the relationship, expectations with regard to media, promotion and marketing, and some strong thoughts on deliverables in the area of financial return, audience penetration and stakeholder engagement.

The recipient non-profit must therefore measure each potential partnership opportunity very carefully and determine the merits of partnering with a specific corporation, any implications with respect to business dealings with other firms in the same sector, and the legal, accounting and public relations responsibilities involved. Because many non-profits have little commercial or business experience you would be well advised to seek professional advice when faced with a partnership opportunity.

Corporate partnerships are pure business transactions and should be thought of and dealt with as such.

Cause related marketing

CRM is a relatively new method of engaging corporations in the non-profit fund development world. Generally, a corporation promotes the sale of a product or service by associating that product or service with a non-profit or a cause. A portion of the sales of the product or service is contributed to the non-profit in exchange for the right to use their name in marketing, promotion or sales campaigns. In Canada, CRM is used infrequently in small non-profits and only modestly in larger, national causes. In coming years, we will see an explosion of corporate interest in CRM who see the practice as benefiting their social marketing and community investment goals while promoting products or services.

Corporate gifts

The Canada Revenue Agency defines a gift as "a voluntary transfer of property without valuable consideration to the donor." Generally a donor will receive a tax receipt for the value attributed to the gift.

Cash donations are always welcomed at a non-profit, and corporate cash donations are no different.

You will find that many corporate cash contributions are tied to employee driven initiatives, staff matching programs or causes related to executive priorities. Cash contributions not designated for these programs are often managed by a corporate foundation or through the community investment unit. Be prepared to show how your cause matches the criteria for foundation gifts or company gifting policies as many corporate gifts result from rigorous analysis.

Canada Revenue Agency states[10] that corporate gifts eclipse sponsorship by a factor of four or five to one and would on the surface be the logical place to search for funding. In my experience, corporations contribute funds to non-profits as gifts in significant amount, but not as freely or as frequently as many expect.

As previously mentioned, employee matching programs and the priorities of senior management oftentimes run roughshod over a Community Investment Manager's budget plans. Multiyear commitments and consistent long-term support for a few well known events or charities can also drain the corporate gift vault.

If you intend to spend a significant amount of time cultivating a corporate gift, ensure that you know all of the company's rules and criteria for giving before you venture too far. Most large companies post their giving criteria on their websites or have printed material that they can send you. There are commercial sources for information about corporate giving policies that can save you hours of research, making your efforts more cost effective and efficient. Any search engine will quickly provide you with dozens of firms across the country that are able to provide corporate research for you. If you do not have the internal capacity (either staff or volunteer) to undertake some basic research, you would be well advised to try a research service in your area. Moving forward with a corporate solicitation without having completed some level of research into the historic giving, priorities and processes required by your prospect is a major waste of time and resources.

Corporate gifts have their own special rules with respect to valuations, receipting and recognition. There are significant implications to a non-profit and to the donor with respect to the valuation of a gift, the real or perceived "advantage" that a donor enjoys as a result of their gift and whether or not a tax receipt has been issued. You are strongly urged to seek assistance in understanding CRA regulations with respect to what is and what is not considered a "gift" and how a gift has been valued, especially if it is a gift-in-kind.

From the CRA website, "Gifts-in-kind, also known as non-cash gifts, are gifts of property. They cover items such as artwork, equipment, securities, and cultural and ecological property. A contribution of service, that is, of time, skills or efforts, is not property and, therefore, does not qualify as a gift or gift in kind for purposes of issuing official donation receipts." For more information, see Pamphlet P113, *Gifts and Income Tax* and *Income Tax Technical News, Issue 26*.

A 2008 Imagine Canada survey[11] suggests that companies and corporations in Canada contribute significantly more gifts than they invest in sponsorship or other business-related contributions. In reality and as discussed earlier, the evolution toward more strategic contributions is moving the boundary between sponsorship and what the CRA defines as a "gift." This suggests that non-profit managers would be wise to focus their corporate programs on providing higher levels of impact with respect to corporate missions, visions and investment policies so as to be able to demonstrate the advantages offered.

GUIDING PRINCIPLES OF A CORPORATE SPONSORSHIP PROGRAM

In order to fully realize the potential for corporate sponsorships, you need to first measure the extent to which your organization is prepared to cultivate, accept, manage and steward relationships with multiple corporations. In addition, your organization must adopt policies to guide the development of sponsorships so that all participants know and adhere to the rules and expectations prior to, during and after the relationship. An organization will need to identify the boundaries within which it is prepared to offer sponsorship and beyond which no discussion will be entertained: what kind of sponsorship will be accepted and how you propose to service and recognize

10 Canadian Revenue Agency (2009) *Financial Data and Charitable Donations Record.* (number: 4106). Retrieved from *http://www.statcan.gc.ca/start-debut-eng.html*. For a listing of CRA definitions see: *http://cra-arc.gc.ca/chrts-gvng/chrts/glssry-eng.html*

11 Hall, Michael H. (2008). *Corporate community investment practices, motivations and challenges: findings from the Canada Survey of Business Contributions to Community.* Toronto: Imagine Canada.

contributors. Finally, you will need to establish some strict ground rules for the staff and volunteers that are involved in the corporate sponsorship program. Duplication of effort, competition for corporate accounts and stumbling over colleagues in front of corporations will set you back significantly.

Remember, corporations enter into sponsorships to gain recognition, add value to their brand and gain access to their target market. The more professional you and your organization appear; the better chance you have of landing a sponsor.

Do your homework

Research need not be exhaustive or expensive but going ahead with a fund development campaign or sponsorship program without doing basic research can be very damaging. You need to know what exactly you are going to ask a corporation for and how that fits into *your* operational needs and *their* community investment objectives. Bob Hamilton, a senior executive at RBC and a respected philanthropist and fundraising volunteer, reinforces the value of research. "Know the facts about what it is that you are proposing and never underestimate or undersell yourself. Be straight up with people so they know exactly what your expectations are. Know what you're asking for."

This applies as much to the volunteer influencer that you take with you as it does for yourself. Everyone going into a meeting should know exactly what is going to be proposed, who will introduce the topic and who will make "the ask." Researching what a corporation sees as important, what they have invested in before and how your project can benefit them is critical information to have in your back pocket. The last thing you want is to be embarrassed in a meeting because you didn't know the areas that they support, their historic funding record and especially – what's important to them. The more research you do the more professional you appear and the more effective you will be.

Research will also help you organize your portfolio of prospects. A system of sorting, prioritizing and assigning prospects to individual staff and volunteer teams is a very effective way to reduce "collisions" on the fundraising trail. Gordon Schneider, President of Sponsorship Management Software Inc. sums it up this way, "Using software to sort through fundraising prospects, rank them by their importance to you and

then managing your relationship building efforts only makes you look better in the eyes of corporations."

Institution preparedness

A culture of entrepreneurial, business or corporate behaviour is not hard-wired in Canadian non-profits. In the past, many organizations have not required a significant level of business or corporate acumen and have, for the most part, relied on governments for funding. As funding models change and organizations are increasingly challenged to find innovative ways to provide for the cost of services, they need to explore more businesslike approaches to funding issues.

Non-profits that have historically relied on government funding for operating revenue would be well advised to establish fund development initiatives that move them closer to sustainability. If a non-profit cannot count on support from their clients, constituents or supporters, than why should governments be expected to carry the financial burden?

Following the success of industry and institutional relationship building done in many large Canadian non-profits, the exploration of corporate sponsorships is a logical and responsible step for small non-profits. This will require that employees update their understanding of the opportunities and responsibilities associated with corporate sponsorship.

Objectives

Non-profits must identify those areas which they believe would benefit from increased involvement with industry and set specific objectives. It is insufficient to state that an organization wants to entertain corporate sponsorship without providing a framework within which sponsorship will be encouraged. For example, an organization may wish to engage sponsors in the development of facilities, schools, classrooms, studios, etc. They may not, however, be prepared to engage corporations in the development of curriculum or allow the sponsor to access the student body for marketing purposes.

Establishing objectives for corporate sponsorship will allow staff and others to cultivate relationships in areas where mutually beneficial activities can be brought to fruition. It also avoids misunderstandings, wasted time and inappropriate or embarrassing situations. In order to establish the areas of interest and objectives for sponsorship, organizations must be aware of the types of sponsorship available.

Areas of sponsorship potential

Corporations have vast reserves from which they can draw to support a sponsorship. Funding and cash contributions are areas most often referred to when people speak about sponsorship. In reality, cash and the transfer of money from the corporation to the recipient generally constitute about 25% of an established sponsorship program. More common is the provision of services and/or products. In addition to money, products and services (and often more important to corporations) is the area of human resources. Employees in corporations represent a pool of talent that if identified and targeted toward a non-profit program could enhance the effectiveness and efficiency of the organization. Corporate employees are generally motivated to provide assistance to their clients and as such bring a wealth of experience and expertise to the table.

Intellectual property, training, mentoring and volunteer time can greatly assist non-profits that are heavily weighted in human service but who find it difficult to attract volunteers of their own. Corporations, their retirees and the organization itself should be viewed as a vast reservoir of potential.

Finally, many corporations have large, experienced marketing and promotions departments. Assistance in the promotion of your organization, cause related marketing or the creation of communication, marketing or promotional and media material can either save or generate thousands of dollars in value.

Sponsorship policies

As in all business transactions, it is desirable to have written policies that provide guidance to those involved. Policies define what can and cannot be done. The development of polices in advance of launching a gifting or sponsorship campaign will save a significant amount of angst and avoid having to pause discussions with a motivated sponsor so that issues can be debated inside the organization.

Policy issues that need to be addressed include:

- To what extent will you engage the sponsor in decision making in the program or project?

- Who will manage the media and public announcements associated with the sponsorship?

- What areas, departments, programs or projects will (or will not) be included in the potential sponsorships?

- Are there certain industry sectors that will not be included in any potential sponsorship discussions? (example: tobacco, liquor, munitions, pharmaceuticals)

- Is program delivery or program content open to sponsor involvement?

- What are the parameters with respect to marketing materials, visual identity and the use of name, logo and images?

- To what extent, if any, can the sponsor access your audience?

- Are you offering exclusivity to the sponsor and if so, in what geographic, program, equipment or project areas?

- How will the resources being contributed be utilized and will the sponsor have any say in how their contribution is used?

- Will you provide an endorsement of the sponsor, their product(s) or service(s).

- Will you have any say in the activity (the way they tell their audience about their involvement with your organization) by the sponsor?

Sample policy statements

1. The corporate sponsorship will do no harm to existing programs, projects, finances, relationships or property.
2. Sponsorships and all items relating to sponsorship activity must be coordinated in advance with <insert the Executive Director or President's Office>.
3. The sponsor will fully disclose all existing ownership, partnership, subsidiary and sponsorship relationships prior to the execution of a sponsorship agreement.
4. Sponsorships and all items relating to sponsorship activity will be recorded in writing and retained in the office of the <insert Exec Director or President>.
5. Sponsorship contributions will be administered, valued and recognized in

accordance with current Canada Revenue Agency policies, guidelines and regulations.

6. We will not enter into sponsorships for products, services or with corporations or associations related to tobacco, alcohol, firearms, munitions, or any element that is contrary to our general policies and procedures.

7. Direct access to staff, clients, patients, students, teachers, researchers, professionals and executive is as a general rule prohibited, however under special circumstances and within the policies, guidelines and regulations of <insert your organization's name>, the Provincial Privacy Commission and any other relevant government agency, sponsors may be granted the right to access certain defined groups with the written permission of the <Exec Director or President>.

8. Contact with our personnel or clients, when granted by mail, electronic or any other medium will be managed and facilitated by our organization.

9. Anything resulting from this relationship will not be used by the sponsor without our written consent and if necessary signed release forms from the subject.

10. The sponsorship will not result in loss of revenue, value, reputation or standing of our organization.

Exclusivity

Eventually you will be asked about exclusivity, and/or the right to exercise exclusivity in relations to your fund development program. You need to determine whether you are prepared to offer exclusivity with your sponsorships. In some cases, corporations enter into relationships with non-profits to benefit their market position and/or the public perception of their organization vis-à-vis their competition. They may want to exclude others in their market sector from participating in the campaign and as such gain increased market exposure over their competitors.

If a corporation makes a very significant contribution to your organization, you may offer them the right to exercise sector exclusivity. The company may choose to exercise that right or not, depending on the circum-stances. In my experience, corporations are generally willing to share space in a campaign or program with others in their sector as long as everyone is contributing relatively equally.

You need to understand that once exclusivity is built into a proposal it is virtually impossible to reverse. In addition, the fact that you offer a corporation (or multiple corporations) the opportunity to exclude their competitors may be perceived by others to be counter to your efforts to be inclusive. Depending on the sector your organization occupies, this may be an ethical or even legal issue. Exclusivity may deter potential sponsors who want to support the institution but cannot compete at the higher levels or who object on philosophical grounds to an "exclusive" position.

Legal advisors and fund development professionals who specialize in corporate partnerships and sponsorships will be able to guide you through the benefits and costs of exclusivity offerings. You may be well advised to avoid exclusivity issues until you have more extensive experience with corporations.

Sponsorship properties

Ultimately you will need to identify recognition opportunities for corporations if you want to pursue sponsorships. It is important to remember that when you build your recognition program you may be wise to separate the specific areas where the contributed funds will be used from the property that is being used for recognition. You want to say "here is how we will recognize your gift" not "here is where we will spend your money." Separating the recognition of the contribution from the place where the contribution will be invested offers you some flexibility in both recognition and the use of the funds. While adhering to CRA regulations, you generally want to move as much funding into "undesignated" funds as possible.

To accomplish this you will need to identify, value and prioritize your sponsorship properties. These may include programs, building spaces, positions or some other entity. Examples of sponsorship properties include:

- The environmental sustainability program for your agency or program

- A faculty, program or area of study

- The XYZ Suite at the school of ABC

- Artist in residence
- The XYZ summer sabbatical for Executive Directors
- Client, patient or student travel, wish or dream programs
- The resident information technology specialist at ABC
- The student commons, patient lounge, guest suites or classroom
- Events, tents, booths and services at annual gatherings
- Vehicles, trailers, information and service kiosks
- Open House and "Meet the…instructor/coach/ counselor/president night."

Recognition of corporate sponsors goes beyond naming rights. Elements that may be included in sponsor recognition are:

- News and media coverage either paid or editorial
- Signage both on-site and in public spaces
- Speaking opportunities at functions related to the sponsored property
- Public recognition of the corporation's involvement
- Participation in meetings, conferences and conventions
- Tickets for staff, clients and shareholders to attend events
- Sponsors activation by way of co-branded products, materials or retail items
- Access to your audience for marketing and promotional programs
- Introductions to your other partners and facilitating industry meetings
- Use of your logo, visual identity, images and personalities

Valuation

Subject to the identification of the sponsorship properties, you will need to calculate a value for each of the properties. Valuation of sponsor properties is done in several ways and the resulting monetary value begins

to establish where the property resides on the menu of sponsorship opportunities. Valuation is not necessarily (or often) the retail value of a product or the cost of providing a program. The sponsorship value is calculated based on a number of parameters including the costs, promotional value, perceived value, exclusivity value, tangible and intangible benefits and promotional impact. In addition, the term of the sponsorship and the unique nature of the property impact the valuation.

The practice of valuation is specialized and you are advised to seek professional assistance. In addition, financial and legal issues exist that require counsel to ensure compliance with CRA regulations. There are several very qualified philanthropic and sponsorship consultancies in Canada that can assist you in this regard.

Cultivation

How your organization cultivates sponsors or gifts will determine much of the value and longevity of a corporate relationship. If you know what you need from a corporation, what you are prepared to offer in return, what they need and what they are capable of offering then you stand a good chance of running a successful corporate program. Lose any of these elements and you cripple your efforts and chances for success.

It is important to remember that the corporation is waiting for you to ask them for something *and* they are responsible to others to ensure that the corporation gets something in return whether that is a tax receipt or a building name. All the research and preparation in the world will be wasted unless you ask for what you need.

The "ask" is simply the act of having the right person ask the right representative from the prospect corporation for the right amount of support for the right project at the right time. The "ask" is always conducted by more than one person and generally handled by a staff person and a volunteer influencer – preferably someone known to the corporation, respected in their field and who can influence the prospect toward a positive answer.

The agreement

A gift agreement or sponsorship contract is an essential piece of the fund development process when dealing with corporations. The agreement is a written document that clearly sets out all conditions and summarizes all conversations, decisions and commitments. Templates for agreements are available online[12] and most legal advisors can provide you with assistance to make the process easier. Remember that in the case of corporate sponsorships you are entering into a binding legal contract as opposed to most gift agreements which record intent and are not necessarily binding or enforceable. Corporate sponsorship agreements must pass the scrutiny of legal advisors on both sides of the transaction. Leave sufficient time for review and signing.

Sponsor servicing and stewardship

Corporate sponsors are accustomed to a high level of engagement and services as a result of their contribution of resources to the recipient organization. It is incumbent therefore that you understand that once a sponsorship agreement is signed and a corporate sponsor engaged, the real work begins. The delivery of recognition, approval of advertisement copy, tickets, entertaining and reporting are all time consuming activities that must be planned and executed in a professional and timely manner.

Nothing will damage an existing relationship and endanger future relationships with the sponsor and other sponsors faster than a failure to deliver on the promises made during cultivation, negotiations and the sponsor agreement. The costs associated with servicing sponsors must be included in the valuation exercise noted previously and must constitute part of the operating budget of the sponsorship program, marketing program, media and executive units.

Stewardship of corporate sponsorship defines everything that happens from the moment the agreement is signed until the sponsorship is either cancelled, expires or is renewed. The largest single failing of non-profits in Canada is a lack of attention to the stewardship of sponsors. Communication, delivering on promises, collecting the money, recognizing the sponsor, listening to their opinion and concerns, engaging the sponsor after all of the money has been received and keeping the sponsor informed about the impact of their invest-

ment all takes time, effort and resources. Stewarding a corporate sponsor can pay very large dividends as the sponsor revisits their strategic marketing needs, realize the true value of what they receive in the sponsorship transaction and are seen by their peers to be gaining a strategic advantage. Manage your sponsors well and you will retain them for years. You may even attract their competitors.

CONCLUSION

If you choose to enter into the arena of corporate and business relationships you need to understand all of the benefits and the costs of the method you select. It is advisable to recruit business, retail and legal expertise to your committee or board so that you can benefit from their knowledge and experience.

There are significant advantages that can be gained through corporate support, many unexplored opportunities and years of positive, creative and valuable contributions to be realized for those who are prepared and who approach corporations in a business-like manner.

ADDITIONAL RESOURCES

▶ COLLETT, PIPPA & FENTON, WILLIAM. (2011). *The Sponsorship Handbook: Essential Tools, Tips and Techniques for Sponsors and Sponsorship Seekers*, Jossey-Bass.

▶ MARTIN, PATRICIA. (2003). *Made Possible By: Succeeding with Sponsorship.* Jossey-Bass.

▶ SCOTT, K. (2000). *Successful Corporate Fund Raising: Effective Strategies for Today's Nonprofits.* John Wiley & Sons Inc.

▶ WELLS, CHRIS. (2000). *Finding Company Sponsors for Good Causes.* Directory of Social Change.

---

12 Templates for fund development pledges, receipts and agreements are available at multiple sources in the internet. For examples see: *http://office. microsoft.com/en-us/templates/results.aspx?qu=donation* as well as *http://www. fundraisingtemplates.com/*

ABOUT THE AUTHOR

Richard L.H. Walker, BSc

Richard Walker is the Principle Partner and President of the Walker Resource Group, a consultancy based in western Canada. A professional Project Manager by training, Mr. Walker holds a Bachelor of Science Degree from the University of Victoria and is an alumni of the Banff Centre School of Management.

Richard was former President and CEO of WorldSkills Calgary 2009, CEO of the Jubilee Auditorium Foundation, V.P. of Ducks Unlimited Canada and Managing Director of the University of Alberta office in Southern Alberta.

He has been a guest lecturer at the Saskatchewan Institute of Applied Science and Technology, the University of Victoria and a guest presenter at Cambridge University in the U.K. Mr Walker has been a key-note speaker at several conferences including the Canadian Council of Ministers of Education, the Association of Canadian Community Colleges and has made several presentations to the Parliament of Canada and provincial governments across the country.

CHAPTER 14

Online Fundraising
MICHAEL JOHNSTON

The online environment has become much more important to fundraising much too quickly for most of the charitable sector. We work with the systemic reality of: not enough money, not enough human resources, and not enough comfort with change and risk management. *read more...*

Many fundraisers have heard – and learned – that channels cannot exist in silos yet that is more of a problem than ever before. As online fundraising has quickly become more important, organizations are struggling to decide how to raise not only small, but large gifts, online as well as hire, structure, and execute online.

When organizations (big and small) begin to raise money online it cannot be done in isolation – it needs to be connected to many other parts of the organization (whether it's other fundraising channels, advocacy activity, or mission-based activity).

This chapter tries to compliment content in other chapters by answering a few key questions for any Canadian nonprofit organization concerning the online channel:

- How can a nonprofit organization use online to build, and strengthen, its brand with the public before using it for fundraising?

- How can a nonprofit organization use online to find major and planned gifts?

- How a nonprofit organization can get started by having an online (and integrated schedule) and staff it properly

Finally, it's important to note that this chapter wants to shout out one key fact for anyone who wants to do more – or better – online fundraising: "it's all about integration!"

In fact, it would be easier to shout out that "it's all about donor choice!" This chapter will touch upon research, case studies, and new fundraising thinking that show that all age sub sets of donors (from young, to middle aged, to older) are comfortable in many channels and want many different options available when they give (including online).

This chapter is a call to all fundraisers to better leverage online for brand building and fundraising (of all kinds). It's also a warning that to keep online in a silo is to waste the huge potential of the channel to be the connector that the sector has been looking for over the last forty years of fundraising.

THE BIG PICTURE

The furious adoption of the Internet for fundraising has brought the issue of multichannel marketing to the forefront. In the past, direct mail, television, and the telephone have been effectively combined to help improve fundraising results. In general, the evidence from multichannel marketing before the emergence of online giving was that using a more active channel (e.g., the human voice of a phone call) was an effective way to upgrade donors who were regularly swimming in the channels of a more passive medium like direct mail.

Why does this happen? A wonderful Canadian fundraising colleague, David Love, once said, "No one has ever made a wet dash out of the bathtub to open a letter, but they have to answer a ringing telephone." And that's the difference between active and passive channels. The phone is much more active and more human, and it still has a place in multichannel fundraising.

At the outset, it's important to understand how multichannel fundraising is connected to online giving. Unequivocally, the examples that follow in this chapter (which show a combination of online and traditional channels, especially the telephone) can make huge improvements to online fundraising. The web is a passive medium and can often be helped by more active media like the telephone.

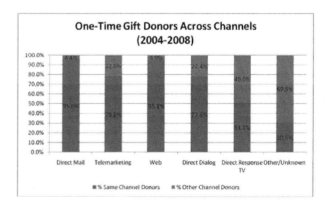

Figure 14.1: Will onetime donors who come in on one channel move to another channel over time?

One of the most frequently asked questions about multichannel marketing is the question of whether donors who come in on one channel (e.g., direct mail) are likely to stay in that same channel or choose another channel to make a donation. The answer is mainly anecdotal, and here we endeavor to give the reader some larger cross-channel statistics to help in the decision to invest more in multichannel fundraising.

Each year, the Cornerstone Group of Companies provides clients with detailed historical trend analyses of their donor activity. In 2008, it provided a benchmark study based on the combined historical results of many of the leading fundraising organizations in Canada (see Figure 14.1).

Cornerstone's analysis looked at close to $400 million dollars-worth of giving to dozens of charities over five years. It's as good a study as we have seen, and its results need dissection. The main result shown in Figure 14.1 is that both direct-mail and web donors have similarly low conversion rates to other channels. After five years, donors who first came in by those two channels remain in the same channel (95.6% for direct mail and 95.1% for the web).

George Irish, an online fund-raiser for almost fifteen years, offered his very trenchant perspective in commenting that those percentages don't necessarily mean that first-time donors in either channel want to remain in those channels. Instead, charities have constructed direct-mail and web fundraising channels that are silos, with little cross-channel solicitation for either kind of donor. Without a doubt, many direct-mail and web donors want to stay in the channel they first gave to, but examples show that, when offered compelling opportunities to give in other channels, many donors do so.

So, we believe that the jury is still out on whether direct-mail and web donors want to stay in their first gift channel. Only with proper cross-channel testing can we know whether donors from the two channels want to live in splendid isolation.

With other channels, there is a higher crossover from the channel donors first gave to, into another channel (78%, 77.6%, and 51.1% for telemarketing, street fundraising, and direct-response television [DRTV], respectively). The initial offer for some charities (like DRTV's prompt to use the telephone) often occurs through another channel, and therefore cross-channel usage is immediately high.

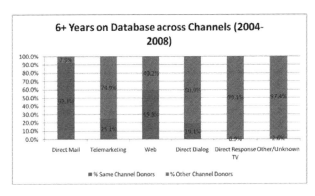

Figure 14.2: Do donors (including regular monthly debit card donors) who come in on one channel make gifts through other channels as well?

Cornerstone's analysis in Figure 14.2 looks at all donors (not just onetime donors but also the important category of monthly donors) and whether they use multiple channels. It's obvious that the most mature channel, direct mail, keeps most of its donors in the same channel.

In some ways, this is self-fulfilling, in that the programs are often not linked to other giving channels, and the customer service model, upgrade system, and re-solicitation programs are complete, sophisticated, and isolated. We have constructed direct mail to be self-enclosed and have received donor results that prove that it has worked.

In addition, DRTV programs often follow up with direct mail, which leads to the use of other channels for giving. And direct dialogue (or face-to-face or door-to-door giving) is the same. We have often followed up door-to-door giving with a telephone call and then direct mail. Donors respond with multichannel solicitation by giving through multiple channels.

Web donors are no different. Many organizations put web donors into the direct-mail stream, and Figure 14.2 shows that 40.2% of web donors do give through other channels, too (most likely direct mail).

Overall, this analysis is very important in that it provides real-world data sourced from many charities. It highlights that donors in direct-mail and web channels tend to stay in the same channel over time; those in other channels do so less often.

All in all, we urge each organization to construct, and test, more multichannel solicitation programs to find out the right combination of online and offline giving to make the most money and lead to the happiest donors.

Significantly, there is a new study which challenges the idea of silos and which gives nonprofit decision makers a very strong statistical backing to invest more into online and integrated fundraising programs. The reader can go to http://www.hjcnewmedia.com/next-gencanadiangiving/ and download the report.

What you will read will not only challenge many of your fundraising assumptions but will give you backing to do more online.

BUILDING BRAND STRENGTH THROUGH ONLINE LEVERAGING

The online environment is an incredibly cost effective place to help a nonprofit organization conduct market research, find (or rediscover) citizens who care about its mission, and ultimately fundraise. The easiest way to show how the online environment can help build and strengthen a nonprofit brand is to show a sample plan from a Canadian organization. What follows is a draft strategy that explains how the online environment can help the Brahmananda Saraswati Foundation (BSF) Canada strengthen its brand and ultimately, fundraising. This foundation has as its mission to bring about world peace, in part, through transcendental meditation (TM).

What's important is that this kind of plan can be crafted at low cost – and executed – at a reasonably low cost. Whether the organization is large or small and no matter the mission, this approach will truly leverage the online environment for brand building (and eventually fundraising).

An online plan was put together that would help BSF connect or re-connect with these millions of practitioners and inspire them to become "Founders of World Peace" by supporting their mandate:

Year 1: Building a community and initial outreach to past TM practitioners. This requires an online destination, blogger outreach, SEM, technology. In year one, BSF will reach out to past TM practitioners to rebuild this list, to re-engage and encouraging them to support BSF's work. At the same time, social media assets will be built to help brand BSF, promote its mission and build an online audience.

Year 2: Continued Outreach and Engagement. BST will build on Year 1 growth through targeted outreach to selected demographic groups. This year will be about engaging BSF's list through regular communications and building opportunities that require BSF's networks to provide more detailed biographical and demographic data. In year two, BSF aims to reach out to a larger network comprised of anyone who shares this vision of attaining "World Peace." This time will be used to grow BSF's online audience of supporters on social networks, while building BSF's list.

Years 2 and beyond: converting supporters. BSF will systematically convert it's followers and supporters to become donors. This effort will be focused on monthly giving and will use the phone, email, and direct mail. The one caveat to conversion timing would be an early conversion testing of past-TM practitioners who are found in the first year community building. Some conversion testing of these constituents could happen in Year 1. (Note the cross-channel conversion methodology being introduced as a partner to the online environment.)

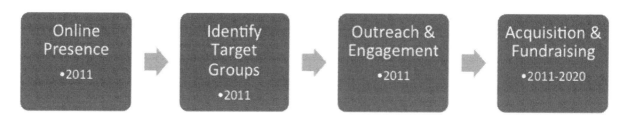

Figure 14.3

A phased approach to using online to build brand and fundraise

PHASE 1: **An official online presence for Brahmananda Saraswati Foundation**
In order to be mission-successful, BSF must first create an engaging, excellent online asset (an official self-branded website).

PHASE 2: **Identify target groups based on interests and demand**
These groups may include:

- Self-help individuals

- Current TM practitioners

- Previous TM practitioners

- General meditation practitioners (past, present)

- General yoga practitioners (past, present)

Figure 14.4

We already know that over 6 million individuals practice TM but this number grows even larger when we look at related health and wellness programs/activities. These groups can be categorized based on their levels of engagement.

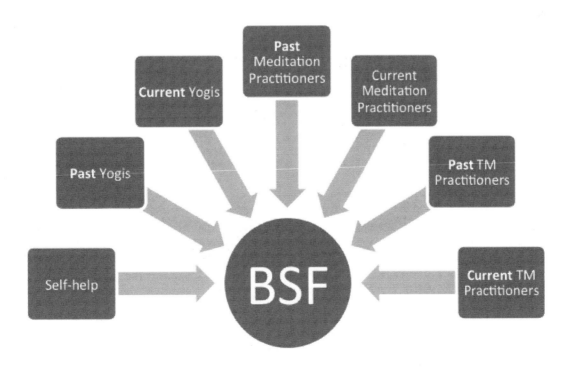

Figure 14.5

PHASE 3	**Outreach & Engagement**
	BSF would begin with re-engaging past TM practitioners. The next step would be initiating contact and stewarding any new constituents. This might be accomplished through a variety of means. Given the broad range of target groups, a marketing plan might include social media marketing, blogger outreach, search engine marketing and optimization and paid advertising.
PHASE 4:	**Acquisition and Fundraising**
	In conjunction with the online brand and engagement work, an integrated call conversion strategy would be necessary to ensure that any acquired leads can be followed up with.
	In order for this to be accomplished, BSF must first have a list of individuals with either:
	Name and full address for which to append a phone number
	Phone number

following ways which rely on users having to submit their personal information in order to take part:

- Virtual meetings/conferences
- Religious books or meditations to receive by mail
- Quarterly newsletter

There you have it. A short but sweet outline of how a non-profit organization can use the online environment to build brand, find people interested in the mission and prepare to convert them into donors. But as mentioned earlier, online MUST go hand-in-hand with other channels (in this case the telephone) to be successful. That's why we want to move to the next section – connecting online and the telephone.

THE TELEPHONE AND ONLINE FUNDRAISING

The fundraising world has been transformed by social network fundraising tools, and before this chapter details some online and offline tactics, let's step back and remind ourselves what social network fundraising is and where it's come from.

What is Social Network Fundraising?

Social Network Fundraising differs from direct response fundraising in that it recognizes the idea that the individual people who support and donate to non-profits do not live in isolation: they live in social circles of family, friends, coworkers and neighbors, all of whom play an important part in their daily lives. Where traditional direct response fundraising seeks to establish a direct one-to-one relationship with each

Using social media and paid marketing support to systematically build BSF's file, the organization would first convert through email followed by the phone. Figure 14.6 demonstrates an online marketing continuum.

Figure 14.6

Before a full calling strategy can be put into place, BSF would use the online environment to cost effectively grow its file of individuals connected to the mission and organization. This can be accomplished in the

supporter, social network fundraising instead focuses on recruiting and mobilizing a smaller set of high-value contacts, known as "multipliers" who will act as communication and fundraising agents for your organization, passing your message into their social circles, and bringing in donations and other forms of support from their "team members."

Examples of straight-forward social network fundraising initiatives:

1. Run for the Cure

One of the earliest models for online social network fundraising was pioneered by the Canadian Breast Cancer Foundation (www.cbcf.org) as a part of the annual charity marathon they organize to raise money for cancer research. They were one of the first organizations to offer online pledge-seekers a set of web and email tools they could use to fundraising from their personal networks. Over eight years, the online fundraising element of the Run for the Cure has grown to become the largest single source of revenue for this multi-million dollar fundraising event.

2. The Night of 1000 Dinners

The Night of 1000 Dinners (www.1000dinners.com) is an annual fundraising event held for the global anti-landmine network. The event takes place on a single day around the world, and involves individual people signing up to host a dinner party at their home where they invite their friends, family and coworkers to join them. A suggested donation is collected from each dinner guest. In this way, the landmines network has been able to organize hundreds of small fundraising events with a single very small office and staff.

3. Amnesty Canada Writeathon

An excellent example of a social network fundraising event is run by Amnesty Canada, who has added a social network fundraising initiative to every year's December 10th Writeathon.

For the annual Writeathon, Amnesty has adopted the model of a charity marathon sponsorship site – asking individual letter-writing participants to go out and seek sponsors for their activity as part of the Writeathon. As an incentive for participants, Amnesty is including prize premiums and a contest draw for the highest pledge earners.

As much as these social network tools are effective in raising money through technology alone, we have found that the tactical and strategic use of the phone further accelerates and improves fundraising results.

Let's look at the following examples of how non-profit organizations (especially grassroots organizations) can further leverage social networking fundraising online.

1. Harry Rosen Spring Run Off

The Princess Margaret Hospital Foundation in Toronto is a cancer-related hospital foundation on par with Sloan Kettering Memorial in the size and sophistication of its fundraising—though in online giving it is probably the most capable in the world.

The organization was intrigued by how the telephone could help improve personal-page fundraising results, and the Harry Rosen Spring Run Off was chosen as a test. This event has been going on for more than 20 years and was founded by the Canadian men's clothier Harry Rosen.

In 2007, a test was conducted on 200 individuals who had made personal fundraising pages. Using an even split, 100 of the individuals were contacted by telephone. The callers thanked the individual for making a page and asked whether they needed any help in raising money online with their social network tool. The other 100 individuals were not called.

The results were encouraging: Individuals who were given a quick (three minutes on average) call got 20% closer ($75 more per registrant) to their fundraising goal than did those individuals who were not called. The calling test was repeated in 2008, and the results were again encouraging and profitable. A call in 2008 improved personal page fundraising by $131.42 per participant reached.

2. Yogainmotion

Another good example comes from Mount Sinai Hospital Foundation and its Auxillary. In spring of 2009, the Mount Sinai Auxillary launched a new pledge based event, a Yoga-thon called Yogainmotion, www.yogainmotion.ca.

Like the Princess Margaret Hospital Foundation, this organization used the telephone to call registrants who made personal pages online to raise money. It was no surprise when the results showed a bit difference when someone was spoken to on the phone.

Figure 14.7 shows how calling and online strategies together can work for pledged based fundraising success.

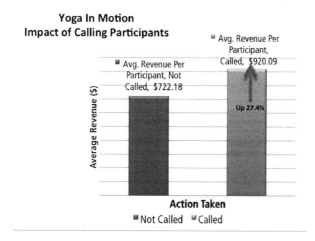

Yoga In Motion
Impact of Calling Participants

Figure 14.7

These examples show the value of testing and rolling out calling for social network fundraising. E-mailing participants is not enough; it is passive, a human voice is active and more effective.

There are a few key investment issues to keep in mind when considering using callers:

1. What will it cost to train internal or external callers to provide expert service to those called?
2. Will that initial investment be recouped by the improved results?
3. Should the calling happen in-house or externally? The answer may be based on the issue of scale. If the organization knows that a successful test would lead to a high number of calls in the future, then an outside solution may be best.

With statistical evidence that a brief call can improve the bottom line results of social network fundraising, a charity needs to think of what to say and when to call.

A phone call to stimulate fundraising can come at different times during a campaign. If you can call more than once, then there are three key points at which to call: at the beginning, middle, and end of a campaign. A social network fundraising campaign has a natural momentum—the ball starts rolling at the beginning, picks up speed and urgency in the middle, and accelerates to the conclusion (event day).

A phone call at the beginning to welcome people and get them comfortable with the technology is key; then a call in the middle of the campaign urging the individual to keep raising money (or to get started because it's not too late!) or to keep raising money to reach a certain incentive is also important. Finally, a final call close to the event to stimulate someone to meet their final goal or exceed it, is a natural denouement to any call campaign. Organizations should investigate how this can be done—and how they can afford it.

At a minimum, if an organization can afford to call only once, it should be a welcoming, introductory call when someone first makes their social network fundraising page.

ONLINE AND LARGE GIFTS

Online fundraising can even find large gifts (like planned gifts). Estate lawyers are reporting that more and more of their older clients are using email to correspond with them when discussing and making changes to their wills. The legacy giving chair of a hospital foundation indicated that it's become such an issue that they've had to implement PDF-policies (in order to create unalterable documents) for client's wills because changes to the will had been going back and forth via email and final versions were becoming hard to agree upon when in Word format.

You may still be doubtful about getting planned gifts online. Recent evidence makes a strong argument.

YOUR PLANNED GIVING WEB LANDING PAGE

If there are large numbers of older donors online going to other organization's legacy web pages then you don't want your organization left behind. In North America, on average 50-60% of adults have made a will. In addition, upon further research, approximately 85-95% of direct mail donors have made a will.

But what should your planned giving page include? How does any nonprofit organization inspire visitors to make a legacy gift?

Figure 14.8 shows an example of best practice on-line construction for a nonprofit organization market-ing a planned giving program

Here are some additional elements that may be integrated into your online legacy presence:

- Incorporate your vision statement

- Include a contact person's details on the page for direct response

- Explain types of legacies (planned gifts) with an emphasis on wills

- Provide "suggested wording" for legal purposes

- Downloadable legacy information/brochure or a web form to request it

- Glossary of legal terms

- Targeted messaging to dispel myths – e.g. you don't have to be old or wealthy to have a will, writing a will and including your favourite charities is easy

Once you've made a planned giving page on your site that can do an excellent job of inspiring and ex-plaining legacy giving then, you need to ensure that people can *find* the legacy section as they navigate your web site.

Once the material is ready and easy to find, then it's time for promotion. Below are a number of important planned giving promotion possibilities that can sup-port your website pages:

- Inclusion of planned giving message in every supporter newsletter (including examples of small and large legacies, explanation of tax benefits, vision, response to named contact, etc.)

Figure 14.8

- Inclusion of planned giving message in Annual Review/Report

- Inclusion of planned giving message in e-mail signature

- Include tick box for requesting planned giving information in other supporter communications (test on appeal coupon)

- Google Ad Words - A large number of older donors use search engines to find what they need and this includes planned giving

This brief example of how online can serve planned or legacy giving, can be similarly adopted for major gifts or even middle donor gifts. Online serves all areas of giving!

HIRING STAFF FOR ONLINE FUNDRAISING

Over the past ten years, charities have often been allocating online fundraising responsibilities to a part-time staff person. The amount of money that online giving has brought in (traditionally a small percentage of overall giving) has made it difficult to justify the budget for a full-time position.

But that time has come and gone. Online giving is one of the few areas of growth in fundraising for charities, and every organization should make an immediate investment in a full time e-philanthropy position to take advantage of that fact.

With dozens of charities over the past six years, there has been one overwhelming human resources recommendation: to create a full-time e-philanthropy, or integrated, fundraising position. That position could be occupied by a present charity staff person if he or she possesses the skill set required for the position.

If your organization is not large enough to afford a full time e-philanthropy person then how do you manage to integrate online fundraising in your plan? Currently, for most charities, there are a number of staff positions that touch on e-philanthropy and integrated fundraising, but none is fully committed to tying online and offline together. We have consistently found that building internal skill sets and internal expertise is the best way to guarantee the success of online and integrated fundraising. Your outside vendors are important resources for any new e-philanthropy and integrated-focused staff person, but those people are still outsiders. They may not be your vendor in a few years, and continuity is important for any donor base that is built. In addition, an internal expert will be able to adapt more quickly to changes in technology (e.g., social media).

Many charities have web-related committees with both volunteers and staff. The e-philanthropy and/or integrated fundraising staff person can provide leadership to such committees. For example, if a staff person were to direct a web committee, then the committee would have to include the following high-priority tasks:

1. Create a one-year plan for online fundraising that outlines integration tactics, media tactics, testing schedules, technology testing, and goal setting.

2. Provide creative and testing direction to an application service provider (ASP) to maximize use of technology for integrated fundraising.
3. Provide input to an integrated stewardship plan for existing and future donors.
4. Coordinate with public relations and other departments to obtain online and offline media to support online fundraising.
5. Coordinate with the IT and marketing departments on online fundraising.

What could this new position look like? Ideally, the e-philanthropy manager or integrated manager would be a full-time staff position. This person would be responsible for delivery of the entire e-philanthropy program and areas of online and offline fundraising integration, which includes:

- Managing online and offline marketing and media relationships that relate to online giving

- Acting as the primary person for interacting with ASP on maximizing the use of the technology for online and integrated fundraising

- Integration of social network fundraising with online and offline channels

- Integration of all direct response media as it relates to online fundraising

This position would have middle management, non-director status; would report to the director of fundraising; and would be independent of the public relations, marketing, IT, and communications departments.

This new staff person should also have the following qualifications:

- Reasonable technical background (especially in technology implementation)

- Good interpersonal skills

- Good communication skills

- Experience working in directorship positions

- A leader with experience in the field

- A track record of success

- A team player

- Good blender

- Online marketing experience

- Experience in other area of direct-response fundraising

It is vital that this position be seen as—and be allowed to be—a connecting position. The point is not to create another silo in fundraising but to be open and collaborative.

An e-philanthropy or integrated fundraising position allows for open channels of frequent communication among other departments and development teams and a new, additional, resource of expertise on matters that brings together fundraising, the Internet, and new marketing.

THE FUTURE OF ONLINE FUNDRAISING

One of the last things to be discussed in this chapter is the power and potential of the Internet to give us – finally – truly personalized, completely individualized giving experiences.

This goes beyond the tactical examples of using online to acquire warm leads or using multiple channels to create greater customer loyalty or a higher average gift. This gets much, much deeper. This is about letting every citizen get a completely different and unique experience with your brand. Goodbye mass marketing and hello personalized marketing.

The Internet has created the tools and the opportunity for individuals to make their own places online; to do their marketing; and pursue their own goals – whether commercial or civic minded – at very low cost.

Traditionally, non-profit organizations have created template, non-personalized online fundraising marketing initiatives to a mass audience e.g. large email marketing campaigns or online fundraising tools for a broad group e.g. the Weekend to End Breast Cancer.

The following outline provides an outline or "skeleton" of a strategy to create a unique, separate community of engaged individuals focused on a specific cause - in this example, one type of cancer:

GOAL: An online destination to call their own

To help build a sense of shared purpose and control, there would be a landing page – or micro site – that would provide a look and feel for the group; give them shared functionality to market, share, and fundraise on their type of cancer; and be a destination for the community to drive their own online and offline traffic.

For example, the URLs could be something like www.PMHFmyway.org/typeofcancer (this is a make-believe URL) At a minimum, the URL would give a sense of personal control within PMHF and be connected in some way to what we can call PMHF micro-communities.

A micro-page would not be created until there was a committee struck – or an existing committee is empowered and educated – to make their own online destination. If there is an existing committee, they would be asked to assign an online champion to help guide and steward the page (and tools) and the committee would be trained, as appropriate, to use some of the functionality of the site.

It's important to note that if a group makes the commitment to have a community site, then they would work with PMHF to set a financial goal and work with PMHF staff to set a calendar of online and offline events to raise that money.

The micro site would use functionality that could include:

1. An online forum to discuss their cancer-type research; breakthroughs, etc. There would be an explicit agreement that PMHF would have the right to monitor, and edit, material as needed.

2. Online personal pages for 3rd party events related to their type of cancer.

3. Online personal pages for tribute/memorial giving.

4. A micro-site ranked of the top fundraisers for this type of cancer.

5. A yearly financial goal set for the community.

6. A video tool that would allow individuals to create their own stories about treatment at PMHF – laying in templated music/beginning and end calls to action.

7. Social media tools to get out the message on their type of cancer. This could include

personal use of social media tools and/or creation of social media pages for each created community.

8. The publishing of, and the ability to comment on, research at PMHF done specifically for their type of cancer. If the committee could connect directly to the researchers, there could be some direct publication of research material for their type of cancer. As stated above, PMHF would have the right and ability to edit content as needed.

Before the creation of a micro-site and accompanying tools, PMHF would conduct in-person, telephone and/or online surveys of what the organization wants to accomplish with their own site and tools. Individuals would be asked which tools would they use – and what skills could they bring to the enterprise.

The online environment holds the possibility of empowering supporters to create online communities of like-minded individuals around one particular kind of cause and market for you.

There is a growing tradition of individuals and groups using online tools to raise money for you in a more templated – and generic – fundraising environment e.g. the Ride and the Weekend.

However, this brief outline points to an even more personalized (and community-controlled) online environment in which like-minded individuals are given a more complete and powerful set of online tools: trained to use them; given a collective goal; and encouraged to raise more money for PMHF on one type of cancer they care to beat the most.

Every courageous non-profit organization should explore how this kind of empowered community could be built, and tested.

CONCLUSION

The furious growth of online giving (and social media and social network fundraising) has challenged every organization to not only master online giving but the integration of all fundraising channels together.

The idea of combining online and offline fundraising to make more money and improve donor relations has not been definitively proved. The study referenced at the start of this chapter clearly demonstrated that many direct-mail and web donors stay in their channel, never leaving, and after six years of giving, continue to give the way they did at the start. However, comparative studies from both the U.S. and Canada, such as those found at http://www.hjcnewmedia.com/nextgencanadiangiving/ are less instructive.

Nevertheless, this chapter has tried to show that online is a hugely powerful tool to build or strengthen a non-profit's brand and ultimately fundraising when combined with other channels such as the telephone.

The thoughtful combination of mail, phone, and the web can increase average donations, response rates, and net income. Clearly, individual case studies do not forge a broad definitive study that everyone can rely on. The only way you will discover whether integrated fundraising can be effective for your charity is to create a testing model appropriate for the organization.

If your organization is good at pledge events, then it makes sense to test how the telephone can support online pledge pages. If your organization has a strong direct-mail program, then it makes sense to investigate how e-mail and web activities can work in conjunction with the mail to increase net revenue. And if your organization has a symbolic gift campaign (like those best personified by the World Vision Canada holiday catalogue in which you buy a loved one a gift of a chicken, goat, or another sustainable livelihood object instead of a REAL gift), then the combination of online and offline giving will lead to a larger gross and net income.

But even if you have a test structure for integrated fundraising and are ready to execute a program, who will do it? Do you have the internal resources and skill sets to run an online and offline fundraising program? That person could be a volunteer or part-time staff person if you are a small organization, or full-time if you have a larger budget. Take a look at the work description earlier in this chapter and see how you can make it happen.

People are vital in fundraising and it's no difference online. Nicolas Locke, now the fundraising head of the Alberta Cancer Foundation made sure a full-time online giving person was hired seven years ago at the BC

Cancer Foundation. Today, it's the main reason they are, per capita, the most effective online fundraisers in the country.

Online is here to stay. And it's here to stay in ways that help it support other areas of fundraising and communication. You may want to begin by using online to strengthen you brand, message, and mission. If so, the example from BSF Canada will be a helpful start.

If you see online as supporting traditional fundraising, then our look at planned giving hopefully piqued your interest.

However, there is one central point in this chapter that resonates throughout the entire book: the only way your organization will be truly successful online is if you truly believe, plan, and execute an integrated fundraising plan with online deeply embedded in all activities. Even more important is finding, training, and hiring the right staff person (part-time or full-time) or a very loyal volunteer to relentlessly execute your online initiatives.

You should have started yesterday but there's still time! There always is in fundraising.

ADDITIONAL RESOURCES

Books

▶ GEIER, PHILIP H., GREENFIELD, JAMES M., HART, TED & MacLAUGHLIN, STEVE. (2010). *Internet Management for Nonprofits: Strategies, Tools and Trade Secrets.* John Wiley and Sons

▶ GREENFIELD, JAMES M., HART, TED & HAJI, SHEERAZ, D. (2007). *People to People Fundraising - Social Networking and Web 2.0 for Charities*, John Wiley and Sons.

▶ GREENFIELD, JAMES M., HART, TED & JOHNSTON, MICHAEL W. (2005). *Nonprofit Internet Strategies - Best Practices for Marketing, Communications, and Fundraising Success.* John Wiley and Sons

▶ JOHNSTON, MICHAEL W. (2000). *Direct Response Fundraising, Trends for Results.* John Wiley and Sons.

ABOUT THE AUTHOR

Michael Johnston

Michael Johnston is President and founder of the Hewitt and Johnston Consultants and co-founder of two globally based companies, The Global Legacy Giving Group and the sports-based Fantasy Fundraising.

Michael has been a fundraiser for 22 years, and has worked with 100's of nonprofit organizations in Canada, the U.S., Europe, Latin America, and Asia Pacific. He is an expert in direct response fundraising innovation and integrated campaigning – most especially in the use of new media technologies like the web, and their integration with traditional direct response methods. He is the author of The Fund Raiser's Guide to the Internet, The Nonprofit Guide to the Internet and the editor of two books: Internet Strategies: Best Practices for Marketing, and Direct Response Fund Raising: Mastering New Trends for Results.

Mike was a founding Board Member of the Washington-based e-Philanthropy Foundation, and was the first chair of its Education Committee. In addition, Michael was the founding Foundation Chair for the first global charity online lottery, www.globelot.com.

CHAPTER 15

FOUNDATIONS
LESLIE WEIR, ACFRE

"If you've seen one foundation, you've seen one foundation…"

Richard L. Frost, CEO, The Winnipeg Foundation

read more…

INTRODUCTION

This statement is frequently repeated by Rick Frost, CEO of the oldest community foundation in Canada when he is asked to comment on foundations generally or community foundations specifically. As a fund development practitioner seeking to successfully secure grants from foundations, it is of paramount importance to recognize the fundamental uniqueness of each foundation. The process for securing foundation grants is the same as it is for the other two private sector groups – individuals and corporations:

- Identifying predisposed prospective foundation supporters;

- Assessing and ranking "predisposed" foundations based on degree of shared interests, values, priorities and financial capacity;

- Creating tailored grant applications for top-ranked foundation prospects; and

- Building mutually fruitful relationships based on shared interests.

This chapter will examine the history, growth and diversity of foundations and the varied ways they support philanthropic activities in Canada. It will also outline how to successfully attract foundation grants using targeted tailor-made approaches.

Shifting landscape sparks growth in philanthropy and foundations

While the first community foundation was founded in Winnipeg in 1921, it was drastic reductions in government funding in the 1980s and 1990s that prompted community benefit organizations to seek greater investments from philanthropic individuals, families and corporations. There was an acknowledgement that it would require a $6 increase in philanthropic gifts for every $1 reduction in public funding to "fill the gap." As a result, charities were able to make stronger cases for support on the basis of preserving services valued by donors or the community. Long-standing perceptions of what Canadians expected governments to provide with public funds and what was perceived as appropriately reliant on private philanthropy began to blur, gradually shift and often overlap.

At the same time, many Canadians were accumulating more wealth than their parents and grand-

parents had. As the millennium drew to a close the multi-trillion dollar wealth transfer was trumpeted as a potential boon for the philanthropic sector. The theory, developed by Dr. Paul Schervish of Boston College, anticipated that as the Depression and World War II generations passed away, their estates would transfer to individual beneficiaries, to governments in the form of taxes (especially capital gains taxes) or to charities (which would generate tax credits). Canada, with its more pronounced baby boom cohort, the first of whom will turn 65 in 2011, would have a similar opportunity to encourage and promote the idea of creating or leaving a legacy that would benefit future generations.

In the early 1990s many charities developed Planned Giving programs to promote and encourage supporters to consider deferred gifts, like bequests. Planned Giving takes place when one or more advisors help people develop a tax-efficient plan to take care of their family and loved ones and fulfill their philanthropic intentions and goals in the context of their personal and financial circumstances.

By 1996 a consortium of proponents advocated for changes to Canada's Income Tax Act that would enhance and broaden tax incentives for gifts to registered charities and public foundations, especially bequests, other estate gifts and gifts-in-kind of appreciated securities. A series of regulatory changes did just that. Indeed, Malcolm Burrows, CFRE Head of Philanthropic Advisory Services makes the argument that Canadians now enjoy more generous tax benefits for philanthropic giving than American taxpayers, challenging the long-held perception that America's system of charitable tax deductions was the reason why Americans contribute a higher percentage of their income than Canadians.[1]

Regulatory changes that have had a favourable effect on philanthropy began in 1996 and continued up to and including those introduced in the 2010 federal budget. Incorporating philanthropic provisions has become a means of preserving the value of inheritances for loved ones or optimizing the value of philanthropic provisions. The number of current gifts secured through the process of discussing deferred gifts has had a substantial effect on reshaping some Planned Giving programs. While in the early years there was a

---

1   (2009) Dialogue - Mars & Venus: Made in Canada 2. *Gift Planning for Canadians: The Arts and Science of Charitable Gift Planning*, Volume 14, Number 9, p. 7.

tendency to focus exclusively on deferred gift options rather than immediate outright gifts, the elimination of capital gains tax on gifts of appreciated listed securities, (initially to public foundations and later extended to private foundations) also helped to encourage more and larger gifts during a donor's lifetime.

The combined effect of constraints on government funding at all levels, greater wealth being held by individuals (especially in listed public securities) and tax incentives that enhanced the benefits of making more and/or larger gifts during life and as part of an estate plan created opportunities for charities, public and private foundations to attract and secure assets. Philanthropic organizations hired staff specifically to seek significant gifts from donors' assets, while not impinging on annual gifts from their donors' income. Endowment funds were recognized as a source of revenue to bolster financial security and invest in a stronger future. The number of public and private foundations multiplied and donor-advised funds became a popular option. As well, two new types of foundations emerged, each signifying the blurring of lines and roles between the private, pubic and philanthropic sectors: corporate foundations and foundations affiliated with banking or other financial institutions.

Another tangible result of these trends was the emergence of public-private partnerships (PPPs or 3Ps) as a means of funding large capital projects. The Canadian Council for Public-Private Partnerships (CCPPP) was established in 1993 as a member-sponsored organization with representatives from both the public and the private sectors. Public-Private Partnership Canada relates to provision of public services or public infrastructure and involves the transfer of risk between partners. The Canadian Council for Public-Private Partnerships definition is:

A cooperative venture between the public and private sectors, built on the expertise of each partner that best meets clearly defined public needs through the appropriate allocation of resources, risks and rewards.

This has emerged in an increasingly competitive global environment in which governments around the world are exploring new ways to finance projects, build infrastructure and deliver services. Public private partnerships (PPPs or P3s) bring together the strengths of the sectors. Benefits accrue from maximizing the efficiencies and innovations of private enterprise and providing capital to finance government programs and projects. This frees public funds for core economic and social programs. One or more foundations may be among the partners providing funds needed to make a project viable, adding one more "p" to the acronym: philanthropy. The lines of demarcation between the sectors become blurred as each responds to challenges and opportunities that arise in a dynamic environment.

An overview of foundations in Canada

There are over 160,000 not-for-profit organizations in Canada of which about 80,000 are registered charities. Almost 10,000 of Canada's registered charities are categorized as foundations. About half (4,690) are public foundations that seek public support for their missions and depend on diverse revenue sources to sustain their activities. Income generated by permanently invested capital held in endowment funds provides one stream of annual revenue for these foundations. The other 50% (4,526) of foundations in Canada are private foundations controlled by a single donor or family. They are governed by a board of trustees whose members form a majority (more than 50%) not at arm's length from each other or the founding donor.

According to Philanthropic Foundations of Canada, foundations tend to be clustered in central Canada with 61% in Ontario and Quebec, 33% in the Western and Northern provinces and 6% in Eastern Canada or the Maritimes.[2] In 2008 the asset base of public foundations was $16.6 billion and that of private foundations was $17.3 billion.

Foundations usually invest their capital in endowed funds that last forever and use the annual income generated from the investment to fulfill their mission by providing grants to registered charities or qualified donees in Canada. Foundations may also handle "flow-through" gifts to a greater or lesser extent. This occurs when foundations accept certain donations or revenue for disbursement in the year of the gift or in accordance with an agreement between the foundation and the donor.

Foundations differ from other registered charities in that they seldom provide direct services. Rather, they support and advance the missions of operating chari-

2   Retrieved from the Private Foundations of Canada website: *http://pfc.ca/en/resources/foundations-in-canada*

ties that align with: their funding interests, geographic scope, priorities, and, in the case of corporate foundations, their target markets through their grant-making activities. Every foundation is a unique reflection of its history, culture, size, scope, breadth or narrowness of their objectives and many other characteristics. They share a common interest in assuring that their grants have a positive impact in their areas of interest. If your organization is in a position to help a foundation fulfill its mission and have a positive impact, it is likely to be predisposed to support your programs.

The next section examines public foundations in general, with a more detailed look at community foundations that grant to a wide spectrum of charities on the basis of competitive grant applications and the expressed wishes of donors.

PUBLIC FOUNDATIONS

There are over 4,500 public foundations in Canada. Though they are separately incorporated and governed by an independent board of trustees, most are intended to support the activities of a related charity or institution, such as a hospital, university, school or community service organization. In addition to annual income generated by permanent endowment funds, most tend to have multiple sources of revenue, generated by an array of fundraising programs (i.e., direct mail, tele-fundraising, capital campaigns, major and planned giving and grants from other foundations) and activities (i.e., special events, lotteries and cause marketing).

The endowed funds in public foundations are pooled and invested to provide a relatively stable stream of income every year, which may be for discretionary or specified purposes determined by the Board. The amount available to spend depends on the policies, market conditions and investment results of each foundation. Growth is proportional to the amount of new capital invested within this framework. Grants generally benefit the related "parent" or beneficiary organization. Such public foundations would rarely entertain grant proposals from unrelated charities and then only in the case of a partnership or other mutually beneficial opportunity.

Community foundations are a subset of the public foundation category. They make grants to many and diverse charitable organizations within their geographic focus, so are worthy of a closer look.

Community foundations - A Canadian movement for community vitality

Community foundations have a long history in Canada, beginning with the establishment of The Winnipeg Foundation in 1921. The Victoria Foundation was the next to be established in 1936, followed by The Vancouver Foundation in 1943 and The Calgary Foundation in 1955. By 1990 there were 30 community foundations. They were largely a phenomenon of Western Canada until more recent years.

With the establishment of Community Foundations of Canada (CFC) in 1992 (the national membership organization for Canadian community foundations) foundations began to work together to build stronger communities by enhancing the philanthropic leadership of foundations.

CFC was there to provide organization, coordination and support at a time when government funding was diminishing, philanthropy was becoming more important to communities and tax regulations were beginning to change, providing philanthropic individuals with new incentives to give more and larger gifts.

It is notable that the T.R. Meighen Foundation in New Brunswick and the Thomas Sill Foundation in Manitoba provided incentives and funds to encourage and support the development of rural foundations in their provinces. Manitoba is home to 45 community foundations, almost one quarter of the total number across Canada.

Today Community Foundations of Canada describes itself as the Canadian movement for community vitality. It represents 176 member foundations that serve 89% of Canadians from coast to coast. It connects and supports a growing network of community foundations that, in 2009 held $2.85 billion in assets and made grants totaling $140 million. This marked a decrease compared to $169 million granted in 2008, prior to the effects of the recession and coincidental market turmoil.[3] Canadians also gave new capital of $194 million to community foundations in 2009.

---

3 Retrieved from the Community Foundations of Canada website: *http:// www.cfc-fcc.ca/about-cfc/index*

Canada's oldest community foundation: The Winnipeg Foundation

The Winnipeg Foundation, Canada's first community foundation, was established in 1921 with a cheque for $100,000 from William Forbes Alloway. This new form of philanthropy had sprung up in the United States in 1914, when The Cleveland Foundation was created by a gift from a wealthy banker named Frederick H. Goff.[4]

Alloway, a successful Winnipeg banker, saw the creation of the Foundation as a way for him to give back to his community. He intended his gift to help realize his vision of a culturally-rich city with opportunities for young people and those challenged by hardship, poverty or illness.

> **"Since I first set foot in Winnipeg 51 years ago, Winnipeg has been my home and has done more for me than it may ever be in my power to repay. I owe everything to this community and feel it should receive some benefit from what I have been able to accumulate."**
>
> *— William Forbes Alloway, Founder,*
> *The Winnipeg Foundation*

In 1924, the Foundation received an envelope labeled "The Widow's Mite" containing its second gift: three $5 dollar gold coins. Modest compared to Alloway's initial donation, this gift truly set The Winnipeg Foundation apart as a community foundation and came to symbolize the spirit that drives the Foundation: that any contribution, no matter the size, can make a difference in the community. This principle remains deeply entrenched in the Foundation's values.

A few years later the Foundation also received substantial bequests from Alloway's estate and that of his wife, Elizabeth. Since then, thousands of people from all walks of life have followed in their footsteps with gifts of all sizes. Every year their gifts help fulfill the Foundation's vision of a Winnipeg where community life flourishes.

Gifts made to The Winnipeg Foundation are pooled and permanently invested to help ensure the city flourishes today and tomorrow. Income generated from endowment funds is distributed as grants to local charities in the areas of: community service, education and employment, health, environment, heritage, arts and culture and recreation. These grants meet the changing needs of the community and proactively address challenges as they arise. Grants also faithfully carry out expressed wishes of donors and support particular charitable projects. The Foundation places emphasis on initiatives that are sustainable, long-term and have broad community impact.

Throughout its history, the Foundation has played an important role in Winnipeg's community life. It has supported the community for almost nine decades, thanks to the foresight, generosity and trust of everyday philanthropists. Imagine the profound impact of cumulative grants of almost $250 million for hundreds of projects and organizations that have contributed to the vibrancy of Winnipeg and the well-being of its citizens. Today it is the second largest foundation in Canada with assets of almost $450 million, the largest being The Vancouver Foundation with assets of $720 million (2009).

Highlights of The Winnipeg Foundation's history[5] depict some of Canada's social, economic, cultural, technological and regulatory changes over nine decades (Figure 15.1).

---

4   Kelly, Kathleen S. (1998). *Effective Fundraising Management.* Laurence Erlbaum & Associates.

5   Retrieved from The Winnipeg Foundation website, *http://www.wpgfdn.org/ aboutus-history.php*

Year	Highlight
1921	The Winnipeg Foundation is founded by William Forbes Alloway with a gift of $100,000.
1922	The first grants are made -- $6,000 equally shared by the Margaret Scott Nursing Home, Knowles Home for Boys, Victorian Order of Nurses, Children's Hospital and the Children's Aid Society.
1924	"The Widow's Mite," an anonymous donation of three $5 gold coins, is made to the Foundation. This modest, second gift, comes to represent the value of every donation, no matter what the size.
1925	The first designated fund is established at the Foundation by Mr. A.R. McNichol, to benefit the Victorian Order of Nurses, Knowles Home for Boys and Margaret Scott Foundation.
1930	William Alloway leaves his estate to the foundation following his death, and that of his wife, Elizabeth Alloway. Together, their estates totaled more than $2 million. This greatly expands the resources of the Foundation to support the community. Though it had been originally decided that member organizations of the Community Chest would not receive operational support from the Foundation, the hardships brought on by recession in 1930 caused the Foundation to change its policy.
1935	The "In Memoriam Fund" was established for donors to make a gift to the Foundation in lieu of flowers as their tribute to family or friends who had died.
1937	The Foundation receives its first gift of a life insurance policy.
1941	All capital accounts awaiting investment are invested in Victory War Loans.
1944	Surplus funds from each year for the next five years are put into the Community Emergency Reserve, which by October 1949 represents $100,000 in bonds.
1950	A Legislative amendment made April 1st, 1950, expands the scope of the Foundation. It can now "accept and administer gifts for educational and cultural purposes." Before this change, the Foundation could only administer grants for charitable uses. $25,000 is granted to the Manitoba Flood Relief Fund, payable from a community emergency reserve account.
1952	A large grant is awarded to the Children's Hospital to help address the polio outbreak.
1958	The Foundation begins establishing and managing the funds of any recognized agency in the field of welfare, education or culture. This enables other organizations to have designated trust funds managed by the Foundation with all profits going to the organization.
1965	A one-time $15,000 grant is given to the fledgling United Way, formerly known as the Community Chest.
1968	The Canada Assistance Plan is put in place to provide for the operating budgets of many agencies, allowing The Winnipeg Foundation to concentrate on more experimental and innovative projects.
1972	Total assets of the Foundation exceed $10 million.

Year	Highlight
1977	This year's grants exceed $1 million.
1980	The Act of the Foundation is revised to expand grant-making activity to include conservation of human, natural and heritage resources.
1981	The Foundation's assets now total over $20 million.
1983	Grants totaling more than $2 million are paid out.
1996	A bronze bust of William Alloway is sculpted by Leo Mol in celebration of the Foundations 75th anniversary. Capital assets are now over $100 million dollars.
1999	The Foundation begins Youth in Philanthropy, a program that gives high school students the opportunity to administer grants and explore the world of philanthropy.
2001	The Foundation sees unprecedented growth in endowment funds, including a $10 million gift from Israel Asper and a $100 million gift from the Moffat family, one of the largest single donations ever made to a philanthropic organization in Canada and the largest ever made to a community foundation in Canada. Cumulative total grants made by the Foundation surpass $100 million.
2002	The Foundation launches its website, **www.wpgfdn.org**
2003	The Foundation makes the largest grant in its history -- $6 million to the Canadian Museum for Human Rights. The Literacy for Life Fund is established at the Foundation to support family literacy programs in Manitoba. The Fund is a partnership with Literacy Partners of Manitoba and the Winnipeg Public Library. The Foundation launches the Centennial Neighbourhood Project, a multi-faceted five-year initiative to help revitalize one of Winnipeg's most challenged neighbourhoods.
2005	The Manitoba government partners with the province's community foundations to develop new bursary programs for rural students, committing $500,000 to be administered by the Foundation over five years. The Foundation's Summer Internship Program begins, matching four Youth in Philanthropy participants with 8-week paid summer jobs at local registered charities. The Foundation is the presenting sponsor of CancerCare Manitoba's 75th anniversary Bears on Broadway project.
2007	The Foundation injects $675,000 over five years into child nutrition programs. The funding is provided through the Moffat Family Fund and administered by Manitoba Council on Child Nutrition.

Year	Highlight
2008	Cumulative total grants made by the Foundation surpass $200 million.
	The Foundation commits $3 million over the next five years to downtown Winnipeg with its Downtown Green Spaces Strategy.
	Electronic grant applications and payments are implemented.
2009	The Foundation stands by its long-standing policy of granting 5% of the average market value of its endowments, calculated over 12 quarters to moderate any market fluctuations in a single year. The 2008 recession and investment losses of over 8% triggered a provision that called for a modest change in its spending rate to allow rebuilding of capital: spending began decreasing in increments of 0.2% annually, to a low of 4.2% by 2013. Then, it will gradually begin to recover. Nonetheless, grants grew to $20.8 million in 2009, from $19.2 million distributed in 2008, despite losses and market turbulence.

Figure 15.1

PRIVATE FOUNDATIONS

Most of the 4,500 private foundations in Canada are family foundations; independent philanthropic holding companies governed by boards of trustees that are not at arm's length from the founding donor. The founding donor and family members are usually involved during the donor's lifetime. This may carry forward to future generations. Some may have a sunset clause that triggers the wind-up of the foundation and a process for spending down of the capital. Other foundations may carry on in perpetuity by appointing a corporate trustee, transferring the assets to a community foundation or other service provider entrusted with carrying out the founder's intent without the involvement of family members or other representatives.

The type of approach and proposal will differ depending on whether a foundation employs professional staff officers or not. If so, the staff likely oversees the grants process and makes recommendations to the governing board. If the foundation is governed and administered primarily by family members, they alone likely determine the openness to proposals and make grant decisions.

CORPORATE FOUNDATIONS

A few corporate foundations have existed for many years, often associated with the philanthropic endeavors of a family enterprise. They have become more common and function as a repository for funds designated from corporate revenue, raised through employee donations or events and contributed to by customers or the public. Granting patterns usually align with the interests of their employees or target markets. Its corporate foundation is integral to a company's brand and image.

FOUNDATIONS AFFILIATED WITH BANKING AND FINANCIAL INSTITUTIONS

A new commercial option emerged in 2004 when the Toronto Dominion Bank created the TD Private Giving Foundation, providing clients with philanthropic planning and granting services through donor-advised funds. Pioneered in the 1990s by Fidelity Trust in the United States, the model had proved popular and highly successful in attracting philanthropic capital. Today it ranks among the largest American foundations. Most Canadian banks, financial and insurance institutions have followed TD Bank's lead; creating foundations that enable clients to have their philanthropic interests remain under the stewardship of their financial advisor and institution. It is not as expensive as setting up and administering a private foundation, though the fees are higher than those offered through community foundations. They tend not to be open to proposals, though the donor-advisors may choose to make a grant in response to a specific appeal for support.

FOUNDATIONS AND CHARITIES: IT'S A FINE BALANCE

Foundations are established to give money away. They must make grants annually to registered charities providing services or undertaking projects relevant to their missions. Many charities depend in part on grants from foundations to help meet new or increased needs, take advantage of opportunities, develop and implement new programs, support capital projects or fund research. This interdependence is at its best when each is respectful and appreciative of the other's role in pursuing the common good and enhancing some aspect of community life.

Foundations either seek out partnerships or strive to attract proposals from philanthropic organizations whose missions and values align with their own. By the same token, registered charities that have done a good job of defining their mission, vision, values and priorities are better able to identify foundations with overlapping interests that make grants in their geographic scope.

FINDING THE RIGHT FIT

Research is important to initiating a mutually beneficial and respectful relationship. This is true whether you are working on behalf of a charity to seek grant funding or on behalf of a foundation to make effective grants. Foundations and philanthropic organizations are two halves of a whole. The challenge is to identify those with overlapping objectives, whether from the perspective of a foundation or an operating charity.

Searchable online databases can facilitate identifying the best prospective foundations that may make a grant to a particular organization or program, that is, any that may be predisposed to your cause for some reason.

FREE ELECTRONIC RESOURCES

Just like registered charities, foundations are registered with the Canada Revenue Agency and listed on their Charities and Giving website. Every foundation must submit its T3010 charity return annually. The public portion of each return is posted on the Canada Revenue Agency website,[6] which has a searchable database. Most foundations are proud to publish their past grants in their annual reports and on their websites. This provides a rich source of information about their geographic scope, scale of granting, areas of interest or granting priorities.

CharityVillage.com also provides electronic links to grant-making foundations at no cost. Many useful resources are available free on their grant-seeking page.

FEE-BASED SUBSCRIPTION SERVICES

There are also subscription-based databases with software tools to support key word searches that locate grants by location, recipient, type, field of interest, value and year. They enable analysis of giving trends over time:

Imagine Canada's Canadian Directory to Foundations and Corporations[7]
- 3,000-3,500 foundations that are relevant to grant-seekers; must have a history of making grants within Canada to more than one or two designated charities

- includes a "How-To" Manual on building foundation partnerships and is fully bilingual

Metasoft's FoundationSearch[8]
- FoundationSearch is a North America wide resource of fundraising information for non-profits and charities including more than 120,000 foundations

- It has tools to locate grants by type, value, year, recipient, donor and historical giving trends and board directors

6   Canada Revenue Agency Charities website: *http://www.cra-arc.gc.ca/charities*
7   Retrieved from Imagine Canada: Canadian Directory to Foundations and Grants website: *http://www.imaginecanada.ca*
8   Retrieved from Metasoft: FoundationSearch Canada website: *http://www.foundationsearch.ca*

As with any successful fund development program, start with those foundations closest to you. Become familiar with the public and private foundations in your area, focusing on any that have an affinity for the organization or cause for which you are seeking support, especially if they have made grants to your organization in the past.

Review each foundation's website. This will help you identify the ones that you think would be the most receptive and responsive. Some will have a wealth of information that will give you insight to strengthen your case. Others may provide limited information beyond the foundation's geographic scope, funding interests or priorities and when and how to apply.

Prioritize the foundations that seem to fit well with your organization's values and mission, and where your organization's priorities and services are congruent with and would advance the foundation's purpose and objectives. Assess each foundation against some measure, such as "LIA":

- **Linkage** (Do any of your board members know members of the foundation's board?)

- **Interest** (Would your proposal address one of the foundation's funding interests?)

- **Ability** (What is the foundation's annual funding capacity, average grant, largest grant?)

Develop your case for support and proposal targeted to the interests and requirements of the best of the prospective foundations you identified. Adapt that case proposal, tailoring it to align with that foundation's unique philanthropic aspirations and submitting it in accordance with its grant application processes and timelines. Highlight mutual benefits related to your project (how the proposed grant would further your mission). Include appropriate gestures of appreciation, reporting and evaluation mechanisms.

Early success with grant proposals from foundations in your geographic area will help you make a stronger case if and when you widen your research to reach other foundations with granting criteria that align with your cause. Take advantage of opportunities to get to know the people behind the foundations.

Avoid the temptation to chase funding that is not congruent with your organization's mission – stretching or reshaping your proposal in order to better fit a foundation's funding criteria. The result can be that your organization begins to drift away from its mission. Such departures can compound over time, in effect diverting programs and activities further and further from your organization's stated mission in order to gain or retain outside funding.

A natural tension exists between organizations seeking funding and their prospective funders. This is especially true for many foundations as high proportions of their granting capacity may be restricted. Finding a balance between shared and diverging interests is a challenge best resolved through dialogue with a goal of reaching mutual agreement without compromising the integrity of the foundation or the organization seeking funding.

APPLYING FOR A GRANT

Carefully follow the guidelines and process that may be prescribed by a given foundation. Each foundation's grant-making process is unique. However, four progressive steps are common to many:

1. A letter of inquiry to the appropriate person

   - Follow-up by phone to establish degree of common interest.

   - In the case of no shared interest being found, send a thank you letter acknowledging the foundation representative's time and consideration and to preserve the connection and pave the way for future opportunities.

2. An initial interview to discuss degree of shared interest

   - Dialogue that concludes with recommendations from the foundation representative about how to proceed, what to include and emphasize in the proposal, suggested dollar range for the grant request, anticipated timeline and any other pertinent information.

3. Creation and submission of a grant proposal

   - This is your opportunity to use all of the information you have gathered and the insight you gained to present a compelling case that will convince foundation board members that your proposal is an excellent investment in furthering the foundation's mission.

4. An on-site visit or project interview

- Depending on the type and size of the foundation and the proposal, this may involve foundation staff, board members and/or family members. It is an opportunity to showcase your cause and project and establish or enhance your organization's relationship with the foundation representatives.

- If possible involve a board member as well as the person most knowledgeable about the project and a potential beneficiary if appropriate; the goal is to enable the foundation representatives to envision how their foundation's support would help create the better future that will be possible as a result of the project.

WHY PROPOSALS ARE NOT FUNDED

1. The proposal is poorly written. It may be confusing or the project description, budget and timelines are not consistent.
2. You are outside of the geographic area.
3. You have not shown how your project meets the goals of the foundation.
4. There is no sense of urgency for the project.
5. The dollar amount you asked for is out of the foundations range.
6. The foundation does not know you.
7. The foundation has already allocated all of its budget.

WHAT TO DO IF YOUR PROJECT IS FUNDED OR REJECTED

Say thank you no matter what!

It's easy to be effusive with gratitude when a proposal is successful... or even partially successful! Tried and true donor-centred stewardship practices described in several other chapters are effective for foundation grants as well. Indeed, foundations tend to have clear expectations about recognition, expressions of appreciation, progress reports and final reports or evaluations, so there are few surprises.

No matter how worthy your organization's mission or how thorough and compelling your proposal, you will inevitably receive some polite letters declining your appeal. As fund development professionals, we yearn to know where we went wrong; what we could or should have done better to magically turn a no into a yes. But before pursuing that information, be mindful that foundations face an age old challenge expressed in the words of Aristotle:

> "**To give away money is an easy matter and in any man's power. But to decide to whom to give it, and how large, and when, and for what purpose and how, is neither in every man's power nor an easy matter.**"
> – *Aristotle (384-322 B.C.)*

Each letter of decline signifies due consideration of a proposal in the context of a foundation's mission, values, financial situation, priorities, previous commitments and other considerations at a particular point in time. Take the time to acknowledge and express appreciation for their consideration. After all, a decline rarely means "no, never." It usually means: no, not right now; no, not for this project; no, not this year; no, not until... or some such conditional decline that leaves the door open to a subsequent application. Do your part to ensure that your organization's relationship with a foundation that declines a grant application preserves a positive tone that will reflect favourably on you and the organization.

CONCLUSION

As we have seen, foundations in Canada are vital funders and partners in the burgeoning philanthropic sector. They number over 10,000, with a total asset base exceeding $34 billion, about evenly split between public and private foundations. Tax and regulatory changes in more recent years provided attractive incentives for making more and larger gifts and greater flexibility in regulations governing foundations.

Foundations tend to take a sustainable long-term approach to fulfilling their missions by investing endowed capital prudently and wisely to generate a steady, reliable, source of annual revenue to support grant-making activities. They share characteristics such as a primary focus on building and preserving capital funds and granting a portion of annual income generated to carry out its mission. That being said, each is unique in the way it supports philanthropic activities in Canada.

Given the unique nature of each foundation, seeking grants on behalf of a particular charity, cause or program can be likened to securing support from individuals or corporations with particular interests or affinities:

- Identify predisposed prospective foundation supporters;

- Assess and rank "predisposed" foundations based on degree of shared interests, values, priorities and financial capacity;

- Create tailored grant applications for top-ranked foundation prospects; and

- Build mutually fruitful relationships based on shared interests.

A proposal that betrays "the cookie-cutter approach" sends a prospective foundation the message that the grant applicant did not take the time or pay respect to the foundation's uniqueness. You are far more likely to secure support by telling a compelling story that demonstrates the potential your proposal offers for a mutually beneficial endeavor in one of their fields of interest.

URL's

▶ CANADA REVENUE AGENCY CHARITIES WEBSITE: http://www.cra-arc.gc.ca/charities

▶ CHARITY VILLAGE WEBSITE: http://www.charityvillage.com/cv/nonpr/ nonpr17.asp

▶ CHARITY VILLAGE WEBSITE: http://www.charityvillage.com/cv/research/ rprop.html

▶ COMMUNITY FOUNDATIONS OF CANADA WEBSITE: http://www.cfc-fcc.ca/about-cfc/index

▶ IMAGINE CANADA: Canadian Directory to Foundations and Grants website: http://www.imaginecanada.ca

▶ METASOFT: FoundationSearch Canada website: http://www.foundationsearch.ca

▶ PRIVATE FOUNDATIONS OF CANADA WEBSITE: http://pfc.ca/en/resources/foundations-in-canada

▶ THE WINNIPEG FOUNDATION WEBSITE: http:// www.wpgfdn.org/aboutus-history.php

ADDITIONAL RESOURCES

Books

▶ BROWN, MARTIN J. & GOLDEN BROWN, L. (2001). *Demystifying Grantmaking: What you really need to know to get grants.* Jossey-Bass.

▶ CARLSON, M. & O'NEAL-MCELRATH, T. (2008). *The Alliance for Nonprofit Management Winning Grants Step by Step, Third Edition.* The Jossey-Bass Nonprofit Guidebook Series.

▶ CLARKE, CHERYL A. (2009). *Storytelling for Grantseekers: A Guide to Creative Nonprofit Fundraising, 2nd Edition.* Jossey-Bass.

ABOUT THE AUTHOR

Leslie Weir, MA, ACFRE

Leslie helps people focus and plan their philanthropy offering information, resources and consulting services, and she coordinates the Foundation's Legacy Circle program. She brings to her role thirty years of experience in a variety of roles and philanthropic settings. She holds the Certified Fundraising Executive (CFRE) and Advanced Certified Fundraising Executive (ACFRE) professional designations and is a Master Teacher for the Association of Fundraising Professionals (AFP) International. She has a M. A. in Philanthropy and Development (Saint Mary's University of Minnesota) and a BA (University of Manitoba).

She is a faculty member for the AFP Fundamentals of Fundraising course at Red River College.

Leslie serves on the Rotary Club of Winnipeg board and as a trustee of her Club's Permanent Endowment Fund. She is a board member of the Canadian Association for Family Enterprise Manitoba Chapter and a judge for the Future Leaders of Manitoba Awards (Community Service Award). Her volunteer service has included various AFP roles (formerly President of Manitoba Chapter, member of the Canada Council and the Publishing Advisory Committee), CAGP (founding chair of Manitoba's Leave a Legacy Program)

and CFRE International Accreditation Board roles (currently on the Committee on Directorship, formerly member of the board and assorted committees).

CHAPTER 16

STEWARDSHIP

LUCE MOREAU, CFRE

When I was invited to contribute to this book, I asked myself "What path led me to become a fundraiser? Where did it all begin?" As a Francophone from Quebec, I enjoy embracing and savouring the many experiences and wonders that life offers and before I share a very personal story with you, I would like to ask you to prepare yourself by getting in a certain frame of mind. If you enjoy wine, select a good bottle, red or white, but neverthe-less Canadian from one of the great houses such as Mission Hill in the Okanagan or Domaine les Bromes, in the Quebec Eastern Townships. With wine in hand, please nestle into your favourite chair, relax, turn on some good, soft music – perhaps classical if that is your taste – take a sip and start reading. *read more...*

Il était une fois…Once upon a time, when I was a young girl, before I knew there was such a thing as a fundraiser, I learned the importance of the gift of giving. I truly believe that fundraising is not about asking, but all about giving and finding a way to help others release their heart's desire!

When I was seven years old, my family moved from Montreal to a small village called Lavaltrie. In addition to being the new kid in town, I started third grade a year earlier than all the other girls and was the only red-headed girl in the entire village. I had all the elements necessary to be singled out and rejected by my classmates.

On top of that, the entire town was politically "conservative" and my parents were "liberal." At the tender age of seven, I became keenly aware that we were labelled as "outsiders" and that my family was not welcome in Lavaltrie at all.

Like every child, I wanted to fit in; belonging was my primary objective from the moment I woke up and went to school until the time I drifted off to sleep every night. Even in my sleep, I would have recurring dreams of being like everyone else and being liked by everyone.

I was the eldest of four children and Rachel was the second born. She was 15 months younger than me and arrived in this world with a severe handicap as a result of my mother being exposed to measles while pregnant with her. This was in 1959, before there was a medical health care system in Canada and Rachel needed extensive care.

She weighed only two pounds at birth and had to stay in the hospital for many months to undergo several surgeries just to survive. Rachel was blind at birth but an ophthalmologist operated and managed to gain 2% vision in one eye. In spite of her difficult start in life, Rachel was an amazing sister who brought incredible joy into our lives and ended up living happily until the age of 42.

The Quebec Health Insurance Act was enacted in 1970 to help ease the financial burden that faced families like ours but by this time our family was deep in debt.

In those years it was uncommon in Lavaltrie - as in most villages in Quebec - to see a family where the mother worked outside the home. My parents marched to the beat of their own drum and, in doing so, broke some rules. My father worked as an investigator for Canadian Pacific Railway all his life. My mother worked, part time, as a waitress in nice restaurants and made good money in tips. My parents arranged their schedules so that one of them would always be at home with the children; they worked night and day so that we would never feel alone.

Every morning, before I went to school, my mother would pull her waitress apron out of her bag. It had two special pockets and she always asked me to empty them, separately and to count the money. I was so very proud of my mother because every time we did this, there was so much money on the table. To me, this meant that she was very good at her work. It was her moment de gloire! (moment of glory) to share the significant contributions that she was making to her family and I felt honoured that she was choosing to share those moments with me.

The beautiful part that will remain with me forever is that, although my parents needed the money to pay for Rachel's medical treatments, I was allowed to take all of the pennies, nickels and dimes and make my own budget.

There were some rules that accompanied this budget. I had to demonstrate that I was able to save some money to deposit weekly in the school bank, some to help the poor and some to keep as fun money to spend any way I chose. With all the change that I was able to collect from my mom's apron each week, I usually had a dollar fifty to manage. Every Tuesday, I would add a dollar to my savings account. My parents thought that this was a good budget but asked that I set aside 10 cents of my "fun money" to give to the church on Sundays. I agreed with this demand and my budget was set.

I now needed to find a cause to invest in. One day, a nun – Sister Dominique - came to our school and spoke to us about the many children in China who needed our help; she asked us to consider adopting a child for 25 cents.

Sister Dominique called upon Nicole - the little girl who had adopted the most Chinese children in the previous year - to be in charge of all the children's adoption tally cards. Each Friday, Nicole would determine how many adoptions had taken place and receive our donations in exchange for the card. Every month she had to report the number of adoptions to Sister Dominique.

Burning inside of me was a strong desire to change something and to really become part of my school group. The minute Sister Dominique left, I knew that I wanted to adopt all the children and be the girl who would be called up to the front of the class and be recognized next year.

I was so touched by Sister Dominique's story that I ran home and asked my parents to give me all their money so we could adopt all the children in China. They explained that I had my part to do to solve the problem. By helping one child at a time, I, Luce, at the age of seven, would be able to make a significant difference in the lives of each and every one of those individual children.

I argued strongly and told my mother that she could give me all the quarters out of her apron so I could make a bigger difference. She adamantly refused and reminded me that those quarters added together were needed to pay for Rachel's medication and treatments and that we could not afford to give more than what I was allowed to take. My mother told me that if I wanted to do more than I had to find a way to do it. She said to think about it, and when I was ready to come back to discuss it.

The next day I returned with the best idea in the world, or so I thought! I realized that I was helping with different tasks around the house including helping Rachel go outside, pushing her in her swing and taking her to milk her favourite cow in the morning so she could feed the kittens at the farm. I thought that I could ask to be paid for all that. I had been doing all those tasks and never asked for money up to that point in time, so I thought it was the right time; a "sure-fire" thing.

Ouch! As it turned out, my "sure-fire" plan backfired. This was not the kind of idea my mother was waiting for! She quickly and emphatically reminded me of the values of being part of a family and of a community and what this meant. The time invested was definitely a requirement and not something you could lightly choose to do or not to do and it was certainly not something to be remunerated for.

I took a few days to think it over and then came back with another idea. Lavaltrie is a beautiful village between Montreal and Quebec on the north side of the

St-Lawrence River. In the 60's there were no highways and "Route 2" was the only road to travel between those two big cities. Our house was located on the "Chemin du Roi" by the River.

In those days, many drivers would roll down the window of their moving car and toss bottles and trash out into the ditch along the side of the road.

With this in mind, I presented my parents with two ideas to make extra money. In the spring, I could sell lilac bouquets on the main road and I could collect all the empty beer and soft drink bottles from the ditches, wash them and sell them for 2 cents apiece. They thought those ideas were good ones but they insisted that I abide by strict safety rules because cars drove by at 40 miles an hour.

So every day after school and on weekends, I collected bottles and was soon able to adopt not only one child a week but two. I consistently met that goal for the full year. The sweetest moment was when I stood in front of the class and introduced my "protégés" to my classmates. I felt so very important and proud!

Sure, there was some pride involved but even more satisfying was the realization that I was responsible for bringing "light" into the lives of those children in China. They had now become part of my family. For many years when we came back from church and enjoyed our weekly Sunday brunch, there was a special time at the table where I was asked to introduce the new members of our family. The recognition by my peers at school was important but even more gratifying was the recognition that my family gave me for doing the right thing for the wellbeing of others.

The next year when Sister Dominique came to our fourth grade class, it was my name that she called and I was in charge of the children's adoptions for the coming year. That was a very good year for me!

This early experience has served as both a motivation and a foundation for my career as a professional fundraiser. It instilled a sense of passion, compassion, purpose, satisfaction, understanding and perspective on what inspires people to make a difference and what continues to motivate them and rivet their resolve to a specific cause.

At the time I didn't realize that I, as a donor, was responding to a number of different messages and activities - touch points – that served to increase my desire and resolve to help adopt the orphans in China.

Looking back, the program that the nuns had set up and the systems that they had in place were effective in recruiting, engaging and reinforcing the actions of little girls like me who were devoted to the cause of making a better life for disadvantaged children in China. In my work, I refer to this process as *stewardship*.

As a professional fundraiser, I remember the feeling I had as I introduced the "protégés" to my classmates and worked at creating a moment that in a way replicated that same sort of feeling for our donors. My life has unfolded in a manner consistent with those values that this experience left me with. I learned the value of giving and helping others. I realized that working in philanthropy is truly a gift and I came to appreciate how much I want to share this feeling and practice with others.

Having parents that showed up for a long list of community activities including everything from coaching hockey teams to fund drives, my parents never talked about showing up, they just did. So it seemed inevitable - fate if you will - that I became a "natural professional fundraiser." I sincerely believe that I am practicing the best profession in the world and hope that you share this belief as you progress on your own career path.

In my office I have a "gong;" an Asian musical instrument that resounds deeply and goes straight to the core of your soul when struck. Striking the gong is understood to be almost a sacred privilege. Every time a donor makes a significant gift according to his budget or every time an employee makes a momentous achievement they are given the right to strike the gong. Once the gong is struck, everyone in the office runs towards the gong to hear the good news and rejoice with the person who struck it. Donating is about celebrating the moment - created by freely giving part of one's self to another!

INTRODUCTION

Stewardship: "the practice that ensures future gifts."

But what *is* stewardship?

Merriam-Webster's Collegiate Dictionary defines stewardship as "the careful and responsible management of something entrusted to one's care."

Stewardship, writes Henry A. Rosso: "is a reflection of many values critical to the practice of philanthropy and its working partner, fund raising. Stewardship is trust, responsibility, liability, accountability, integrity, faith, and guardianship."[1]

From the point of view of Andrea McManus, CFRE, stewardship is essentially an expression of two core human experiences – building relationships and building community. In order to "get it right" there are techniques and there are the values that lie behind what you do. The underlying values of stewardship include integrity, sincerity, warmth, appreciation and diversity.[2]

Those definitions are a good beginning. They identify the essential components of stewardship: the concept of being responsible for something of value and the recognition that what is cared for actually belongs to someone other than the caretaker.

We can understand stewardship, then, as being responsible for something valuable on behalf of someone who has entrusted it to our care. In other words, it has to feel right for those who are the givers and it has to be expressed in the way that they expect to be appreciated.

A simple and easy way to understand stewardship, is to think of every move you do *after* you send the receipt and thank you note to your donor. Stewardship starts right at this moment. As a professional fundraiser, you want to bring people close to your organization - stewardship is one way of doing so.

PRINCIPLES OF ACCOUNTABILITY

According to Webster's Collegiate Dictionary, the word accountability entered the English language in 1794 and means "an obligation or a willingness to accept responsibility or to account for one's actions."

"However, few non-profit organizations have paid serious attention to how they might be more accountable to the communities they seek to serve."[3]

It is important to keep in mind that each non-profit organization holds a public trust to improve the quality of life of those they serve. The accountable

---

1   Rosso, Hank. (2003). *Achieving Excellence in Fund Raising,* John Wiley & Sons, Inc. (p. 432).
2   McManus, Andrea. (2010). Retrieved from *http://www.thedevelopmentgroup.ca*
3   Ebrahim, Alnoor. (2010). *The Many Faces of Non-profit Accountability.* Harvard Business School.

organization clearly states its mission and purpose, articulates the needs of those being served, explains how its programs work, how much they cost and what benefits they produce.

Like Wayne Olson says in his book *Think Like a Donor,* "Treat money like donors do." Be frugal, he recommends, donors will give more money when they have confidence that a charity respects their funds the way they do.[4]

The accountable organization freely and accurately shares information about its governance, finances and operations. It is open and inclusive in its procedures, processes and programs consistent with its mission and purpose.

"Accountability is the charity living up to its role as a steward of the public trust," advises Paulette V. Maehara, CFRE, CAE, former president and CEO of AFP (Association of Fundraising Professionals).

According to Guy Mallabone and Tony Myers's study, *Motivators and Barriers to Philanthropic Giving by Entrepreneurs,* the two top reasons donors stop giving to charity are unreliability (i.e. you didn't do what you said you were going to do with my money) and loss of credibility. However, proper performance by the charity organization is an important motivator for increasing a gift.[5]

As these thoughtful definitions suggest, accountability means an organization's wide commitment to the principles of honesty and transparency. Acting on that commitment translates to self-assessment of operations against a set of standards, and of best practices in governance, financial integrity, program evaluation, fundraising and stewardship.

Non-profit organizations must therefore measure intangible elements such as their quality of service and overall performance which are part of stewardship. In Canada, charities follow the generally accepted accounting principles set forth by the Canadian Institute of Chartered Accountants (CICA). The intent is to provide a uniform methodology in all fiscal reports for public access and understanding as well as consistency in disclosure of financial details to meet government, accreditation and other public reporting requirements.

4   Olson, Wayne. (2009). *Think Like a Donor.* White Trout Press.
5   Mallabone, Guy & Myers, Tony. (2000). *Motivators and Barriers to Philanthropic Giving by Entrepreneurs.* Saint Mary's University of Minnesota.

GIFT PROCESSING

A non-profit organization may receive gifts of all sizes and types, with or without restrictions, or with conditions or instructions that may vary with each individual donor.

The key to proper handling is to establish a standard gift processing routine for all fund-raising activities. Use of a uniform set of procedures will help ensure that all gifts are handled accurately and that bookkeeping errors are kept to a minimum.

To process gifts appropriately, the staff must understand the legal and accounting procedures that must be followed. Effective staff training is essential. Typical gift processing policies and procedures might concern the following: checks, cash, credit card transactions, and pledges; gifts of securities; gifts of personal property; gifts of real estate; legacies and bequests; gifts-in-kind & employee gifts by payroll deductions.

Gift processing procedures should include:

- **Accurate and timely recording of gifts**: a record is made and kept of each gift on its arrival that includes details such as full name and addresses of the donor, amount or value of the gift, form of gift, date the gift was received, date of its acknowledgement, it's stated or implied purpose or use by the organization, areas of donor interest, and the solicitation method and/or volunteer who procured the gift. There must be good communication and coordination regarding gift processing between the development program and the accounting function of the organization.

- **Prompt gift acknowledgments and forwarding of receipts**: in most cases, a formal letter and gift receipt is prepared and sent within 48 hours to the donor to report the safe arrival of his/her gift along with a statement of acceptance by the organization of the gift for the purposes or uses that the donor defined.

- **A donor records profile**: accumulate all information available about individual donors and amounts contributed.

- **Gift reports**: these reports eflect all performance activity within each of the solicitation methods used. Gift reports must be maintained faithfully and accurately. It provides campaign results, identifies which fundraising methods were the most successful, compares current performance against long-range goals and objectives, helps prepare for budget requirements and it establishes relationships between dollars spent, program by program, and individual results in each program, allowing for analysis of donor performance.

Examples of the different areas of activity to report are: source of gifts, purpose or uses of the money, results of each fundraising program and methods used.

Examples of different types of analysis available from gift reports include: percentage of participation, renewal rates and average gift size, volunteers' personal solicitation performance, donors' response to recognition, special and benefit event ticket sales.

In addition to the policies and procedures governing, accepting, recording, and acknowledging gifts, the staff also has an obligation to manage all funds, from small contributions to major gifts. Written policies governing these activities must be firmly in place and strictly followed.

REPORTING ON THE IMPACT OF THE GIFT

In Harvey McKinnon's book, *The 11 Questions Every Donor Asks*, he talks about the core questions and the answers all donors crave. Here are some examples:

- Why are you asking me?
- Will one gift make a difference?
- Do I respect your organization?
- How much do you want?
- Is there an urgent reason to give?
- How will I be treated?
- Will I make a greater difference here or should I give to another cause?
- Will I have a say over how you use my gift?
- How will you measure results?

It is important to show donors that they *can* make a difference - it is your job to do so. There are many tools inside your organization that will help to answer all those questions.[6]

"To give away money is an easy matter in any man's power. But to decide to whom to give it, and how much and when, and for what purpose and how, is neither in every man's power nor an easy matter."
– Aristotle, Nicomachean Ethics

According to the *Survey of Donors* done by the Canadian Centre for Philanthropy (now Imagine Canada), there are three reasons donors don't give: failure of charity to be accountable, insensitivity to donor differences and interests and lack of knowledge of the prospect's donor history or existing connection to the charity.

It is also important to know that the three reasons donors stop giving is 1) reliability 2) credibility and 3) a shift in charity's mission.[7]

The impact of the donor's gift is crucial and well presented in the study conducted by Guy Mallabone and Tony Myers, in three Canadian cities: Calgary, Winnipeg and Toronto. *Motivators and Barriers to Philanthropic Giving by entrepreneurs and non-entrepreneurs*[8] consists of a review of the literature on motivations and barriers to giving in general and by entrepreneurs specifically, as well as a contextual look at general giving trends in Canada and a review of key definitional concepts for the term entrepreneur.

The study examined the specific factors that affect: (a) the giving of a next gift, (b) increasing a gift amount, (c) giving an "ultimate gift" (d) refusing to make a specific philanthropic gift, and (e) ceasing to give to a non-profit organization.

Five key characteristics of entrepreneurial behaviour were identified and defined. This definition was applied to the national survey to identify and segment entrepreneurs from non-entrepreneurs. These characteristics included the ability to identify opportunities; the ability to pursue opportunities; the ability to find/lever new resources; the ability to make decisions on

---

6   McKinnon, Harvey. (2008). *The 11 questions every donor asks.* Emerson & Church.
7   *Survey of Donors*, Canadian Centre for Philanthropy.
8   Mallabone, Guy & Myers, Tony. (2000). *Motivators and Barriers to Philanthropic Giving by Entrepreneurs,* Saint Mary's University of Minnesota.

the direction of the enterprise; and the willingness to accept risk.

Key findings in this study included:

1. The more entrepreneurial characteristics a donor group has, the more likely that group is to respond highly to motivators to a) give their next gift, b) increase their philanthropic giving, and c) to make an ultimate philanthropic gift.

2. The top five motivators for giving the next gift by entrepreneurs are:
   • belief in the vision and mission of the organization
   • desire to help those in need
   • desire to give back to the community
   • the accountability of the charity
   • "my gift makes a difference"

3. There are no significant differences in barriers to giving. Entrepreneurial donors and non-entrepreneurial donors alike are equally apt to be dissuaded from supporting an organization. Once the donor has become turned off by the organization or cause, they tend to react with the same intensity, to the same degree and to the de-motivators.

4. Entrepreneurial donors report they will give their next gift (in order) to the following sectors: health, education/research, social services, and religion. Non-entrepreneurial donors will give their next gift (in order) to the following sectors: health, religion, social services, and then to education/research.

5. The top four motivators for increased giving to a charity by an entrepreneurial donor are:
   • I am financially able
   • the cause is consistent with my personal values
   • the quality and reputation of the charity
   • the performance of charity

6. High-end donors (those giving $10,000+ per year) are more apt to have given a gift of some size during the past week.

7. The more a donor gives per year, the greater the chances are that they made a gift during the past week.

8. The top three motivators for making the ultimate gift (defined as the largest gift a person can make in their lifetime) by entrepreneurs are "belief and trust in organization," "charity demonstrates results" and "desire to make a difference."

9. The two top reasons donors stop giving to charity are reliability (i.e. you didn't do what you said you were going to do with my money) and loss of credibility.

10. The more donors give on an annual basis, the more likely they will know where their next gift will go. Conversely, the less donors give on an annual basis, the less likely they will know where their next gift will go.

11. There is a measurable unasked capacity in the bequest market. While 11% of entrepreneurial donors report they have given a gift in their will, a further 28% indicate they are willing to give a gift in their will.

DONOR RECOGNITION

"Silent gratitude isn't much use to anyone."
– Gladys Browyn Stern

Donor recognition is a key element in maintaining excellence in donor relations. Ongoing donor support enables the development office to provide much needed funds for the organization's mission. The value of recognizing donors goes far beyond showing appreciation for a gift. Recognition can motivate donors to become steadfast supporters of your organization.

Donor recognition is the start of a long-lasting relationship between donors and the organizations in which they invest.[9]

Non-profit organizations have little choice but to reach out to donors in ways that go far beyond sending a receipt for their gifts. Today's donors expect to become involved in the organization and valued by it.

All programs should be designed to recognize and to ensure continued communication with donors. The objectives of recognition are to thank donors properly for their gift support and to establish the means for

---

9   Greenfield, James. (2002). *Fund Raising Fundamentals.* AFP/Wiley Fund Development Series.

continued communication that will help to preserve their attentive interest in our organizations.

"Donor recognition should be thought of not as the end of the fund-raising process, but as the beginning: donor recognition should be treated as the preamble, not the post-mortem. Done well, and done often, it should be the beginning of the next ask."[10]

There are an unlimited number of ways to express appreciation to individuals, foundations, and corporations for their generosity. Very often their gifts make possible the quality valued in the organization.

Donor recognition is an important part of donor cultivation. "Thank you is not enough," according to Judith Nichols. Out of every 100 individuals who stop giving to your organization, only four move away or die, fifteen have decided to make their gifts to other organizations, fifteen are unhappy with your organization and sixty-six think you don't care about them.[11]

A thank-you system should be put in place for the entire office. Setting policies and procedures for donor recognition is important (kinds of policies, acceptance policies, identifying issues that need to be considered) to ensure that donors are treated equally and fairly, and that no donor is overlooked or under-thanked.

The development officer should be the lead organizer in gift celebration and include every person involved in the asking.

A majority of people simply believe in the value of giving and most of them also believe if the value of being recognized and being thanked. Even though most donors will never bring up the topic of recognition, you should assume they want it.

For some donors, the "thank you's" are less important than the fact that the organization is putting "their" money to work in the way they want it, in the way they've been promised, and in a way that is helping to achieve results. For others, it is about sincere expressions of warmth and belonging, a connection with an organization they want to be part of and which they admire.[12]

Penelope Burk, long considered one of the continent's foremost experts on donor recognition, summarizes key points:[13]

A donor needs to know:

- that the gift was received… and that you were pleased to get it
- that the gift is "set to work" as intended
- that the project or program to which the gift was directed had/is having the desired effect

By simply saying thank you, organizations can satisfy a donor's first two needs immediately. All it takes is a prompt acknowledgment letter that includes confirmation of the receipt and intended use of the funds, in a communication that is a pleasure to read. The third need can only be addressed over time, and the length of time depends on how the gift is being applied.

Happily, donors are very generous as long as they are given satisfactory information in a timely manner.

Too often, fundraisers concentrate too much on asking for money. More time and attention should be given to the relationship with the donor and information needed to sustain donor interest.

In the book *The Seven Faces of Philanthropy,*[14] Prince and Maru File remind us that major donors respond positively to non-profits who recognize and attend to their philanthropic personality by creating opportunities for individual involvement. Donors hope to be channelled into roles most appropriate to their strengths, and they hope for an ongoing relationship built on mutual benefit. Sustaining relationships through donor centered strategies is the key to success.

Remember that recognition is one of the ways of building and maintaining relationships. Donor relationships do not end with a gift, they *begin* with the gift.

DONOR CONFIDENTIALITY

It is particularly important that all staff members understand the need not only for complete accuracy but also for donor confidentiality. For those donors who wish to remain anonymous, your organization must

10 Lawson, Charles E., (2001). Capital Fund Appeals, in Greenfield, J.M. (ed.) *The Nonprofit Handbook: Fund Raising, Third Edition.* NSFRE/Wiley Fund Development Series: New York.
11 Nichols, Judith E. (1994). *Pinpointing Affluence.* Precept Press.
12 McManus, Andrea. (2010) Retrieved from *http://www.thedevelopmentgroup.ca*

13 Burk, Penelope. (2003). *Donor Centered Fundraising.* Cygnus Applied Research.
14 Maru File, Karen & Prince, Russ Alan. (2001). *The Seven Faces of Philanthropy.* John Wiley & Sons.

have procedures in place that address how anonymous donors will be coded in the database, how they will continue to receive mailings and how their gifts will be included in fundraising reports.[15]

According to the AFP Code of Ethics, all members shall protect the confidentiality of all privileged information relating to the provider/client relationships.

DONOR RIGHTS

To make sure that philanthropy deserves the respect and trust of the general public, and that donors and prospective donors can have full confidence in the non-profit organizations and causes they are asked to support, a *Donor Bill of Rights* has been introduced to the public by a group of associations who have great respect for donors.

CONCLUSION

Treat donors gently, respond thoughtfully to their requests, and let them know that they are very important people, because they are.[16]

Contrary to commonly accepted wisdom, a fundraiser, even a skilled one, can never give the donor a reason to give. Either the donor has a passion for the mission or the donor does not. Good fundraisers identify the donor's passion, nurture it and then reward it.

"In the first place, I advise you to apply to all those you know who will give you something, next to those whom you are uncertain whether they will give you anything or not and show them the list of those who have given and lastly, do not neglect those whom you are sure will give you nothing, for in some of them, you will be mistaken."

— Benjamin Franklin

According to Kathleen Kelly,

"The fundraising process is not complete without stewardship. Obligations and responsibilities to the donor must be met. Furthermore, the last step proves an essential loop back to

the beginning of the process for new efforts... acquiring fund raisers' attention and action: reciprocity, responsible gift use, reporting, and relations nurturing."[17]

I strongly recommend that you follow and apply the best practices applicable to donor stewardship established by Andrea McManus:[18]

- Always keep donors in touch with what is happening with the organization. If you don't steward donors all the time, you don't deserve to have the money in the first place.

- In these tough economic times call your donors and thank them for staying with you when times are difficult all around – it means more than ever.

- Have your board members call donors on a regular basis, preferably within 24 hours of receiving the gift, just to say thank you... and nothing else.

- Strive to build authentic relationships with donors that are based on trust, honesty and good communication.

- Be prompt, personal and genuine with your gift acknowledgements.

- Send timely, customized correspondence to donors that demonstrate impact (for example, individual update reports or donor stories in the annual report).

- Take the time to know what donors want – some will want recognition and some will want anonymity - but they will all want to see their gifts in action.

- Try to diversify your communication channels so you have something for each stakeholder group – letters, phone calls, website stories, media releases, e-newsletters and tours are just a few ideas.

- In certain organizations volunteering can also be considered a donor stewardship opportunity – it keeps donors in the loop, makes them feel useful

---

15 *Donor Policies and Procedures,* Association of Fundraising Professionals Ready Reference Series.
16 Rosso, Henry A. (1996). *Rosso on Fund Raising.* Jossey-Bass.

17 Kelly, Kathleen S. (1998). *Effective Fund Raising Management.* Routledge.
18 McManus, Andrea. (2010). Retrieved from *http://www.thedevelopmentgroup. ca*

and provides regular face-to-face communication opportunities.

- Bring the organization to the donors – for instance, in an educational institution offer opportunities for donors to see a program in action or speak with student scholarship recipients. In this age of media, there is no reason why you can't video a student's thank you message to a donor and send it via email with a link on YouTube. Make it personal, make it concise and make it count.

- Consider flexible funding arrangements. To support flexibility, develop a range of donor fund agreements that reflect the diversity of arrangements available.

- Despite the economy, keep your stewardship going strong. Let donors know that it is business as usual; that you are not sitting around bemoaning the economy and that you continue to fulfill your mission because it is still relevant. Continue to send updates on your work and new opportunities, continue to invite your donors to events, continue to send them your annual report.

- Broaden the conversation beyond the ask itself and try to understand your supporters' circumstances to ensure the conversations are open and not defensive.

- Conduct a philanthropic audit and find out what your donors really think. Engage them; get their feedback; let them know it is important.

In closing this chapter, I would like to share a wonderful quote by Mahatma Gandhi learned while visiting South India in the fall of 2009:

> **"You must be the change you wish to see in the world."**

Le mot de la fin… stewardship applies to all aspects of fundraising and it's my personal belief that it should also rule every moment of our lives. Stewardship and fundraising come together like the chicken and the egg; fundraising cannot be effective without stewardship.

When you think that everything has been said and done, remember to thank again, again and again! Namaste et merci beaucoup!

ADDITIONAL RESOURCES

▶ AHERN, TOM & JOYAUX, SIMONE. (2007). *Keep Your Donors.* AFP/Wiley Fund Development Series.

▶ BORENSTEIN, LCSW. (1992). Recognition: The Stepchild of Fundraising, *Fundraising Management.* April, (pp. 19-22)

▶ BURK, PENELOPE. (2003). *Donor Centered Fundraising.* Cygnus Applied Research.

▶ CICONTE, BARBARA L. & JACOB, JEANNE G. (2008). *Fundraising Basics, A Complete Guide, Third Edition.* Jones and Bartlett Publishers.

▶ DESSOFF, ALAN L. (1997). Creativity Counts. *Case Currents.* February, (pp. 31-34).

▶ EMLEN, JULIA S. (2007). *Intentional Stewardship.* CASE.

▶ GREATRAKE, JOAN M. (1990). Beyond the Donor Wall. *AHP Journal*, Spring, (pp. 45-47).

▶ GREENFIELD, JAMES M. (1999). *Fundraising: Evaluation and Managing the Fund Development Process, 2nd Edition*, John Wiley & Sons, Inc.

▶ HARRISON, BILL. (1996). When a Plaque Isn't Enough… How Do You Thank Major Donors? *Fundraising Management.* July, (pp. 36-39).

▶ LEVY, REYNOLD. (2009). *Yours for the Asking.* John Wiley & Sons Inc.

▶ LINZY, JERRY A. (2000). Donor Recognition and Relations. Greenfield, James M. (ed.) *The Nonprofit Handbook: Fundraising, 2nd Edition.* John Wiley & Sons, Inc. (pp. 121-133).

▶ MACDONALD, LAURA J., & GOETTLER, JOHN G. (1997). Revolving Around the Donor. *Advancing Philanthropy* Fall, (pp. 33-37).

▶ McKINNON, HARVEY. (2008). *The 11 Questions Every Donor Asks.*

▶ MALLABONE, GUY H.E. & MYERS, TONY J.A. (2000). *Motivators and Barriers to Philanthropic Giving by Entrepreneurs,* In Partial Fulfillment of the requirements for the Degree of Master of Arts in Philanthropy and Development, Saint Mary's University of Minnesota.

▶ ROSSO, HENRY A. & ASSOCIATES (1991). *Achieving Excellence in Fund Raising.* Jossey Bass.

▶ SPRINKEL GRACE, KAY. (2005). *Beyond Fundraising: New strategies for Nonprofit Innovation and Investment.* Wiley.

▶ WATTS, SUSAN, (1997). Recognizing Your Forgotten Donors. *Fundraising Management,* June, (pp. 32-33).

▶ WILSON, THOMAS D. (2008). *Winning Gifts, Make your Donors Feel Like Winners.* John Wiley & Sons Inc.

ABOUT THE AUTHOR

Luce Moreau, CFRE

Luce Moreau is a professional fundraiser with more than twenty years of experience. She possesses a Certificate in Public Relations from the Université de Montréal, and currently is the President & Chief Executive Officer of the Orchestre Métropolitain in Quebec.

Luce has served as President and CEO for both the Fondation du Centre hospitalier Jacques-Viger, and also the Fondation Centre de santé et de services sociaux (CSSS) Jeanne-Mance.

In her career, Luce has received many Awards, grants and bursaries. She annually attends major national and international conferences and provides professional training sessions and conferences in North-America and abroad.

CHAPTER 17

Governance & Boards
ANDREA MCMANUS, CFRE

"conundrum – 1. A riddle whose answer is or involves a pun. 2. A question or problem having only a conjectural answer. 3. An intricate and difficult problem."

I have always thought that one of the real conundrums in fundraising is the involvement, engagement and interaction with boards of charitable organizations. It seems to be such a natural assumption that your board will be involved in fundraising activities, and not just involved but actually exercising its "ownership" and "responsibility." The reality is usually much more of a mystery and, in fundraising, probably the one single area that presents fundraisers with the most frustration and a never-ending discussion topic. *read more...*

In my 24 years of experience, I have worked with a number of boards who are thoughtfully and fully engaged in fundraising and I have coached numerous boards that are learning how to be engaged. But, I also have encountered many boards who simply don't believe it is part and parcel of their governance responsibilities and because of that, many fundraisers who are stymied by the challenge of getting their boards involved in organizational fundraising.

Over the years I have learned a great deal about how to work with boards but I have also realized why it is essential for us as fundraisers to understand the context of boards and fundraising in order to successfully enable them to collectively and individually maximize the organization's philanthropic potential.

In this chapter I will cover three main topics on what you need to know about working with boards:

- the actual legal responsibilities of all boards and how this relates to fundraising;

- why boards should be engaged in fundraising; and

- how to engage boards of all types and sizes in the philanthropic and fundraising processes.

THE BOARD'S GOVERNANCE RESPONSIBILITIES

While there is no one definition for governance that applies to all types of organizations, in the non-profit sector it typically refers to how an organization makes its big picture and strategic decisions. Basically, the board is legally responsible for all of the organization's actions and specifically for ensuring that:

  a. it is complying with all laws at the municipal, provincial and federal levels;
  b. it is achieving and staying on track with its mission and setting strategic direction; and
  c. it is financially healthy and spending its money wisely and carefully.

All boards, regardless of the size of the organization or the board, have governance responsibilities that fall within these three areas and when boards and organizations get into governance trouble it is usually because there is lack of clarity surrounding the board's specific responsibilities. The Management of Non-profit and Charitable Organizations in Canada outlines the seven

common areas of responsibility in which boards may become involved:[1]

  1. Mission, values, goals, strategic priorities and performance assessment: setting the overall purpose for the organization – why it should exist, who it should serve, what services it should provide, and what values and ethical guidelines it should follow in providing them. This area also includes the setting of objectives and the development of broad strategic plans for achieving them. To do this properly requires assessing how well the organization has performed in achieving the goals set for it as well as understanding the challenges and opportunities that lie ahead.

  2. Fiscal and legal oversight: ensuring that the organization behaves in a fiscally and legally responsible manner. This includes such matters as overseeing operating and capital budgets, investments, property management, and compliance with various laws applying to the organization. It is also includes risk assessment – attempting to identify areas in which the organization is subjected to high risk to its assets or reputation.

  3. CEO selection and evaluation: ensuring that the best person holds the position of Chief Executive Officer and performs it at a satisfactory level of competence.

  4. Community relations (also known as "boundary spanning"):
     a. representing the interests of the organization to its external publics
     b. building alliances and partnerships with others that benefit the community
     c. ensuring that the interests of key external stakeholders are made known inside the organization

  5. Resource development: Ensuring that the organization obtains adequate funds to enable it to achieve its objectives.

  6. Management systems: Ensuring that the organization is managed efficiently and effectively, e.g. that it has the right

---

1   Murray, Vic. (2009). *The Management of Nonprofit and Charitable Organizations 2nd Edition.* LexisNexis, (p. 60-61).

administrative structures and policies, information systems, human resources, etc.

7. Board self-management: activities aimed at ensuring the board itself is as effective as it can be. E.g., recruiting, selecting and training its members, evaluating the effectiveness of its meetings and committees.

Of course, exactly how any given board fulfills these responsibilities depends on many things, not least of which is where the organization is in its own evolutionary process. If it is a working board then clearly the board and the individual board members will be much more engaged in operations than if it is a management board, other type of mixed-model board or a policy board, which operates at the highest governance level.

Role clarity can become even more complex and confusing when the size and infrastructure of an organization is factored into the mix, e.g., the board of a large institutional organization may not fulfill its governance role in each of the responsibility areas as does the board of a medium-sized social service agency. Fundraising seems to be a lightning rod for controversy and discussion when it comes to role clarity.

THE BOARD'S ROLE IN FUNDRAISING

Surveys of board members and EDs assessing their satisfaction with the board reveal that most of them believe that boards should be "responsible" for fundraising but few think the board does a good job of it."[2] This is directly attributable to confusion over the meaning of "responsible" and is relevant to large institutional organizations (health care/post-secondary), foundations and small social service agencies alike.

I guarantee that at least once in your fundraising career you will be challenged by a board that doesn't believe fundraising is part of its responsibility, that "it is a staff job" or "I will do anything but raise money."

This is where it is essential to understand the governance and fundraising context and be able to articulate it to your board. Consider these three key arguments in support of board engagement:

1. If philanthropic donations generated through fundraising are an important revenue source for an organization, i.e. mission critical, then

it warrants a strategic approach, thoughtful planning and maximum use of available resources in order to ensure success.

2. The Board's input and approval of the long-term fundraising plan is a governance responsibility carried out at the board table – just like any other strategic direction.

3. There is no "one size fits all" in governance and neither is there a one size fits all in how a board is engaged in fundraising. It depends on what my organization needs now to keep fulfilling its mission in the future.

INDIVIDUAL BOARD MEMBERS AND FUNDRAISING

The Rationale

If we accept that fundraising is really about relationship building then the argument for individual board member engagement is actually pretty clear and is directly related to both ensuring fiscal health and appropriate resources, and the community relations aspect of board responsibilities.

I was facilitating a discussion on communications at a professional development event and at my table there were two women from the same small organization. They were curious about how a case for support is actually developed. I gave them a few tips that included involvement of their lead fundraiser and the conversation went something like this:

Me: "*I would have your lead fundraiser work with volunteers to identify why your organization is so important to the community and begin to capture this in your materials.*"

Them: "*We don't have any fundraising staff.*"

Me: "*Ok, well then, is your Executive Director responsible for fundraising?*"

Them: "*No, we don't have an Executive Director.*"

Me: "*Then I guess it would be the fund development committee of your board.*"

2   Ibid, p. 73.

Them: *"We are a Carver board so we don't have board working committees."*

Me: *After a pointed pause, "Well, then who does the work?"*

I tell this story often when I am working with boards and staff on roles in fundraising because it is such an excellent (albeit extreme) but poignant example of just how confused we can be over roles in fundraising.

The bottom line is...someone needs to build those relationships and wouldn't you rather start with your best options leading the charge. Why keep your strongest horses in the barn?

KNOW WHY YOUR BOARD MEMBERS ARE BOARD MEMBERS

Board members are busy people, which is exactly why we want them on our boards, but they have joined the board for a reason. It is useful to give regular opportunities for board members to share why they are on your board. Whether you do this in retreat introductions or by asking one or two board members per regular meeting, give board members the opportunity to tell why they care enough to be sitting here today.

Of course the common factor is a belief in and passion for the cause but in addition I want to know what else drew them to board service. Perhaps it is a professional career booster, or providing networking opportunities, or pushing the leadership envelope by gaining different skill sets they can use in the workplace. I always like to find out what that reason is because I figure if I know that, then I can be far more effective in encouraging their engagement in a way that is both comfortable for them, meets their own personal needs and maximizes their individual strengths. You do not always get influence, affluence and passion in equal doses in one package so understanding what drives a board member will help you to align their needs with the organization's fundraising needs.

It is essential to work with board members one-on-one but as a group communicate these messages in support of their individual involvement in fundraising:

• As individual board members you have huge opportunity and potential to bring your networks, contacts and influences to our organization and along with it the potential to maximize philanthropic support, all of which directly advances our mission. No one is as well positioned as our board members to undertake this critical role. We can do it alone as staff, but we can't do it as well.

• Simply by being a member of our board and advocating on our behalf you bring credibility to our mission and demonstrate that the work we do and the people we help is crucially important to our stakeholders and our community. It is instant validation with prospective donors.

• When you speak on behalf of our organization and make connections with donors you are inviting those donors to share in the passion you feel for what we do. You are offering them the same opportunity you have had. This is much stronger and more persuasive coming from a volunteer peer than from a staff member.

ENGAGING BOARD MEMBERS

Setting your board members up for success is approached from two perspectives: firstly, through structure and expectations and secondly, through individual engagement.

The 2009 Canadian Fundraising & Philanthropy study on governance structures and practices in Canada found that organizations "...with formal board structures and procedures are better organizations, have better board and individual board members..." yet it also found that only 68% of organizations have job descriptions for the board, its directors and its committees.

It is absolutely essential that expectations of the board as a whole and of individual board members are clearly and consistently communicated to prospective new board members before they agree to join your board, particularly as it relates to fundraising and giving expectations. Imagine how you would feel if you joined a board and at your first meeting discovered that not only were you expected to give at a certain level but you were also expected to raise money from your friends and neighbours. Surprised and chagrined might not be too strong a description! To prevent this:

- Pay attention to both the governance and engagement roles when recruiting new board members. Yes, you want specific skill sets at the table but your organization also needs leaders who are willing to lead by example, open up their personal networks and ask for gifts from the philanthropic community.

- Be involved in the recruiting process. Whether you are the leader of a charitable foundation or the development director of a smaller nonprofit, make sure your voice is heard when board recruitment takes place. Include your requirements in your long-term and annual development plans and link your fundraising success back to board engagement at every possible opportunity.

- Make sure there is a reference to fundraising engagement and board giving expectations in the board role document.

- Make sure there is a reference to fundraising engagement and board giving expectations in the board member job description document and/or annual board commitment letter.

Board members who are recruited properly with clear expectations are going to be much more open to being involved in fundraising than if it comes as a surprise. Consider this part of the ongoing education of the organization and the board as to the role that fundraising and philanthropy plays in fulfilling the mission.

THE FUND DEVELOPMENT COMMITTEE

The development committee is where fundraising leadership typically comes from at the board level. Not all non-profits choose to have a development committee, particularly fundraising foundations where the primary purpose is to raise philanthropic revenue. However, for many organizations a committee provides focus, leadership and entrée to engagement of the full board in the fundraising process. The development committee should be staffed by the senior development person and is primarily responsible for developing the long-

term development program goals, keeping the annual development plan on track, assisting with identifying, qualifying, cultivating, asking and stewarding donors, and being the go-to support group for the chief development officer.

The development committee also leads the board giving program and encourages other board members to be involved in fundraising. However, there is a caution here about the use of development committees. It is vitally important that the development committee not be considered to be solely responsible for fundraising to the extent that the board, intentionally or not, abrogates its collective responsibility. In the world of relationships, strategic partnerships and highly-savvy and informed donors, there is both a need for and expectation that all board members will be involved in some way. To contain the responsibility within a sub-committee of the board is, quite simply, shutting the organization off from the potentially beneficial outcomes of relationships other board members may have with prospective donors – to the detriment of the organization and ultimately its mission.

The development committee also provides an opportunity to recruit non-board members to the important work of fundraising. This not only offers a natural training ground for new board members but opens up the field to volunteers who may not be interested in the time commitment and responsibility associated with a board seat. Even better if these volunteers are donors themselves who are willing to talk about why they gave to your particular cause. It is hard to be more compelling than that!

In her little gem of a book that is part of the AFP Ready Reference Series, *Building an Effective Board of Directors*, Linda Lysakowski, ACFRE lists the following development committee tasks:[3]

- Work with appropriate staff to develop a long-range and short-range development plan.

- Plan and oversee all fundraising activities of the organization.

- Contribute financially to the organization and ensure full board participation in all campaigns and projects.

---

3   Lysakowski, L. *Building an Effective Board of Directors*, AFP Ready Reference Series. Retrieved from *www.afpnet.org* (p. 19).

- Identify and recruit leadership and volunteers for development activities.
- Educate the full board on the theory and techniques of development programs.
- Encourage the participation of all board members in fundraising activities and programs.
- Attend all fundraising events and encourage board members' attendance.
- Work with or assume the duties of the public relations committee.

The development committee is also a way to connect with the board if you don't have direct access to them through your day-to-day work. Make the committee your champion and let them lead you to direct contact with individual board members.

BOARD GIVING - LEAD BY EXAMPLE

"I gave at the office."

"I give elsewhere."

"I give my time here and my money somewhere else."

"I'm on three boards, I can't give to them all."

"I can only make a small gift – what difference can that possibly make?"

These are all typical responses and objections to the expectation that board members should give to your organization. But the reality is, that it takes time *and* money to provide services and fulfill missions – and *both* matter. The board, as the ultimate leader, can and should reasonably be expected to lead by example. In fact, the trend clearly indicates that donors increasingly have this expectation and are not shy at asking about it. As well, more and more foundations are making 100% board giving a requirement of getting the grant. Interestingly, in the 2009 CF&P study 53% of organizations agreed or somewhat agreed that all of their board members provided financial support with 32% indicating this was not the case.

As a consultant I am often brought in to facilitate this always sensitive and often contentious discussion at the board table. It is something that I believe all boards, if they are not already fully engaged in fundraising, should be encouraged to take the time to discuss.

In my first or second year of fundraising I went to a workshop on working with boards that was led by Ken Wyman, a nationally known fundraising leader and contributing author to this book. The workshop was on staff/board relationships around fundraising and participants were encouraged to register both a board member and a development professional in the half-day session. There were probably about 60 people in the room representing about 25 or so organizations. Ken asked the participants how many of the represented organizations enjoyed 100% board giving on an annual basis. Two people – yes, only two - raised their hands. They were a board member and staff person from a national organization that worked with people at or below the poverty line. They went on to very proudly inform the group that by virtue of their by-laws, something like 80% of their board members had to be below or recently below, the poverty line. There was a moment of silence where you could hear a proverbial pin drop and then a very heartfelt and admiring standing ovation.

In fact, I reminded Ken about this incident just a few years ago and told him how often I have used it and how influential it was for me in shaping my approach to board giving. It is a powerful illustration of passion, commitment and leading by example. When I tell other boards this story it really puts the conversation into perspective and heads literally nod in understanding all around the table.

Approach	My Observations	Pros	Cons
Set specific expectation levels	This is not one of my favourites but one that often works well for boards that have a narrower focus. You are more likely to find this in arts organizations where the artistic direction and general operations are clearly separated and board members are primarily recruited for their networks and fundraising prowess. Another example is AFP which, as a professional association, has a clearly stated expectation in the Board role document that board members will contribute at minimum at the President's Level ($1,000) annually.	• Sets a clear minimum level • Establishes a baseline where everyone is recognized for their time and giving equally	• Sets up a false ceiling which can result in board members giving below their capacity or stretch gift level • Can prevent some potential board members from joining even though they would be coming to the table with other critically important skills and/or networks • Can be offensive to some people who may consider it a demand or an intrusion of their privacy
Make a meaningful, stretch gift	This works well for many organizations. It is soft but personal and is likely to tap into the individual motivations for being on your board.	• Emphasizes the donor's choice in giving – because I want to not because I have to • Not as likely to offend anyone who is already committed to your mission	• Can be too open-ended resulting in board members giving below their capacity of stretch gift level • Can still set up a "is my stretch gift good enough" syndrome
Make it one of your top three philanthropic priorities while you sit on this board	This is my personal favourite and the one that I find resonates with most organizations. Particularly after I have told them my powerful board giving story.	• It is a reasonable expectation that makes sense to most board members • It puts the expectation squarely in the sphere of the "realistically achievable for me" category • It is less likely to result in giving under capacity • It acknowledges and celebrates that the board member is a generous and sharing philanthropist who supports broader community betterment	• Small likelihood of giving under capacity but this should be ameliorated by personal cultivation and asking

Figure 17.1

In addition to including the expectation of personal giving in the board roles document and job description, here are some other suggestions to gently reframe your board's thinking on personal giving expectations:

- Start the discussion at the development committee level and have them bring it to the board. This creates a peer-to-peer discussion which automatically reduces the "pressure" and focuses instead on the "let's do this together."

- Make sure that each board member is heard both at and outside the board table. We know from working with donors that people have deep relationships with their money – so do our board members.

- Acknowledge that your board has other factors to consider in its leadership composition, e.g. diversity, geographical scope, stakeholder representation, that may make this a tough decision.

- Research other organizations in your community that have board giving policies or expectations and present them as benchmarks. If you don't do it first you can bet at least one of your board members will. So be prepared.

- Tell your board members that you want them to be able to answer proudly when a prospective major gift donor asks if they have personally given. This could be "Absolutely, it was the largest gift I have ever given to any organization." or "Yes I did. It was a stretch but it was worth it to me to support my organization."

- Tell my story above – but do it at the right time when your board is moving close to a new way of thinking.

- Present options and empower your board to make not only a good choice but the right choice for them and for the organization. Table 17.1 lists three approaches to the often thorny issue of board giving. Options 2 and 3 are very similar but are communicated in a slightly different way. Consider which one will resonate best with your board.

And finally, a word about adopting "give, get or get off" or "time, talent or treasure" policies. While both of these recognize the importance of giving both time and money and are widely used and articulated in fundraising literature, I personally have never been that comfortable with them or found a great deal of resonance with volunteers.

"Give, get or get off" always strikes me as a bit harsh and grasping and "time, talent or treasure" a bit trite.

These phrases are fundraising jargon that I believe are best left to our internal discussions and not with our volunteers. I'd rather talk to board members about passion and philanthropy.

ENGAGING INDIVIDUAL BOARD MEMBERS

Providing context for fundraising

As fundraisers we generally have a pretty clear idea of what we need and want from our board members when it comes to fundraising. But do we always take the time to ask the right questions so we understand what our board members need from us? One of the exercises I like to do in board fundraising workshops is to break the participants into groups ensuring there is at least one staff member in each group. Then I give them plenty of time (30 minutes or so) to have a conversation guided by the following questions:

1. What does the staff think its board members could do and how would they make that work?
2. What do Board members think they can do and how can staff help them to be successful?
3. What specific tools do board members need to be successful?

I do this exercise towards the end of what is usually a half-day workshop so we have already covered a lot of enlightening materials from the board perspective and I often find that staff are more, or at least as equally, surprised at the conversation flow than the board members. They realize they have missed an important piece of the puzzle or they have put the puzzle pieces together incorrectly and the picture is skewed. They have probably provided goals, success factors, trends, reports, tools and techniques but they may have missed the real context, the essential fabric of why fundraising is important. They haven't pulled it all together.

Here are four critical puzzle pieces to build a picture for your board members which includes them:

1. Make sure your board "gets" the importance of fundraising – right from the beginning.

If you want your board to think strategically about fundraising then you must present it to them from a strategic perspective, starting with the board orientation and including regular reinforcement aligned with planning cycles. Without this context you will likely not get the action. Make sure your board knows:

- why private support is required and how important it is to your budget, i.e., how it allows you to fund new programs but also the impact on programs if you don't meet your goals;

- how it determines programming and mission-fulfillment;

- how it is used, both restricted and non-restricted gifts, and particularly the importance of the latter;

- successes, challenges and lessons learned in previous fundraising;

- how fundraising goals are set, based on past history, current and appropriate resources and realistic growth, i.e. that goals are not set based on the budget deficit;

- that it is not just about reaching a single dollar goal in any given year but about building a sustainable program over the long-term that includes acquiring new donors, retaining current donors, filling the pipeline and numerous other measurable activities; and

- who your current donors are, both generally and specifically, and how they have become donors (particularly when they can be linked back to board member engagement).

2. Talk about philanthropy, not fundraising.

I appreciate that this may seem contradictory to my first point but it really isn't. It's about using the right terminology at the right time, i.e. how we frame the message. I believe that if there is one cardinal sin we make as fundraisers it is in talking too much about "fundraising" to our boards and not enough about "philanthropy."

Yes, fundraising is our business, our profession, our tools and techniques and we want to build a strong and viable internal fundraising structure. But "phi-lanthropy," now that is an amazing thing. It is about mission support and it is a wonderful, warm, caring, generous, feel-good concept that has an external focus. We must build a strong philanthropic culture that our boards can enthusiastically support. They don't want to talk to their networks about fundraising – but they will talk to them about contributing, giving back, paying it forward, bettering the community and the world.

As Gail Perry so eloquently says – fundraising is the "F-word" and by always talking to our board members about fundraising, we not only play into that fear but we feed it. We focus our board members on their fear, their discomfort, their great unknown, instead of focusing them on what they can achieve, what donors want to achieve and how they can contribute to the great process of doing good. Really, fundraising is simply the enabler of philanthropy so let's focus on the good stuff where it really counts.

And while you are building this philanthropic culture remember to focus on the day-to-day jargon that undermines engagement. Find new words for "target," "hit-up" and "moves management." Again, they are internally focused and that is exactly where they should be kept – in the office and not communicated to board members like you are planning to cold call every single name that escapes their lips!

3. Make your board "feel" why people give.

Make sure your board members know why people give generally and to your organization specifically. Do the following:

- Regularly celebrate gifts to your organization at board and committee meetings and actively create other opportunities to share how and why a donor came to your organization and why you appealed to his/her philanthropic inclination, how the cultivation process unfolded, and why he/she ultimately decided to make the gift. Don't just advise that a gift was made by Mr and Mrs. Smith and you thank them very much. Bring your board into the passion of Mr. and Mrs. Smith.

- Give your board members the opportunity to interact with donors at individual meetings, on tours and at events. This is just part of good stewardship but also gives your board members deeper insight into giving motivations. And insight = understanding.

Gail Perry has a terrific exercise that addresses both the fear of fundraising and juxtaposes the reticence for making the ask with your own personal giving. It effectively allows board members to get their own feelings out but also opens their eyes to why they, and other people, give. I like to do this right at the beginning of a workshop as it effectively frames the remaining time we have together. I also keep the flip charts up and refer back to them during the day.

Ask your board members to pair up and talk about how they feel about soliciting and asking for money. A good question is "*How do you personally feel about raising and soliciting funds?*" Give them a couple of minutes to discuss with each other – you will see lots of animated discussion – and then share with the group. The words are often "rejection," "embarrassed," "charity," "begging," "hitting-up," "nervous," "unpleasant," "guilty" – you get the picture.

Next, ask them to pair up again and discuss a different question.

"Think of a time you recently made a gift to an organization you really care about or that has touched you personally. How did you feel when you wrote that cheque? Why did you write that cheque and what do you hope to achieve by it?"

Again, give them a couple of minutes for discussion and to process with the group. This time you are very likely to hear all the reasons we, as fundraisers, know of why people give: to give back, to improve or save lives, to help people in need, to give people a hand up, because they felt a personal responsibility to others, and many others. This is the perfect time to compare the two sets of answers and relate their giving to the same reasons that other people give. It is a very powerful exercise.

Kay Sprinkel-Grace has a great quote that I have seen her use in her workshops that works particularly well with this exercise.

"Nonprofit organizations exist to fulfill community needs. People do not give because an organization has needs. They give because your organization meets needs."

Board members really get this quote. It can be like a light going on and puts the focus where it should be – on the people you are serving and the opportunities that are available for the donor.

4. Focus on the whole fundraising cycle, not just the "ask."

When we tell our board members that "we need your help in fundraising" I guarantee you that 95% of them immediately think we are asking them to "ask" others. In other words, we want them to say to their friends and colleagues those fateful 12 words "I'd like you to consider a gift of $10,000 to my organization."

Hence – the fear of fundraising. Instead of talking about the "ask," talk about the fundraising cycle and all the various entry points for volunteer leaders. Emphasize:

- There is a role for everyone in fundraising. You can be an "asker," but you can also be an ambassador and an advocate. And within these categories there are many other roles to play.

- The "ask" is about 1% of a continuous fundraising cycle.

- It is vitally important that you, as a volunteer leader, contribute where you are most comfortable. This is going to lead to greater success.

When I ask board members if they want to fundraise most of them usually don't. But when I ask them if they can open doors, make introductions, go on an advice visit with a staff member, thank donors, bring people to events, host events or tours and anyone of the myriad pieces of the cultivation and stewardship process, they say "sure, I can do that." The fear literally falls away.

Gail Perry has another great exercise and visual (see Figure 17.2) which shows board members how complex and cyclical the fundraising cycle is.

Graph 1 depicts the time and energy involved in the fundraising cycle. It clarifies that there are many important roles to play of which the actual ask is only one small part. I find this a real eye-opener for board members and can tell they are already realizing where they too can play an important role and make a difference.

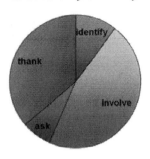

The Fundraising Adventure
TIME AND ENERGY INVOLVED
in each step of the cycle

Graph 2 is the second step, focusing on the root cause of the fear of fundraising and breaks the actual ask into three stages – warm-up, ask and follow-up. I also add percentages to this stressing that the actual ask is simply 1% of the whole ask, which in turn is perhaps 5% of the full cycle. Again, a message that really reverberates with board members and gets to the heart of their reluctance and discomfort with fundraising.

The Fundraising Adventure
A ROLE FOR EVERY BOARD MEMBER

Figure 17.2

TIPS FOR SUCCESS

Engaging your board in fundraising can be challenging, frustrating, time consuming and exhausting. But when you work with a board that is truly engaged it will be exciting, exhilarating, gratifying and the peak of your fundraising career. Anything that good is surely worth the hard work you must put into it. My top twelve strategies are summarized here:

Top 12 tips for governance & boards and fundraising

1. Understand the legal context of governance.

2. Develop your approach to engagement based on how it fits within and for your organization – there is no one size fits all.

3. Know why your board members are on your board and use that information to their and your organization's benefit.

4. Work with board members one-on-one for personalized support and maximum engagement.

5. Make sure that fundraising is part of board and board member responsibilities and communicated to them during the recruitment process.

6. Be involved in the recruitment process – get the board members you need.

7. Use your Development Committee to access the full board. Make them your champion.

8. Encourage your board to fully discuss and adopt a board giving program that will allow them to proudly give within their personal capacities.

9. Present fundraising strategically and don't box yourself into being measured simply on the basis of raising $xxx's.

10. Build a philanthropic culture that overlays your internal fundraising culture.

11. Make sure your board understands why people give and are able to relate that to why they personally give – to you and other causes.

12. Build a web of engagement opportunities that encourages each and every board member to be involved according to their individual skill sets and comfort levels.

Figure 17.3

ADDITIONAL RESOURCES

Books

▶ CANADIAN FUNDRAISING & PHILANTHROPY AND INNOVATIVE RESEARCH GROUP. (2009). *Assessing Not-for-Profit Boards, Governance Structures & Practices.* Civil Sector Press.

▶ LYSAKOWSKI, LINDA. (2004). *Building an Effective Board of Directors.* AFP's Ready Reference Series, Association of Fundraising Professionals.

▶ MURRAY, VIC. (2009). *The Management of Non-profit and Charitable Organizations in Canada.* Second Edition. LexisNexis.

▶ PEACOCK, ROBERT I., (2009). *Engagement, A Resource For Canadian Volunteer Boards.* Civil Sector Press.

▶ PERRY, GAIL. (2007). *Fired-Up Fundraising, Turning Board Passion into Action.* The AFP Fund Development Series, John Wiley & Sons.

▶ SPRINKEL GRACE, KAY. (1997). *Beyond Fund Raising: New Strategies for Innovation and Investment in Non-profits.* John Wiley & Sons.

ABOUT THE AUTHOR

Andrea McManus, CFRE

Andrea has over 26 years of strategic philanthropic experience in fundraising, and currently serves as President of The Development Group.

Andrea is a well-known leader in the nonprofit sector locally, nationally and internationally, and is the current Chair of the Association of Fundraising Professionals (AFP) International Board – the first non-American to hold that position. Andrea also served as former President of the Calgary Chapter of AFP, and was the founding chair of the AFP Foundation for Philanthropy Canada.

Andrea is an active community volunteer and leader and is a board member and immediate past-Chair of the Calgary Chamber of Voluntary Organizations; sits on Imagine Canada's Ethical Code Advisory Committee; and is a member of the Canada Revenue Agency Charities Technical Issues Working Group. She is a past member of the Advisory Council for the Institute of Non-Profit Studies at Mount Royal University.

Andrea was recognized by the Calgary Chapter for her contributions to the profession as the inaugural recipient of its Outstanding Fundraising Professional Award. Andrea serves as a Master Teacher and speaks frequently at conferences and workshops in Canada.

CHAPTER 18

VOLUNTEERS IN FUNDRAISING
BOYD MCBRIDE, CFRE

When I was asked to contribute a chapter on volunteers in fundraising my first instinct was to "go to the source" – to seek out the insight of those who know the business of volunteering in Canada better than any of us. Maybe there were things I could learn and share with you, beyond my own insights gained working with fundraising volunteers over almost thirty years.

So off I went to the offices of Volunteer Canada. *read more...*

Set in a modest three story building on the eastern edge of Ottawa's Byward Market, the office seemed typical of many I've visited in the voluntary sector: modest, frayed carpets and crowded with bright, creative people.

When I arrived, the first hurdle to overcome was an elevator that refused to budge. After puffing up three flights of stairs I was greeted by a young woman who explained that the elevator problem was a recurring one. She then went out of her way to make me feel welcome.

Volunteer Canada oversees the "big picture" work around volunteering in Canada. Their latest study, *Bridging the Gap,*[1] provides fascinating insight into what Canadians are looking for today as they contemplate volunteer service. It also explores how organizations are (or are not) successfully meeting those needs and engaging volunteers to advance their work.

Bridging the Gap has found that volunteers are younger now, and more likely to be new Canadians. It notes that, for many, finding the right kind of volunteer experience is difficult. Although millions of volunteer hours are provided every year, our organizations report that they "do not have the tools, training, and strategies in place to engage youth, families, baby boomers, and employer-supported volunteers."

The study goes on to explore a series of gaps between what today's volunteer wants in order to get engaged and what our organization's are, or are not, able to offer. An insight for me: "Many people are looking for group activities BUT few organizations have the capacity to offer them."

Fortunately, the study goes on to offer some very practical insight into what the changing volunteer landscape means for organizations that want to maintain and build even stronger volunteer programs. It urges greater flexibility in accommodating the interests and schedules of today's volunteers. It reminds us that we must "be sensitive to gender, culture, language and age" in communities where diversity has become the rule. For younger volunteers particularly, it urges that organizations fully embrace online and social media technologies that are so much a part of their lives.

While commissioning valuable studies and providing these kinds of insights, Volunteer Canada operates very much like so many of the organizations it serves

– engaging volunteers in its own work in the areas of fundraising and communications. Wendy Mitchell, Director of Corporate Citizenship & Fund Development, spoke highly of their Corporate Council on Volunteering. Its members open doors, make introductions and generally support Volunteer Canada's efforts to broaden the base of corporate support for the work they do. I'll return to the importance of "door opening" volunteers later.

So what, I asked, does someone involved in fundraising need to know about volunteers in Canada these days? And what advice would they offer a fundraising professional challenged to make the best possible use of volunteers raising funds?

VOLUNTEERS ARE A VALUABLE FUNDRAISING RESOURCE

This, of course, is an insight many successful fundraisers and fundraising managers already have. Those who have had some success with volunteers are generally keen to do more with them. The result? Tens of thousands of volunteers are engaged in fundraising on any given day in this country.

Just how many volunteers am I talking about? *The Canadian Survey of Giving, Volunteering and* Participating (CSGVP) is the best source of data on volunteerism in Canada. Every four years it reports on the level of volunteer involvement. The 2007 data is instructive.

Almost 12.5 million Canadians reported volunteering of some sort in 2007. Of those, 9% reported volunteering in fundraising. Many more reported working on events and other activities, which may well, have had a fundraising objective. Even the 9% minimum, however, yields a startling number: 1.12 million Canadians volunteered in fundraising!

---

1   Volunteer Canada. *Bridging the Gap: Enriching the Volunteer Experience to Build a Better Future for our Community.* 2010.

Top five volunteer roles in Canada

1. Organizing and supervising events

2. Fundraising

3. Sitting on committees and boards

4. Office administration

5. Teaching and/or mentoring

Source: Statistics Canada, *Canada Survey on Giving, Volunteering and Participating, 2007*

Figure 18.1

Fundraising volunteers: Are you getting yours?

Canadians volunteer a lot. In 2007 they volunteered for the equivalent of 1.1 million full time jobs. Of this, fundraising volunteers put in the equivalent of 100,000 full time jobs! These fundraising volunteers worked with 86,000 registered charities: that makes for the equivalent of almost one full time fundraising volunteer per registered charity! Are you getting yours? Is your charity getting its fair share? If not, why not?

Source: Statistics Canada, *Canada Survey on Giving, Volunteering and Participating, 2007*

Figure 18.2

Those volunteers gave our sector a total of about 189 million hours of volunteer fundraising – the equivalent of almost 100,000 people working full-time as volunteer fundraisers. These are remarkable numbers and, in my view, are lowball estimates. Canadians either enjoy their volunteer fundraising commitments, or they are so motivated by the causes, the leadership or the perceived payback involved, that they continue to step up in startling numbers.

Paula Speevak-Sladowski, Volunteer Canada's Director of Applied Research and Public Policy, describes volunteering for fundraising events as a "gateway" to broader and deeper volunteer engagement for many Canadians. Event volunteering is time-limited, can be done with friends or family, carries with it no ongoing responsibilities and taps skill sets most volunteers have to share. It may also "give back" – offering volunteers a chance to get certain kinds of experience, rub shoulders with people they would like to meet etc. It may not be the most effective fundraising, but it has broad appeal and engages many.

Of course there are many other kinds of volunteer work in fundraising beyond events. You may have volunteers at work in your office, on your Board or on a fundraising committee; perhaps contributing material from their homes... or you may not have any at all.

Which agencies are taking advantage of this rather remarkable volunteer engagement? The fact is Canadian fundraising volunteers are doing their work for a wide range of charities and non-profit organizations. The top six broad categories of organizations (see Figure 18.3) account for just over one third of volunteers. The other two thirds are hard at work in a diverse range of other agencies – including my own international development organization.

What types of organizations are Canadian volunteers supporting?

11% - Sports and recreation and social services

10% - Education and research and religious organizations

6% - Health

4% - Development and housing

3% - Environment and arts and culture

2% - Hospitals and law, advocacy and politics

Source: Statistics Canada, *Canada Survey on Giving, Volunteering and Participating, 2007*

Figure 18.3

Perhaps the better question for you to consider is "How many volunteers are assisting with the fundraising in which I am involved?" If the answer is "None," "Not so many," "Some, but not doing the right things" or even "Not enough," it will be worth reading on.

Keep in mind, however, that volunteers are not "free." Mobilizing more of them will require an additional investment by you and your agency. To use volunteers effectively in fundraising you will have to have systems in place, tasks and expectations made clear, and time set aside to manage and support their efforts. I'll return to these practical matters later in the chapter.

VOLUNTEERS ARE MOTIVATED TO GET INVOLVED FOR A NUMBER OF REASONS

Whether I am with volunteers or donors, one of the questions I pursue at every opportunity is "what motivates your involvement with my organization?" The answers are always illuminating, though rarely the same. They reflect the wide cross-section of people in our community, and often say as much about people's perceptions of the organizations I have worked for as they say about the backgrounds of the people themselves.

One thing I can say with confidence, however, is that when it comes to motivation to fundraise, people rarely get involved because they like asking people for money.

More often it is because they are passionate about a cause. When I worked for the Canadian Paraplegic Association (CPA) I met dozens of volunteers in cities across Canada who were willing to spend countless hours organizing wheelchair events, selling raffle tickets or working on corporate appeals. Most often these volunteers were motivated by their knowledge of just how crucial the CPA's services and supports are to those who have mobility impairments.

Why are Canadians getting involved?

Statistics Canada's 2007 Survey of Giving, Volunteering and Participating found that people are likely to volunteer because of a desire to contribute to the community; to use and build upon skills and experiences and have a personal connection to the cause. Statistics Canada also reported that many people see volunteering as an opportunity to build networks and meet new people.

Source: Statistics Canada, *Canada Survey on Giving, Volunteering and Participating*, 2007

Figure 18.4

It is a similar story when I think about the volunteers I currently support at SOS Children's Villages Canada. Whether it is event organizers in the South Asian community in Toronto, "thon" participants in Western Canada and Southern Ontario, letter writers at our national office in Ottawa or corporate leaders opening doors in Montreal and Calgary, it is the plight of orphaned and abandoned children half a world away that inspires their commitment.

Common to all of this volunteer effort in fundraising is the universal desire to make a difference. Volunteer work becomes a means to that end. Every volunteer I have ever known has made it clear to me – sometimes quite explicitly – that they hope to make that difference through their voluntary service. They talk to me (and to the pollsters) about how successful volunteering adds meaning to their lives. So, as you read this, you need to be thinking about how your agency positions itself while recruiting and managing volunteers.

Are you mission-driven and proud to be that way? Are you giving your volunteers a chance to make a difference, and then to measure and celebrate the difference they have made? If you're not, ask yourself and your colleagues what you can change to add meaning to the work you want volunteers to do.

There are often secondary motivations for volunteer involvement, and these can be as varied as the hair and skin colour of the volunteers themselves. Someone who cares about orphans can volunteer for at least a dozen agencies that serve that constituency. Why choose SOS Canada over Compassion, World Vision or PLAN? It may be because one agency can provide a valuable quid pro quo that isn't available or clearly identified by another. I mean things like specialized training, entry level work experience, the promise of a strong reference, an opportunity to "rub shoulders" with certain people, or perhaps a chance to build a writing portfolio that they can share with potential employers.

Often, it can be as simple as opening your facilities to volunteers so that they can meet, work and develop relationships with people who share common program interests and values. Some potential volunteers, particularly youth volunteers, will only get involved if they can do it with family or friends (see Figure 18.5).

Safety in numbers

Sometimes people are more likely to take risks, try new things and get involved with new organizations if they have the support of friends, family or coworkers. Statistics Canada reported that over one quarter of volunteers (26%) in 2007 volunteered because of a family project. Forty three percent of respondents stated that they became involved with their friends, neighbours or colleagues. Volunteers may be more willing to get involved in fundraising for your organization if they can do so with a friend, family member or colleague.

Source: Statistics Canada, *Canada Survey on Giving, Volunteering and Participating*, 2007

Figure 18.5

What lesson can you draw from this? It is not enough to have a good cause to offer. You need to do an inventory of what else you can provide and be ready to share it with prospective volunteers. Don't be shy about telling the recent university graduate who shows up wanting to help that, after 60 hours of volunteer service in fundraising, you are prepared to provide a written reference for that crucial first paying job.

Similarly, if your organization can offer any of the other benefits noted above, or others of your own creation, make a list and build some of them into your recruitment copy. At the same time, talk to new volunteers during their orientation to find out what they expect or might like to gain from their involvement

with your agency. Make deals. Volunteer satisfaction levels will rise if you make a commitment and deliver. It will also aid you with volunteer retention.

VOLUNTEERS ARE REMARKABLY FLEXIBLE – THEY CAN DO MANY THINGS

Remember I am talking only about fundraising volunteers, but even with this tight focus, people who come forward to volunteer can do a wide range of things for us. Naturally, there are many other kinds of volunteer tasks in the areas of service delivery, financial oversight, governance etc., but let's consider the many and varied roles for volunteers in fundraising.

We think of envelope stuffers as the classic fundraising volunteer. Too bad. This sells many of the people considering volunteering for us short. It does the same for our own agencies, and the increasingly complex nature of most mature fundraising programs.

Whatever your needs, make sure your recruitment materials and your selection process make them clear. Jerold Panas has a few suggestions about the qualities you should be looking for in a fundraising volunteer in Figure 18.6. It is safe to say these characteristics should also be sought as you recruit great fundraising volunteers.

Top five qualities of a good fundraiser

Impeccable integrity

Good listener

Ability to motivate

Hard worker

Concern for people

Source: Panas, Jerold. (1988). *Born to Raise: What Makes a Great Fundraiser; What Makes a Fundraiser Great*. Chicago: Pluribus Press.

Figure 18.6

FUNDRAISING VOLUNTEERS IN THE COMMUNITY

For many years volunteers have taken on traditional fundraising tasks in the community: organizing events, door-to-door canvassing, bottle drives, and selling raffle tickets and products ranging from candy to fertilizer to greeting cards. All of this still works, and is still largely done by volunteers. I say "largely" because some organizations are now using paid canvassers in door-to-door work. That bright young Greenpeace canvasser, for example, is motivated by her interest in the environment as well as the payments she receives for each new monthly donor signed up on your street. Paid telephone solicitors and in-bound call centre workers move a lot of lottery tickets. There is still plenty of room, however, for a range of volunteers in our community fundraising.

FUNDRAISING VOLUNTEERS IN THE OFFICE

In many fundraising offices the work of professional researchers and writers is supported by volunteers doing elements of the same jobs. Recent university graduates are as comfortable doing online prospect research as their parents were canvassing their block for the Canadian Cancer Society. A good writer, whether paid or volunteer, can generate copy for a charity's website, its donor newsletter or its reporting and stewardship packages. The more specialized tasks of writing compelling direct mail copy or legacy giving promotions may still have to be handled by seasoned professionals, but there is much a capable volunteer can assist with.

FUNDRAISING VOLUNTEERS IN ADVISORY ROLES

We who raise funds for a living know that we could not afford to engage the high level of professional insight our organizations need if we had to pay for it. The best lawyers, accountants, marketing minds and experts in a range of matters can only be drawn into our work, and make their invaluable contributions, if we can offer them something, in return for their volunteer service. Consider the following examples:

- I have a highly qualified family law expert whose law firm encourages her to do *pro bono* work

for us on estates and legacy gifts. She reviews provisions in wills, assesses the quality of work done by executors; and helps us frame language for wills that will meet the needs of donors who want to leave something for my charity.

- Another partner at the same firm reviews every important contract before we sign. I know that he has steered us clear of what might have become major problems a number of times.

- No less than three leading chartered accountants meet monthly on my Audit and Finance Committee. They review our financial statements, manage our modest investment portfolio, refer me to other specialized advice when we need it, and generally keep us tracking toward our fundraising and financial goals.

As a relatively small charity, SOS Canada could simply not afford to pay for all of this. Yet without it, our chances of success would be diminished; our chances of making costly mistakes enhanced. Allow me to say a public thank you to all five of these folks right here, right now! And for you, as readers, please consider what roles you could offer to folks like these. They are out there and they want to help.

FUNDRAISING VOLUNTEERS AS AMBASSADORS, ADVOCATES AND ASKERS

Some volunteers can do things that NO staff person, no matter how well trained or experienced, can do. Serving as ambassadors and advocates for our charities, and as "askers," are roles that these specialized fundraising volunteers can play with enormous success.

A motivated volunteer ambassador can open doors and provide introductions for your charity, sometimes at the highest leadership levels in your community. He or she can lend their own personal and professional credibility to our charities, helping persuade people who may not know the charity itself to get involved. A personal endorsement delivered friend-to-friend or peer-to-peer is a form of volunteer service that is invaluable. So too is a more public endorsement from a community leader.

The very best of our fundraising volunteers in this category can ask people to join them in making a gift.

These volunteers are able to inspire others through their own visible commitment to a cause. They have no vested interest and no pay cheque on the line when they say, "I believe so strongly in this that I give my time and my money. Join me."

Good fundraising is, after all, built on relationships. It is not about one-time gifts from strangers (although these are a starting point), but about longer-term relationships with people who, over time, can be persuaded of the logic of even greater support for your cause and your organization's service to that cause. More volunteers serving as ambassadors, advocates and askers means more support; it's that simple.

FUNDRAISING VOLUNTEERS ON YOUR BOARD OR FUNDRAISING COMMITTEE

Every charity, and certainly every fundraising foundation, needs to have board members who are committed to the notion that raising funds for the organization is part of their responsibility. They must also provide leadership in the areas of strategic planning and policy making, as well as in monitoring the performance of the organization. They must recruit, then supervise (and if necessary sanction) the CEO. But if the organization is to be truly successful in fundraising, board members must embrace their fundraising responsibility and lead here, just as they do in their governance work.

A Board can, to a degree, delegate some of this to a fundraising committee or campaign cabinet, but its members cannot delegate their responsibility to provide leadership as a Board. For Board members it starts with their personal gift. Similar gifts must follow from each volunteer recruited into a leadership role in the fundraising. A leadership gift empowers the volunteer to ask others to join them in giving. Without it, the message to others is confused and unsatisfying: 'I am asking you to give and to help us with fundraising, but I am not yet convinced to make my own gift…'

The chart below indicates one way in which volunteers in fundraising can be organized around a Board of Directors committed to the task. The overlap of the Fundraising Committee with the other three groups is deliberate. The board must be represented, on the committee, and its representative is often expected to lead. An engaged honourary leadership group may have a few members who will go beyond their honorific role and work on fundraising. There may also be people in advisory roles inspired by the case for giving and wanting to help raise funds. These folks, and others drawn from the broader community, become the Fundraising Committee.

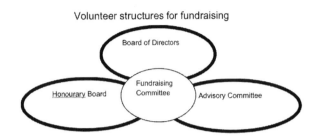

Figure 18.7

The actual work of fundraising starts with case development. The board must confirm the charity's case for support. Staff is likely to do most of the legwork in developing and refining the case. The involvement of fundraising volunteers is, however, critical to the ability of the case to motivate giving. When fundraising volunteers inside each of the fundraising groups can say "I truly believe we must raise funds in support of this project and I will start by making my own donation," we can be pretty sure, as fundraising staff, that the case will motivate giving in the broader community.

Board members and active fundraising volunteers can continue to assist in the work of prospect identification and qualification. Who out there has the links, interest and ability to support our programs? Well-connected, case-driven volunteers can help with the sifting and sorting so essential to confirming top quality prospects.

Next, volunteers can help cultivate the interest of good prospects. One of the criteria for a top prospect is some personal link with the organization. This link may be a fundraising volunteer. If it is, the volunteer has a unique role to play in helping draw the prospect into your agency's work.

Fundraising board members may also have a role to play in opening doors for the kind of encounters that are so critical in enhancing relationships with a prospective donor. The initial meeting may be nothing more than a discussion of philanthropic interests over coffee, but the very fact of it taking place helps position the charity as a potential recipient of the prospect's financial support. A carefully managed social event can further engage prospective donors as well as existing donors judged able to give much more.

The more important meeting is one where the fundraising volunteer can witness, or participate in, a solicitation. This is where the rubber hits the road for any fundraiser. While the actual ask may be made by the staff person, there is a crucial supporting role for the right volunteer. He or she adds *gravitas*. And he or she will also, in the company of a seasoned major gifts person, learn about and become more comfortable with the process of leading a prospective donor to a decision to give.

Finally, at least in the context of the donor cycle, and after a gift has been secured, there is lots of room for board members and fundraising volunteers to assist with stewardship. The many ways that we can thank and recognize donors for their gift can involve fundraising volunteers in meaningful and rewarding work – sending notes, making thank you calls, presenting awards etc.

Many boards create a fundraising or development committee to advance the board's work in fundraising. Its members must include a few board members, but the Committee can be further populated by people who are involved in other ways – as donors, volunteers, or friends of the organization. Some boards are willing to recruit community leaders onto their development committees in order to increase the organization's range of connections into the community it serves.

VOLUNTEERS COME IN ALL SHAPES AND SIZES THESE DAYS

At the risk of oversimplifying on this point, my experience tells me that volunteers generally fall into one of two broad categories:

- The traditional reliable long-term volunteer; and,

- The time-limited volunteer.

Both are valuable resources, but each has a particular character, special needs and offering to make.

Where to find fundraising volunteers

They're out there! Here are a number of possible sources:

- Your personal network: friends, family, neighbours, parishioners at your church

- Your Board/Honorary Board/Advisory Council members.

- The networks of your Board/Honorary Board/Advisory Council members.

- Your donors. They have already embraced your mission and understand what you do, why you do it, and who you serve.

- Volunteer Bureaus. Almost every community in Canada has one.

- The community newspaper. It is probably willing to do a story about your agency, increasing your agency's publicity, and drawing attention to your need for volunteers.

Figure 18.8

The former is usually older, better educated, often retired, and more likely to be female. She likes routine, familiarity, and appreciates the opportunity that her volunteering provides for socializing. She likes to be known to her co-workers and likes spending time with them each week in a way that allows her to befriend them, even as she gets her volunteer tasks done.

The latter, the time-limited volunteer, is often younger, sometimes looking for career launch experience and professional references. He or she may be between jobs and looking for an opportunity to learn a new skill or get exposure to a new industry. These folks are generally only prepared to commit for a limited period of time – often the time it takes to secure the paying job they need – although they may be able and willing to work up to full-time hours for the period they are available.

The traditional long-serving volunteer is well suited to carrying out routine tasks in the fundraising office: dealing with basic repetitive correspondence, following up phone or email messages asking for information, preparing and mailing packages in response to web-based inquiries etc.

A seasonally available volunteer of this type might play a role in an annual event, the critical path for which is flexible enough to accommodate her travel plans.

The time-limited volunteer is a bigger management challenge. Time-limited, volunteer- appropriate tasks must be confirmed for the time slots available to each volunteer. The front-end costs of orientation and training must be amortized over as little as a few days or weeks of service, often with an explicit understanding that the charity will not likely see the volunteer again once the task is complete.

Here are two fine volunteers who, for me, capture the essence of the long-term and time-limited volunteer. As you read their words consider their demographic profile, their motivations and their terms of engagement. Ask yourself whether your fundraising program is structured in a way that would encourage people like them to get involved.

THE TRADITIONAL LONG-TERM VOLUNTEER – MARIA VIRJEE'S STORY IN HER OWN WORDS

"Born and raised in Austria, I immigrated to Canada in 1962. During my first few years here I continued to make donations to SOS Austria. In 1969 I learned about the newly founded SOS Children's Villages Canada. I got in touch and have been involved with SOS Canada ever since.

During the 1970s and 1980s I was a donor, sponsored two children, and helped with office duties. In 1991 I joined the Board of Directors as Secretary. Over the next 10 years I held various positions, including two years as President.

My activities as a committed volunteer over the years - decades really - have changed with the needs of the organization. I have written letters, organized Christmas card sales, volunteered at golf tournaments, managed database tasks, helped organize events like open houses, been the contact person for the Legacy Program, maintained records and followed up with complaints from supporters.

Because I have been with the organization from the beginning, I sometimes feel that I am its corporate memory. There have been many changes at SOS and I've had to adapt my roles and activities over the years. But what has not changed is my support of an organization that has consistently fulfilled and exceeded its mandate and has done so with enduring enthusiasm and commitment. SOS is in *my* blood. "

Volunteer Loyalty: once they're yours they could be yours for good

As with brand loyalty, most people who begin volunteering for a charity will stay involved with that organization for the long-term. Slightly over half of volunteers (51%) gave their time to only one organization in 2007 while 28% and 22% volunteered for two and three organizations respectively. These statistics reinforce the special status your volunteers attach to your organization's work. Cultivate them; make the work they do as interesting and meaningful as possible, and the reward can be extraordinary loyalty.

Source: Statistics Canada, *Canada Survey on Giving, Volunteering and Participating, 2007*

Figure 18.9

THE TIME-LIMITED VOLUNTEER – JULIA EHRHARDT'S EXPERIENCE IN HER OWN WORDS

"I first became involved with SOS Children's Villages in the summer of 2007. I had just finished my second year at Carleton University and was working in retail. While that suited my schedule because of the flexible hours, it was neither particularly meaningful nor did it provide me with skills to build my resume. I looked to SOS Canada to bring some meaning to my summer and some depth to my work experience.

When meeting with Boyd, I described my expectations and schedule. I was able to volunteer a few days a week, around my work schedule. I am an outgoing person and Boyd decided that helping with the FIFA U-20 World Cup of Soccer Canada would be a perfect fit. SOS, as the official charity of the games, had a national role to play. I was able to do many great things that summer, including researching activities for children attending the games, helping organize logistics and promoting SOS and its relationship with FIFA through social media. By the end of the World Cup my work experience had grown exponentially.

I appreciated the confidence that Boyd and the rest of the SOS staff had placed in me and was grateful for the opportunity to work in an office where I had the opportunity to meet new, interesting and dedicated people. Everyone made me feel that my volunteer work was important and made a difference; sentiments that aren't bestowed upon many 21 year olds at work! Is it any wonder that, the next time I found myself temporarily between jobs, I turned to SOS again to help fill my time, improve my skills and contribute to an organization that is working to create international change?"

VOLUNTEERS IN FUNDRAISING NEED TO BE MANAGED

Like the management of staff, managing volunteers requires insight and discipline. It also requires the application of some widely recognized management principles. Ideally it will be handled by someone with human resources training or training as a volunteer coordinator.

You may have asked yourself "Is it worth the time?" My bias is yes. However, I have often observed on the wide variation in the amount of time it takes to care for and manage certain volunteers.

Who are youth volunteers?

According to Volunteer Canada's 2010 Pan-Canadian research study, youth volunteers (ages 15-24) are career-focused, open-minded, energetic, tech savvy and enjoy the social benefits of volunteering. Many youth are obligated to volunteer as part of a high school community service initiative. Volunteer Canada reflects that one of the primary barriers to youth involvement is an inability to make a long-term commitment. So why not engage youth in projects with clear and feasible deadlines? This could help turn their community service into a life-long relationship with your charity.

Source: Volunteer Canada, Bridging the Gap: Enriching the Volunteer Experience to Build a Better Future for our Communities, 2010

Figure 18.10

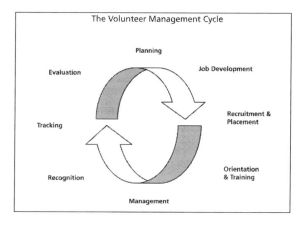

Figure 18.11

Some seem to need little more than a kind word and a desk to work at. Others need constant supervision and feedback. Still others require only the time necessary for quality social interaction. This variation so intrigued me that I took it up with my hosts at Volunteer Canada.

Is there a rule of thumb, I wanted to know, that will help Canadian fundraisers understand what they are getting into as they begin to expand the volunteer ranks in their work?

It turns out there once was, but it no longer holds. I was told that long ago, in a simpler fundraising world, a staff team could expect to devote as little as one hour of its time to garner as much as forty hours of volunteer assistance. Even with my thirty years of experience, I cannot recall that time. Although there are still volunteer roles in fundraising where the work is simple and rewarding enough that, for certain people, it almost takes care of itself.

There is also a range of other complicated, one-off and sometimes not so rewarding tasks that volunteers can do, but which require higher levels of interaction with staff to achieve success. My experience suggests that in small shops without a human resources staff person, fundraising staff should expect to devote an hour of their time for every two to five volunteer hours your organization gains. The ratio will be more appealing as you engage volunteers who enjoy the relationship and stay longer. It gets less so with volunteers who come in for short-term, project-specific tasks, and then move on.

Fortunately, there are lots of resources devoted to the challenge of working with volunteers more generally. There is also a range of material available specific to the challenge of mobilizing and supporting fundraising volunteers. Trainers can be found to prepare volunteers for the dreaded 'ask.' Whole books have been written about helping bring people from initial objections to a generous commitment of funds to a cause. Codes of conduct for volunteers, and for the management of volunteers, are easily found on the web. No one charged with the management of fundraising volunteers needs to feel they are breaking new ground or that they must develop resources from scratch. For examples of where to turn see the additional resources section.

A word about volunteer – staff partnerships

Much has been written about the management of fundraising volunteers. More should probably be said about the notion of "partnership." When staff is searching for ways to work more effectively with volunteers who have agreed to participate in major gift "asks," the notion of partnership is what we should aspire to. We need each other to be truly successful.

Certainly our "askers" need to be managed. They must be recruited with sensitivity; they must know what is expected of them; they must be briefed and debriefed around their meetings with donors and prospects; their efforts must be rewarded and their successes celebrated.

They must also be supported in practical ways. Customized case documents must be in hand. Prospect bios need to be updated. Timely news items must be clipped and available for review prior to a meeting. They must have meeting dates, times and venues clear.

Finally they must be nurtured. Asking for money, even with the strongest case for support, is challenging. For some volunteer askers it is downright frightening! Professional fundraising staff must be aware of this and be able to instil confidence in the process. The best ask is usually a team ask, with the volunteer and the staff person involved. Tag-team follow-up can be a great option too.

As fundraising professionals, the work we do with our best volunteer askers goes way beyond the traditional notion of volunteer management. And when we work together in a true partnership new levels of fundraising can be achieved.

Figure 18.12

Show appreciation

Let volunteers know when they're doing a good job. A little recognition and appreciation can go a long way in helping to motivate volunteers. Volunteer Canada's 2010 report reflected that youth, in particular, are looking for both positive and constructive feedback in order to improve their skills and become more marketable as future employees.

Source: Volunteer Canada, Bridging the Gap: Enriching the Volunteer Experience to Build a Better Future for our Communities, 2010

Figure 18.13

CONCLUSION

Working with volunteers can be immensely rewarding. Last year I can attribute about 30% of my organization's fundraising directly to the involvement of key volunteers. A million dollar legacy gift was prompted by a discussion of philanthropy that took place between one of our Board members and a friend grappling with a life-threatening illness. A corporate partnership generated another $300,000 and can be traced back to an exercise spearheaded by a CEO who opened a door for us two years earlier. Another $50,000 resulted from the Board's discussion of its own giving commitment.

Good things happen when high-level fundraising volunteers get engaged in the fundraising challenge.

Don't deny yourself the opportunity to discover just how much volunteers can mean to your organization, particularly if you have been reluctant to make the commitment necessary to move into volunteer-led and volunteer-supported fundraising.

Remember, the volunteers you bring into the fundraising challenge will, if all goes reasonably well, make your work easier. They will also make it more meaningful, and much more satisfying. The volunteers in my office make me feel like a hero, even as they carry out the really heroic tasks themselves. Your own volunteers will make you feel like a hero too.

ADDITIONAL RESOURCES

Books

▶ CONNORS, T.D. (1999). *The Volunteer Management Handbook.* New York: John Wiley & Sons Inc.

▶ GRAFF, L. (1997). *By Definition: Policies for Volunteer Programs: a Manual for Executive Directors, Board Members, and Managers of Volunteers.* Dundas, ON.

▶ LYSAKOWSKI, L. (2005). *Recruiting and Training Fundraising Volunteers.* New Jersey: John Wiley & Sons Inc.

Online documents

▶ ASSOCIATION OF FUNDRAISING PROFESSIONALS. (2011). *Orienting and Training Volunteers for Success.* Retrieved August 22, 2011 from http://www.afpnet.org/ResourceCenter/ArticleDetail.cfm?ItemNumber=5841.

▶ GOULBOURNE, M., & EMBULDENIYA, D. (2002). *Assigning Economic Value to Volunteer Activity: Eight Tools for Efficient Program Management.* Toronto: Canadian Centre for Philanthropy. Retrieved August 21, 2011 from http://library.imaginecanada.ca/resource_guides/volunteerism/management.

▶ GRAFF, L. (2006). *Declining Profit Margin: When volunteers cost more than they return.* The International Journal of Volunteer Administration, 14(1), (pp.24-32). Retrieved from http://www.ijova.org/.../IJOVA_VOL24_NO1_Profit_Margin_Linda_Graff.pdf

▶ GRAFF, L. (2009). *Reconceptualizing the Value of Volunteer Work.* Retrieved August 22, 2011 from www.lindagraff.ca.

▶ KNOWLEDGE DEVELOPMENT CENTRE: IMAGINE CANADA. (2005). *Attracting and Keeping Youth Volunteers: Creating a Governance Culture that Nurtures and Values Youth.* Retrieved August 22, 2011 from http://library.imaginecanada.ca/resource_guides/volunteerism/recruitment.

▶ LYSAKOWSKI, L. (2005). "Why and How to Use Volunteers in Fundraising." *Recruiting and Training Fundraising Volunteers* (pp. 1-13). New Jersey, John Wiley & Sons Inc. *from* http://media.wiley.com/product_data/excerpt/85/04717064/0471706485.pdf

▶ McCLINTOCK, N. (2004). *Understanding Canadian Volunteers: Using the National Survey of Giving, Volunteering and Participating to Build your Volunteer Program.* Toronto: Canadian Centre for Philanthropy. Retrieved August 22, 2011 from *http://www.energizeinc.com/art/subj/trends.html.*

▶ NOBLE, R. *Volunteering in Canada: Practical Findings from Research, 2000-2007.* Toronto: Knowledge Development Centre: Imagine Canada. Retrieved August 22, 2011 from http://ic.andornot.com/.

▶ QUATER, J., MOOK L., & RICHMOND, B. (2002). *What Volunteers Contribute: Calculating and Communicating Value Added.* Toronto: Canadian Centre for Philanthropy. Retrieved August 22, 2011 from http://library.imaginecanada.ca/resource_guides/volunteerism/management.

▶ STATISTICS CANADA. (2009). *Caring Canadians, Involved Canadians.* Ottawa: Statistics Canada. Retrieved August 22, 2011 from *http://www.statcan.gc.ca/bsolc/olc-cel/olc-cel?catno=71-542-X&CHROPG=1&lang=eng.*

▶ VOLUNTEER CANADA. (2006). *The Canadian Code for Volunteer Involvement.* Ottawa: Department of Canadian Heritage. Retrieved August 22, 2011 from *http://volunteer.ca/about-volunteerism/canadian-code-volunteer-involvement.*

▶ VOLUNTEER CANADA. (2010). *Bridging the Gap: Enriching the Volunteer Experience to Build a Better Future for our Community.* http://www.volunteer.ca/files/English_Research_Fact_Sheet_Bridging_the_Gap.pdf

Organizations

▶ CANADIAN VOLUNTEER DIRECTORY, http://www.canadian-universities.net/Volunteer/index.html

▶ CENTRE FOR VOLUNTARY SECTOR RESEARCH AND DEVELOPMENT (CVSRD), http://www.cvsrd.org/eng/home.html

▶ CHARITY CENTRAL'S FUNDRAISING RESOURCES, www.charitycentral.ca

▶ CHARITY VILLAGE, www.charityvillage.ca/cvnet/volunteer.aspx

▶ IMAGINE CANADA'S Nonprofit Library, http://library.imaginecanada.ca/

▶ VOLUNTEER CANADA, www.volunteer.ca

▶ VOLUNTEER VALUE CALCULATOR from Image Canada's Knowledge Development Centre, http://volunteercalculator.imaginecanada.ca/eng/default.asp

ABOUT THE AUTHOR

Boyd McBride, MA, CFRE

Boyd McBride has served as the National Director of SOS Children's Villages Canada since 2001, and worked in the international development community for most of his career, beginning with CUSO (now CUSO/VSO) over 25 years ago. He gained further experience while in fundraising and in leadership roles at the Canadian Red Cross Society, the Canadian Organization for Development through Education (CODE) and the Canadian Paraplegic Association.

His work and professional consultancies have taken him to South and East Asia, Latin America and Africa.

Boyd is also an experienced educator. For many years he coordinated the National Program in Fundraising Education for Algonquin College and was deeply involved in curriculum development for that Program. He has presented numerous workshops and has worked with Boards of Directors and staff groups for organizations across Canada and as far away as Brazil and Guyana.

Boyd received his BA from the University of Alberta and earned his MA in International Affairs from the Patterson School at Carleton University. He earned his CFRE (Certified Fundraising Executive) in 1994 and is currently Vice President of the Association of Fundraising Professionals' Ottawa Chapter.

CHAPTER 19

DATA MANAGEMENT
TANIA BRANDSTROM, CFRE

In a business based on relationships, organizational memory represented by its data sources - including electronic, print files, and staff memory - is a critical business asset. *read more...*

Similarly, the business know-how reflected in its processes and systems ensures this organizational memory is nurtured and leveraged to optimal benefit for your organization and your mission. Both components are critical for an effective fundraising operation. An efficient data management system without historical data is just pretty programming and workflow charts; and data without a system and business rules for storage and access is akin to a filing cabinet full of paper but without any files. Neither are very functional, and neither allow the fundraising practitioner to employ the information on-hand effectively.

Have you ever joined a new organization and struggled with understanding why someone chose to support the organization in the past? Or maybe the issue you encountered was more fundamental - and left you spending months assembling information to build a basic donor list? Perhaps you inherited beautiful-looking donor files, which over time were revealed to be only 70% complete – leaving you blindsided with undocumented history on three out of ten donor visits? While the catchy topic of data management might not appear so fundamental at first glance, it is these very issues that a sound data management system is designed to address.

At the end of this chapter you should:

- Have an understanding of the importance of data management to a successful development operation;

- Understand the principles of good data management; and

- Be in a position to evaluate practices within your own organization and identify opportunities for improvement.

This chapter focuses on data management within the Canadian fundraising context, and will address database selection, implementation, ongoing management, and regulatory frameworks. The principles being reviewed can be applied, regardless of the software platform you have, and will benefit small and large fundraising operations alike.

PRINCIPLES OF GOOD DATA MANAGEMENT

Regardless of whether you work for a large fundraising operation, or are starting the first fundraising efforts for a small not-for-profit, adhering to a few, simple, data management principles will ensure the information you gather can be used to support and enhance fundraising efforts over time. Regardless of the state of the data we inherit, as practitioners we do a disservice to the organization and the mission we serve if we do not strive to improve organizational memory during our tenure: try always to leave a file, electronic or otherwise, in better shape than it was when you started working with it. The scope of information to be tracked will depend largely on your organization, and should be a conscious decision made with a view to long-term plans. There is, however, information that charities are required to record and report to ensure compliance with the legal and regulatory framework in which we operate. A reference list of provincial and federal resources is included at the end of the chapter.

There is a lot that can be done with simple office programs: if you follow good data practices, these can offer efficient support for a small organization, and position you well for upgrading into a specialized fundraising software program when volume and sophistication warrants.

First, let's review some basic principles that will help newcomers to data management set a good foundation:

1. Define a common vocabulary

Between organizations, and even between development activities within the same organization, language can be used for different, contradictory purposes. In some instances this is driven by the software applications we use. While there are industry-standard definitions and application of terms, many of which are discussed in other chapters, the important thing from a data/knowledge management perspective is that terms should be well defined and consistently applied within your own organization.

For instance, when building a stewardship plan for a major gift donor, the use of the word "gift" often means total value of commitment, to be paid over a period of years, whereas this description may more accurately define the word "pledge". Already we can see how easily a misunderstanding may emerge between staff, or a report be misinterpreted, if a definition is not developed and applied consistently for your organization. For this example, consider the interaction between a stewardship officer and data specialist seeking to identify donors for a specific recognition opportunity – and the difference a query based on gift amount, versus pledge amount, might result in.

2. Develop documentation

Without current reference documentation, understanding can change over time; implications of certain classifications can be forgotten altogether, or inferred where they don't exist, further clouding understanding. Good documentation, including up to date process flows or desk references and procedure manuals, will ensure that the value of the information contained in your databases grows over time. This will also ensure the information is strategically applied to support your fundraising efforts. As new information is introduced, and processes adapted, changes should be communicated both verbally and through updated documentation. A regular schedule for reviewing and refreshing data should also be established.

3. Use one data field for one type of information

Allow me to use a simple example to illustrate this point. In the last three months, I've received direct mail appeals and stewardship letters from a number of charities I support, with varying degrees of successful personalization: Dear Mrs. Brandstrom, Dear Tania (both good) Dear Tania Brandstrom (While not incorrect, this is an odd salutation), Dear T. (inappropriate - clearly does little to engender a sense of relationship). While the odd and inappropriate could be a result of either human or process errors, both are also likely to have arisen from a data structure (either in the database or the output file used to generate the letters) that was not designed with an understanding of the ultimate intent.

This very simple, but important, example, illustrates the need to structure your data with an understanding of the ultimate uses it will need to support – begin at the end, when designing or selecting the data structure to meet your needs. Recognizing that data is gathered through many vehicles (e.g.) event attendee lists, captured from credit card/cheque payments, and

that it is not always possible to secure a "complete" file of information from these sources - the data management processes should accommodate the permitted variances in the database. For example:

Problem:	Dear Tania Brandstrom
Likely Cause:	First and last names captured in single data field
Solution:	Data Structure: Keep one piece of information in a single field
Problem:	Dear T.
Likely Cause:	Record missing first name details
Solution:	Develop data management process that identifies missing/abbreviated information, and address distinctly through merge data logic. For example, your database may allow you to flag records with incomplete name information. This flag can then be used as a guide where preparing your salutation output:
	Where the flag exists for a record, use the prefix and last name: the outcome is more formal, but appropriate.
	Where no flag exists (meaning a record is complete) use the first name, resulting in the warm personal tone intended. If your database does not allow this flexibility in generating the output file, simply have the incomplete flag displayed in the output, and use "If..then" formula logic in your spreadsheet to build the desired salutation.

Processes utilizing data should be able to accommodate gaps in information. In the proposed solution for the organization that does not appear to know my first name, I have suggested that a special handling flag be applied against the record to ensure special cases can be easily pulled-out and treated distinctly during the mailing process. If you have this problem in your database and are now haunted by visions of lengthy manual review to apply a newly created code for each record, don't worry! Instead, consider incorporating data cleaning steps into your mailing process.

Use the power of your spreadsheet program to make this process easy. In the following table (Figure 19.1) I've demonstrated how combining two formulas in excel can allow you to quickly identify first name fields containing only an initial, and to construct a salutation field that results in appropriate treatment of each record. Using formulas in this way avoids manual review or special handling, and can create appropriate letters in just a few minutes.

If your system allows for a bulk upload of information, routinely adding the cleaning steps to your process, and using the result to upload a special handling code, will ensure consistent improvement over time.

4. Establish a shared commitment to information gathering, and define accountability

Who is currently accountable for the quality of the information in your database? Who is responsible for gathering and inputting? If this is limited to a handful of people, I would suggest you are limiting the value of this resource. If we are truly committed to building the organizational memory through accurate, complete donor and prospect files, we must also ensure that this commitment translates into accountability for infor-

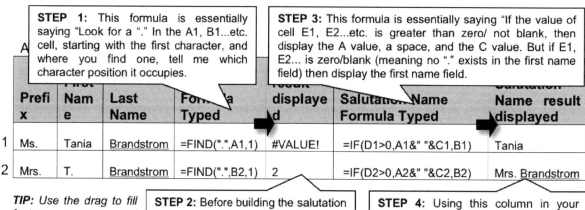

STEP 1: This formula is essentially saying "Look for a "." In the A1, B1...etc. cell, starting with the first character, and where you find one, tell me which character position it occupies.

STEP 3: This formula is essentially saying "If the value of cell E1, E2...etc. is greater than zero/ not blank, then display the A value, a space, and the C value. But if E1, E2... is zero/blank (meaning no "." exists in the first name field) then display the first name field.

	Prefix	First Name	Last Name	Formula Typed	result displayed	Salutation Name Formula Typed	Salutation Name result displayed
1	Ms.	Tania	Brandstrom	=FIND(".",A1,1)	#VALUE!	=IF(D1>0,A1&" "&C1,B1)	Tania
2	Mrs.	T.	Brandstrom	=FIND(".",B2,1)	2	=IF(D2>0,A2&" "&C2,B2)	Mrs. Brandstrom

TIP: Use the drag to fill feature, or copy and paste, to quickly replicate the formulas throughout the whole column.

STEP 2: Before building the salutation formula, copy this entire column and right-click to paste as values, then use the find & replace feature to replace #VALUE! <u>with</u> "0" or blank cells.

STEP 4: Using this column in your letter merge will ensure you are addressing your donors appropriately, without the time involved in manually updating each record.

Figure 19.1

A similar process can be used to address invitations, where you might prefer to address formally using the prefix and last name, but have data with prefix or gender missing. If you construct your salutation to use the prefix and last name where the prefix exists, and otherwise to use the first name, you will again have an appropriately addressed list in little time.

If you're not sure how these steps would be applied using the tools you have available, I recommend investing the time to master the functionality of your spreadsheet program – any number of courses are available that can provide a solid foundation in applying and working with formulas, many of which can be used to shortcut the process of perfecting a mailing list.

mation gathering being attributed to all roles in your team. I don't mean your Vice President should be expected to enter address updates or gifts in the database. However, this person will have unique insight into the motivations of your leadership donors, and capturing this intelligence will ensure it can be used to shape future cultivation and solicitation strategies. Within your fundraising team, establish processes for staff to feed information into your database, and reflect the expectation of performance through individual and team performance measures to reinforce this accountability.

What might this look like? Consider formalizing a meeting debrief with leadership and volunteers that includes a staff member designated to capture key information. This allows the call team to share information gathered while the information is fresh, and communicate any follow-up action required. An added bonus is the support provided to key personnel reduces the time burden for documentation, allowing you to make the most of their time by having them involved in donor calls.

How you address information gathering for fundraising staff will depend on your organization's culture. Whatever process you choose, ensure there is a checkpoint for measuring performance. This will reinforce the importance of contributing to the information resource, and provide a mechanism to reward information gathering. The key is to design processes that support the capture of information that is right for your organization, articulate and agree to each team member's obligations with respect to the process, and then provide a method to evaluate.

While pushing accountability out to staff increases training and monitoring requirements, the organization benefits from the holistic profile of the relationship with a prospect that emerges. The information that is shared in each interaction with the organization will vary depending on context, quality of relationship with the fundraiser. It is through the compilation of these various bits of information, and the unique insights each individual gleans from an interaction, that the most comprehensive view of a prospect can be developed. The value of the combination of information included in fundraiser call reports can be critical in guiding future cultivation plans.

Decentralized data gathering and input emphasizes the necessity for establishing processes and standards for data. As you establish these standards, consider:

- how information is gathered

- how it is input, and by whom

- how compliance with data entry standards will be assured

- who will monitor for accuracy

Some software programs will allow you to pre-populate frequently used values, reducing the risk of inconsistent data entry, or establish forms that require certain information to be provided before a record can be saved. These systems provide greater certainty of consistent entry and reduce the need for monitoring. Regardless of the structure of your system, periodic monitoring of data for accuracy and cleaning efforts

should be accepted as part of an essential support framework.

SELECTING AND IMPLEMENTING SOFTWARE

When you begin looking for software to manage data, processes and analysis, it quickly becomes evident that there are a wide range of options and costs to choose from.

Should you host your own system, or look for a service arrangement? Customize a program, or build from scratch? Select a fundraising-specific package, or use a more general relationship management solution? While this discussion cannot answer these questions for you, it will provide a structure you can apply to your own decision-making process, and provide you with an example check-list and comparison matrix intended to bring some clarity to what can be an overwhelming process.

Start by looking at what you are currently doing. Who is tracking what information? Who accesses it, and for what purpose? What are the key pieces of information you are currently using to make business decisions? What pieces are missing? Working through these questions as an organization will help determine whether the time is right to move forward with the selection of a new system, and identifies core functionality that must be present in the selected software.

You must also consider the technical proficiency of the staff that will enter, retrieve and analyze information. Is there a common level of competency, or do skills vary widely between team members? Is your team tech-savvy and eager to adopt new technology, or more likely to rely on the tried and true unless encouraged? It is important that the system become a tool for the entire organization – recognizing that each individual may have different needs/requirements for input and retrieval; the system must be able to meet those needs, without presenting a barrier to usage.

While you might task your most technically proficient staff to select and lead the implementation of the new system, it is important that they select a system that the entire team will be able to use, to ensure successful adoption and integration into the business culture of your organization. The risk here, if collective proficiency is not considered, is a system that can meet all your needs, but does not suit the expertise of your users. This becomes a barrier to gathering, accessing, and applying data, undermining the value of this business asset.

Understanding what you need, is key to ensuring your selection will serve the organization effectively. Investing the time to meet with users and review their current use and "wish list" of functionality is a great way to develop a comprehensive view of the organization's data and process needs. These sessions also provide the opportunity to assess proficiency and identify individuals who can serve as champions, as well as anyone who may be "latent adopters" or outright resistant. As with any change within an organization, it is important to pay attention to human dynamics.

Respect and understand individual perspectives and attitudes, and seek to involve them in the process. It is unlikely to succeed without a team ready to embrace the new program and the changes it will bring.

To ensure the system you ultimately select can support your growth, review your organization's strategic plans and fund development plan. Are there new fundraising streams planned that will need support for the next 3-5 years? Is there a campaign on the horizon? This may make implementing a new system a challenge, but may also serve as a motivator if prospect identification is a challenge in your existing structure. While it is important to plan for future expansion, working with software that greatly exceeds your requirements can not only be costly, but result in overly complicated processes, which may deter your users from fully using the capacity you are intending.

Once you've completed your assessments and identified the functions that are critical, and desirable, begin to evaluate how various programs meet those requirements. Where are the gaps? Identify where they exceed expectations and where they fall short, and begin to make decisions about ease of use, functionality and cost. As you work through the evaluation, also consider the ability of each option to integrate with other functions that will not be replaced – finance, for example, or perhaps a tel-a-thon program.

Develop a matrix based on the current needs and growth areas you've identified, such as the example in Figure 19.2, and use this framework to evaluate potential software options. Keeping your needs clearly iden-

tified will help retain focus on core requirements and prevent the glamour of the extra functionality from unduly influencing your decision. As new products are reviewed, additional functions can be incorporated into the comparison. When you move to the evaluation stage, remember that additional functionality, beyond your core needs, will add to the complexity and maintenance overhead. Selecting a product that greatly exceeds your needs may help position your organization to accommodate long-term growth, but the complexity may impair usability in the short-term.

Required
Growth Plan (3-5 years)
Extra Functionality

	Organizational Requirements	Software Option 1	Software Option 2	Etc.
Development Processes				
Constituent Classification, Segmentation	R	Y	Y	
Gift & Pledge Management	R	Y	Y	
Receipting & Acknowledgement	R	Y	Y	
Online Giving	G	N	Y	
Membership Sales	E	N	N	
Etc.				
Communication Processes				
Mail Management	R	N	Y	
Event Management	G	Y	N	
Etc.				
Reporting & Analysis				
Standard Reports aligned with Business Needs	R			
Custom Report Creation	R			
Import/Export to/from Excel	R			
Etc.				
User Interface				
Core Processes are Well Structured for Efficient Entry	R			
Easy, Intuitive Navigation (from user's perspective)	R			
Etc.				

Figure 19.2

The categories and functions included on your decision-making matrix will be tailored to your organization; this illustration includes some basic examples to demonstrate how the tool can support your evaluation. A consideration to be mindful of if you are considering going with a hosted service is the location of the data. If your vendor will be hosting or transferring data through the United States, contents may become subject to the *USA Patriot Act* which permits American law enforcement and anti-terrorism agencies to access the electronic content.

Selecting and implementing a new software program can be a daunting task. Following a structured process that engages key staff in defining the requirements, builds enthusiasm for the capacity and capabilities of the new system and focuses on core requirements of your organization, will ensure you are able to make the switch happen effectively.

WHAT DATA TO TRACK: DECIDING WHAT'S IMPORTANT

As you consider enhancements to your existing database, or implementing a system with additional functionality, you may be overwhelmed with the scope of information that can be captured. In determining what data is appropriate for your organization to focus on, I would recommend beginning with the end in mind. Identify:

- external requirements

- stewardship and accountability reporting needs

- prospect identification and qualification indicators meaningful for your organization

- key performance measures, processes and business functions that will require regular access to direct, analytical and summary information

- moves management criteria

EXTERNAL REPORTING REQUIREMENTS

First, your data management system needs to contain those items that enable your organization to comply with regulatory requirements for charities and fundraising for the area(s) in which you operate.

The ability to issue charitable tax receipts stems from the *Income Tax Act (Canada)*. The Canada Revenue Agency's Charities Directorate is responsible for establishing the regulatory framework based on the Act, and ensuring registered charities comply. The activity of fundraising, however, falls within provincial jurisdiction, and a number of provinces have enacted legislation to oversee these activities. At the end of this chapter you will find a reference list that will help you locate the regulations that apply for you.

The *Canada Revenue Agency* (CRA) website provides a detailed listing of the information that must be included on all Charitable Tax Receipts issued. The CRA characterizes gifts in a few key ways that provide useful categories to assess your fundraising performance (e.g. type of gift, level of benefit accruing to the donor, official donor name and so on). The CRA website also provides electronic copies of the *T3010 Charity Return* and related guide. Considering the information required to complete the return and structuring your data accordingly will minimize the time required to complete the filing. It is much easier to establish a coding structure that distinguishes membership revenues from outright gifts, for example, than attempting to make the determination retroactively at the end of the year.

At the time this book is being written we are witnessing an unprecedented rate of change in the Canadian regulatory framework, most notably:

- The 2010 federal budget which:

  - eliminated the disbursement quota's charitable expenditure rule (previously requiring charities to spend 80% of all gifts receipted in the prior year) and the enduring property definition;

  - increased the minimum threshold for application of the capital accumulation rule to $100,000; and

  - introduced anti-avoidance rules applied to transfers between non-arms length charities.

- The CRA's introduction of a comprehensive fundraising guidance in 2009;

- The Repeal of Ontario's Charitable Gifts Act in 2009, replaced by the Charities Accounting Act; Good Government Act.

In coming years the full impact of these changes on the charitable sector will become clearer, as supporting regulations, enforcement practices and precedents are established. Understanding the changes in filing and reporting requirements for your organization will ensure you are able to structure your data to easily provide the information needed.

Umbrella organizations that represent charities and fundraising practitioners (including Imagine Canada, the National Charities and Not for Profit Law Section of the Canadian Bar Association, Association of Fundraising Professionals and the Canadian Association of Gift Planners) have been influential in pushing for some of these changes. Going forward, we can expect these organizations to evaluate the impact of the new regulations, and identify additional policy measures government could enact to further support fundraising efforts. Connecting to these groups through membership or publication subscription can help ensure you and your organization are kept informed of additional changes. There are also a number of free newsletter services that can help in monitoring trends impacting the sector; a list of these is included at the end of the chapter.

A solid understanding of the regulatory framework that applies to your organization will inform your processes and systems and help ensure compliance. Further, changes in requirements should be monitored and reflected in your organization's gift acceptance and management policies and practices. A good gift acceptance policy is broad enough that it will not require constant revision as regulations change and interpretations evolve, but establishing a regular schedule for review and revision will ensure changes are made proactively, before any compliance issues arise.

Policy development is also an appropriate venue to articulate the values of an organization as it pertains to gift cultivation, solicitation and stewardship, and to demonstrate commitment to the *Donor Bill of Rights* and ethical principles developed for the various aspects of development. It is beneficial if both the regulatory framework and professional code of ethics statements are reflected in the organization's policies with respect to gift acceptance, endowment management, recognition and naming and corporate sponsorship.

STEWARDSHIP AND ACCOUNTABILITY

Next you should think about the information requirements your donors will have, and how you can use data to enhance your stewardship activities.

If you allow donors to direct their contributions towards a specific restricted purpose, are your gift processing and finance functions able to accommodate separate accounting and reporting? Have you established internal controls to ensure expenditures align with the donor's intent?

The optimal system provides the gift processor with the ability to differentiate gifts, and portions of gifts, for unique purposes, and allows this distinction to carry through to the management of the funds. It is important to ensure that those responsible for managing and approving expenditure of donor dollars are aware of the limitations placed on them by the donor. Segmenting donations by purpose in a restricted fund is only part of the solution. The intended use also needs to be clearly communicated to the operational team responsible for implementation.

While easy stewardship is the immediate beneficiary of consistent gift management practices, and may in fact be responsible for establishing these structures, the ultimate benefit for the organization is in strengthened donor relationships that emerge from a process that sees their dollars well managed and set to work as intended. Pragmatically, these systems and structures are essential for good stewardship, and can prevent hours of tedious work retracing transactions should you begin preparing a donor report and realize information is not available in the format you need.

Keeping track of key donor information is also a necessary support for important stewardship activities: being able to easily access *cumulative giving value*, monitoring for key milestones (e.g.) five years of consecutive support, or number of clients served, all provide unique opportunities to remind your donors how grateful you are for their support, and demonstrate the difference their contributions are making to your service community and your mission. Chapter 16 discusses stewardship in more detail, and will provide insight into the types of information and process structures that can support a donor focused stewardship program.

One final note: When designing your stewardship policies and specific program elements, ensure that the Canada Revenue Agency Guidelines addressing token gifts and value in return for a tax receipted contribution are honoured (See the CRA de minimis and split receipting rules).

PROSPECT IDENTIFICATION AND QUALIFICATION

As we've seen in the discussion on prospect research, to identify new prospective donors for your organization, it is important to know who your current donors are. And that means more than knowing their names. Consider these other important factors:

- How many of your donor's first connected with your organization through a direct mail appeal?

- Attending an event?

- Through the phone-a-thon?

- As a volunteer for your organization?

- It is also useful if your database allows you to identify similarities between donors: age, gender, and other demographic characteristics, for example, may highlight similarities that can help you focus attention on prospective donors with a similar profile to your existing donors.

As your database is populated with information over time, this internal data will become a valuable resource in identifying and qualifying prospective donors. Identifying commonalities between your best donors, in term of demographic information and connections with your organization, is an excellent way to build a list of characteristics you might use to help identify other potential donors already in your database. For example, if all your major gift donors attend your special speaker series, including a systematic review and rating of other attendees is a prudent research activity likely to result in the identification of a number of major gift prospects.

KEY PERFORMANCE MEASURES

Each aspect of fundraising operations has its own key measures that drive decision-making – many of these have been outlined for you throughout this book. The Key Performance Measures (KPM's), and Key Performance Indicators (KPI's) you adopt for your organization may deviate somewhat from those presented here. Depending on your organization's overall operational priorities, age, strategic focus, etc, you will need to identify which measures you will use to evaluate individual and team performance, and select or build a report process that consistently evaluates progress over time.

Defining meaningful measures, which are both an accurate reflection of a particular business activity and align with strategic goals, is an important process that should involve your organization's leadership, management and fundraising team.

Measures you adopt will ideally include a blend of lead and lag indicators. Lead indicators (sometimes referred to as Key Performance Drivers), are essentially measures that allow you to forecast performance and revise operational plans where indicators demonstrate that you are not on target to reach a key goal. Lag indicators celebrate success and showcase achievement of goals. The following table (Figure 19.3) provides some examples of lead and lag indicators for a major gift operation.

Examples of a Lead Indicator	Examples of a Lag Indicator
• Number of discovery calls made	• Gift commitments secured
• Number of donor contacts	• Average gift size
• Number of asks completed	• Pledge fulfillment rates
• Average ask value	• Total dollars secured (raised)
• Ability level of qualified prospects	• Total dollars received

Figure 19.3

There are almost unlimited numbers of measures that can be applied to fundraising. Over-measurement can be as crippling as no measurement, as staff becomes torn between which activities and measures to focus on. Organizations with an effective measurement culture have aligned individual, team, and organizational measurements with strategic objectives, and use a balance of lead and lag indicator to manage the operation. Select the indicators that best reflect the nature and stage of fundraising operation at your organization.

A sample of lead and lag performance indicators aligned with strategic goals, are shown in Figure 19.4 (below and on page 302).

STATEGIC GOAL: Increase financial resources aligned with organizational priorities		
KPM	**Leading KPI's**	**Lagging KPI's**
For each priority area: • Donations secured (pledged) during the year • Donation revenue received (gifted) during the year Compared with prior year(s) to evaluate growth over time.	For each priority area: • Number of asks made • Average ask value • Pipeline value (planned ask value)	For each priority area: • Success rate for asks • Average pledge value • Pledge fulfillment rate • Number of upgraded donors

STRATEGIC GOAL: Sustained growth in donor base		
KPM	**Leading KPI's**	**Lagging KPI's**
Number of donors who made a pledge commitment or outright gift, compared with prior year(s).	• Number of acquisition channels • Size of connected prospect pool in database • Number of discovery calls made • Number of qualified prospects	Rate of donor: • Acquisition • Renewal • Reactivation
STRATEGIC GOAL: Cost-effective fundraising operation		
KPM	**Leading KPI's**	**Lagging KPI's**
Appropriate: • Cost to raise $1 • Return on Investment For current stage of development cycle, age and composition of fundraising program	• Composition of prospect pool by gift level • Ratio of committed donor base to prospect pool • Forecast of pipeline (based on application of past success rate)	• Cost of donor acquisition • Cost of donor fulfillment • Lifetime donor value

Figure 19.4

MOVES MANAGEMENT AND PORTFOLIO MONITORING

Providing fundraising staff with tools to monitor their activity, analyze the composition of their portfolio and forecast the donation in the pipeline is a key means of supporting development activities and increasing productivity. In addition, these tools allow the fundraiser to set accurate goals, and support performance management efforts. Elements commonly found in a fundraiser's performance management report include:

- *Portfolio Composition:* Presenting a few different views of a portfolio (by project, by stage of the development cycle, by gift level) enables the fundraiser to understand the composition of their portfolio in relation to performance objectives.

- *Move Activity:* A balance of moves at stages throughout the development cycle, and aligned with fundraising objectives, supports the likelihood of completing goals (to understand more about the *moves management* methodology, see the chapter on major gift fundraising).

- *Pipeline Forecast:* Summarizing the likelihood of gifts at various stages in the pipeline (identification, cultivation, solicitation).

- *Gift Commitments:* Total of commitments secured, often presented as new for current period, year to date, compared against goal and/or forecast.

An example of the types of information that can be gathered in a monthly fundraisers report is included in Figure 19.5.

Fundraiser Report
September 2011

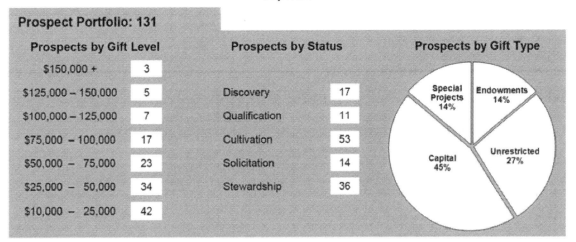

Prospect Portfolio: 131

Prospects by Gift Level

$150,000 +	3
$125,000 – 150,000	5
$100,000 – 125,000	7
$75,000 – 100,000	17
$50,000 – 75,000	23
$25,000 – 50,000	34
$10,000 – 25,000	42

Prospects by Status

Discovery	17
Qualification	11
Cultivation	53
Solicitation	14
Stewardship	36

Prospects by Gift Type

Special Projects 14%
Endowments 14%
Capital 45%
Unrestricted 27%

PART 2

Pipeline, Year to Date

Value of Gifts in the Pipeline

	Total Value	% Probability
Discovery	$ 235,000	$ 58,750
Qualification	142,500	71,250
Cultivation	578,000	375,700
Solicitation	120,000	96,000

Results by Target Area

	Year to Date	Target	%
Capital	75,000	$ 200,000	38%
Endowment	5,000	60,000	8%
Special Projects	20,000	50,000	40%
Unrestricted	35,000	100,000	35%

PART 3

September Activity Summary

38 Moves in September

Moves by Gift Level

$150,000 +	4
$125,000 – 150,000	3
$100,000 – 125,000	5
$75,000 – 100,000	6
$50,000 – 75,000	7
$25,000 – 50,000	9
$10,000 – 25,000	4

Moves by Gift Type

Capital	13
Endowments	5
Special	8
Unrestricted	12

Moves by Status

Qualification	9
Cultivation	17
Solicitation	3
Stewardship	5

Number of Ask(s) Made	2
Valued at	$ 75,000
Number of Pledge(s) Secured	1
Valued at	$ 20,000
Number of New Leads Identified	3
Number of Planned Giving Leads Identified	1

Figure 19.5

DONOR PRIVACY AND CONFIDENTIALITY

As you make decisions about what to track, privacy legislation will dictate parameters for how information is saved, who has access to it, and where and how it is used.

Depending on the type of organization, you may be subject to one or more pieces of privacy legislation (the Office of the Privacy Commissioner link in the resource section will help you navigate to recent legislative bodies). Being familiar with restrictions on the use and sharing of information for your organization will ensure your data structures and practices are established within allowable guidelines.

As you develop data standards, establish a consistent privacy lens for your team that is easy to remember and use. As contact reports are prepared, ask staff to consider whether your donor or prospect would be comfortable with how a particular piece of information has been captured, and ensure only information that meets this expectation is recorded. An easy way to frame this could be to ask: Would I be comfortable sharing this with the prospect? If the answer is no, consider whether the information belongs in your database. Some organizations ask, "If this ended up on the front page of the paper, would we be comfortable?" Consistent framing of privacy considerations ensures that the database is free from personal judgements or evaluations that would be uncomfortable to share with the prospect.

Privacy concerns must also be considered as you structure your security and data access protocols. Individuals must have access to information that they are required to gather, record, and use in the regular course of business operations. Others may need access to only select information. So while your fundraising team may require complete access to view contact reports and donor profiles, the operational team involved with implementing a particular gift would not need this level of information (although they should understand the donor's priorities and intended outcomes to ensure these are delivered). If your organization uses volunteers or consultants as part of your fundraising operation, ensuring a confidentiality agreement is in place, and that these individuals are briefed on internal guidelines, will safeguard your donor's privacy.

Your prospect research team will commonly provide guidelines for balancing confidentiality and data management issues. If you do not have these resources, or if you are responsible for developing these policies and practices for your organization, consider consulting resources published by the *Association of Professional Researchers for Advancement (APRA)*. These resources provide extensive discussion of balancing privacy and confidentiality issues with data collection, tracking and dissemination.

USING YOUR DATA

Data management - the systematic gathering, recording, application and analysis of key information regarding your donors and fundraising efforts - is critical to the long-term success of any fundraising operation. As we've seen, a good data management system functions as a support for your operation, drives key business decisions, enables communication and cultivation plans that respond to the unique characteristics of your donors, and relieves the development practitioner from relying on memory, allowing them to focus on relationship building.

Here are some specific ways the data contained in your system can be used to enhance your fundraising operation.

I) Mass personalization of communication materials

Increasingly, development practitioners are looking for ways to provide a personalized communication experience, embedded in the traditional and evolving mass communication vehicles (direct mail, email, social media, stewardship reports etc). This mass-personalization speaks to unique relationship elements – beyond personalized greetings – and can be accomplished by structuring the source data file to include a set of variables that can be incorporated directly into the text of your communication. In addition, treating these variables as indicators will allow messaging to be tailored to reflect what you know about each donor.

II) Trigger events

Acknowledging significant milestones in a donor relationship communicates that you value the individual, and provides you with an opportunity to celebrate with them. Consider the impact of a letter announcing the 100th program participant that shares that individual's story and highlights how the donors' support has contributed to their success. You might opt to celebrate anniversaries, giving milestones or dollar value thresholds. Each affords a unique opportunity to remind the donor how their gift allows your organization to further your mission, demonstrates accountability and strengthens the relationship.

III) Data mining and predictive modelling

Data mining and predictive modelling are excellent prospecting tools for organizations with a large database of potential donors who have not yet made a financial contribution – schools with large alumni populations, for example. The process involves using your data to identify correlations between personal characteristics/behaviours and giving.

These behaviours can then be used to identify and isolate a set of non-donors who you predict are more likely to give than the baseline population, based on the presence of similar factors. When you are evaluating your data to identify correlations, be sure to look for patterns that exist outside of your giving and stewardship program.

For example, that a high percentage of your donors participate in recognition events is not a good indicator, as their inclusion in the event is predicated by their donor relationship with your organization. Look instead for activities outside of your giving program that are present at a higher rate in your donor segment than your total population, and use those factors to identify a group of prospects to focus on.

For example, you might notice that individuals who respond to your advocacy calls-to-action have a higher giving percentage – and you might therefore want to focus an acquisition campaign on these individuals, with customized messaging.

CONCLUSION

Does it seem like a complex maze of requirements to be navigated? Well, in some ways it is. Those practitioners responsible for data management and reporting do fulfill an internal compliance and monitoring function. But data management is not only about compliance. Once you have built your structure, understand your regulatory framework, and have the team supported by the organization's information resources, you can truly begin to see the benefits of good data management. Looking at data mining and donor modeling activities, prospect identification, trend analysis and predictive modeling, all rely on a robust set of data; well-structured and cultivated by practitioners within your organization. Good data - appropriate, well structured, accessible, and informative - can mean the difference in focusing your development operations for the highest degree of success.

ADDITIONAL RESOURCES

Provincial fundraising legislation

▶ **ALBERTA:** Charitable Fundraising Act

▶ **BRITISH COLUMBIA:** Charitable Purpose Preservation Act

▶ **MANITOBA:** Charities Endorsement Act

▶ **ONTARIO:** Charities Accounting Act; Good Government Act

▶ **PEI:** Charities Act

▶ **QUEBEC:** Taxation Act

▶ **SASKATCHEWAN:** Charitable Fundraising Businesses Act

Resources for legal and regulatory issues concerning Charities

▶ NOT-FOR-PROFIT UPDATE (Borden Ladner Gervais)

▶ CHARITY TALK (Canadian Bar Association)

▶ CHARITY LAW UPDATE (Carters.ca)

▶ CHARITY INSIGHTS (Drache LLP)

▶ CHARITIES & NOT-FOR-PROFIT NEWSLETTER (Miller Thomson LLP)

URL's

▶ OFFICE OF THE PRIVACY COMMISSIONER: Personal information and electronic documents act; Privacy act, and links to provincial sites for Freedom of Information and Protection of Privacy Acts http://www.priv.gc.ca/index_e.cfm

▶ CANADA REVENUE AGENCY: Charitable Tax Receipt content requirements, T3010 Charity Return forms, interpretation bulletins addressing explaining application for specific regulations. http://www.cra-arc.gc.ca/chrts-gvng/menu-eng.html

ABOUT THE AUTHOR

Tania Brandstrom, MA, CFRE

Tania Brandstrom came to the charitable sector in 2002 with a Bachelor's Degree in Political Science from the University of Calgary, and diverse industry experience that includes shareholder relations, event management, and public company compliance. In her role as Associate Director of Development and Advancement Services with SAIT Polytechnic in Calgary, she has established a culture of partnership-based service that reflects her strong commitment to team engagement and collaboration.

In 2008, Tania completed her Master's Degree in Philanthropy and Development from Saint Mary's University of Minnesota, where her capstone focused on the use of citizen engagement as a tool for advancing social justice causes in the Canadian not-for-profit sector.

An Active member of AFP (Association of Fundraising Professionals) and AASP (Association for Advancement Services Professionals), Tania is a frequent presenter on issues and trends impacting Advancement Services functions and performance, and is the sole Canadian representative on AASP's Best Practices Team.

CHAPTER 20

FUNDRAISING COUNSEL
PAT HARDY, ACFRE

The number one job of fundraising counsel in Canada is to solve problems for your organization. It may be as simple as making an inventory of naming opportunities or as complex as running a major capital campaign. Fundraising counsel in Canada are knowledgeable, qualified women and men who passionately practice fundraising as a career. Rather than working full-time at one organization, fundraising counsel offer their services on a contractual basis. *read more...*

Fundraising counsel give organizations of all sizes and levels of sophistication access to a range of skills and knowledge they may not have in-house.

Hiring fundraising counsel can be an effective way for an organization to get things done, to supplement staff skills and knowledge or to get an objective view, an expert opinion or an outside voice. Beyond helping organizations to achieve their immediate financial objectives, fundraising counsel can be a powerful agent for change, building total organizational capacities.

This chapter will examine four types of professional counsel, how to hire the right firm or individual, how to keep counsel accountable and the type of work professional fundraising counsel can do to help your organization.

TYPES OF PROFESSIONAL FUNDRAISING COUNSEL

In Canada there are basically four types of fundraising counsel available for hire by community benefit organizations:

1. Large, full-service international/national firms;
2. Small to mid-sized full service firms that confine their practice to one region of Canada;
3. Small firms that specialize in special events or technical support such as prospect research; and
4. Independent practitioners.

International or national full-service companies have the capacity to provide any and every service including onsite staff. The international/national full-service firms have in-house prospect research, technical expertise and a large staff with skills in every area of fundraising. The large staff ensures you will get the knowledge and advice you need based on best practices and on your special circumstances. The professional fee is likely the most expensive of the four types but you can be assured they know what they are doing and have a record of success.

Local full-service firms are usually based in individual cities with a practice focused in that city and the surrounding region. These firms are often small to mid-size where the principals are well-trained,

knowledgeable and certified professionals who can offer many of the services of a national or international firm. The local firm's professional fee may be less than the large international/national companies.

There are also small firms that offer specialized services. These range from prospect research to direct mail, special events, social gaming like raffles and lotteries as well as technical service for things such as geographic mapping of donors for analysis and strategy development, recommending and installing donor management systems, and mining donor databases. The advantage to this type of counsel is that you get the exact technical expertise you need to get the job done.

Last but not least are individuals who are self-employed consultants who may provide advice, fill staff roles or take on a particular part of your campaign or act as your fundraising staff on a contract basis.

The four types of professional counsel each have their own strengths and advantages and only you can determine what's best for your organization. In many cases your organization will want the depth and breadth of a large firm and in other cases may find a local firm has an in-depth understanding of the local fundraising scene. Technical support from experts may be the only thing you need or you may choose a self-employed individual because you want personalized service that fits your budget. Each type of professional counsel has advantages and disadvantages to consider when deciding what support you want for your organization.

In order to help you determine the best type of fundraising counsel for your organization, you'll want to identify what you need and the role that counsel will play.

WHAT TYPE OF COUNSEL IS BEST FOR YOU?

The role counsel will play is largely up to you. Identifying what you want to do and what resources you need to accomplish it, will help you decide what type of counsel is best for your organization. In some situations you may simply need a person to come in and help you get a particular task done and in others you may need professional counsel to assist in deciding how to proceed and what strategies to adopt for a successful fundraising program. Your organization may choose to have a close relationship with one firm who can be called on when required or you may wish to use different counsel for different things. In any case your first and most important task is to hire appropriate fundraising counsel.

FIVE STEPS TO HIRING PROFESSIONAL FUNDRAISING COUNSEL

Step 1: Define what role counsel will play. (What do you want done?)

- Prepare for a capital campaign
- Manage a special event
- Coach staff and volunteers
- Conduct a feasibility study
- Design your first direct mail program
- Advise on the best donor management system
- Design a bequest program
- Anything else?

Step 2: Define your expectations.

- Timeline for task, project or campaign
- Will counsel work onsite?
- How often will you meet?
- What deliverables do you want?
- Who will counsel work with at your organization?

Step 3: Establish fair compensation.

- Do you need to check on market prices?
- Do you understand what professional fees cover?
- What budget do you have to work with?
- What investment can your organization make?

Step 4: Begin your search.

- What firms will you contact?
- How will contact them?
- What will you request from them?
  - Information Meeting
  - Response to an *RFP (request for proposal)*

Tip: Request for Proposals (RFP)

RFPs (Requests For Proposals) are a transparent and effective way of finding fundraising counsel, however not all firms or individuals respond to RFPs. They may not respond because the firm already has enough work, they are unable to meet your timetable or they are too busy. Word of mouth becomes another way to find good fundraising counsel. Organizations often simply ask other people or funders they trust for recommendations.

Step 5: Hire with special emphasis on reference checking.

Choose a good method to decide what fundraising counsel is right for you. You may like one person best but does he or she have the skills and knowledge you need? It's tempting to take the lowest price but will it be the best investment for your organization? Think about how you hire a lawyer or an, accountant, or select a dentist – would you go to a dentist that doesn't have professional certification or a degree in dentistry?

Whatever method you use to identify and contact potential counsel, the decision making process is important. Here is list of things to consider when hiring fundraising counsel:

- Who in the firm will be assigned to work with you? Is that person a Certified Fundraising Executive (CFRE)? The CFRE accreditation is an international standard for fundraisers working in the field for a minimum of five years. Hiring a CFRE ensures you are hiring someone with no less than five years of theory and practice.

- Does anyone in the firm have academic credentials in philanthropy, organizational development and behavior, or management?

- What organizations have they worked with as fundraising counsel? What were the results?

- Does the staff assigned to you have a history of being a volunteer and working with volunteers?

- Is the firm clear about what they are offering to you?

- Does the role counsel proposes for themselves coincide with the role you see them in?

- Are you buying the firm's or person's knowledge or are there other products being offered as well?

- Does the person assigned to your organization seem like someone you would want to represent your organization? Are there sufficient shared values?

- What is their quote for professional fees based upon? A daily or hourly rate? A fee for a particular project? Are fees tied to deliverables? Or to a specific time period?

Hiring fundraising counsel for the first time can be a demanding process. You may not be sure how to interpret the different proposals that you receive or you may feel that you don't know enough to be sure of what you want in counsel. Your organization may also be suspicious of fundraising counsel if people are not clear on what counsel will actually do for you.

As long as you can articulate what you are looking for and the fundraising counsel you hire can articulate what they will do to assist you, you are off to a good start.

One very important consideration: as you select your fundraising counsel make sure you really do trust their competence, their values and their commitment to your mission. If you do, you will be able to make the best use of their advice and expertise. If you are uncomfortable with your fundraising counsel and end up spending your time (and theirs) second-guessing advice and decisions, chances are you will be wasting your money and time.

ACCOUNTABILITY

If your fundraising counsel is selling you knowledge, how can you measure what you're getting? This may be the hardest part for both counsel and those hiring them. The dissemination of information happens in many different ways but how do you measure whether people are actually becoming knowledgeable?

Ideas for holding counsel accountable about knowledge:

- Establish formal activities where knowledge is shared and applied to solve problems

- Create interactive workshops with board and staff members

- Conduct small seminars focusing on particular topics

- Have a weekly mentoring session with the executive director and/or the board chair

- Ensure knowledge sharing activities are delivered on time

Ideas for holding fundraising counsel accountable for tangible services:

- Establish timelines for activities

- Establish target dates for interim and final reports

- Establish deadline dates

- Before starting the work, outline what kind of things reports will cover - then monitor them to ensure everything has been addressed

- Expect to see prospect lists, rating and ranking charts from volunteers and profiles containing research information

- Have a good, positive feeling of making headway

Each area of your fund development/fundraising program will have activity goals and timelines. Many of these are the same things you will use to hold your fundraising counsel accountable for doing their part of the work. In some cases, organizations wish to tie the financial goals to the performance of fundraising counsel but we all know that fundraising is everyone's job and fundraising counsel can't raise the money alone.

WHEN TO RETAIN PROFESSIONAL FUNDRAISING COUNSEL

Organizations can benefit from fundraising counsel anytime fundraising or preparing for fundraising is going on, when you want an outside view or external objective opinion or you have tasks that your internal resources just don't have time to complete. The value of professional fundraising counsel cannot be overrated. Inevitably, working with professional fundraising counsel will strengthen your organization.

Don't underestimate the impact an accredited and objective outsider can have in helping you move your organization forward, and establish and develop the missing links needed for successful fundraising. The nature of counsel's involvement may vary depending on circumstances and the size of the organization, however community benefit organizations of any size will find value in working with fundraising counsel.

Professional fundraising counsel comes to you with experience and knowledge of the challenges you face and can help you and your organization better understand options and develop strategies more quickly. You can save a lot of time and money by using your counsel's expertise, often saving multiples of the fees that you are paying that counsel!

ESTABLISHING A CULTURE WHERE PHILANTHROPY CAN FLOURISH

What exactly is "philanthropy?"

Most people, answering that question, without thinking, would say something like "giving money away for a good cause" and, of course, that's true. But it's not good enough for community benefit organizations to sit back and assume that because they have a good cause the money will come rolling in from well-meaning donors.

It's just not that simple. Creating an environment and culture where philanthropy flourishes demands clear and constant communication about the public good contributions will help create. It demands reassurance that funds are used effectively; at its best, it includes opportunities for donors to feel directly involved, building the deep relationships you want with your donors.

Good fundraising counsel can effectively coach staff and Board members on these matters and champion their importance. Curiously, it can often be hard for staff and volunteers to understand the power of philanthropy – donors' motivation – and the power of the relationships you can establish with them.

The first step is to understand the distinctions between philanthropy, development, and fundraising.

"*Philanthropy* is the giving and receiving exchange that fundraisers facilitate; development is the management of all the required relationships; and fundraising encompasses

the methodologies and functions themselves."[1]
– Karla Williams

Professional fundraising counsel will provide tools that can guide staff and volunteers in assessing their philanthropic culture and identifying areas of strength, and the specifics that need more development.

IS YOUR ORGANIZATION ACCOUNTABLE AND TRANSPARENT?

Professional fundraising counsel knows what it takes to ensure donor confidence in what the organization is doing and how it is spending its money. Fundraising counsel understands that fundraising is at the centre of any organization and they understand that fundraising can change the way an organization operates. Good governance is vital for successful fundraising and counsel can help to identify gaps in accountability and transparency that are so important to donors.

Fundraising counsel's involvement in governance may include clarifying the vision, reviewing the mission, strategic planning, and annual assessment of the board and organization, as well as reviewing how the board structure supports the mission and strategic objectives, and helping to define the role of the board in fund development.

What can counsel do to help you?

- Review bylaws and policies
- Review practices and procedures
- Develop gift acceptance policies
- Assist with defining ethical fundraising practice
- Facilitate strategic planning for fundraising

EVALUATION AND ANALYSIS OF FUNDRAISING ACTIVITIES

Fundraising counsel can offer real value in the areas of evaluation, analysis, and planning for fundraising. Don't be too surprised to hear this, but many community benefit organizations don't know what's working and what's not when it comes to their fundraising activities; nor do they have a handle on the costs of

---

1 Williams, Karla. (1997) *Donor Focused Strategies for Annual Giving.* Aspen.

their fundraising. Fundraising counsel can help you conduct evaluations and analysis that digs down to see the real fundraising picture.

These services may be called development audits, campaign analysis and evaluation, development or fundraising reviews. In general terms the process is the same. Counsel will gather facts about your organization's past and current fundraising activities; they will assess perceptions about fundraising from staff, board members, and donors and weigh the results of those investigations; asking pertinent questions about the numbers and the stories that unfold.

Fundraising counsel may perform a development audit and assessment and then make recommendations for a strategic fund development program. "The audit and assessment will enable the organization to focus its vision, establish its priorities and recognize opportunities; measure progress toward long term goals; inventory organizational assets and debits; connect aspirations and strategies; predict changes within and outside the organization and add a sense of fairness to even the most painful changes."[2]

Some fundraising counsel will work on their own to do an audit, some may work onsite so staff is available to answer questions. Others may incorporate a facilitated workshop into the task. To get the most value out of your process, talk to your counsel ahead of time about how he or she works, what information is needed before hand and who should be involved.

Guy Mallabone and Ken Balmer's book, *The Fundraising Audit Handbook,*[3] is an excellent resource to help begin the process.

MAJOR GIFT PROGRAMS

Managing and operating major gift programs should be part of your organization's core capacities. When it is not, hiring fundraising counsel can be appropriate in designing a program, identifying infrastructure needs, assisting with prospect identification, research and ranking, and coaching staff and volunteers on how to make personal visits. The objective can be to move your major gifts program to another level or to develop

your internal capacities so you can start a major gift program.

One of the most important contributions your fundraising counsel can make is to help in developing your organization's internal capacity for a successful major gift program – growing your people and your systems.

HIRING FUND DEVELOPMENT STAFF

Fundraising counsel is often used when an organization wishes to hire new fundraising staff. Fundraising counsel may be engaged to assist with developing a position description and job posting, to do the search, screening and preliminary interviews.

COACHING AND MENTORING STAFF

Fundraising counsel may be used to coach or mentor staff through a fund development program by offering advice and options for action. Coaching and mentoring may also be appropriate in an effort to help less experienced staff gain needed skills and knowledge. In some cases CEOs or executive directors hire fundraising counsel to help them gain knowledge of how to supervise fund development staff, how to work with board members on fundraising matters or even to give advice about strategies for working with donors.

ESTABLISHING A FUND DEVELOPMENT DEPARTMENT AND/OR AN INTEGRATED FUNDRAISING PROGRAM

Today, many community benefit organizations receiving philanthropic gifts have core capacities in a development department staffed with professional fundraisers and support staff. Many others have not yet evolved to that extent and may have little or no fund development programming or staff support for fundraising. As organizations begin to realize the power of philanthropy, hiring professional counsel to develop and establish integrated fundraising departments is money well spent.

2   Ibid. p. 54
3   Mallabone, G., & Balmer, K. (2010). *The Fundraising Audit Handbook.* Civil Sector Press.

Setting up the infrastructure, including the donor database needs a seasoned professional who knows tried and true practices and how to adapt them into workable systems and procedures in your particular organization. Fundraising counsel can also help to recruit fundraising staff and mentor them during the first year as things are being set up.

BOARD DEVELOPMENT

Fundraising counsel is often used to design and deliver board workshops or facilitate board-planning retreats related to fundraising. Specific workshops to help board members identify, rate and rank prospects or to understand their role in cultivation, recognition and stewardship activities may be conducted by fundraising counsel. Coaching board members on how to have strategic conversations with donors and how to articulate the organizations case for support are also appropriate roles for professional fundraising counsel.

Ideally all of the above items would be part of the core capacities of your organization through the Executive Director or Director of Development. In situations where these skills are not in-house, you can't afford not to hire professional fundraising counsel. They have the knowledge and facilitation skills to get the job done.

DIRECT MARKETING PROGRAMS

Fundraising counsel is valuable when you need specific technical advice that is not part of your core capabilities. For instance, you may need someone to help design a direct marketing program, write copy, design packages and offer advice about acquisition techniques.

It is essential to have someone who knows direct marketing theory and practice to help with direct mail for retaining and acquiring donors; for driving people to your website and for using social media most effectively.

PROSPECT RESEARCH

Prospect research is time consuming and there are people who can do this for you. The fee is usually based on a per prospect rate and the information is delivered as a prospect profile. Fundraising counsel will often have skilled staff that is expert at doing the data mining necessary to create first-rate prospect profiles.

CAPITAL CAMPAIGNS

Fundraising counsel is commonly used in capital campaigns. After all, capital campaigns generally involve more ambitious fundraising targets than the organization usually addresses, and executives recognize that additional skills and human resources will be required.

FEASIBILITY AND PLANNING STUDIES

Typically organizations going into a capital campaign will hire fundraising counsel to conduct a feasibility or planning study to forecast campaign success and to identify what needs to be done to get ready for a successful campaign. The organization and counsel identify a limited number of prospective donors and then counsel conducts individual, confidential interviews. Following an evaluation of the interviews, counsel provides a written report outlining findings and making recommendations to the organization.

Recommendations usually involve suggestions for cultivation, governance, stewardship and relationship building that need to be in place before launching a campaign.

While feasibility and planning studies can be helpful in guiding organizations through the initial readiness phase of a campaign, many organizations ignore counsel's recommendations and plough ahead with their campaigns. This is a waste of time and money. Don't bother paying for a feasibility study unless your organization is prepared to seriously consider and implement the recommendations from fundraising counsel.

CASE FOR SUPPORT

The advice of fundraising counsel can be an invaluable part of developing your case for support – the narrative intended to persuade potential donors to support your cause. Whether the organization is large or small, people close to the organization may be capable of writing a case but often they are too close and may insist on including ALL of the good things they do, why and how, muddying a clear focus on the real case. This "kitchen sink approach" can often backfire.

Conversely, those intimately involved in the organization may be so familiar with its operations that they take for granted that people are already aware of potentially persuasive aspects of the case and neglect to mention them at all.

Fundraising counsel is able to guide the development of the case by asking the right questions and pushing for pithy answers that volunteers can articulate and donors can understand. Donors today want to know the impact of their gifts and the case for support should provide this information.

CAPITAL CAMPAIGN READINESS

"What do I need to do to get ready for a capital campaign?" Every organization faces that question in one form or another and the answer is not always the same. In a large organization with a mature integrated fundraising program, experienced fundraising staff, a strong strategic plan and volunteers who are used to participating in calls, campaign readiness may begin with getting the case statement written and identifying and recruiting a campaign cabinet.

In a smaller organization, preparing for a capital campaign may start with a board workshop to establish or reaffirm the vision, mission and values of the organization; then move on to developing a strategic plan, finding staff, installing donor software, and ensuring policies and procedures are in place - all before even starting to write the case for support or identifying potential cabinet members. In a small or mid-size organization fundraising counsel may be used to assist with all of these aspects of a campaign start-up; and the organization will benefit from fundraising counsel's expertise and outside view.

One potentially critical element for campaign readiness is a systematic effort to talk to donors and communicate their values and concerns to the board. In one recent board workshop that I facilitated, board members decided that a particular aspect of the organization was not important to their fundraising efforts. When staff reported on donor interviews, it became immediately apparent that, contrary to the board's assumptions, that particular aspect was one of the most important elements motivating donors to make philanthropic gifts.

CAPITAL CAMPAIGN IMPLEMENTATION AND ONSITE MANAGEMENT

As stated earlier, one of the most well-known uses of fundraising counsel is in the direction and management of capital campaigns. Organizations may not have enough or the right staff resources and expertise to implement a capital campaign, in which case hiring professional counsel to oversee the campaign makes sense.

When fundraising counsel is engaged to implement a capital campaign, the onsite counsel staff works on a daily basis alongside the organization's staff and volunteers; in some cases, counsel may supervise existing or new staff hired by the organization.

The roles and responsibilities of the onsite staff generally depend on the size of the fundraising counsel's firm. In the case where a large national or international firm is hired, in addition to onsite staff, one of two other senior counsel may come in to work with the board or cabinet, deliver workshops and volunteer coaching, or offer ongoing strategic advice. This not only helps achieve immediate fundraising goals, but also contributes to knowledge transfer as fundraising staff learn from the more seasoned and professional fundraising counsel.

JUMP STARTING A STALLED CAPITAL CAMPAIGN

Capital campaigns almost never go quite as smoothly as we wish they would. Occasionally dysfunctional practices or simply bad timing will cause a campaign to grind to a halt entirely. The reasons for this are as varied as the organizations that have experienced a stalled campaign. Too often, campaigns simply didn't follow the basics of planning that would have allowed for success.

In this case, counsel's role is invaluable. Providing an outside, objective perspective, counsel can reaffirm the case for support, help identify top prospects, motivate volunteers and establish new timelines. In short, professional fundraising counsel can offer objective expert advice to help reach the goals, complete the capital campaign successfully and achieve the financial targets.

CONCLUSION

It is easy to see that fundraising counsel can be appropriate for every element of fund development or fundraising. However, at the same time, it is important that organizations build their internal core capabilities with their own staff and resources.

Fundraising counsel can't replace internal core capabilities; counsel should really be used to supplement staff resources and knowledge and to assist with implementing best practices when starting or expanding your fundraising programs.

One of the most important lessons taught by the St. Mary's Master of Development Program was to ask the right questions and find out what is really going on, instead of what people think is going on. If community benefit organizations are open to assessment and evaluation by fundraising counsel and learn to use counsel to take their fundraising to the next level, they will find it to be a valuable investment.

In the future, Canadian community benefit organizations will rely even more on professional fundraising counsel not only for capital campaigns, but also for assessment, analysis and advice on best practices. Fundraising counsel will always be appropriate for supplementing staff and knowledge and for offering an important outside viewpoint. It will be wonderful to see more community benefit organizations celebrating successful campaigns, developing their core capabilities and using professional fundraising counsel to push them to new heights.

ADDITIONAL RESOURCES

▶ BURNETT, KEN. (2002). *Relationship fundraising. A donor based approach to the business of fundraising, 2nd Edition.* San Francisco, CA: Jossey-Bass.

▶ GREGOR, A. G. AND HOWARD, D. (FALL 2009). *The non-profit starvation cycle: Stanford Social Innovation Review.* 7(4), 48.

▶ JOYEAUX, SIMONE. (2011). *Strategic fund development: Building profitable relationships that last* (3rd ed.). Mississauga, ON: Wiley.

▶ KELLY, KATHLEEN S. (1998). *Effective fund raising management. Mahwah, NJ:* Lawrence Erlbaumm Associates.

▶ SCANLON, EUGENE A. (2009). *Fundraising consultants: A guide for nonprofit organizations.* Hoboken, NJ: Wiley.

▶ WEINSTEIN, STANLEY. (1998). *The Complete Guide to Fund-raising Management.* New York, NY: John Wiley & Sons.

▶ WILLIAMS, K.A. (2003). *Donor Focused Strategies for Annual Giving.* New York, NY: Aspen.

ABOUT THE AUTHOR

Pat Hardy, MA, ACFRE

Pat began her career as a fundraiser in 1982 with the United Way of Winnipeg and since that time has worked for numerous non-profit organizations, including the University of Winnipeg.

Pat teaches "Essentials of Fundraising" at Red River College and is certified as a Master Teacher through the AFP Faculty Academy. Her fundraising courses are popular with fundraisers, executive directors and board volunteers alike.

Pat was the first Canadian to achieve certification as an Advanced Certified Fundraising Executive (ACFRE), and also holds a

Masters in Philanthropy and Development.

A recognized leader in the profession, Pat was instrumental in starting AFP Manitoba and "Leave a Legacy Manitoba" which included the first Winnipeg fundraising conference in the launch. Pat mentors fundraisers working toward their CFRE and was honoured by the Association of Fundraising Professionals with the establishment of the Patricia Hardy Scholarship for Advancement.

Pat is a member of the Association of Fundraising Professionals, the Association for Research in the Non-Profit and Voluntary Sector and Arts Consultants Canada.

Glossary of Canadian FundraisingTerms

JOHN BOUZA, CFRE

This glossary is an abbreviated and updated version of the original Canadian Glossary of Fundraising Terms published in 1993 by myself and Doris Smith, CFRE. At that time there was no comprehensive guide to terms commonly used in the profession. The Association of Fundraising Professionals had not yet published its Dictionary and, regardless, there were, and still are today, terms that are uniquely Canadian. For example, the Canadian T3010 forms versus the American Form 990. *read more...*

Since the original, new words have come into our profession; particularly in the world of online fundraising. Others, such as "webbing" (coined by Ken Wyman) do not appear in the current online AFP Fundraising Dictionary.

This glossary focuses on terms that have a special place in the field of fundraising in Canada. If a term is used by non-profits and charities – audited statement, for example – but has the same common meaning as in any business it is not included here.

A

ACFRE (Advanced Certified Fund Raising Executive). A professional designation indicating senior and highly professional status in the field. The ACFRE credential signifies mastery of professional standards in leadership, management and ethics, at an advanced level of practice. Available only to senior-level fundraisers who have worked in the profession for 10 years or more, the ACFRE is a distinguished achievement earned by fewer than 100 professionals to date of which ½ dozen are Canadian.

ADOA Alberta Development Officers Association

AFP (Association of Fundraising Professionals) Professional association of individuals responsible for generating philanthropic support for a wide variety of nonprofit, charitable organizations with a membership of more than 30,000 members in 225 chapters throughout the world. AFP fosters development and growth of fundraising professionals and promotes high ethical standards in the fundraising profession. There are some 2,700 Canadian members and 16 Canadian chapters.

AHP (Association for Healthcare Philanthropy) The professional association for fundraising in health care institutions. This international association has an active Canadian Regional Cabinet. Its 4,700 members represent more than 2,200 health care facilities in the United States and Canada.

Accountability In fundraising, the principle that donation recipients must be able to inform the donor how their gift was used; as well as account for the fundraising costs incurred. (*see Stewardship*)

Acknowledgment A letter or note sent to thank the donor for the gift.

Acquisition Mailing A mailing to attract new donors or members. (*see Prospect Mail, also Cold Mail*)

Acquisition Program A process or plan to identify prospective donors and secure initial donations.

Activity Based Costing A method of developing a project budget that includes all direct and related indirect expenses so that a portion of overhead, administration, and routine maintenance are included. By spreading these costs over all activities or projects, the true cost of the initiative can be identified and funds sought. Also known as Project Based Costing.

Admail The trademarked term used by Canada Post for its targeted direct mail services; can be addressed or unaddressed.

Advancement A term used primarily in universities, colleges, institutes, independent schools, and cégeps across Canada for the promotion of all phases of an institutions public activities including fundraising, development, alumni, media relations and government relations.

Advance Gifts Gifts made to a campaign prior to the public launch which serve to build momentum. Such are usually solicited from supporters already close to the organization. Advance gifts are often crucial to the success of a campaign.

Advocacy Support of a particular public program or cause; advocacy work may limit an organization's ability to qualify for charitable status.

Affinity Card Credit cards that are issued to supporters of a non-profit organization, usually bearing the logo of the organization, and for the use of which the charity receives a small benefit, generally a fraction of one percent.

Affinity An assessment of the strength of the relationship of a prospect with the organization; usually used when assessing the potential for a major gift and in association with the term "capacity."

Affirmative Statement A phrase that appears prominently on a reply coupon to encourage quick agreement to donate. Often begins "Yes, I will…"

Alumna/Alumnae/Alumnus/Alumni (singular female/plural female/singular male/plural male) People who have attended/graduated from an educational institution. Sometimes used for former clients of a social service agency.

Anniversary Giving (1) Donations made at a set date, usually commemorating a major holiday or significant event in the donor's or charity's history (2) A method of encouraging donors to contribute on the anniversary of their last gift.

Annual Fund A fundraising program that seeks donations, often multiple times, from donors to support (in full or in part) yearly budgets or general operations. Also known as Sustaining Fund.

Annual Gift A donation given annually, usually without restriction.

Annual Giving The term used to describe an ongoing, regular fundraising program that seeks repeat and upgraded gifts annually; distinct from a capital campaign or planned giving.

Anonymous Gift A gift which the donor requests not be acknowledged publicly.

Arm's Length Canada Revenue Agency defines "at arm's length" as a tax concept used to describe the relationship between taxpayers. Generally, individuals who are related by blood, marriage or adoption are considered not to deal with each other at arm's length. The arm's length concept is of prime importance in determining whether a charity is designated as a Charitable Organization, a Public Foundation or a Private Foundation by Canada Revenue Agency.

Ask, The The act of asking for a donation, either in person or in writing.

Associated Charity Two or more registered charities may apply to Canada Revenue Agency to be designated as associated. If approved, income that a charitable organization disburses to a registered charity that has been designated as associated with it will be considered a resource devoted to the charitable organization's own charitable activity.

Auction A popular special fundraising event, normally disposing of donated items or services.

Auction, Silent An auction during which bids are submitted in writing, either anonymously, or publicly with name and amount of bid listed, during a fixed period of time at an event.

Audit, Fundraising An objective evaluation of an existing fundraising program to assess strengths and weaknesses and propose improvements, often conducted by outside professional consultants. Also called Diagnostic Report. (*see Fundraising Audit*)

Average Gift Gross donations revenue divided by the number of donors. A rough measure of effectiveness.

Awards Dinner A popular form of donor and volunteer recognition; frequently used as an occasion for fundraising.

B

BADS Negative or hostile replies in direct mail as well as undeliverable addresses.

BRE Business reply envelope, with pre-printed return address used for direct mail appeals. Frequently includes pre-paid postage.

BRE Permit Permit obtained from the post office to use BRE's when the postage is pre-paid. The permit number is shown on the top right corner of the envelope.

Bang Tail An envelope with an extended flap which can be torn off and used as a self-contained reply device.

Bazaar Popular special event organized by churches and other community groups with a large local membership. Goods and services are usually donated by members of the organization.

Benchmarks Specific levels of contributions reached at various stages of a campaign or project by which the success or lack of same can be measured at pre-set intervals.

Benefactor Contributor, usually in monetary terms and usually the source of significant dollar amounts. Often a term used as one of the upper levels of donor categories in donor recognition programs.

Beneficiary A person or an organization that receives support from any source (usually monetary support or gifts-in-kind); a charity that is named as the one to whom the benefits of a life insurance policy will be paid or is named in a last will or testament.

Benefit Any special event in which proceeds are to be designated as a contribution for a non-profit organization.

Benefits The special ways of showing recognition to members and donors who have contributed to a cause. Different levels of benefits are usually assigned to the several categories of members and donors. Benefits that give significant market value rewards to the donor affect the tax-credit status of the donation.

Bequest The gift of cash or property by will or testament that a registered charity receives from the will of a deceased person.

Bingo A popular game of chance used as a fundraising event where provincial licensing rules allow.

Block Captain Person in charge of a team of canvassers who cover a block of streets during a house-to-house canvas or campaign.

Block Funding A funding arrangement with a government agency whereby a non-profit organization receives a large block of funds for a variety of projects.

Blown-in A reply coupon or card that is mechanically inserted (or blown into) a publication before mailing and is not bound, stapled or glued in place.

Board In this context usually refers to Board of Directors or Board of Trustees who are responsible for the governance of charitable and non-profit institutions.

Board Member Volunteer director who is elected, appointed or assigned to serve on the board of a charitable institution.

Bonding A precautionary insurance agreement (bond) for persons who handle significant amounts of cash.

Bounce Back Gift An additional donation that comes from including a BRE in a thank-you letter (or in a package of goods sold).

Bound-in A reply coupon or card that is stapled or stitched into the fold of a publication before mail-out.

Bowl-a-thon One of the many "thons" that are popular with charities, tailored to the preferences of target groups; participants usually obtain pledges from family and friends. In this case the participants go bowling for charity.

Break-open Tickets A game of chance in which the player pays for a ticket which has covered tabs and which is opened to reveal a combination of figures similar to those on slot machines and can provide for instant winners. Also known as Nevada.

Building Fund A campaign that is specifically targeted to pay for the construction and/or renovation of buildings belonging to the charity; may suggest a longer term effort than a capital campaign.

Bulk Mail Large quantities of letters mailed simultaneously that qualify for special postal rates. Bulk mail must correspond to the sizes and configurations accepted by Canada Post and must be sorted as regulated by the post office.

C

CAEDO Canadian Association of Education Development Officers. (*see CCAE*)

CAGP (Canadian Association of Gift Planners) The professional association for development officers who specialize in planned giving, including professionals in such related fields as law, accounting, and financial planning.

CARD (Canadian Advertising Rates and Data) A publication that lists all newspapers, journals, and magazines in Canada with the advertising rates and details such as circulation figures; now available as CARDonline.

CASE (Council for the Advancement and Support of Education) An international professional association serving educational institutions and advancement professionals in alumni relations, communications, development, marketing and allied areas.

CCAA (Canadian Charitable Annuity Association) A group of Canadian charities that jointly provide education, information and guidance to charities about gift annuities, life income gift plans, and other forms of sophisticated charitable gifts.

CCAE (Canadian Council for the Advancement of Education) CCAE is a professional association for educational advancement professionals working at universities, colleges, institutes, independent schools, and cégeps across Canada; some 1,400 members represent more than 140 educational institutions.

CFRE (Certified Fundraising Executive) An internationally-recognized baseline professional credential for philanthropic fundraising practitioners; a practice-based designation signifying knowledge, achievement and commitment to the profession of fundraising. It is administered by CFRE International with an independent board of directors.

CMA (Canadian Marketing Association) Canada's largest national organization for businesses and non-profits that use direct marketing. Its Not-for-Profit Council serves the interests of Canadian charity and non-profit fundraisers through education, advocacy, and engagement with other marketing professionals.

CRA (*see Canada Revenue Agency*)

CTRAD Cost To Raise a Dollar (*see Cost per Dollar Raised*)

Call-to-Action A statement in an appeal telling prospective donors how much you hope they will contribute and urging them to give now; a campaign slogan or phrase that defines the campaign theme in terms of the need to act.

Campaign A special, organized effort to raise funds and generate support for a particular cause, organization or institution.

Campaign, Annual An annual effort made to raise funds or increase membership usually lasting a certain number of weeks; may have follow-up components.

Campaign Cabinet In a traditional campaign, the group of people appointed to lead the fundraising. They meet regularly, under the leadership of the Campaign Chairperson; each member leads a Campaign Division.

Campaign, Capital An intensive, time-limited appeal to raise funds for construction or renovation of buildings, or the purchase of equipment needed by the organization.

Campaign Chair Also referred to as "Chairperson," the person who leads all volunteers working on the campaign and generally makes a major gift.

Campaign Division Any one of the numerous groupings that are created during a traditional capital campaign to segment the target audiences by logical categories such as major gifts, corporations, employees, etc.

Campaign Director The person who manages the overall campaign - either a professional on staff or a paid consultant hired on contract to handle a specific campaign.

Campaign, Endowment (*see Endowment Campaign*)

Campaign-for-One The concept of considering each major gift prospect in a campaign as a series of individual mini-campaigns with their own campaign plan to ensure that the best opportunity is presented to them, at the best time, by the best person.

Campaign Timetable The plan devised before the start of a campaign, determining the beginning and completion of the different activities that make up the campaign as a whole.

Canada Revenue Agency (CRA) The federal government agency that, among its multitude of responsibilities, has a section called the **Charities Division** which is charged with registering and monitoring Canada's 85,000 charitable organizations.

Canvass Direct solicitation usually done face-to-face, house-to-house or by telephone.

Canvasser The person doing the canvass.

Capacity An assessment of the financial potential of a prospect to make a philanthropic donation at a given level; usually used for major gifts and capital campaigns and in association with the term "affinity."

Case Statement A carefully prepared document describing the reasons an organization needs support during a special campaign, as well as the reasons for meriting this support. Case statements can be external - prepared for the general public and special prospects who will be solicited for major gifts, or internal - prepared to brief board members, staff and volunteer solicitors. Also known as the Case for Support.

Case for Support (*see Case Statement*)

Cash Flow Projection A plan showing the expected timing for incoming revenue; especially necessary when obtaining significant pledges for future donations.

Casino A special event at which gambling is allowed; a technique used by some charities where legal, and when gambling is not frowned upon by the supporters of the charity.

Cause The organization or activity on whose behalf support is being sought.

Cause-Related Marketing The process by which a company markets its products or services by offering to make a contribution to a designated charity each time a consumer participates in the marketing program. The term was coined by American Express to explain their marketing effort in support of the restoration of the Statue of Liberty – each time a card member used the credit card a donation was made by the company to the restoration fund.

Celebrity A high profile person whose presence or participation at an event will act as an inducement to others to participate in and support the cause.

Certified Cultural Property Property deemed by the Canadian Cultural Property Export Review Board to be of "outstanding significance and national importance" to Canada. If a gift comes under the Cultural Property Export and Import Act, the institution receiving the gift must apply with the donor or on the donor's behalf to the Board to have the property certified. Cultural property may be paintings, sculptures, books, manuscripts or other objects, whether manufactured or natural. The objects need not be Canadian in origin.

Chairman, Honourary Usually a high profile individual who lends his/her name to the organization to increase the organization's credibility in the community.

Challenge Gift/Grant A gift or grant promised on the condition that matching gifts will be given by other donors; the challenge gift acts as an inducement for others to give.

Channel The various fundraising techniques through which donors can be acquired or asked to renew their contributions to an organization: such as direct mail, email, face-to-face, telemarketing, special events, direct response television, website.

Charitable Contribution A donation in cash or in-kind to a charitable organization; if within the regulations of the Income Tax Act, it is eligible for an income tax credit.

Charitable Deduction The amount allowable for deduction under the Income Tax Act for a gift given to a registered charity. (*see Tax Credit and Tax Deduction*)

Charitable Donation A gift of cash or in-kind given to a registered charity.

Charitable Foundation (*see Foundation, Charitable*)

Charitable Gift Annuity An irrevocable contribution of capital to a charity in exchange for immediate guaranteed payments to the individual for life at a specified rate depending on life expectancy; the donor generally receives substantial tax savings. This is a common fundraising technique in the United States, but is more limited in Canada because "while a charitable organization may enter into such arrangements without jeopardizing its charitable status, a charitable foundation may not do so." *(Source: Canada Revenue Agency)*

Charitable Organization Canada Revenue Agency characterizes a Charitable Organization as an initiator of charitable activities (as opposed to an organization that funds the activities of others). Typically, it is controlled by an independent board of directors and is responsible for administering a charitable program and arranges for the conduct of its affairs through its own paid or unpaid employees, agents or representatives. Over 90 per cent of registered charities are charitable organizations.

Charitable Registration Number Identification number given by Canada Revenue Agency to each organization that meets the definition of a "charity" under the Income Tax Act. A complete charity registration number has three parts: the Business Number

(first nine digits), the program identifier (two letters), and the reference number (four digits). The registered charity program identifier is "RR". (*Source: Canada Revenue Agency*)

Charitable Remainder Trust A donation wherein the donor establishes a trust and an irrevocable gift of the remainder interest is made to a charity. The donor receives an immediate charitable tax receipt for the present valuation of the remainder interest.

Charitable Status A status accorded to an organization if it has been accepted by Canada Revenue Agency as a registered charity.

Charity A cause, organization or institution doing "good work." The term is often used to include both registered charities and non-profits that are not registered charities.

Charity, Registered An organization that meets the definition of "charity" under the Income Tax Act and that has been registered by Canada Revenue Agency. To be registered, an organization must promote one or more of the following: relief of poverty, advancement of religion, advancement of education, or other purposes beneficial to the community as a whole in a way the law regards as charitable. Registered charities are strictly regulated and must supply information about their activities annually to Canada Revenue Agency. A charity may lose its registration if it does not conform to the laws governing all registered charities.

Coin Box A collection container placed by some charities in banks, shops and other public outlets to collect loose change; need to be regularly serviced.

Cold List A mailing list of names that has no connection to the organization.

Cold Mail (*see Acquisition Mailing*)

Commission A fundraising practice by which a person is paid based on a percentage of income received by the charity; a practice considered unethical by profession fundraising associations.

Commitment Promise of a gift or pledge by an individual or an institution to support a particular cause. Also used to describe involvement by a person or institution in the activities of a cause.

Community Foundation (*see Foundation, Community*)

Community Investment A term, becoming increasingly common in the corporate world, used to describe a company's charitable donation activities; implies a responsibility on the part of the company to invest funds for the betterment of the community in which it operates.

Community Service Sentencing Requiring people convicted of minor crimes to work a set number of hours for non-profit groups instead of paying a fine or going to jail.

Competitive Situation Analysis A methodology for evaluating your event or project that includes *Cause-Related Competition* (organizations that have similar mandates), *Audience-Related Competition* (targets a similar market audience), *Sponsor-Related Competition* (targets similar sponsors) and *Event-Related Competition (similar event).*

Computer-Generated Upgrade Matrix A method of putting a different suggested gift grouping on the reply device of a direct mail piece depending on the size of the donor's most recent (or largest) gift.

Concentric Circles of Giving The fundraising principle which demonstrates that the most likely sources of support of an organization are those closest to it; moving progressively out to clients/users, and then the general public. *(see Chapter 1: Figure 1.3)*

Constituency Those people with an interest in the organization, such as board, staff, volunteers, clients and donors.

Consultant (*see Fundraising Consultant*)

Contingency Fund Cash reserves set aside by an organization for unpredictable situations or in the event that other funding does not materialize.

Contribution A voluntary gift of money, property, equipment or services to a non-profit or charity.

Control or Control Package A direct mail package that has performed successfully over time so as to become the standard against which new ideas or packages are tested and measured.

Corporate Donation A philanthropic gift given freely by a company to a charity without expectation of a benefit, other than a minor token.

Corporate Donations Committee A group of staff and/or board members of a company who decide on donations based on company donations policies; increasingly customers or outside community members are being recruited to the committees.

Corporate Foundation (*see Foundation, Corporate*)

Corporate Sponsorship A method of corporate support for charities in which the company clearly expects a marketing or product sales return; not to be confused with corporate philanthropy or charitable donations.

Cost Benefit Analysis A method for calculating the financial costs and the revenues earned from a particular fundraising activity or technique; the concept suggests a concern for getting the most of something for the least cost.

Cost per Dollar Raised also **Cost to Raise a Dollar** A term used to analyze the value of a fundraising appeal or program; usually expressed as XX¢ per $1.00.

Cost to Service a Member The total dollar value of benefits given to members, such as newsletter, booklets, and so on; the figure may exceed the dues charged.

Cow Patty Bingo A game of chance in which a field is marked in numbered squares and participants bet on which square a cow will deposit a cow pie.

Crowdfunding Use of the Internet to ask for small amounts of money from a large number of people to finance a particular project, venture or organization.

Cultivation The process of involving potential supporters in getting to know an organization before soliciting a gift.

Cultural Property Export and Import Act (CPEIA) The Canadian Cultural Property Export Review Board (CCPERB) is responsible under the CPEIA for certifying that an object is of such "outstanding significance and national importance" that its loss to Canada would diminish the national heritage. The Income Tax Act and the CPEIA provide tax incentives to people who want to sell or donate significant cultural property to Canadian institutions.

Cut-off Date In direct mail, the term for the date when the campaign can be considered to be completed. For analysis and planning purposes a consistent cut-off date must be used even though donations may come in over a longer period of time.

D

Deferred Giving (*see Planned Giving*)

Designated Gift A donation for a specific purpose clearly stated by the donor. (*see also Restricted Fund*)

Development A term used to define the total process of fundraising; usually includes public affairs and marketing and takes a long-term approach to fundraising with a focus on the development of relationships with donors.

Development Office The organized function within a charity charged with carrying out a development program.

Development Program The overall fundraising and donor relations activities of a charitable organization; may include annual giving, capital campaigns, gift clubs, planned giving, special events, etc.

Diagnostic Report (*see Audit, Fundraising*)

Direct Dialogue Like solicitations for major gifts, direct dialogue involves face to face asking but usually refers to street corner, mall or front doorstep solicitation.

Direct Mail Solicitation of funds by mail; usually divided into in-house appeals to previous contributors and acquisition or prospect mail to potential donors.

Direct Response Any of several fundraising techniques that are targeted to specific individuals or groups for an outright donation and which are completely measurable in terms of cost per dollar raised; includes such channels as direct mail, telemarketing, email.

Direct Response Television (DRTV) Television programs that provide emotional stories and a sense of urgency asking the viewer to respond with an immediate donation; often with a monthly giving component.

Director of Development The individual who heads an organization's fundraising program.

Disbursement Quota The amount a registered charity must spend each year on its own activities or on gifts to "qualified donees" to meet Canada Revenue Agency requirements for continued registration. The quota differs for each category of registered charity. (The disbursement quota is being discontinued by the federal government.)

Discretionary Funds Gift income that can be used by the organization's board and/or management as it wishes; that is, without conditions attached by the donor.

Do-Not-Trade List A list of donors to an organization who have indicated they do not want their names traded or exchanged with the list of another charity for cross mailings.

Donation A voluntary gift of money goods or services to a charitable organization with no expectation of a tangible benefit to the donor.

Donor A person who makes a donation to a charitable organization.

Donor Acquisition The process of attracting first-time contributors to a charitable organization.

Donor Advised Fund A private fund administered by an independent entity such as a community foundation or financial institution created for the purpose of managing charitable donations on behalf of an individual or family; donor advised funds offer the donor ease of administration while the donor to maintain significant control over the placement and distribution of charitable gifts.

Donor Centred Fundraising A methodology for fundraising that places the emphasis on the relationship with the donor rather than the transactional act of asking for a gift. "Donor Centered Fundraising" (note American spelling) is a trademarked term of Penelope Burk and Cygnus Applied Research Inc.

Donor Cultivation The process of involving donors or prospective donors in the activities of the organization so that they will be more inclined to make a donation in the future.

Donor, Current A donor who has contributed recently to an organization; usually considered to be within the last eighteen months to two years.

Donor Database Donor records maintained in specialized software which allows for effective use of the information for fundraising and record-keeping.

Donor Fatigue The situation in which people no longer give to charities or respond to appeals to which they may traditionally have responded; causes cited include overstretched budgets, pressure to donate, frustration with mismanaged charities and excessive donation campaigns; it may also refer to inaction on the part of the international community in respond to a humanitarian crisis.

Donor File The list of people, companies and organizations that support the charity, along with the details of their giving history.

Donor Identification The process of understanding the attributes and attitudes of a charity's donors and searching out similar prospects to become new donors.

Donor, Lapsed A donor who has not contributed recently; usually has not given in the last eighteen months or two years.

Donor Life Cycle The process of how relationships with donors are developed: identification, qualification, cultivation, solicitation and stewardship. Modern approaches include such variants introduced by hjc New Media as "branding, engagement, giving, stewardship."

Donor List The overall list of people, companies and groups that support a charity; an extremely valuable asset of a charitable organization, to be treated as such. *(see House List)*

Donor Profile (1) A file containing specific information about an individual supporter gathered through research. (2) A description of the demographic and psychographic attributes of a charity's supporters.

Donor Prospect A person, company or group that fits a profile of the charity's existing donors and therefore would be more likely to support the organization.

Donor Pyramid The graphic representation of the segmentation of donors by type and size of gift with an emphasis on the need to understand the differing techniques required in communicating with donors at each level. *(see Chapter 1: Figure 1.1)*

Donor Recognition A program to thank and acknowledge donors - often based on the size of their contribution or how long they have been contributing. Usually involves listings in public documents such as an annual report or plaques or certificates for the donor placed at the site of the charity.

Donor Renewal Fundraising activities designed to elicit continuing support from donors.

Donor Research The process of understanding the interests and giving history and ability of a potential supporter so that the solicitation is made in the most effective manner possible.

Donor Retention The concept of developing and implementing a program to keep donors actively supporting a charity. Just as in business, it costs much more to attract a new donor (customer) than it does to keep an existing one.

Donor Rights A set of principles based on the premise that donors and prospective donors should have full confidence in the not-for-profit organizations and causes they are asked to support; commonly set out in a Donor Bill of Rights.

Donor Wall A listing of the contributors to an organization or campaign; often showing different levels of support, placed in a prominent public location. It recognizes donor support while encouraging others to join in giving to the organization. A "virtual donor wall" is a similar list on a web site.

Door Prize An item offered as a random prize to participants who attend a fundraising event. If the value of the prize is for more than a nominal amount, Canada Revenue Agency does not allow the charity to offer a charitable donation receipt for any part of the admission ticket.

Door-to-Door Canvassing A fundraising technique involving a concerted drive in a short period of time going house to house soliciting funds. Traditionally done by volunteers, this is now sometimes done with paid canvassers.

Doubling Day The day when half the total donations from a direct mail appeal have been received. This date is useful for planning purposes. Organizations find by experience that they have different doubling days.

Drive A campaign for funds usually with a fixed time element to it.

Drop Date The day scheduled for delivering a mailing to the post office.

Dues, Membership A set amount of money paid by a person to a charity. Membership dues are generally not considered a charitable donation if the member receives tangible benefits in return, such as reduced or free admission to a museum or discounts on purchases.

Dup-elim Duplicate elimination; a term used in the direct mail industry for running a series of mailing lists through a computer program to check for and delete duplicate entries. (*see merge-purge*)

E

80-20 Rule The truism that twenty per cent of an organization's donors will contribute eighty per cent of the fundraising revenue.

Ear-marked Gift (*see Designated Gift*)

Electronic Funds Transfer (*see PAC, Pre-Authorized Chequing*)

Employee Fund Funds in some medium to large companies that are collected from and distributed by workers, separate from the corporate donations budget. A source of grants for charities.

Endowment Principal or corpus maintained in a permanent fund the interest from which provides income for general or restricted use by an organization, institution or program.

Envelope, Carrier The envelope in which a direct mail appeal is sent; also known as an exterior or outside envelope.

Envelope, Window A carrier envelope that has a clear plastic panel through which the address of the recipient is visible.

Ethics, Fundraising A belief system which, in the case of fundraising, requires a high degree of honesty because of the nature of the activity; that is, handling the voluntary contribution of monies by donors to a worthy cause. May also include moral decisions not to seek or accept donations from certain donors, or resulting from certain methods, for instance, gambling.

Event Landscape The range of comparable fundraising events in your city, province or across Canada; assessed to know what is already in the marketplace and who is your competition.

Every Member Canvas (EMC) or **Every Member Visit** (EMV) A fundraising technique used frequently by churches, involving personal conversations and requests in the homes of each congregational member.

F

50/50 Draw A type of raffle in which the winner keeps half the proceeds and the charity gets the other half. Often conducted at a gathering of a group of supporters.

FAHP (Fellow Association for Healthcare Philanthropy) The highest designation for a professional fundraiser in the healthcare field signifying distinction and achievement, earned through successful experience, self advancement and demonstrated commitment to ethical standards of professional practice.

FSA (Forward Sortation Area) The first three characters in a postal code indicating a specific geographic area - a part of town in an urban area and the local post office in a rural area. Used in direct mail.

Face-to-Face (F2F) Approaching top donors privately, not through the mail, phone or events.

Fair Market Value The price a property would command in the open market between a willing buyer and a willing seller acting independently of each other, with each having full knowledge of the facts. An official receipt for income tax credit can be issued by a charity for the Fair Market Value of property donated to it.

Feasibility Study A thorough and professionally conducted examination of the size and approachability of the market for a proposed fundraising drive (usually a capital campaign) (*see Planning Study*)

Foundation, Charitable The Canada Revenue Agency defines a Charitable Foundation as a corporation or trust set up and operated exclusively for charitable purposes which is not a Charitable Organization.

Foundation, Community A foundation that accepts donations and bequests from residents of a city or region; the funds become part of endowment administered by the foundation and distributed to worthy causes in that city or region. The oldest Canadian community foundation is the Winnipeg Foundation; the largest is the Vancouver Foundation.

Foundation, Corporate A charitable foundation established by a corporation to channel corporate revenues in support of charitable activities. Has the advantage of being able to maintain donations in times when corporate profits are lower.

Foundation, Government A foundation established by a provincial government, generally with proceeds from government lottery revenue. For example, Trillium Foundation in Ontario and Wild Rose Foundation in Alberta.

Foundation, Private The characteristics that distinguish this category of foundation from the others is the degree to which it is privately controlled or funded. In short, a private foundation is a registered charity that at the time of registration is controlled by a group of related persons, or receives over half of its funding from one person or group of related persons.

Foundation, Public A public foundation can be loosely described as a separately incorporated body formed for the purpose of funding the charitable activities of a related organization. They are governed by an independent board of directors. The most common are foundations created to fund the activities of a particular hospital, school or museum. While a public foundation is permitted to carry on its own charitable activities, most of its expenditures are made to "qualified donees."

Freemium or **Front End Premium**, that is, a free premium, e.g., a button, ribbon, pencil, decal, or fridge magnet included in a mailing to encourage prospective donors to respond. (*see Premium*)

Frequency The term used in direct mail to indicate how many times and how often a donor has given. Used to segment the donor list. (*see Segmentation, Recency*)

Friend A term used by all kinds of organizations such as museums and libraries to indicate a group of active supporters - often both as donors and as volunteers.

Friend-Get-A-Friend Acquiring prospects by asking current donors to suggest people who might also be interested in donating.

Friendraising Traditionally a term used to denote programs that place an emphasis on developing relationships with potential donors before engaging in active fundraising; this term in now becoming associated with fundraising events where individuals reach out to their peer network for donations when they are doing a walk, run, or other participant-based fundraising activity. Also referred to as "Peer-to-Peer" fundraising.

Fulfillment Rate The percentage of donors who actually send in a contribution after having made a pledge to do so in response to a telethon, telemarketing, or other such effort to elicit their support.

Functional Budget Sub-dividing all expenses into specific projects and programs to show the true cost; including indirect expenses and an appropriate share of overhead.

Fundamental Fundraising Truth A term coined by Guy Mallabone which posits that "people give their money to things in their life that they are closest to."

Fundraising/ Fund-Raising/ Fund raising The process of generating income for a charitable organization other than through the provision of its services. As a noun it is traditionally two words; as an adjective, hyphenated. Increasingly, as the field becomes more professional, the term is being used as a single combined word.

Fundraising Audit An objective evaluation of an existing fundraising program to assess strengths and weaknesses and propose improvements, often conducted by outside professional consultants. Also called Diagnostic Report.

Fundraising Consultant An individual or firm that provides specialized knowledge and expertise in the development, implementation and/or evaluation of a fundraising program. A professional who works for a fixed fee, not on a commission basis.

Fundraising Continuum (see *Donor Cycle*)

Fundraising Costs Expenditures necessary to raise funds. Acceptable percentages can range from 10% for a major capital campaign by a well-established organization, to as high as 50% or 75% for a smaller organization or a difficult cause. Start-up operations may not break even for the first year or two. Also, some types of activities can cost fifteen cents on the dollar such as mail appeals to established donors, while others such as special events tend to be closer to fifty cents spent per dollar raised.

G

Games of Chance Any of the techniques such as raffles, lotteries, Nevada, Bingo, etc. that charities use to raise funds and in which the participants have the opportunity to win prizes and/or cash.

Gift A voluntary transfer of real or personal property from a donor, who must freely dispose of his or her property, to a donee, who receives the property given. The transaction may not result directly or indirectly in a right, privilege, material benefit or advantage to the donor or to a person designated by the donor.

Gift Array The series of check-off boxes on a donation reply form which donors can use to indicate the amount of their contribution. (*see computer-generated upgrade matrix*)

> **Yes, I would like to donate:**
>
> ❏ $25 ❏ $35 ❏ $50 ❏ $75 ❏ $100 ❏ Other_____

Gift Club A mechanism used to encourage donors to consider larger amounts by offering increased benefits and/or recognition at each higher level.

Gifts, Honour Donations made in honour of someone.

Gift-in-kind Donation of property, goods or services instead of cash. Charities can issue tax receipts for the fair market value of most gifts of goods, but not of services.

Gift, Matching (*see Matching Gifts*)

Gift, Memorial Donations made in memory of a loved one or friend.

Gift Processing A term denoting a structured approach to handling donations that includes establishing a standard gift processing routine for all fund-raising activities, use of a uniform set of procedures, and understanding the legal and accounting requirements involved.

Gift Range Table A chart showing the size and number of gifts than are needed to achieve the goal in a capital campaign. The table focuses the efforts of the campaign leaders on securing the largest gifts.

Gift Range Table
($3 Million Goal)

No. of Gifts	No. of Prospects	Gift Level	Amount Raised	Cum. Total
1	3	$300,000	$300,000	$300,000
2	6	150,000	300,000	600,000
4	12	100,000	400,000	1,000,000
5	15	75,000	375,000	1,375,000
8	24	50,000	400,000	1,775,000
15	60	25,000	375,000	2,150,000
30	120	10,000	300,000	2,450,000
50	200	5,000	250,000	2,700,000
75	300	1,000	75,000	2,775,000
200	800	500	100,000	2,875,000
Many	Many	Small	125,000	3,000,000

Gift, Specified A gift from a registered charity to a charitable foundation when the charities involved choose to make the transfer without affecting the disbursement quota of either charity.

Giving Club Similar to an investment club in which a group of people meet regularly, discuss charities they may want to support and make joint decisions as to which to fund; sometimes used for "Gift Clubs."

Government Foundation (*see Foundation, Government*)

Grant A gift made by a foundation, corporation or government, usually for a specific project of activity and after submitting a grant application or proposal.

Grant Application The form used by a charity when submitting a request for support to a foundation or government funding source. Some funders have applications; others require a grant proposal.

Grant Proposal The document used when submitting a request for support to a funding source that does not have its own application form. Grant Proposals usually follow a well-established format in which all the necessary information is presented in a concise yet comprehensive manner.

Grantor The organization making the grant. Grantors are increasingly becoming more pro-active in selecting the type of charities or issues they will support and in demanding accountability and evaluations after the grant has been used.

Grantsmanship The process of developing grant proposals, conducting research, submitting applications, and engaging in the necessary lobbying to ensure that a grant proposal is approved.

H

Healthpartners A workplace fundraising campaign carried out in federal government offices as a joint effort with the United Way campaign to benefit major Canadian health charities.

House List Generally used in direct mail, the list of (usually) individual donors who support an organization. When renting or trading for prospecting lists, the names acquired are run against the House List to ensure that donors do not get prospect mailings.

I

Imagine Canada A national charitable organization that promotes public and corporate giving, volunteering and support to the community; it acts to strengthen Canada's charities and nonprofits and conducts activities such as the "Caring Company Program" and the "Ethical Code Program" for registered charities.

Information Circular Information notices published by Canada Revenue Agency to clarify rulings and laws.

In-Kind Contribution (*see Gifts-In-Kind*)

In Memoriam Gifts (*see Memorial, Gifts*)

Insurance, Special Event Any of various insurance options for special events that limit the liability of the charity if someone wins a major prize, such as hole-in-one insurance for a golf tournament or weather insurance in case of rain or snow.

Inter Vivos Trust A planned giving product whereby a donor promises (or contracts) to give a sum of money to a charity. The donor receives tax credit for the donation before he/she dies. Similar to irrevocable charitable trust.

Interpretation Bulletin Numbered publications produced by Canada Revenue Agency to guide Canadians in the interpretation of government laws and regulations.

Integrated Fundraising (1) a fundraising program that synchronizes all key elements such as direct mail, events, monthly giving, major gifts, planned gifts, and

campaigns (2) a strategy of ensuring that donors are approached across multiple channels with each individual channel reinforcing the others and enhancing the overall effectiveness of the campaign.

J

Jail and Bail A type of special event wherein local celebrities are "jailed" and then must be bailed out by donations from friends and colleagues.

Junk Mail Any unwanted direct mail. With proper targeting most donors do not mind receiving mail from their favourite charities, thus charities must focus their efforts so that fewer people receive mail they don't want.

K

Kill List / Kill File A direct mail list of names that should not receive a particular mailing. The most common use is to avoid sending existing donors a prospect solicitation mailing, or multiple mailings to donors who have asked to be solicited only once a year.

L

LCP (Letter Carrier Presort)The smallest geographic area used by Canada Post. Mail sorted by the sender to this level qualifies for the largest postage discounts.

LYBNT (Last Year But Unfortunately Not This) A special appeal by mail or phone to past donors who have not given in the past year.

Ladder of Effectiveness A commonly used diagram developed by Hank Rosso, which emphasizes that in any activity, direct face-to-face interaction is more effective than less personal techniques such as flyers. (*see Chapter 9: Fig. 9.5*)

Lapsed Donor A donor who hasn't made a donation over the previous 18 months or two years. Requires special appeal techniques to renew. (*see LYBNT and WHYFU*)

Legacy (see *Bequest*)

Letter, Piggy-Back 1) A fundraising letter that is included in a larger, unrelated package, such as a mailing from a union or church; 2) A letter sent as a follow-up to a previous letter.

Lettershop A company used to put together the mailing in direct mail fundraising - collating, inserting, labeling, imprinting of postage, and sorting by postal code walk are all done here. (also known as Mail House)

Life Insurance Gift A method of making a major, deferred gift to a charity by making it the beneficiary and/or owner of a life insurance policy. This may be done with either an existing or a new policy. If the charity is made the owner, the premiums paid by the donor are considered charitable donations which are tax-creditable.

Life Time Value (LTV) (also, Long Term Value) A method for calculating the importance of a donor over time by adding the total of all donations an average donor gives over all the years they support a charity, compared against the long-term costs of servicing that donor.

Lift Letter A secondary letter or note enclosed with a fundraising letter that is designed to add credibility, or additional giving incentives; perhaps signed by a celebrity or other high profile individual.

List The term used in direct mail to refer to the names and addresses of a particular group of people with a common characteristic, such as donors to a particular organization, subscribers to a certain magazine, people of a similar age in a particular postal code, etc.

List Broker An agent who arranges for the exchange or rental of the lists available from various magazines, compiled sources, or organizations willing to exchange

their names. The broker acts as the go-between in the process.

List Exchange (see *List Trade*)

List Rental The process of borrowing the names on a list for direct mail purposes and paying the list qwner a fee for the one-time use. The point is that the list is only "rented" for that single occasion; any future uses must be paid for again and the renter is not entitled to do anything else with the rented list.

List Trade The process of trading one organizations list with another's. The distinction here is that both agencies get to use the others' donor names and no money changes hands as it would with a list rental.

Live Stamp A genuine postage stamp affixed by hand or machine to an envelope.

M

Mail House (see *Lettershop*)

Major Gifts Any gift which is substantially larger than the average for a given organization. May be $1,000 or more for one organization, $100,000 for another.

Marketing, Direct Using techniques such as mail and telephone to reach directly to the customer/prospect, as opposed to broadly-based techniques such as advertising.

Mass Mailing A large-scale mailing campaign usually to prospective donors.

Matching Gift/ Matching Funding The practice whereby a corporation, major donor, or government agency contributes additional funding (up to a specified ceiling) to match donations from the public. Can be used in direct mail, telemarketing, telethon, and major capital campaigns as an incentive to encourage donors to give to a special campaign. Matching funding is often discussed in terms of a 1-to-1, 2-to-1 or 3-to-1 match.

Membership A fundraising method in which supporters are given specific, tangible benefits and responsibilities in return for their contribution. If the benefits are substantial, the fees may not qualify as a charitable donation.

Merge-purge A term used in direct mail to indicate a computer program that merges a number of separate lists together then creates one master list after eliminating duplicate entries. (*see also dup-elim*)

Mission Statement A brief description of the basic principles underlying the purpose of the organization; it's reason for being.

Monthly Giving A payment program whereby donors have their gift deducted from their credit card or bank account automatically and which encourages long-term donor loyalty.

Move A planned, regular, documented step taken to draw a donor closer to the organization. (see *Moves Management*)

Moves Management A system of planned initiatives that "move" a donor through a cycle that furthers their relationship with the organization leading to a philanthropic donation.

N

NDG Presort (National Distribution Guide) The sorting, bundling and labeling by the first three digits of the postal code that must be done to a direct mail piece in order to have it delivered to certain geographical areas by Canada Post on a discounted basis. (*see also LCP Presort*)

Nevada (*see Break-open Tickets*)

No Show Dinner A fundraising event in which all the normal steps in creating a gala dinner are undertaken and tickets are sold as usual, only the participants are told they can stay home, there is no dinner, and therefore the entire amount of the event is a tax-creditable donation.

Non-profit or Not-for-profit An organization that is incorporated without share capital and which operates for social as opposed to commercial benefit. Registered charities are non-profits but there are many non-profits that are not charities, such as professional associations and sports groups. Non-profits that are not registered charities cannot issue receipts for tax credit.

O

Official Receipt (*see Receipt, Official*)

Online Fundraising The overall term for soliciting charitable donations using the internet and email.

P

PAC (also Electronic Fund Transfer) A donor fills out a form authorizing regular, usually monthly, donations from their bank account. (*see Pre-authorized chequing*)

PACE Public Affairs Council for Education. (*see CCAE*)

PSA (Public Service Announcement) An ad placed free of charge on radio or television or in print media promoting a charity or its event.

Package, The The entire mailing piece in a direct mail program. Usually consists of an outside envelope, reply device, return envelope, appeal letter and sometimes a brochure, lift note or premium.

Pay Roll Deduction Plan A method of contributing to a charity by having a regular amount routinely withdrawn from a pay cheque and automatically credited to the charity.

Patron A term generally used to denote a major contributor; often used as one of the upper levels of donor categories in donor recognition programs.

Peer-to-Peer Fundraising A term associated with fundraising events where individuals reach out to their peer network for donations when they are doing a walk, run, a-thon or other participant-based fundraising activity. Also referred to as "Friendraising."

Personalized Mailing A fundraising letter that has the recipients name, address and salutation on it; usually generated by computer. The name may also be laser printed on the outside envelope and reply device.

Philanthropy The philosophy and practice of giving voluntary financial and other contributions to charitable organizations. The word literally means "love of mankind."

Planned Gift A substantial gift usually made with estate and financial considerations in mind. The most common are bequests, life insurance and charitable annuities which often only take effect upon the death of the donor.

Planned Giving A fundraising program designed to generate substantial gifts of cash, bequests, securities, life insurance and charitable annuities which often only take effect upon the death of the donor.

Planning Study A thorough and professionally conducted examination of the size and approachability of the market for a proposed fundraising drive (usually a capital campaign). *(see Feasibility Study)*

Pledge A promise to make a donation at some time in the future. In the case of telethons, pledges are usually paid immediately after the event; in capital campaigns, when the amounts are generally much larger, the pledges are paid over a period of several years.

Pledge Card A pre-printed form used by solicitors to obtain pledges from prospects in a campaign.

Pledge Flow Projection A report showing a future amount of funds due to a charity based on pledge commitments made and the time period when the income is due.

Pre-Authorized Chequing A method of making donations in which the donor signs a form and then a set amount of money is automatically deducted from the donor's bank account and credited to the charity's account on a regular basis; usually monthly. *(see PAC, and Electronic Funds Transfer)*

Premium A product offered to prospective supporters usually as part of a direct mail package as an incentive to respond. A "front end" premium is sent with the mailing (for example, the address labels of War Amps) While a "back end" premium is given after a donation is received and may require a minimum dollar amount.

Product Sales A fundraising technique in which the organization sells items in order to generate income. These may be unrelated to the mission of the charity; such as chocolate bars or raisins, or in some way connected, such as T-shirts with the organization's logo.

Project Based Costing *(see Activity Based Costing)*

Prospect / Prospective Donor A person, company or group considered to be likely to give financial support to the organization based on carefully selected factors.

Prospect Mail A mailing to people who have never before given to the organization to attract them as prospective donors. *(see also Acquisition Mail, Cold Mail)*

Prospect Pipeline A critical element of a fundraising campaign that addresses having sufficient potential donors being solicited at any given time, and at a high enough dollar value such that the campaign can reach its goal using appropriate success ratios.

Prospect Pool The list of qualified potential donors to a given cause, campaign or organization; managing the prospect pool with respect to capacity, affinity and relationship is a critical aspect of major gift fundraising.

Prospect Profile A comprehensive document detailing the results of the prospect research process with an emphasis on capacity, affinity, and any relationships the prospect has with the organization.

Prospect Research The process of identifying potential donors (usually major gift donors) and discovering what part of your work interests them most, who should ask them, and how much to ask for; using databases, the Internet and other current technologies, prospect research collects, evaluates, analyzes, organizes, packages and disseminates publicly available information in a way that maximizes its usefulness and enables accurate and educated decision-making.

Q

Qualified Donee The term used by Canada Revenue Agency for an organization to which a Canadian taxpayer may make a donation that qualifies for a tax-creditable official receipt.

R

Raffle A form of fundraising in which people are offered prizes in return for purchasing a ticket. Raffles are licensed and regulated by provincial statutes. The ticket price, whether large or small, is not eligible for a receipt for tax credit.

Receipt, Official A form used to acknowledge donations of cash and gifts-in-kind. In order to be used for income tax purposes the receipt must conform to specific guidelines established by Canada Revenue Agency. The donor needs such a receipt to support a claim for a tax credit or deduction for charitable donations.

Recency The term used in direct mail to indicate the most recent date of a donor's contribution and used to segment the donor list. (*see Segmentation*)

Records, Donor The system used to track all the essential information about contributors to an organiza-tion; considered to be one of the most valuable assets of a charity. (*see also Donor File*)

Registered Canadian Amateur Athletic Association An amateur sports group that operates on a national basis that does not qualify for charitable status but may issue official donation tax receipts.

Registered Charity (*see Charity, Registered*)

Relationship Fundraising The term used for the method of fundraising which places an emphasis on developing and cultivating the on-going relationship between the donor and the charity rather than simply on seeking donations; first popularized by Ken Burnett.

Remainder Interest (*see Residual Interest*)

Reminder Appeal Any mailing or contact with the donor that is done with the objective of urging the donor to respond to a previous appeal or pledge.

Reply Device / Reply Card / Response Device The pre-printed form on which the donor indicates the amount of the donation to be made. It usually has a gift array and the donor's name and address already on it and often re-states the appeal. Experienced fundraisers consider this one of the most important parts of the mailing.

Reply Envelope The envelope usually enclosed in a fundraising mailing for the donor to use to return the contribution. It has the address of the organization pre-printed on it and may or may not have postage prepaid. Often a #9 business envelope. (If it has postage paid, see *BRE*.)

Residual Interest A term applying to the situations where a donor irrevocably gives real estate or personal property to a charity while retaining the right to use the property for life or a period of time.

Restricted Fund Funds allocated to specific purposes within an organization; the level of restriction may vary to a general program or a very specific project.

Response Rate The rate at which those receiving a mailing respond. Usually expressed in percentage terms, based on the number of donations divided by the number of requests sent out (less the Bads or un-deliverables).

Return per Piece The amount of revenue generated by a mailing divided by the number of pieces mailed. Expressed as a dollar figure.

Roll Out A mailing to the rest of a particular list after it worked successfully in a test mailing. Also known as a "continuation."

Rule of Thirds A commonly used formula for capital campaigns: the top ten donors account for about one third of the campaign goal; the next one hundred donors provide the next third; and all the other donors contribute the final third. While there can be some variation in the amounts received in the top two thirds, the bottom third can never make up the difference for a short-fall from the top 110 gifts.

Rummage Sale A fundraising technique used mostly by smaller charities in which mostly used items are gathered together, usually donated by supporters and offered for sale with the proceeds going to the charity.

S

SMS Giving (Short Message Service) Donors receive a short text message asking them to donate a small amount, often $5 or $10, usually in response to a disaster at a group gathering such as a concert.

SYBNT (Some Year But Unfortunately Not This) A special appeal by mail or phone to donors who have given at some point in the past but have not given in the last year.

Segmentation The practice in direct mail fundraising of sorting donors into different categories based on the recency, frequency and size of their donations.

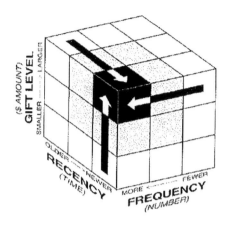

Sequential Giving A key principle in capital campaign fundraising that stresses that the largest gifts must be secured at the beginning of a campaign; followed by the next larger gifts and then on down the gift range table.

Social Network Fundraising Programs that place the emphasis on recruiting individuals to reach out to their own family, friends, neighbours, and colleagues to support them in their fundraising efforts through a multiplier effect for a cause or organization that they believe in; traditionally using printed pledge forms, the predominant method today is email, Twitter and Facebook solicitation and online giving often with personal web pages.

Solicitation The act of asking, usually face-to-face, for a donation for a charity.

Special Event Any of number of fundraising techniques in which the participants are contributing to a charity by virtue of taking part in the event. That is, they are receiving a tangible benefit themselves such as a concert or a dinner. In these cases only the amount of the admission fee that is over and above the value of the event is considered a charitable donation.

Special Names The list of supporters of an organization whose donations are substantially higher than average and who are generally solicited differently than the majority of donors.

Sponsor Someone who is supporting the cost of putting on an event or activity and is receiving substantial exposure in return; usually a corporation.

Sponsorship The act of providing financial support for an event or activity in return for substantial public relations benefit; usually does not qualify for charitable donation status because of the value of the benefit received by the sponsor.

Stamp, Live A term used in direct mail to indicate a "real" stamp as opposed to a metered stamp or a bulk mail indicia. Usually increases response rate.

Stewardship The process of building and maintaining a strong relationship with the donor; including thanking, providing information on how donations were used and making them feel good about giving so that there are inclined to make further and larger donations.

Suggested Amount The gift amount that is being sought from a donor or prospect. Normally found on fundraising reply coupons to guide the donor deciding on the size of his donation.

Supporter In fundraising terms generally synonymous with a donor; someone who assists a charitable organization with a financial contribution.

Suspect A potential donor requiring further research to qualify as a prospect. (*see Prospect*)

Sustainable Fundraising A fundraising principle that measures success not solely on the basis of current gross or net dollars raised but on the capacity to maintain a thriving program over time and on the ongoing relationships developed with donors; such a program builds on the principles of the donor pyramid.

T

T3010, Form Canada Revenue Agency official form that must be submitted annually by all registered charitable organizations on which the executive officers, overall revenue and expenses, and major charitable activities for the year are noted; it is available to the public.

Tax Credit The term used beginning in the 1988 tax year for the tax treatment of donations by individuals to registered charities in Canada. Rather than a deduction against taxable income, the donations (subject to certain limitations) are treated as tax credits which have the effect of reducing the amount of tax payable.

Tax Deduction The term used prior to 1988 in Canada tor the tax treatment of donations by individuals to registered charities. The amount of the gift (subject to limitations) was deducted from the donor's income earned. Corporate donations are still tax deductions, while individuals now receive a *tax credit*.

Teaser The term used in direct mail to indicate information other than the return address that appears on the outside of the mailing envelope. The purpose of the teaser copy is to entice the reader to open the envelope.

Telemarketing The systematic use of outbound telephone calling to donors/prospects to solicit funds. Telemarketing uses either paid canvassers or volunteers.

Tele-thon A fundraising technique in which a variety show is broadcast on television or radio asking viewers or listeners to phone in pledges in support of the charity putting on the show.

Test List A list of prospect names that is being used to see if the profile of the list will result in an acceptable response rate to a mailing.

Test Mailing A new or different mailing letter or package that is being tested against a control to see if it will out-perform the control.

Testimonial An endorsement or acknowledgement that a charity has been helpful to a client; it could also come from a donor. Used in direct mail or a campaign to lend credibility and/or urgency to the appeal.

Thank-you Letter The letters sent to donors along with their receipt after a donation.

Time, Talent and Treasure (TTT) Board members are generally expected to give all three.

Tracking The process of recording the results of a campaign, especially a direct mail campaign.

Transformational Gifts Truly large donations that allow an organization to dramatically grow or achieve its vision; a six figure donation may allow a small charity to hire staff for the first time, while a multi-million dollar gift may enable a college to add a new program.

Walk-a-thon A fundraising event in which participants obtain pledges for walking in the event.

Webbing The process of actively uncovering the network of people you know that you didn't know you knew; who in turn can be useful in fundraising, on boards, as volunteers or as donors.

Welcome Package A more sophisticated version of a thank you letter that focuses on making a first time donor feel that he or she is becoming part of a special cause or organization because of the donation.

Wish List A list of items that an organization would like to buy for its programs or clients but for which it has no funding. The wish list is presented to prospective donors for them to choose something to buy with their donation.

U

Unrestricted Fund Donations which an organization may use for any purpose consistent with its mission.

Upgrading A process of encouraging donors to increase the amount and/or frequency of their support.

V

Volunteer A person who undertakes any of a variety of tasks or duties on behalf of a non-profit organization without financial remuneration.

W

WHYFU Letter A fundraising letter sent to lapsed donors asking "Why have you forsaken us?"

WIIFM (What's In It For Me?) A phrase often asked either directly or implicitly by potential corporate donors when considering a major donation or sponsorship.

ABOUT THE AUTHOR

John M. Bouza, BA, MA, CFRE

John has thirty years experience in fundraising, marketing, and communications principally as the founder and president of Bouza & Associates Inc. and CanFund – Canadian Centre for Fundraising. John has worked for and/or advised a wide range of nonprofit institutions designing effective, unique resource development initiatives. He has successfully organized every type of fund development activity from capital campaigns to special events to direct mail programs.

Major projects and campaigns have included: Canada Science and Technol-ogy Museums Corporation Foundation, Ottawa Rotary Home, University of Ottawa Heart Institute, Aga Khan Foundation, Boys and Girls Club, Ashbury College, Villa Marconi, and Fulbright Foundation, CARE Canada and Ottawa Civic Hospital Foundation.

John was the first person in Ottawa to earn the Certified Fund Raising Executive (CFRE) designation. His longstanding and passionate commitment to the non-profit sector and his tenure as a fundraising professional were recognized by his peers in 1998 when he was awarded the Outstanding Fundraising Executive Award by AFP Ottawa Chapter.

PROFESSIONAL CERTIFICATION AND CANADIAN FUNDRAISING PRACTICE

SHARILYN HALE, CFRE

For fundraisers in Canada (and countries around the world), the CFRE credential sets the baseline standard for professional fundraising practice. In fact, of the more than 5,200 CFRE's worldwide, close to 20% are in Canada. *read more...*

Attaining CFRE certification is an important career milestone for practitioners and is a mark of professionalism and commitment to the profession of fundraising. The CFRE shows you and others that you grasp the fundamental knowledge of the profession. CFRE certification is voluntary, which distinguishes a CFRE's personal commitment to your chosen field, and achieving your CFRE brings a sense of great personal accomplishment and satisfaction.

Furthermore, CFRE's have higher compensation than those who do not hold the CFRE credential. The Association of Fundraising Professionals' Annual Compensation and Benefits Study in 2010 indicated that CFRE's in Canada earned $28,000 more than their non-CFRE colleagues.

CFRE also brings value to the profession. In fact, one of the key markers of any profession is the existence of a credible certification program built upon an identified body of knowledge and practice. And when a profession voluntarily chooses and supports certification, it sends a strong message of accountability to the public. In the nonprofit sector, this includes our donors, organizations and regulatory bodies. In this way, the profession informs the certification and the certification informs the profession in a mutually beneficial relationship.

What is CFRE and how does it work

CFRE International (CFREI) is the global provider of certification for professional fundraising, and the only practice-based credential for career fundraisers. CFREI is an independent corporation led by a volunteer Board of Directors and a small professional staff. CFREI has itself achieved accreditation by the National Commission for Certifying Agencies of the Institute for Credentialing Excellence. You can learn more about these rigorous standards at www.credentialingexcellence.org.

To become a Certified Fundraising Executive (CFRE), practitioners must complete an application which demonstrates that they meet established eligibility requirements (including a minimum of five years paid experience, continuing education and volunteerism), and then pass an examination.

Many candidates choose to devote time to prepare for the exam, and develop a personal study plan. As the CFRE is a practice-based credential there is no set curriculum, but the *CFRE Test Content Outline* provides

the domains and task statements that are covered on the exam and is therefore a key resource. Candidates may also read selected books from the CFRE Resource Reading List, attend workshops or review courses available through professional associations, and/or participate in a study group with colleagues.

Once certified, recertification is required every three years. This means your CFRE remains current through continued mastery, ongoing learning and engagement in the field.

Certification and certificates (or degrees), and their role in professional development are sometimes confused. Certification is an assessment process, whereas a certificate or degree is an educational process. Each are valuable, distinctive, and complimentary, as outlined in Figure A1.1. Consider both as key to your career path and increasing your knowledge and depth of professional practice.

Certification versus Certificate

Certification	Certificate
Results from an assessment process	Results from an education process
Requires some amount of professional experience	For newcomers and experienced professionals
Awarded by a third party standard-setting organization	Awarded by educational programs or institutions
Indicates mastery/competency as measured against a defensible set of standards	Indicates completion of a course or series of courses with a specific focus
Standards set through a defensible, industry-wide process (job analysis/role delineation) that results in an outline of required knowledge and skills	Course content set a variety of ways – e.g. faculty committee, dean/instructor
Typically results in a designation to use after one's name (e.g. CFRE, ACFRE, FAHP, CFP)	Usually listed on a resume detailing education; may also receive a hard copy document to hang on the wall
Has ongoing requirements in order to maintain; holder must demonstrate he/she continues to meet requirements	Is the end result; demonstrates knowledge of course content at the end of a set period of time

Figure A1.1

Details about certification and recertification, including application due dates and preparation resources, are outlined on CFRE's website www.cfre.org.

THE HISTORY OF CFRE

In 1981, the first CFRE examination was offered in the United States and 166 professional fundraisers (including a handful of committed Canadians who wrote the U.S. exam) achieved certification.

Between 1981 and 1996, the Association of Fundraising Professionals (AFP then known as NSFRE) offered the CFRE certification program, and the Association for Healthcare Philanthropy (AHP) offered the CAHP program. In 1997, these certifications were merged into a single certification, CFRE, which was also endorsed by the National Catholic Development Conference, International Catholic Stewardship Council, Association of Lutheran Development Executives and Council for Resource Development.

In 1998, a Canadian version of the CFRE examination was developed with input from Canadian

fundraisers. This was done in order to meet growing demand for certification in Canada and to more effectively test the knowledge of fundraisers within the Canadian regulatory context.

Today, country specific CFRE examinations are available in the United States, Canada, the United Kingdom, Australia and New Zealand. In other regions where the formalized profession is new and emerging, the interest in and demand for CFRE certification is growing exponentially, in part as a key strategy to build and standardize their professional fundraising communities.

In 2001, CFREI became an independent organization. Both AFP and AHP agreed that independence would be in the best interest of the profession and the long-term credibility of the credential. As part of the transition, AFP and AHP retained their advanced certification programs, the ACFRE and the FAHP respectively. These advanced certifications continue to require the CFRE credential as a prerequisite.

Today, in addition to AFP and AHP, CFREI has welcomed formal relationships with a growing number of leading professional associations worldwide including the Canadian Association of Gift Planning in 2001.

CFREI is the voice for fundraising certification around the globe, and this voice is informed by many volunteers. Volunteers are critical to CFRE's core business and are engaged in every aspect of the organization and exam development. Practicing fundraising professionals are thoughtfully selected to ensure a balanced representation of different types and sizes of organizations, demographics as well as regions and countries.

Canadian volunteers have a long history of supporting and leading CFRE: from promoting the benefits of certification and leading study groups for candidates preparing to write the examination, to serving on the Board of Directors shaping policies that support a strong credential, and on committees building awareness and collaborating among partners. With training and support, Canadian volunteers also write and review CFRE test questions for the Canadian exam and analyze the statistical performance of the examination to ensure it remains a valid and reliable testing tool.

CFRE TEST CONTENT OUTLINE

Good certification programs require regular analysis of what professionals are doing and what they are supposed to know. Known as a job analysis study, this is done by all credible credentialing programs.

The only research of its kind, CFREI conducts this rigorous job analysis among practicing fundraisers every five to six years. The results identify what members of the profession say is important to their work, and the knowledge they must master to conduct their work effectively. Simply put, fundraisers tell CFRE what other fundraisers should know. This then forms the specifications and content of the CFRE examination.

In 2009/2010, CFREI conducted a new job analysis engaging close to 3,000 certified and non-certified fundraisers across eight countries (Canada, United States, United Kingdom, Australia, New Zealand, Brazil, Kenya and Italy) and in three languages (English, Portuguese and Italian).

CFREI distils the results of the job analysis into the "Test Content Outline." This is the blueprint of professional fundraising knowledge and of the CFRE

examination. The CFRE Test Content Outline is available to the public, posted on the CFRE website.

CFRE's Test Content Outline for 2011-2015 includes six key subject areas or domains:

- Current and Prospective Donor Research
- Securing the Gift
- Relationship Building
- Volunteer Involvement
- Leadership and Management
- Ethics and Accountability

Within these six domains are 32 identified fundraising tasks, supported by 108 knowledge areas needed in order to effectively perform the tasks.

Candidates use the Test Content Outline to prepare for the CFRE examination, but it is also valuable for the development of job descriptions, recruiting and evaluation, and curriculum development.

For the complete CFRE Test Content Outline see www.cfre.org.

WHAT CFRE'S JOB ANALYSIS SAYS ABOUT THE PROFESSION

CFRE's job analysis in 2009/2010 identified two important aspects about our profession.

First, there is remarkable stability in professional fundraising knowledge. Previous CFRE job analyses conducted in 1997, 2003, and 2009 – each of which Canadian fundraisers actively participated in - provide a longitudinal comparison spanning 12 years.

Stable does not mean static, nor that nothing has changed. Our profession is dynamic and influenced by social and cultural trends, research and technological advancements. Rather, these changes have been incremental and not erratic. This stability reflects a maturity in our professional practice and the depth of our shared body of knowledge. As our profession continues to grow this maturity will deepen.

Study responses from both CFRE's and non CFRE's demonstrated the same stability. This affirms that the CFRE is a practice-based credential and not just the practice of a small subset. It reflects profession-identified best practice regardless of certification status.

For example, Figure A1.2 reflects how study respondents ranked the importance of each of the domains (or content areas) as well as how they spend their time on tasks within each of the domains. Since the first CFRE job analysis in 1997, "relationship building" has remained the most important domain and the one task on which fundraisers spend most of their time.

CFRE domains ranked in terms of importance and time spent on tasks within domains

Importance Rating of Domains (Ranked from Highest to Lowest)	Time Spent on Tasks within Domains (Ranked from Highest to Lowest
Relationship Building	Relationship Building
Securing the Gift	Leadership & Management
Ethics & Accountability	Securing the Gift
Leadership & Management	Current & Prospective Donor Research
Current & Prospective Donor Research	Ethics & Accountability
Volunteer Involvement	Volunteer Involvement

Figure A1.2

The second important finding of the CFRE job analysis is that professional fundraising knowledge and practice is increasingly global. There were differences among the various countries surveyed. In Canada for example, fundraisers rated engaging volunteers in fundraising as more important than did their colleagues in other countries, and as such spent more time engaging volunteers in fundraising and did so more often. Canadian fundraisers also indicated that they reported to constituents about the use and impact of donated funds more frequently than fundraisers in the other countries. However, the variations overall were statistically modest.

Canadians share more things in common with our colleagues around the world - from Banff to Brazil and Kamloops to Kenya - than differences. CFRE articulates this core body of shared professional knowledge.

The most common tasks performed by fundraisers around the globe are:

- Develop a list of prospective donors by identifying individuals and groups (foundations, corporations, government agencies, etc.) who have the capacity and propensity to give, in order to qualify prospective donors for further research and cultivation efforts.

- Ask for and secure gifts from prospects in order to generate financial support for the organization's purpose.

- Acknowledge and recognize gifts in ways that are meaningful to donors and appropriate to the mission and values of the organization.

- Ensure that all fundraising activities are conducted in accordance with ethical principles and standards.

- Clarify, implement, monitor, and honour donors' intent and instructions, and ensure that allocations are accurately documented in the organization's records.

- Comply with all reporting requirements and regulations in order to fulfill commitment to accountability and demonstrate transparency.

What CFRE's job analysis did identify were regional variations in the maturity of the profession of fundraising in the surveyed regions. This was evident based on reported levels of knowledge of and engagement in the broad range of fundraising tasks, the frequency with which the tasks were performed, and the associated knowledge applied.

In Canada, the United States, United Kingdom, Australia and New Zealand, the results pointed to an established profession and professional practice that is both broad and well rooted. In Brazil, Italy and Kenya, the evidence suggested fundraising is an emerging profession, but with a practice that is expanding and entrepreneurial. For example, respondents from Brazil led the way among all countries in the knowledge and use of electronic media in solicitation and relationship building.

You can find out more about the similarities and differences CFRE's job analysis found in fundraising practices among the eight countries surveyed, by reading my chapter "International Perspective on Fundraising," in *Achieving Excellence in Fundraising* (pp. 441-452) published by Jossey-Bass.

CONCLUSION

Whether you are new to the profession of fundraising, have worked in the field for a long time, or it is time for you to recertify, achieving your CFRE is a personal and professional goal that brings benefit to you and your profession. In fact, close to ninety per cent of certified and non-certified professional fundraisers surveyed in Canada said that CFRE was important to them and to the profession of fundraising.

As a CFRE, you can be confident in the breadth and currency of your fundraising knowledge and distinguish yourself as a knowledgeable professional. Your CFRE also serves as a valuable link to the global profession, unified by a shared body of knowledge and practice.

For more information about CFRE or to begin the application process, visit www.cfre.org.

ABOUT THE AUTHOR

Sharilyn Hale, M.A., CFRE

Sharilyn is Principal of Watermark Philanthropic Advising. Sharilyn previously led Canada's largest capital campaign in support of affordable and supportive housing for the YWCA, where women's leadership and philanthropy set new records in the sector. Her background spans fifteen years fundraising for social service and arts organizations, in addition to private sector experience in marketing and communications.

Sharilyn is a strong advocate for voluntary fundraising certification and is Chair of the Board of CFRE International, the global fundraising cre-dential setting standards for effective and ethical practice. In 2009/2010 she led CFREI's job analysis study which explored fundraising across eight countries, in order to identify and articulate the core body of professional knowledge.

An enthusiastic mentor and speaker, Sharilyn has published articles and has contributed to a number of books including Achieving Excellence in Fundraising 3rd ed. (2011).

Sharilyn holds an MA in Philanthropy & Development, and was a member of Canada Advancing Philanthropy, a volunteer driven effort to initiate Canada's first graduate degree program in Philanthropy. A member of the Association of Fundraising Professionals and the Canadian Association of Gift Planning, Sharilyn also serves as a Director of Canadian Feed the Children.

INDEX

Made in the USA
Middletown, DE
02 September 2017